Russian Government and Politic

COMPARATIVE GOVERNMENT AND POLITICS

Published

Maura Adshead and Jonathan Tonge
Politics in Ireland

Rudy Andeweg and Galen A. Irwin
Governance and Politics of the Netherlands (3rd edition)

Tim Bale
European Politics: A Comparative Introduction (2nd edition)

Nigel Bowles
Government and Politics of the United States (2nd edition)

Paul Brooker
Non-Democratic Regimes (2nd edition)

Robert Elgie
Political Leadership in Liberal Democracies

Rod Hague and Martin Harrop
* Comparative Government and Politics: An Introduction (8th edition)

Paul Heywood
The Government and Politics of Spain

Xiaoming Huang
Politics in Pacific Asia

B. Guy Peters
Comparative Politics: Theories and Methods
[Rights: World excluding North America]

Tony Saich
Governance and Politics of China (2nd edition)

Eric Shiraev
Russian Government and Politics

Anne Stevens
Government and Politics of France (3rd edition)

Ramesh Thakur
The Government and Politics of India

Forthcoming

Tim Haughton and Datina Malová
Government and Politics of Central and Eastern Europe

Robert Leonardi
Government and Politics in Italy

* Published in North America as **Political Science: A Comparative Intoduction (6th edition)**

Comparative Government and Politics
Series Standing Order
ISBN 0–333–71693–0 hardback
ISBN 0–333–69335–3 paperback
(outside North America only)

You can receive future titles in this series as they are published by placing a standing order. Please contact your bookseller or, in the case of difficulty, write to us at the address below with your name and address, the title of the series and one of the ISBNs quoted above.

Customer Services Department, Macmillan Distribution Ltd
Houndmills, Basingstoke, Hampshire RG21 6XS, England

Russian Government and Politics

Comparative Government and Politics

Eric Shiraev

First published 2010 by
PALGRAVE MACMILLAN

Palgrave Macmillan in the UK is an imprint of Macmillan Publishers Limited,
registered in England, company number 785998, of Houndmills,
Basingstoke, Hampshire RG21 6XS.

Palgrave Macmillan in the US is a division of St Martin's Press LLC,
175 Fifth Avenue, New York, NY 10010.

Palgrave Macmillan is the global academic imprint of the above companies
and has companies and representatives throughout the world.

Palgrave® and Macmillan® are registered trademarks in the United States,
the United Kingdom, Europe and other countries

ISBN 978–0–230–23585–4 hardback
ISBN 978–0–230–23586–1 paperback

This book is printed on paper suitable for recycling and made from fully
managed and sustained forest sources. Logging, pulping and manufacturing
processes are expected to conform to the environmental regulations of the
country of origin.

A catalogue record for this book is available from the British Library.

A catalog record for this book is available from the Library of Congress.

10   9   8   7   6   5   4   3   2   1
19 18 17 16 15 14 13 12 11 10

Printed in China

*To Lee Sigelman and the enticing elegance
of his research into politics*

Contents

Figures, Tables, Photos, and Maps

Figures

Tables

Photos

Maps

Preface

Every country changes with time, but very few countries alter as dramatically as Russia has done over the past 20 years. Russia has changed as a state, nation, and military power. It transformed its entire political and economic system. After the end of the Soviet Union in 1991—Russia was one of its 15 constituent republics—the country had to totally redefine its role as a reliable partner, global player, and an efficient member of international institutions. These 20 years saw a difficult process of reinventing, rebuilding, and restructuring. Russia keeps on changing today. Therefore, for those who study Russia, grasping these developments and interpreting them will remain a challenge.

Almost everything in Russia these days is "work in progress" marked by sudden accelerations, slowdowns, turnarounds, and paradoxes. For example:

- Russia is a federation (a union of partially self-governed entities), but its political structure defined by the 1993 Constitution allows the central government to exercise almost unlimited power over those entities.
- Russia is a democratic society. Yet the country is remarkably tolerant of undemocratic activity by the government, avoiding transparency and limiting the scope of political competition.
- The Russian government controls television and regulates political speech in many areas of life. However, the internet—uncensored and basically free of government control—is thriving.
- The Russian government controls key profitable industries but continues to encourage private investments in all spheres of the nation's economy.
- Russia has one of the lowest income and capital gains taxes in the world, but simultaneously, maintains one of the worse bureaucratic systems, suffocating free enterprise.
- Russian people are suspicious of the west and its policies, but at the same time they tend to admire western culture, economic prosperity and political systems.

Mikhail Zhvanetsky, Russia's most celebrated comedian and writer, once said that Russia's freedom is like a traffic light with all three lights flashing at the same time. When you study Russia, you constantly encounter inconsistencies and contradictions. This book reflects on these changes, challenges, and paradoxes.

A distinct feature of the book is its structure, the way it presents the materials. After the introductory chapter and two chapters covering history, every chapter focuses first on basic facts, or key developments. These are crucial, formative events that have played an important role in the social and political life of Russia. These events and facts should help us better understand the current processes, their roots, underlying causes, and future possibilities. Chapters frequently refer to the last days of the Soviet Union in the 1980s or the very early years of the new Russia. Some examples are drawn from Russia's more distant history. This background is necessary before we turn to the current state of events. Then the chapter considers major government institutions, laws, and principal decision makers. Next, each chapter moves to discuss various interpretations of these key developments, facts, events, and policies. Presenting the material in a sequence of facts and their interpretations should provide an opportunity to compare various points of view on the same subjects and critically evaluate different assessments and forecasts.

The book incorporates a critical thinking approach. The emphasis on critical thinking should encourage the reader to be an informed skeptic and distinguish facts from points of view. The book also brings together various facts and theories from the fields of political science, international relations, history, sociology, and political psychology. In a nutshell, the structure of each chapter may be presented like this:

| Background, Key Developments | Institutions, Policies, and Decisions | Critical Thinking |

The book incorporates several **pedagogical devices** designed for classroom use and homework assignments. Each chapter contains an opening quotation, a brief prologue, and ends with a conclusion. In every chapter you will find several boxed features including visual aids, tables, and cases in point related to specific facts or individual personalities. Each chapter also has several boxes entitled "Russians speak their mind," featuring the most recent and significant results of national opinion polls. A test bank is available for teachers.

The book has a dedicated **website** which contains the most recent updates, factual data, interviews, editorials, and opinion polls related to current developments in Russia. There is a searchable glossary that defines key terms in Russian politics; these terms are shown in bold type in the text of the book. The website also contains specially selected links for readers who are either studying or already proficient in the Russian language. In addition, practice examination questions for students are posted on the site.

The book is structured in four parts. The first part is introductory. The opening chapter deals with the subject of Russian studies, the methods of studying Russia, and introduces various theories explaining Russian society and politics. The main focus of the other two chapters is a historical background of today's Russia, from early Slavic states to the final days of the Soviet Union.

Part II of the book deals with three major branches of government and Russia's key government institutions. Special attention is given to the executive, the most powerful branch of the Russian government. The chapter about the legislative branch describes both the history and the contemporary dynamics of Russia's parliamentary system. The chapter on the judiciary also pays attention to Russia's law enforcement and administration of justice.

Part III contains three chapters dealing with various aspects of political behavior, participation, and communication. These three chapters are dedicated specifically to political parties, elections, and the mass media in contemporary Russia.

Part IV of the book deals with Russia's policies. They include economic, foreign, defense and security, and social policies. The chapter on Russia's economy also deals with business policies and the interactions between government and private business. Special attention is given to Russia foreign policy and security doctrines. The book ends with a postscript.

No project of this scale could have been realized without the invaluable contributions, assistance, and support of many individuals. I have benefited from the insightful feedback and advice of colleagues and reviewers in the United States, Russia, and Great Britain, from the thorough efforts of research assistants, and from the patience and understanding of co-workers and friends on several continents.

Many things in Russia might change while you are reading these pages. We will try to address them quickly on the book website. Russia will remain for some time a continuing work in progress.

Eric Shiraev

Acknowledgments

This book could not have been realized without the invaluable contributions and support of scores of individuals. It has benefited from the insightful feedback and advice of colleagues and reviewers, from the diligent efforts of research assistants, and from the patience and understanding of my family members and friends. In particular I wish to acknowledge Henry Hale, James Goldgeier, and Henry Nau (George Washington University), Phil Tetlock (University of California at Berkeley), Ariel Cohen (Heritage Foundation), Scott Keeter (Pew Research Center), Dimitri Simes and Paul Saunders (The Nixon Center), Alan Whittaker (National Defense University), Mark Katz, Eric McGlinchey, Peter Mandaville, Jack Censer, Fred Bemak, and Jason Smart (George Mason University), Vladimir Shlapentokh (Michigan State University), Dakhil Elias (Voice of America), and Cheryl Koopman (Stanford University). My special thanks to Robert Dudley, Sergei Tsytsarev, Sergei Andronikov, David Levy, Bill Kinsella, John Ehle, Bruce Mann, Dmitry Shiraev, Dennis Shiraev, Nicole Shiraev, Oh Em Tee, Mike Steward, Alice Steward, and Denis Sukhodolsky.

I received tremendous help from my colleagues and friends in Russia including Konstantin Khudoley, Stanislav Eremeev, Dmitry Mezentsev, Stanislav Tkachenko, Leonid Ivanov, Olga Makhovskaya, Andrei Agapov, and Anton Galitsky. Sergei Pavlov provided photographs for this book. A special word of gratitude to my parents: I can never thank them enough.

I would also like to thank the book's reviewers for their insightful comments.

A special word of appreciation is due to the administrations, faculty, staff, and students at George Mason University and George Washington University and other academic institutions where I have consistently been provided with incredible research opportunities. I also would like to take this opportunity to acknowledge the tremendous support I received at every stage of this project's development from the team at Palgrave Macmillan, in particular, Steven Kennedy, Stephen Wenham, Sarah Fry, and Farideh Koohi-Kamali. Additional thanks go to the management and staff at Curran Publishing Services including Susan Curran. Last, on a more personal note, I wish to express my feelings of thankfulness to Vlad Zubok (Temple University), my colleague and friend, for his continuous support.

Part I

Russia: Continuity and Change

Chapter 1

Studying Russian Government and Politics

Why we study Russia
How we study Russia
Views of Russia and its politics
Critical thinking about Russia
Conclusion

> *There are many bosses but the last word belongs to head of the*
> *state. This is, of course a heavy moral weight.*
>
> Vladimir Putin, former president and
> prime minister of Russia, 2007

Why we study Russia

Russia is a key global power with vast natural resources, significant nuclear arsenals, and growing economic capacities. A country with a rich history and traditions, Russia is now trying to define its new role in the 21st century. Its journey to prosperity and stability has been contradictory and at times ambiguous.

Russia no longer has food shortages but continues to struggle with a painful housing problem. At a time when small businesses are flourishing and expanding, the country's agriculture is decaying. Russia seeks peace and global stability, yet its government maintains a belief in growing foreign threats against it. Russian people enjoy political freedom in most areas of life, yet face restrictions in many others.

Russia today is a constant newsmaker. Many strategic decisions of its leaders domestically and internationally may appear perplexing to an average observer. However, behind Russia's policies there is a comprehensible strategy based on a firm vision of today's world. Russia as a state has its own distinctive strategy. For a future diplomat, journalist, entrepreneur, officer, analyst, or policymaker, it is essential to learn about, understand, and correctly interpret this "Russian strategy."

Why do we have to study Russia? What makes this country important, and in some ways special, in a global world today? Is Russia a reliable partner or

Map 1   *Russia in the world*

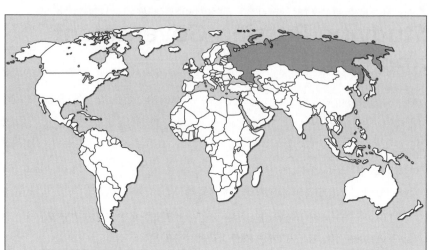

an unpredictable adversary? I hope this book will provide some answers to these questions. For starters, consider a few facts, opinions, and arguments.

Size and geopolitics

The Russian Federation, the world's largest country, stretches over 6.5 million square miles (17 million square kilometers) and 11 time zones. When you arrive at midnight to Baltiysk, Russia's most western seaport, it is already 10 am in Petropavlovsk, a city on the Kamchatka peninsula. Russia borders the Baltic Sea in the west, the Black and the Caspian seas in the south, the Arctic Ocean in the north, and the Pacific Ocean in the east. Its shares borders with five NATO countries (Norway, Estonia, Latvia, Lithuania, and Poland), faces a sixth (Turkey) across the Black Sea, and is separated just by the 53 mile wide Bering Strait from the United States. Overall, Russia borders 16 internationally recognized states. Russia's sheer location becomes an important geopolitical factor affecting policy: anything that happens on Eurasian territories stretching from Central Europe to the Sea of Japan may appear important to Russia and cause it to react.

Regional power

Russia is a key regional power. Located in Eurasia, it pursues its own political, economic, and security interests around the perimeter of its borders. Russia develops its own independent policies toward other states in the region. These policies do not always correspond with strategic interests of the United States, Japan, or the United Kingdom. For example, despite Russia's unenthusiastic view of North Korea's military preparations, Russia continued to maintain economic, political, and cultural ties with the communist government of that country. For many years, Russia also maintained friendly relations with Iran despite this country's growing nuclear ambitions. However, Russia remained one of very few states capable of affecting Iran's nuclear policies to some degree (Graham, 2008a). Russia continues its efforts to build multi-state economic and political coalitions with neighboring countries, including major players such as China, India, and Iran. Finally, although the Soviet Union as a state no longer exists, Russia as the biggest and strongest country of the former Soviet Union continues to claim its own "privileged interests" in the so-called post-Soviet territories (Medvedev, 2009). All these and other facts point at Russia's important role as a regional power.

Military power

Russia remains a very strong military state with immense nuclear capabilities. Having strong military capacities has always been the highest priority of Russian leaders in the past (Pipes, 1984). Russia began to produce nuclear weapons in 1949 and reached nuclear parity with the United States by the 1970s. Today Russia maintains a nuclear arsenal and delivery systems comparable with the arsenal of the United States (Legvold, 2009). Although Russia is no longer an enemy of the western democratic powers, their relations early in the 21st century have been at best lukewarm and sometimes unfriendly. Therefore, one of the most important tasks for the near future will be the creation of new reliable policies of mutual security between Russia and other countries.

Economic power

Russia remains a global economic power. Its Gross Domestic Product (GDP)—one year's market value of all final goods and services—puts the country among the world's top ten economies. In mid-2000 the private sector contributed almost 65 percent of Russia's GDP. By that time, Russia had more than 5 million private enterprises (Åslund, 2007). Although economic slowdowns are possible, Russia is likely to sustain steady economic growth for years to come. Although the country has a wide range of industries, the main source of revenue remains natural resources, including oil, gas, metals, and timber. Russia has nearly 23 percent of the total forested land in the world (WRI, 2009). In the 21st century it also became one of the biggest world energy suppliers. It has vast reserves of natural resources on its territory, which should be available for exploration and extraction in 10 or 15 years: for example, almost 30 percent of global gas reserves (Legvold, 2009: 79). In addition, Russia is near to Arctic gas and oil reserves, a large unexplored source of hydrocarbons. Moscow claims that energy resources could become the key causes of future international conflicts. Because of its size and economic infrastructure, Russia is one of the biggest contributors to greenhouse gases: it is just behind the United States, China, and the European Union. This makes Russia a very important decision maker in global environmental policies.

Cultural hub

Russia remains an important cultural center of both the European and Eurasian civilizations. Despite the country's exceptional geographic location in both Europe and Asia, Russians tend to consider their culture as part of western civilization. Russia has given the world many celebrated composers, such as Tchaikovsky, Glinka, and Rachmaninov. Russian writers including Tolstoy, Dostoevsky, Nabokov, and Chekhov (not the character in *Star Trek*!) became known worldwide. Russian ballet, with its unique choreography and performance, is among the best in the world. Several Russian cities, St Petersburg in particular, were designed by top European architects, including great French and Italian masters. The collections of western art in Russian museums such as the Hermitage are priceless. Today, Russian youth listen to western rock and hip-hop, dress like their peers in London or Boston, and follow European soccer tournaments and NBA games. Yet as we will see later, despite Russia's pro-western cultural orientation, the country overall maintains a very ambiguous, love–hate type of relationship with the west. Understanding Russian cultural inconsistencies and their impact on Russian policies is a very challenging yet important task.

A multi-ethnic state

Russia's population is about 142 million, which makes it one of the ten most populous countries globally. The great majority of the population—nearly 80 percent—are ethnic Russians, who share Slavic ancestral roots with many peoples of Eastern and Central Europe. There are also over 30 million people representing about 70 smaller ethnic groups, which are officially called nationalities in the Russian language (although ethnic groups is a more appropriate term). These ethnic groups are mainly concentrated within 31 administrative units, but there are no restrictions on where their members live. Among the largest are Tatars, Ukrainians, Belarussians, Chuvash, Bashkir, and Mordovans. There are substantial contingents of Russian citizens of German and Jewish origin (these are also called nationalities), but their numbers declined in the 1990s as a result of massive emigration from Russia to Israel, Germany, and other countries. The overwhelming majority of ethnic groups speak Russian, and in most interethnic marriages, Russian is the first language (Gosstat, 2010).

In terms of religious affiliation, more than 70 percent of people in Russia identify themselves in opinion polls as Orthodox Christians (Dubin, 2008). About 10 percent of Russians are Muslim (mostly Turkic groups). It is important to mention that many Russians do not practice religion or maintain firm religious beliefs. For example, only 45 percent believe in life after death and 46 percent think that the devil does not exist (Levada, 2008).

Russians speak their mind ...

... On religion in schools. Percentage of Russians believing that school is not the place for religion: 20. Percentage of Russians believing that based on students' and their parent's consent, schools can teach a history of religion and religious foundations of morality: 60.

Source: Levada (2008).

In sum, Russia is a leading political force, strong economic and military power, a rich energy supplier, a very important international player, which is still building its political structure, and searching for its own firm identity in the 21st century.

How we study Russia

Policymakers and analysts, business advisers, diplomats, and researchers have to rely on dependable and accurate information about Russia, its leaders, its policies, and specific developments taking place in the country. How and where do they obtain this information? Which methods do they use to analyze it?

Official reports

Both government and private organizations in Russia issue official reports and publications related to foreign policy and defense, tourism, employment, fiscal plans and law-enforcement policies. Political parties upload official statements and publish their leaders' interviews and press conferences. How reliable are such reports?

When working with foreign sources, always keep in mind that their accuracy is typically related to the professional prestige of the institutions, quality of previous reports, or competition from other sources of information. On some occasions, governments deliberately distort data in official reports. In the communist Soviet Union, for example, before the 1980s, many government organizations knowingly falsified their published statements to cover up existing problems or create a false impression of success. Most of the published official statistics about crime in the former Soviet Union provided deliberately lowered numbers. Thus it was next to impossible for a scholar to know the number of violent crimes or prison inmates in the Soviet Union. Today the vast majority of published reports in Russia are reliable. In most cases, there are no deliberate government policies to distort statistical information. Every government office on the federal and regional level has its own website containing regular updates, media commentaries, policy statements, and statistical information. In this book and on the book's website you will find links to official sources of information provided by government and nongovernment institutions. Many of these government sites have English versions.

Statements, letters, and communiqués

Official statements and other documents usually explain how government agencies interact with one another, and how the state communicates with other states and international institutions. A communiqué, which is an official report, provides information about the intentions, expectations, or actions of political leaders, government agencies, or negotiating sides. Correspondence between state leaders is an important source of information. For example, official letters exchanged between US President Theodore Roosevelt and Soviet leader Joseph Stalin during the Second World War made clear the difficult bargaining process. Today, Russian politicians including the president and prime minister frequently use televised interviews, press conferences, and live internet chats to convey the government's vision of policies and events. Of course, official lines of communication can be used to distort the facts or mislead an opponent, as has happened in the past (Pearson, 1987). However, with the spread of the internet, the number of independent reporters has also grown dramatically, which makes government distortions and cover-ups more difficult. Keep in mind though that not all web-based stories are reliable.

Eyewitness sources

An **eyewitness account** is a description of an event or other developments provided by an individual who observed them directly. In some cases, eyewitness accounts are the only available source of information. Personal testimonies provide valuable facts and important details that are not necessarily supplied by the official media. Ambassadors sometimes publish their own accounts of most important events they witnessed, such as private negotiations with top state officials, as former US ambassador Jack Matlock did in his influential book (Matlock, 2005). Personal translators to political leaders such as Pavel Palazhchenko (1997), and family members of top diplomats such as Naomi Collins (2007), bring valuable observations and add important details to official publications. Investigative journalism today has brought a new dimension to eyewitness accounts: a reporter specifically looks for facts unavailable to most people or deliberately hidden from them. Unfortunately, investigative journalism frequently faces resistance from Russian local authorities, and many reporters have to overcome threats and violence against them simply because they try to provide truthful information about ethnic violence, corruption, abuse of power, and other serious problems.

Many Russian officials, usually those who are retired from active politics, now write memoirs and provide valuable information about their past decisions (Gorbachev, 1996; Yeltsin, 1994). Beware, though, of their tendency to reinterpret past events. Most politicians do not write memoirs to describe their dreadful mistakes. Instead, they want to defend their legacy and emphasize their achievements, and in the process they may distort important facts.

One useful research technique, used for the quantitative examination of reports, is **content analysis.** This systematically organizes and summarizes both the manifest (what was actually said or written) and latent (the meaning of what was said and written) content of information. A researcher usually examines transcripts of speeches, interviews, television or radio programs, letters, newspaper articles, or other reports. As an example, Shlapentokh, Woods, and Shiraev (2005) examined how Russian newspapers reacted to the events of September 11, 2001 in the United States, describing the common tendencies and the overall tone of the reports.

Intelligence reports

In a general sense, **intelligence** is information about the interests, intentions, capabilities, and actions of foreign countries, including government officials, political parties, the functioning of their economies, activities of nongovernmental organizations, and the behavior of private individuals. Intelligence can be electronic or human. The term is often used to refer specifically to the output of state intelligence agencies. Today, approximately 80 percent of intelligence information about foreign countries comes from open sources such as official reports, press releases, and interviews with government officials. Specially trained professionals gather and interpret "open source" intelligence information.

State leaders can use intelligence information effectively, but they also can manipulate and misuse it. It is customary for many political leaders to "push" their intelligence agencies to produce information that corroborates their own views of foreign policy. In 1982, the head of the Soviet security forces (the KGB) and soon-to-be top Soviet leader, Yuri Andropov, pushed intelligence professionals to generate evidence of US preparations to launch a surprise attack against Russia (Zubok, 2007). In the United States, there were periodic scares in the military and intelligence community that the Soviet Union was getting ahead in the nuclear arms race. As a result, the US Congress periodically voted for huge military appropriations to retain American strategic superiority.

Political leaders often believe that they are better judges of international relations than intelligence and national security professionals. Thus, they often ignore the intelligence gathered, and may suspect that it is misinformation "planted" by the other side. Infamously, Joseph Stalin ignored a

Case in point: Historical fabrications

Government officials may spread deliberate lies about past events. They may fabricate documents, manufacture facts, or produce witnesses of events that never happened. By fabricating sources or creating "fake" facts, officials try to manipulate public opinion, and gather sympathy and support in the hope of justifying their policies or actions. Consider an example.

In 1940 Soviet authorities ordered the executions of thousands of Polish officers captured during the Soviet annexation of a large portion of Polish territory. The event, which became known as the Katyn massacre (after the place where it occurred), was later referred to by both German and Soviet officials for political purposes. After Germany occupied Poland in 1941 and the mass graves of the Polish officers were discovered, Nazi propagandists cited it as an example of Russian barbarism, to sow discontent between the Soviet Union and its allies, primarily the United Kingdom and the United States. Soviet officials resorted to denial. They accused Germany of having committed the murders. The western allies of the Soviet Union, who were anxious to retain their strategic good relations with Moscow, accepted the Soviet government's version and rejected the reports of an international medical commission suggesting that the murders had in fact been committed by the Soviet secret police. For decades, Soviet history books contained this distorted account of the massacre. Only in the 1990s did the Russian government acknowledge these killings, although they played down the tragedy by claiming it as not a political decision generated in Moscow but a "military crime."

Source: Sanford (2009).

number of signals from Soviet intelligence before Nazi Germany's surprise attack on the Soviet Union on June 22, 1941. In retrospect, some intelligence failures are in reality the failures of the leadership to recognize foreign threats.

Media reports

In the days of the Soviet Union, the government controlled the press, and any truthful information about the real state of affairs in the country was difficult to gather. Experts studying the Soviet Union exchanged anecdotes about the "tricks" they used to unravel facts from the accounts in Soviet newspapers, such as studying the order of names of senior party leaders attending public funerals to determine which had moved up or down the bureaucratic hierarchy. Today researchers of Russia use open sources, including the internet, to find valuable information about a wide range of events. There are hundreds of professionals in countries such as the United States, Germany, and the United Kingdom who translate and analyze newspaper articles, public statements, economic data, and other statistical information related to Russia and appearing in Russian sources. These professionals work for a range of organizations including government agencies, research institutions, and marketing firms. Their data are then generalized to appear in various analytical reports about Russia's policies or economic opportunities. It is important to know that as the diversity of the media sources increases, so do the chances that the information will become inaccurate. It is worth repeating that you must learn more about the internet sources you are using, their owners, political affiliations, and sources of their posted materials. The book website provides a sample of relatively reliable sites that deal with Russia, its policies, and people (in English or Russian).

Surveys

Polls or **surveys** are investigative methods in which large groups of people answer questions on a certain topic. Two types of surveys are most valuable: opinion polls and expert surveys. Opinion polls, usually obtained by putting the same questions to a representative sample of people, can provide information about Russian people's views of events and individuals. In the following chapters, you will see results of many surveys. They will illustrate certain tendencies or provide additional illustrative examples. Today's Russian polling companies are highly reputable professional organizations. Many Russian pollsters studied in Western Europe or North America. They use advanced techniques of information-gathering and publish their results immediately after taking a poll. In general, surveys are difficult to design and expensive to administer. Therefore, most organizations that conduct surveys these days are relatively big commercial enterprises.

Opinion polls can give an instant assessment of people's perception of specific events or government policies. For example, in 2009, 41 percent of Russians believed that the country was moving in the right direction, compared with 39 percent who disagreed. This simple fact alone makes it clear that not all Russian people unconditionally support the policies of their government. Surveys also can show changes in people's attitudes about policies. Asked the same question in 2008, more Russians (59 percent) believed that their country was on the right path and only 27 disagreed (Levada, 2009). Based on an analysis of these and other surveys, an expert can try to suggest why people's perceptions have changed. Surveys are not always conducted on national samples. Many researchers use small-scale, personalized surveys to study tendencies in people's opinions on a variety of topics related to their daily lives (Carnaghan, 2008).

Surveys can also provide the dynamics of particular social trends for which information is impossible or difficult to obtain from other sources. For example, how many cellphones do Russians have today compared with the past? This information could be valuable for business and commercial purposes. See Table 1.1.

From other surveys you can also learn that despite the high level of popularity of mobile phones, most families in Russia (67 percent) still do not have personal computers, and only 10 percent of Russians check their e-mails daily. Not very long ago, 74 percent of Russians said that they had never used e-mail in their lives (Levada, 2009a). This lack of technology is certainly a negative factor affecting Russian people's ability to communicate effectively in business, educational, and personal contexts.

Surveys also help in understanding Russian domestic policies (Stoner-Weiss, 2006) and can be used to predict the results of local and national elections. For example, as you can see in the box "Russians speak their mind," in 2009 most Russians said they would support their current president if they were asked to vote tomorrow. However almost 40 percent did not have an opinion on this subject.

Table 1.1   *Percentage of people owning mobile telephones in Russia according to surveys*

2001	2002	2003	2004	2005	2006	2007	2008	2009
2	5	9	19	32	45	58	71	78

Source: Levada (2009a).

Russians speak their mind ...

... **On future elections.** *If presidential elections were held tomorrow, which candidate would you vote for?* Percentage of Russians saying they would vote for the incumbent president Medvedev: 53. Percentage choosing the Communist Party leader Zyuganov: 4. Percentage choosing the Liberal Democratic Party leader Zhirinovsky: 4. Other people remained undecided.

Source: WCIOM (2009).

Other survey-type assessment methods are less expensive than full national surveys. **Focus group** methodology is used in for example foreign policy planning, conflict resolution analysis, and commercial or academic research. The typical focus group contains between seven and ten participants who discuss a particular situation or problem, and express their opinions to the focus group moderator. The United States Information Agency used this methodology for a long time to study people's attitudes in various countries, including Russia, where public opinion studies were impossible or difficult to conduct (Dobson, 1996). Many scholars used this valuable information for their research and assessments. The principal advantage of this method is the opportunity to analyze specific foreign policy issues in an informal atmosphere where people are not necessarily constrained by their fear of government officials or other authorities.

An **expert survey** is another popular method of research, where the respondents are experts in the subject rather than a cross-section of the wider population. Such surveys can reflect reliable professional opinions about Russia's domestic and international actions. For example, Freedom House in Washington, DC, an internationally recognized organization, publishes annual reports on the degree of democratic freedoms in most countries. Based on experts' evaluations, *The Freedom in the World* survey provides an annual rating of a country's treatment of its citizens' most basic liberties. These ratings determine whether a country is labeled *free*, *partly free*, or *not free*. Russia is consistently rated as "not free." Of course, Russian officials are openly displeased with such assessments and call them wrong or irrelevant. Nevertheless, such critical evaluations can affect Russia in a negative way: tourism, international business, educational exchanges, and trade may suffer as a result.

Transparency International (TI) is another well-known nongovernmental organization (NGO) which uses survey methods to create the internationally recognized Corruption Perception Index. It asks international entrepreneurs and business analysts how corrupt they perceive various countries to be, then ranks the countries accordingly. Russia has consistently ranked very low on this list (meaning that corruption is perceived as a major problem): in 2009 it was in 147th place out of 180 countries examined. Senior Russian government officials openly agree, and consider corruption as one of the most serious domestic problems their country faces (Bastrykin, 2008; Medvedev, 2009).

Web

You can check Russia's contemporary ranking on different aspects according to expert surveys by checking these sites:

Freedom House: www.freedomhouse.org
Transparency International: http://www.transparency.org/

However, foreign experts' opinions about the lack of freedom in Russia are frequently disputed in Russian sources. Critics in Russia use data from other surveys that reveal different results. For example, more than 50 percent of Russians said in a 2008 national survey that there was enough freedom in their country. Moreover, 24 percent said there was too much, and only 12 percent believed there was too little freedom (Dubin, 2008a).

Russians speak their mind ...

... On trust. Percentage of Russians who do not believe published reports about Russian public officials' incomes: 70.

Source: WCIOM (2009a).

Such discrepancies in evaluations are among the most common and intriguing challenges for those who study any country. Russia is no exception. Foreign experts studying political freedoms in Russia might focus on violations of liberty, while local experts tend to see mostly positive developments. Disagreements in opinion do not only exist between local and foreign observers. Russian political commentators themselves frequently disagree about how to interpret facts and developments in their country (Shlapentokh, Shiraev, and Carroll, 2008). Therefore, our next step will be to briefly review the most common views of Russia, its government, and politics.

Views of Russia and its politics

Ever since the very earliest studies were made of Russia and the Soviet Union, experts have advised their governments about the best course of action to take towards the country. Their views of Russia and its policies have always been diverse and frequently contradictory, and they still are today. For example, many specialists see Russia as a growing antidemocratic, authoritarian power with aggressive intentions. Therefore, they conclude, democratic countries should maintain a tough approach in their relations with Russia and treat it from a position of strength. Others disagree. They see Russia as a country in transition, a state that has many problems typical to countries going through a similar process of development. For that reason, Russia needs to be treated with patience and goodwill. Yet others may feel that Russia today is not qualitatively different from western countries such as the United States, the United Kingdom, and France, and accuse critical observers of bias toward Moscow.

Web

On the book's website you will find a more detailed description of different views of Russia and its politics.

Russia is an authoritarian state

According to this view, Russia is a typical authoritarian state. In this kind of state, political decisions are made by only a few individuals and are not scrutinized by opposing political forces. The authoritarian leader secures support from a small inner circle and imposes their decisions on the rest of the political elites and the wider population. Therefore, the leader's individual characteristics should play a more substantial role in decision making than in democratic, non-authoritarian political contexts. According to this point of view, generally accepted by most scholars outside Russia, the country pursues expansionist foreign policies because Moscow leaders believe that their country is strong enough to ignore the opinions of the United States and its major European allies (King, 2008). Although the creation of a democratic society was a major goal of Russian reformers after the dissolution of the Soviet Union in 1991, the country turned to authoritarianism. Some experts see such a turn as an unfortunate development: they claim Russia has too much oil, too little economic liberalization, and too little legislative power to reflect the voice of the people (Fish, 2005: 1). Others consider authoritarianism as an "inevitable" stage that any country probably should go through during rapid social transformation (Brinton, 1938; Mau and Starodubrovskaya, 2001).

When it comes to policies toward Russia, many argue that democratic countries should develop ties with it and seek collaboration. However, this collaboration must not cause the west to ignore the fundamental antidemocratic nature of the Russian political system (Gudkov et al., 2009). Therefore, confrontation between Russia and the major western powers will be inevitable for some time. Cooperation with Russia will be possible only in limited areas such as nuclear non-proliferation, anti-terrorist policies, and global security.

There are, of course, other opinions about how best to relate to an authoritarian state.

Russia is a semi-authoritarian state

According to this view, Russia is largely an authoritarian state but with some established democratic traditions. Russia in the 21st century lacks at least three main institutions of accountability: viable opposition parties, fully independent media, and an independent court system (McFaul and Stoner-Weiss, 2008: 83). Elections are held but they are not fully democratic because of the government's interference in the electoral process. The government in Moscow limits people's major civil rights in exchange for providing them with economic security. Scholars sharing this view also agree that Russia in the 2000s has been on an increasingly confrontational course with the United States and most European countries (Sestanovich, 2008: 28).

Although Moscow is largely responsible for its own actions, western powers including the United States, the United Kingdom, and Germany should realize some of their own past mistakes in dealing with Russia, and re-engage with its government in several areas including disarmament, joint international decisions, trade, and cultural exchanges. In terms of future policies, it is necessary for democratic politicians to put aside their differences and focus on the similarities between Russia and western powers. Both sides should acknowledge that the differences between them pale in comparison with the many common challenges that they should address together (Graham, 2008).

Russia is a hybrid state

Supporters of this point of view believe that Russia has most features of a typical state in transition from one political system to another. Russia is neither authoritarian nor democratic. It is a "hybrid" state combining both democratic and nondemocratic features. For example, Russia has achieved success in some areas, such as establishing a free market, but not in others, such as democracy. Russia's wealth has increased over the past ten years, yet the quality of its democracy has eroded (Stoner-Weiss, 2006a).

Opinions vary about what kind of a hybrid state Russia is. There are optimists and pessimists. The first group defends the idea that Russia is moving toward democracy despite many setbacks and authoritarian trends appearing since the 1990s. They emphasize Russia's economic achievements, which imply that economic stability is a key to future democratic changes. The pessimists see a different trend. Russia, from their view, has simply failed to advance toward democracy, and is rapidly turning into an authoritarian anomaly. Russia displays an example of combined economic development and political degeneration (Åslund, 2007: 227). In sum, Russia today has a highly centralized government, combined with a weak civil society.

Others accept the "hybrid" label as a reflection of an old trend of Russian government, where top leaders and their ideas are far more important than the political institutions (Treisman, 1999–2000). Power is rooted to some extent in traditional Russian **paternalism**. This is a popular attitude, and there are many examples of people accepting the decisions of a central authority such as a mayor, governor, or president. To use an analogy, such individuals play the role of a "benevolent father" making decisions on behalf of grateful family members—in this case, citizens. People trust their top leaders, and the leaders in turn accept their exceptional role. Similarly, on the global level, Russian leaders want to see Russia as a great world power that should be feared and respected (Kuchins, 2007).

Many supporters of this view maintain that although Russian political elites are largely responsible for the country's uneasy international situation, most western powers have overlooked Russia's success and placed too much emphasis on its setbacks and mistakes. Russia has been transformed from an expansionist communist empire to a more traditional power (Simes, 2007). Therefore, in dealing with Russia, other countries have to pay attention to mutual possibilities rather than disagreements. Reconciliation between Russia and the leading world democracies is possible, but it will require substantial effort from both sides (Legvold, 2009). In terms of cooperation, the United States, for example, needs Russian help in meeting multiple challenges such as controlling nuclear materials, pressing Iran and other countries to give up their nuclear ambitions, receiving assistance in Afghanistan and other areas of conflict, fighting against international drug cartels, and countering international terrorism (Pifer, 2009).

Russia is a "sovereign democracy"

From this point of view, which is enthusiastically accepted in Moscow (and only by a few western experts), Russia is a sovereign, democratic country which pursues its own national interests and conducts polices that are no different from the policies of most other countries including the United States. From this position, Russia has changed significantly since the late 1990s. From a communist dictatorship it turned to a multiparty democracy.

What used to be a planned economy has been reshaped into a market system. The state does not tell the producers what to make and where to sell. Russia's economic and political systems are far from perfect, but their defects are typical of many other countries in Latin America or Asia at a similar level of development (Shleifer and Treisman, 2004). Most importantly, many Russian authors maintain that their country's type of government—an imperfect democracy—is probably the best option in the current economic and political conditions (Isaev and Baranov, 2009).

Many supporters of this view maintain that the main reason for the lukewarm relations between Russia and the west is the latter's desire to see Russia mostly as a junior partner that is weak and obedient. Russia's rapid and successful economic developments have frightened most politicians in Europe and America because they find it difficult to accept Russia's increasing influence, and the respect given to Moscow by other states. Russia's leaders maintain that to restore good relations with Moscow, western powers, not Russia, must radically change their attitudes and policies, acknowledge Russia's strategic interests, and accept this country as a major international player (Medvedev, 2009).

As you can see, there is no one uniform view explaining Russia, its government and policies. Scholars and politicians tend to see Russia from different angles and interpret Russian policies from different points of view. There are many reasons for such a variety of perceptions, including personal motivation, educational background, life experiences, the types of data experts deal with, and, very frequently, specific political developments which have affected people's individual views.

Domestic politics and views of Russia

The Russian domestic situation has a serious impact on various views of Russia, and on the policies that are developed and pursued in the country. Its recent history can be divided into three major periods. During the **Soviet period**, there were severe restrictions on Russians' ability to criticize their government and society. Typically, people could grumble about small problems of daily life (such as a long wait to see a doctor), but were not allowed to criticize the ruling Communist Party, as we will examine in Chapters 2 and 3. Soviet society and its history had to be interpreted in only one, positive, way approved by the government.

During the second period, in the final years of the Soviet Union and the early years of sovereign Russia, many alternative and critical views of Russia appeared. Russian historians, political and social scientists, economists, and journalists developed diverse views and theories of their country, its history, and its political institutions (Shiraev and Bastrykin, 1988).

The political situation began to change in the late 1990s when President Putin came to power in Moscow. During the third period, the government aided by loyal political forces began to apply substantial political pressure on researchers and other commentators to portray Russia from a uniform point of view. This view is based on several assumptions.

First, Russia has always been and remains a great and independent power that must be reckoned with and respected.

Second, during its long history, Russia has had two types of leaders: those who weakened the country by looking to the west and those who strengthened Russian statehood by all appropriate means.

Third, Russia has been (and continues to be) surrounded by unfriendly foreign powers attempting to undermine Moscow's authority and sovereignty (Shlapentokh, 2009). This point of view of Russia and its history finds support among many Russians (Isaev and Baranov, 2009). To develop this view further, in 2009 the Russian government established a special commission under the Russian president to create policies to resist attempts to falsify history to the detriment of Russia's interests.

In the west, domestic political factors also play a major role in the way Russia is perceived. Although the following generalizations are somewhat simplistic, they show that even in an open democratic society, political ideology may influence the social and political views of researchers and other commentators (Shlapentokh et al., 2008). Most ideologically conservative scholars and politicians continue to emphasize Russia's deficiencies, and interpret Russia's lack of democracy as a major factor that has to define western policies toward the country. These experts frequently support a tough approach toward Russia, and believe that any attempts to "please and appease" Moscow will be ineffective or even counterproductive. In sum, most ideologically conservative experts tend to see Russia as an adversary or opponent rather a friend or partner.

On the other hand, many ideologically liberal experts disagree with these critical arguments and maintain that the disapproval of Russia by conservatives is exaggerated for political purposes. From their point of view, Russian democracy is far from perfect and Moscow's foreign policy is not always friendly. Yet it would be a mistake to maintain confrontational attitudes toward Russia. In the past, the frequent failures of western politicians to reach out to Moscow were based on their unwillingness to do so. Foreign governments should engage with Russia, and use cooperation rather than confrontation in solving bilateral and global problems.

As you can imagine, supporters and opponents of these views continue their debates about how to understand Russia and what decisions will be best suited to their countries' foreign policy. We will study these views in some detail later in the book.

Critical thinking about Russia

Critical thinking is not all about criticism and rejection. It is an active and systematic intellectual strategy that helps us to examine, evaluate, and understand facts on the basis of reasoning and valid evidence (Levy, 1997). It is a skill (or, a set of skills) that can be successfully taught, learned, and mastered. It is a process of inquiry that is sometimes skeptical and cautious. The use of the critical thinking method requires the observer to display three important virtues: curiosity, doubt, and intellectual honesty. Here we look at several important ways in which critical thinking is used in this book to evaluate factual information.

Emotions and judgments

Emotions frequently affect our judgments. Our personal interests and preferences may bias our thinking: often we equate our description of what "is" happening in the world with our perception of what "should be" from our emotional point of view. For example, a supporter of democracy may be displeased that the process of democratic transition in Russia is taking such a long time, and consider the Russian political system to be fraudulent. This person might easily miss many positive developments taking place in the country. On the other hand, an enthusiastic supporter of Russia's policies could tend to overlook many obvious examples of political corruption, censorship, or human rights violations. We have to be critically careful about published reports containing predictions of inevitable "collapse," "fall," or "failure" (Shakhnazarov, 1997: 19). Such predictions make headlines but frequently lack scientific validity because they are based largely on emotional assessments.

"Convenient" assumptions

The power of assumptions frequently challenges the wisdom of facts. There are many things that we don't know; yet we assume that we do know them. Based on assumptions we create theories to support our ideas.

For example, there is a common opinion, frequently expressed in the media, that the process of transition in Russia is only about nationalizing industries and increasing the role of the central government in business affairs. This claim is valid, but only partially so. It is true that the government intervenes in many areas of the Russian economy, but there is also a wide range of government policies promoting deregulation and encouraging people's participation in managing their own affairs. We will discuss these policies later in the book. In fact, one of the most serious political fights that the Communist Party of Russia is engaged in now is about preventing the denationalization (selling into private hands) of many industries in Russia. In a similar fashion, convenient assumptions of Russian politicians about western powers' desire to undermine Russia, weaken its influence, and create internal turmoil there are largely inaccurate. Yet such assumptions are so convenient that they become easily believable, and they are quite popular in Russia these days.

Case in point: Convenient perceptions and misperceptions of Russia

Which of these assumptions are true and which are false?

During the Second World War, the United States and the United Kingdom fought against Nazi Germany and Communist Russia.

Answer: False. The Soviet Union, the United Kingdom, and the United States were allies. Together they fought against Germany and Japan from 1941 to 1945. The Soviet Union lost almost 26 million people in that war.

The Soviet Union and Russia are just different names for the same state.

Answer: False. Russia before 1992 was just one part of the Soviet Union (or Union of Soviet Socialist Republics, USSR), a federative republic that also included 15 other, smaller states (such as Georgia and Azerbaijan). It was then called the Russian Soviet Federative Socialist Republic. The Soviet Union was dissolved in the end of 1991, and since then we can talk of Russia as an independent state.

The Soviet Union was the first country to launch a non-piloted satellite and then a piloted space ship into orbit.

Answer: True. The Soviet Union completed these launches in 1956 and 1961. The first person in space was Yuri Gagarin, a national hero. He died in 1968 in an accident.

Russia continues to have food shortages.

Answer: False. There were some food shortages in the early 1990s. These days, however, Russia's stores are filled with products. A typical Russian food store resembles a typical western store or supermarket in many ways.

Most Russian people would love to see radical changes in their country.

Answer: False. According to a national poll, only one-third of people in Russia want to see radical changes. About two-thirds expect and hope for more cautious change (Dubin, 2008a).

Multiple causes of events

As a critical thinker studying Russia (or indeed any other country), you need to consider a wide range of factors affecting any event, decision, or policy. For example, some people might think it is easy to explain the collapse of communism in the Soviet Union: it was the result of US President Ronald Reagan's polices of military and political pressure. That is a simplistic view and not a fully critical one, however. In fact most international experts agree that the end of the Soviet Union was caused by several intertwining factors, including the Russian people's disillusionment with communist ideology, a growing economic crisis in the country, and the reforming policies of the Soviet leader Mikhail Gorbachev. An increasing amount of evidence suggests that the military pressure from the United States played only a marginal role in the remarkable ending of the Cold War and the Soviet Union (Zubok, 2007).

Political pressure

Theory allows analysts and decision makers to turn a seemingly formless heap of data into a logical construction that makes sense of events. Many foreign-policy debates ultimately rest on competing theoretical visions (Walt, 2005). We tend to believe that scholars should be ideologically neutral: they find facts and build their theories based on their findings. But there are many ways of creating theories and finding facts to justify them, and the political climate, and personal tendencies, have a role in determining which theories scholars develop. Sometimes this process is very apparent: governments "suggest" to scholars how they should interpret the facts. For example, different presidential administrations in the United States have required different interpretations of information about Russia to substantiate their policies. President Nixon's advisers needed data to supported his policies of detente (peaceful cooperation with the Soviet Union) in the early 1970s. President Reagan in the 1980s liked advisers whose theories supported a "tough" approach in dealing with Moscow. Similarly, President Clinton's advisers in the early 1990s welcomed research data suggesting that Russia had lost its competitive edge to justify a period of general inaction in US foreign policy toward Moscow. Studying various views of Russia we should try to identify, whenever possible, what has motivated an expert to present a particular point of view.

Overall, studying Russia, it is very important to realize that each theory describes only a fraction of reality, and this description is taken from a particular, and almost certainly biased, viewpoint. This viewpoint is just one light, one reflection of reality. A critical thinker ought to look for many reflections.

Case in point: The importance of definitions

In the English language, the word "Russian" refers to something or somebody associated with Russia. However, if you translate this word in the Russian language, you have to be careful because there are two different meaning of this term. One refers to "Russian" as an ethnic category (*"Roos-ski"*). The other (*"Rossiy-ski"*) refers to something or somebody belonging to or associated with the Russian Federation as a sovereign state. This one is a civic, not an ethnic category. Both these adjectives are translated in English as Russian, which may create confusion. Some people from various ethnic groups living in Russia may be sensitive to the way you apply the term "Russian" to them. They might have been born and raised in Russia and keep Russian citizenship, but ethnically not be Russians (Sakwa, 1993: 116). If you speak Russian, you can avoid this confusion by using the right adjective. In English, you have to provide additional explanations of the word "Russian" as referring to either an ethnic group or citizenship.

Conclusion

There is good news for students and scholars: Russia is "back" as a subject of studies and debates. After the Soviet Union disappeared from the map in 1991, Russia, both weakened and isolated, was becoming a less popular area of studies than it had been before the 1990s. Many politicians also believed that Russia was "finished" as a key world power, and in the best-case scenario, it would become an automatic ally of the free world. In the worst-case scenario, they thought Russia would remain somewhat irrelevant as an economic and political power. Unfortunately, over past 20 years many Russian studies programs in European and North American universities began to downsize. The justification was: Why do we have to invest our time and resources in something that is no longer important?

Those who argued that Russia was "irrelevant" now realize their error of judgment. Russia is back as a military, economic, and political power. It has tremendous energy resources. Its people are educated and talented. Russia actively pursues its interests near its borders and around the world. However, it is wrong to believe that Russia is destined to be an adversary to the democratic world. Russia itself is part of the west, culturally, historically, and politically. Yet it also remains a Eurasian power with interests and aspirations that have to be acknowledged. We should not forget that Russia's national symbol is a double-headed eagle looking both east and west. We have to study and understand this new and strong Russia to engage with it in a mutually productive and reliable cooperation.

It is difficult to understand a country and its politics without learning about its history. In the next two chapters we will learn about the most important past events, and individuals who have played significant roles in the development of the Russian state and its people. Very often, the seemingly chaotic and incomprehensible developments of contemporary politics have grown from the roots of earlier political battles, reforms, wins and failures. That is where history often comes in to help us understand what we are seeing today.

Chapter 2

The Roots: The Russian Empire and the Soviet Union

> *We continue to be happy about the fact that we have gone away from a partisan and ideological coverage of history of our country. But we won't allow falling into another extreme ... these books should contain facts of history, they have to form a sense of pride for our history, our country.*
> Vladimir Putin, 2003, during a speech in the Russian State Library on new history textbooks

History is often an unappreciated teacher: its lessons are not always obvious and its students tend to have a very short memory. Yet in the history of Russia we can identify a range of issues and developments that have had an obvious and memorable impact on today's state of affairs. The impact is mostly indirect, and different events have had different impacts. There are at least two major types of impact of history on the events of today.

The first type refers to material, substantive, tangible developments that create legacy or material heritage for future generations. For example, territories conquered and retained, wealth plundered and retained, or roads and bridges built or destroyed—all these developments of the past should matter for future generations. The second type refers to mostly non-material, subjective factors that make up the **political culture**, or predominant institutions, beliefs, and ideas that have played their roles in politics and social developments. These are political traditions, habits, and values directing the behavior of political leaders, elites, and the masses.

What do we have to know about Russian history when we study Russian government and politics today? What sorts of events in the past

25

have had the most significant impact on today's developments in Russia? Let's answer these questions by reviewing Russia's history.

Early Russian states

Russia is a multi-ethnic state. The majority of Russian citizens are ethnic Russians. Historians have a compelling body of evidence suggesting that the Russian people have their roots in Eastern Slavic tribes who practiced agriculture and populated a vast territory in Europe, roughly between the Baltic and the Black Sea.

The early consolidation of these Eastern Slavic tribes, and the forming of an early Russian state, was a key development which took place probably in the ninth century. Whether the Viking rulers from Scandinavia took part in the creation of the Russian state, or whether this founding story is a myth, is still being debated. First Novgorod, then Kiev, became political and economic centers of the Russian lands. The term *Kiev Rus* refers to the time of a centralized Russian state headed by Kiev, a large city and a trade center with several thousand inhabitants. Russian rulers called *Knyazes* (translated as princes or dukes), despite unremitting internal disputes, continued to expand their lands and possessions through the 11th century. Dukes and other property owners began to retain servants, or serfs—people legally attached to the land. However, there were also plenty of free peasants living in communes across Russian lands.

The Slavic people were pagans: they believed in multiple gods. In 988, Duke Vladimir accepted Orthodox Christianity as the official state religion, which Russia maintains today. The acceptance of Christianity is commemorated today as a very important spiritual and cultural event. By this time, the Russian alphabet (which is rooted in the Greek alphabet, and continued to evolve) was already in use. Kiev Russia had its own legal code based on practiced customs and previous legal rulings.

This consolidation period had ended by the 12th century, and the process of dissolution of the unified Kiev state began (although some researchers maintain that the Kiev Rus was never consolidated). It was succeeded by a number of smaller states, which grew from 15 in the middle of the 12th century to almost 250 two centuries later (Orlov et al., 2008: 35). This separatist tendency went hand-in-hand with strengthening of the **boyars**, the emerging regional elites who possessed most military, economic (as landowners), and political power. New cities grew rapidly. One of them was Moscow, first mentioned in records in 1147. Princes consolidated power in their hands, sharing it commonly with the boyars, and also, in states such as Novgorod, accepting governing councils and plebiscites—referendums to make important collective decisions and elect religious authorities. Some historians say that the city of Novgorod was a prototype of an early democratic state. This is the basis of the common Russian claim that Russia has inherited an older democratic tradition than many other countries (Yanin and Aleshkovsky, 1971: 56).

Mongol rule

In the 13th century Russian states lost their political independence to the khans—the rulers of the *khanates,* vast Eurasian territories east of Russian lands and spreading thorough Central Asia and China. These territories are frequently identified as the Mongol world empire. The western Muslim khanate called the Golden Horde began to control Russia after a series of devastating invasions in the 1230s and 1240s. The Russian states fell under the political, economic, and military power of the Golden Horde. Politically, Russian princes retained their titles and most territorial possessions, yet they had to receive licenses or permissions from the khan to rule. After conducting a census, the Golden Horde forced Russian city dwellers and peasants to pay various tributes. Russian princes were also allowed to collect taxes from their own people. They had to send warriors to participate in the khans' military operations, but Russia was allowed to retain its Christianity, and Orthodox priests did not pay the tribute to the khans. Some Russian princes also fought battles against western conquerors, especially against the Teutonic knights who represented a Catholic religious and political order. Russians today commemorate Alexander Nevsky (1220–1263), grand prince of the cities of Novgorod and Vladimir, who defeated the Teutonic knights in 1242.

From the 14th through the 15th century, the influence of Mongol-Tartars (the most common Russian name for the rulers of the Golden Horde) began to deteriorate. After a series of battles, the power of the Horde weakened considerably. From the 1480s, Russian rulers began to annex the lands of several khanates located east of Russia. A new consolidation of Russian lands began (Skrynnikov, 2006).

The strengthening of Moscow

The consolidation of Russian lands took place during a period of strengthening for Moscow's rulers. Moscow enjoyed economic, military, and political dominance after the end of the Golden Horde's rule. After refusing to reach a deal with the Catholic Church in Rome and after the Ottoman capture of Constantinople, the heart of the former Byzantine Empire, in 1453, Moscow unilaterally assumed the role of the center of Orthodox Christianity.

During the reign of Ivan III (1440–1505), the independence from the khans was completed. Assuming the title of great prince, he expanded Moscow's possessions and acquired lands around Tver and Novgorod in Russia's northwest, Yaroslavl in the north, and Rostov and Ryazan to the east of Moscow. He contained the Crimean khan, and fought against the rulers of Lithuania. Most Russian princes received the status of boyars, which placed them under direct control of the great duke, or as he can also be called, the great prince. The most powerful of them joined the **Boyar Duma**, an advisory council serving the great prince. Although many of these boyars had lost some of their land possessions, they gained political power.

Ivan III introduced a new symbol of his power: a double-headed eagle, which would later become the official state emblem of Russia. Ivan's comprehensive legal code established property rights and a legal foundation for slavery (thus legalizing the possession of people by other people) and **serfdom**, a system of legal dependency for individuals who worked on leased lands belonging to landowners. Serfdom would become a key legal and economic foundation of Russian society until 1861 (Skrynnikov, 2006a).

Under Ivan IV, known as Ivan the Terrible, the first Russian to take the title of czar (1530–1584), the Russian state grew in size. In accepting this title, Ivan IV underlined the importance of the Russian throne, whose occupants were no longer "dukes" but sovereigns who claimed to be equal to European kings. Among his most significant acquisitions were large territories of the Astrakhan and Kazan khanates, which expanded Moscow's possessions to the Volga River. Russian military detachments penetrated deep into the territories of the Ural Mountains and western Siberia. Several strategic fortresses were built there. Less successful were Moscow's attempts to expand its territories westward. Russia faced tough resistance from Poland, Sweden, and Denmark.

Ivan IV continued the redistribution and consolidation of economic and political power in the hands of boyars, strengthening authoritarian methods of government. Although historians mention his use of various councils including the Boyar Duma, in fact he had unmatched individual power as a ruler. Yet he had to fight for his throne against various boyar families and clans. One of his most significant moves was the establishment of **Oprichnina**, the declaration of his own rule over vast areas of Russia, and a significant expansion of political prosecution and terror against his political opponents and the civilian population. The supporters of this policy maintained that it was necessary to preserve the state. Many Russians refer to Oprichnina as a brutal policy of coercion and injustice.

Until the beginning of the 16th century Russia experienced a difficult period of political and social instability coupled with significant economic difficulties and foreign invasions. Historians often call this period the **Time** of Troubles to indicate the dismal state of affairs in the country, including starvation, violence, and significant territorial losses to Lithuania, Sweden, and Poland. This period lasted for almost two decades until the installment of Czar Mikhail (1596–1645) on the Russian throne in 1613 by a Grand National Assembly. He was the first representative of the Romanov family, which remained in power until 1917. In Russian history, the Time of Troubles is also associated with the popular movement led by Kuzma Minin and Dmitry Pozharsky, who headed a large army of volunteers to fight against the ongoing Polish occupation of Moscow. For many years, Russian patriotic and nationalist forces continued to use this popular revolt as an example of Russia's victorious struggle for independence. Today, unfortunately, some commentators also use this episode of Russian history to scorn Poland (Brazhnikov, 2008).

Significant land acquisitions took place under Czar Alexis I (1629–1676). Russia took control of important lands west of Moscow stretching to the Baltic Sea, and continued its colonization of Siberia. Among the most significant events was a treaty of unification with Ukraine in 1654. Planned by Ukraine as a strategic union against Poland, the treaty resulted in the effective Russian annexation of Ukraine. This event, as you can imagine, still receives different interpretations in Ukraine and Russia today. Nationalistic forces in both countries use the 1654 treaty to draw different conclusions: while many Ukrainians claim that their country never volunteered to lose its independence to Russia, many Russians argue that it means Ukraine has long been a legitimate part of Russia.

A new legal code strengthened Russian peasants' dependence on their landlords, and restricted the migration of free peasants as well as residents of cities and towns. The Church reform of the 17th century standardized the liturgy, religious scriptures, and rituals across Russia. The size of the central government in Moscow grew. Existing small local administrative units were assembled into larger entities governed by officials appointed in Moscow. This was the beginning of Russia's transition toward absolutism, which is a type of generally unrestrained monarchical power (Platonov, 1937/2009).

Russia as an empire

The transition toward absolutism is associated with Czar Peter, who was Alexis's son. Peter remains one of the greatest figures in Russian history. During his reign, Russia grew in size and became a major power in European affairs. Peter was also responsible for a significant transformation of Russia's government and the further "Europeanization" of Russian culture.

Reforms of Peter the Great

Czar Peter I (1672–1725) is frequently referred to as Peter the Great to emphasize the grand scale of his polices and significance of his reforms. During his reign, Russia fought several wars. Defeating Sweden after a 12-year conflict, Russia by 1721 had acquired the lands of contemporary Latvia, Estonia, and a portion of the northwestern territories of the Baltic coast. In the south Russia fought, with mixed results, to gain access to the Caspian Sea. In the east, expansion continued as well. Russia was building new fortresses as far east as in Omsk in Siberia and Semipalatinsk in today's eastern part of Kazakhstan (see the maps on the website). However, the significance of this period in Russian history is also determined by the scope and depth of political and social reforms. Peter strengthened his absolute power, and after the victorious war against Sweden, assumed the title of emperor. European monarchies gradually recognized this title, which may have seemed symbolic, but also indicated that Russia was indeed becoming an empire—an increasingly multi-ethnic but centralized state.

In reforming the government, Peter generally followed western patterns of statehood and governance. He followed his own designs in other cases. Peter moved the new Russian capitol from Moscow to St Petersburg, a city on the Baltic Sea built in 1703. He dismissed the Boyar Duma and established the Senate, an appointed collective institution which played supervisory, taxation, and some legislative roles. Peter established a Prosecutor's office to supervise the activities of the expanding government's institutions. Following the Swedish model, he founded eleven Collegia or departments (prototypes of ministries). Each department was responsible for a particular state activity, including foreign affairs, military affairs, taxation, mining, naval affairs, and spending. New departments regularly appeared. For example, in 1721 a new institution in charge of religious affairs, called the **Synod**, was added to the Collegia. Thus Peter eliminated the institution of patriarchs as heads of the Church, destroying the autonomy of the Russian Orthodox Church. Now the government was in charge of religion.

At this time Russia adopted a uniform system of administrative protocol, document circulation, and other bureaucratic procedures borrowed from Europe. A new Table of Ranks provided a novel hierarchical system of formal ranks and official responsibilities for state employees and the military. A new administrative system was set up, establishing eight large provinces (each headed by a governor), with local units below them. The rights of the Russian nobility or landlords were formalized. By the end of this process, a vast and growing bureaucratic system supported the absolute power of the emperor. Several main components of this system are basically still in place today.

Peter reformed the armed forces and built a brand new, formidable navy. He replaced the old military force by one recruited under a new system according to which each 20 peasant households chose one young male for military service. Military regulations established the responsibilities of officers, soldiers, and sailors. Male members of the nobility also had to serve in the armed forces. Military schools began to train and educate officers. The government became an active organizer and sponsor of manufacturing, trade, and commerce. Peter hired thousands of foreign experts to teach engineering, mining, and scores of other disciplines to local specialists. Russians began to study in Europe, and Europeans began to discover Russia.

In the social sphere, Peter mandated compulsory education for the nobility, and established new European-style fashions for the aristocracy, including pantaloons, shoes, and wigs. He ordered all upper-class males to shave their beards off. Only peasants and clergy were allowed to grow beards, along with other individuals who were willing to pay a "beard tax." Previously prohibited, tobacco smoking was legalized. Formal receptions and balls for dancing and socializing became a custom. Peter simplified the Russian alphabet, and changed the traditional Russian calendar to a more European version. He founded the Academy of Sciences and the University in St Petersburg. Russia began to employ scores of West European artists, architects, musicians, and scientists. The architectural style of major Russian cities began to change dramatically. When he died, Peter left a country quite different from the one he had inherited (Hughes, 2004).

Becoming a major power

In the 18th and 19th centuries, Russia continued its territorial expansions and became a vast multi-ethnic state stretching to the Pacific Ocean. It contained about 30 million people by the end of Peter's reign in 1725, and grew to 125 million according to the first Russian census of 1897. By that time Russia had acquired the territories of today's Baltic states (Lithuania, Latvia, and Estonia), Poland, and western parts of Ukraine. It also added to its possessions Finland, the Crimean peninsula, the Caucasus states (Armenia, Georgia, and Azerbaijan), and Central Asian states (Kazakhstan, Turkmenistan, Tajikistan, Uzbekistan, and Kyrgyzstan). In the east, Russia possessed Siberia and vast areas of the Eurasian continent north of China, spreading to the Bering Straits which separate Russia from North America (see the map on the book's website).

The Romanov dynasty remained in power. It survived several palace plots and assassinations. The dynastic foundations of the monarchy were preserved and the administrative structure of the country was strengthened.

Map 2   *The expansion of the Russian state, 1613–1914*

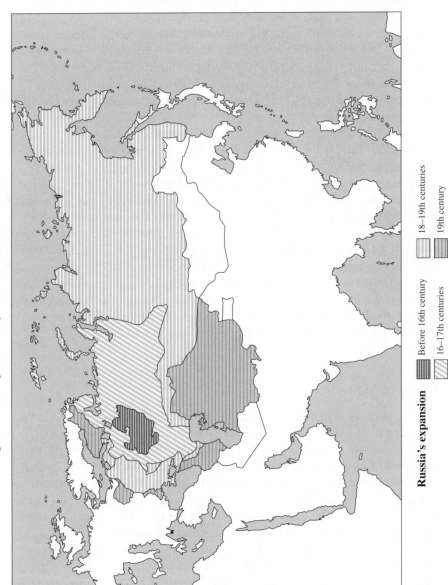

Russia's expansion

Before 16th century

16–17th centuries

18–19th centuries

19th century

Two empresses, Elizabeth (1709–1761) and then Catherine II (1729–1796), together spent 54 years on the Russian throne. By the end of the 18th century, Church lands had become the property of the state. The majority of Russian peasants were dependent on either local landlords or the government. In the ethnic provinces, however (those with a majority non-Russian population), local governments were allowed to apply their own rules related to the peasantry (Orlov et al., 2008).

Russia began to take an active part in European affairs. One of the major events of the end of the 18th and the early 19th centuries was Russia's confrontations with France. It fought against the armies of Emperor Napoleon. The Russian Emperor Pavel I (1754–1801) joined a coalition with England against France, and Russia began its military actions in Europe far away from its own borders. This policy continued under Emperor Alexander I (1777–1825).

The French invaded Russia in 1812 and captured Moscow, but this did not bring victory to Emperor Napoleon. He had to retreat from Moscow, and eventually the whole of Russia, suffering significant casualties in the process. This retreat and final defeat in 1814 is viewed in Russia as the biggest Russian military and political triumph of the time. Pursuing stability and order in Europe, Alexander I and the sovereigns of Prussia and Austria signed a treaty in 1815 founding the so-called **Holy Alliance**, a military and political alliance to preserve the existing dynastic principles of government and prevent democratic revolutions in Europe.

Inside Russia, the executive branch of the government grew. During the tenure of Alexander I, a system of ministries appeared and their number increased. The Emperors' Chancellery assumed several important executive functions. The Senate began to play legislative and judicial functions including discussion on and initiation of new laws. The State Council appointed by the Emperor became an advisory board to the monarch.

Emperor Nicholas I (1796–1855) expanded the bureaucratic system developed by his brother, who died in 1825. During his reign Russia also gained multi-ethnic territories between the Caspian and the Black Sea, and fought a difficult and costly war there. This war and the annexation of the region would remain in the collective memory of many ethnic groups populating the northern Caucasus. In addition, Russia suffered a painful defeat in the so-called Crimean War of 1853–56, in which it fought against the Ottoman Empire allied with England and France. This war was a historic lesson, suggesting that western powers were not willing to accept Russia's growing influence.

Nicholas strengthened the executive branch, consolidated the law under the code system, and introduced and developed the Emperors' Chancellery, including the **Gendarmerie**, the highest law-enforcement and investigation agency. Despite these reforms, Russia retained serfdom, allowing a small

A case in point: The Decembrists

The revolt of 14 December 1825 remains one of the most remarkable events in Russian history. Several young officers and civilians (informally known as the Decembrists) attempted an armed revolt in St Petersburg after the death of Emperor Alexander I. Russia had witnessed many revolts and palace coups in the past. This time, the plot was different because of its magnitude and visibility. The plotters wanted to achieve several goals. First, they wanted to arrest the new emperor or force him to abdicate, and replace him with a provisional government. The second goal was to proclaim a constitution which would establish basic political freedoms, end serfdom (thus liberating the peasants), and establish mandatory military service for all men regardless of their social status. The constitution would also guarantee jury trials and free elections. The plotters gathered their troops on the Senate Square, just a few blocks away from the official emperor's residency. After unsuccessful negotiations, the revolt was put down by artillery fire. It was followed by an investigation and trial, and five leaders of the revolt were sentenced to death.

Debates about the Decembrists and their role in history continue (Solonevich, 2005). Anti-monarchist forces have always considered the plotters as revolutionary heroes, an early wave of the Russian liberation movement. In the Soviet Union, the revolt was romanticized in school textbooks as a heroic and patriotic attempt to fight against autocracy and serfdom. The revolt was also used by official propaganda as an example of the inherent weakness of a plot not supported by the masses (in contrast to the strength of later revolutionary movements which did have mass support). On the other hand, some contemporary commentators in Russia are less happy to emphasize the fact that the Decembrists had taken up arms against the legitimate state authority.

group of landlords and the government to keep legal, political, and economic control over millions of peasants, almost 40 percent of the Russian population. Although many people understood the immoral nature of this virtual half-slavery, they had other compelling reasons to support serfdom. For example, most dependent peasants lived in the southern parts of Russia on humus-rich soil, and the landlords needed them to work the land and produce income. The other reason was political: the government could not find an acceptable system allowing a transition from serfdom to freedom. However by 1861, Emperor Alexander II (1818–1881) had seemingly found a solution.

The reforms of the 1860s–70s

The emperor's decree was called the General Statute about Peasants Released from Serfdom. According to the law, all peasants would gradually become free. They could leave their homes at will and keep their personal belongings. However, if they wanted to stay and take ownership of the land they farmed, they had to first lease it from their former landlords for nine years. Only after this time could they claim possession of their plots. Peasants could also purchase land outright, without leasing it, if they could afford to pay for it.

Alexander II's second set of reforms modified the structure and functioning of local governments in Russia. More power was given to local elected bodies called **Zemstvos** in areas including running elementary schools, managing medical care, sanitation, and street planning. Each Zemstvo could institute local taxes. According to the 1864 law, any land or other property owner received the right to help elect representatives to a local Zemstvo for a three-year period. These local representatives could then elect their own representatives to regional bodies.

The third set of reforms eliminated the old recruiting system in the military, established universal mandatory service for all men, and set up a military reserve. In addition, there was judicial reform which mandated transparency for court hearings. It established new procedures including an appellate system, trial by jury, and legal defense.

Alexander II was assassinated in St Petersburg in 1881 by the members of a small radical organization. His son, Alexander III (1845–1894), rolled back some of his father's reforms. He strengthened the power of aristocrats by increasing their presence on local councils (the Zemstvos) and in courts. Universities gave up their autonomy, some literary journals were closed, and elementary schools returned to the control of the church authorities. These policies were meant to preserve the authority of the czar, strengthen the state, and support the Orthodox religion (Highest Manifesto, 1881: see Kukushkin, 1996). Alexander III's official social policies were also nationalistic: their goal was to unify the country and promote everything Russian (Odelburg, 1949/1991).

The revolutions

Russian history books call the events of the early 20th century "the three revolutions." This refers to the events and political changes of 1905–07 (the first revolution) and fundamental political transformations in 1917 (the second and third revolutions). These events marked the end of the old political system and the creation of a communist state.

Of the more than 125 million people who lived in Russia during the reign of Nicholas II (1868–1918), about 65 percent were native Russian speakers. Still behind most European countries in terms of living standards, Russia was becoming a major economic power. The global economic slowdown of the early 1900s turned into a massive economic recovery. Russia was building new factories, roads, bridges, and railroads. The total length of railroads was second only to America's network. On the global scale, Russia was second in oil production, fourth in machinery building, and fifth in coal extraction. Russia was among the top five nations in steel manufacturing, and first in production of wheat—the main ingredient of bread (Orlov et al., 2008).

A combination of factors contributed to the boom. First, there was a global increase in demand. Second, the government created favorable conditions for private business. The number and size of manufacturing corporations grew. The government pushed forward with new labor laws, mandating health and accident insurance for workers in large factories. Factories began to pay pensions to retired workers. The third reason was a massive agrarian reform conducted by Prime Minister Pyotr Stolypin (1862–1911). A series of laws first allowed and then forced peasants to leave their residential communes, to which they had been legally attached. They could now receive their share of land for free. Special banks allowed them to borrow money to purchase more land. The reforms created a supply of new laborers for industries. Many of the new workers, however, were unable to compete in a free market and ended up in poverty. Overall, Stolypin remains a divisive figure in Russian history. His supporters maintain that his reforms turned the country around economically. His opponents associate his name with deepening economic inequality and the brutal suppression of political opposition. Why did this suppression take place, and what did the opposition do to cause such a harsh response from the government?

The revolution of 1905–07

In the early 20th century, Russia had gone through a period of political instability. By 1905, the country was in crisis. In the international arena, it suffered a painful defeat in the Russo–Japanese war of 1904. Both countries were competing for territories and influence in the Eurasian Far East. Both believed they could win. Russia lost, and not only ceded some territories to Japan, it sustained almost 50,000 casualties and accumulated a huge debt. Taxes went up to pay for the war, and the prestige of the government was as low as ever.

Next, socially and politically, Russia was in a dismal state. The law divided the population into social castes (such as nobility, clergy, and peasants) and preserved a system of social inequality. The peasants, who represented more than 75 percent of the population, and the growing working class had very few economic rights and received few social benefits. Most of them remained in poverty. Unlike most countries in Europe, Russia did not allow political freedoms. People could not form political parties or unions, publish a critical political pamphlet, or speak negatively about the government or the Orthodox Church. Many representatives of educated elites believed that reforms were necessary.

Anti-establishment movements and parties began to appear. In 1898, the Russian Social Democratic Workers' Party was formed illegally in Minsk. The group dedicated its activities to the liberation of the working class, and was an early prototype of the future ruling Communist Party. The Socialist Revolutionaries (SR) Party appeared in 1902 and claimed the right to defend the interests of the poor peasantry. Many Russians had joined various pro-reform movements by 1905. On the other hand, supporters of the monarchy gathered strength too. Various nationalist, anti-Jewish, anti-socialist groups began to appear, claiming to defend Russia's heritage, order, and religion.

In 1905, massive strikes and demonstrations paralyzed many industrial regions of the country, including St Petersburg, the Russian capital. Political pressure on the czar continued. Trying to ease tensions, Nicholas II introduced a law establishing a new legislative body, the Duma. On 17 October, he released a manifesto proclaiming basic political liberties including freedom of speech, assembly, and conscience (Manifesto, 1905: see Chistyakov, 1994). The Manifesto, in general terms, called for universal voting rights and promised the Duma broad legislative rights. The first national elections were called in 1906. New laws eliminated political censorship. Political prisoners obtained their freedom.

Despite these significant political concessions from the government, tensions in Russia continued. Although many supporters of the reforms believed that their goal had been accomplished, many critics disagreed. The old bureaucratic and corrupt machine of the empire remained in place. Peasants had received neither enough land nor the freedom to move out of their communes and villages. Using all available legal means including the Duma floor, the growing antimonarchy opposition began its relentless attacks against the government. Political extremism grew and became rampant. Anarchists, socialists, nationalists, and other groups clashed openly with the government and among themselves. Social instability grew.

These developments caused a harsh response from St Petersburg in June 1907. New decrees ordered the suspension of certain freedoms and prohibited several political parties, most liberal newspapers, and student groups. A biased proportional representation in the Duma replaced the previously established direct voting, allowing the government to nominate, promote, and elect many loyal deputies. Remarkably, almost one hundred years later, the Russian Duma of the 21st century is also not elected by direct vote. A complicated party list system is in place. We will study this electoral arrangement in Chapters 5 and 7.

The revolutions of 1917

Political reforms in Russia did not reduce the tensions in society and within the ruling elites. A consensus grew about the necessity of further political changes. Different social and political groups pursued different goals, however. Supporters of moderate reforms endorsed the idea of a refined, progressive constitutional monarchy. Other reformists believed in a parliamentary republic of the French type. Yet others argued for a socialist revolution and a radical transformation of the entire country. The open struggle among these and other groups determined the course and outcome of the historic events of 1917. Several developments contributed to this struggle. Among them were the devastation caused by the First World War, the continuing ineptness of the government, and the growing economic and social polarization of society.

Early in the 20th century, Russia remained a major international player. It continuously sought ways to preserve a stable international peace. Russia was also building major international coalitions to address its own security concerns. Alarmed by the rapid economic and military developments in Germany, it joined the Great Britain and France to form a military bloc. Germany, in response, gathered its own allies and wanted to diminish the growing power of the rival states. The First World War started in 1914, and brought unprecedented and devastating consequences to many nations.

Initially, many people in Russia supported the war out of patriotic feelings. An anti-German mood swept the country. As an illustration, St Petersburg, capital of Russia, received a more "Russian" name, Petrograd. However, this nationalistic elation soon diminished. The Russian army began to lose battles, suffering heavy casualties. The country mobilized more that 15 million people over the four years of the war. More than 1.8 million perished and 2.8 million were wounded. Socioeconomic conditions worsened significantly. Many influential politicians began to believe that to reverse the situation, a new, efficient, and popular government was necessary.

The czar and his close supporters meanwhile showed ineptness in handling both military and civil affairs. The reputation of Nicholas II suffered because of his alleged connection to Grigory Rasputin (1869–1916), a flamboyant religious healer with a questionable reputation. Rasputin, a priest and alleged practitioner of black magic, was accused of having too much influence over the czarina (the czar's wife) and the royal family. Although historians are uncertain about the extent of his influence, the public's perception of this situation was very unflattering to the czar. Rasputin was killed in December 1916 in a plot. To this day, many Russians perceive him as a mysterious, almost legendary villain.

The events of February 1917

By the end of February 1917, the central government could not control the situation in the capital. Severe economic problems, food shortages, the continuing war, disunity among government forces, and strengthening of the political opposition, all contributed to instability. Several military detachments in the capital joined the opposition to the throne. Bread disappeared from stores in St Petersburg and the city was shaken by riots. On February 28, the Duma formed a provisional committee, which announced that it was taking power in the country. In March 1917, Czar Nicholas abdicated the throne.

From March to October, Russia was a state with **dual power,** a situation in which a country is run by two institutions both exercising executive and legislative functions. On the one hand, there was the Provisional Government formed by the Duma. The main task of the Provisional Government was to run the country's affairs before the Constituent Assembly was elected. This assembly, a national representative body, was intended to decide on future governments. On the other hand, there was a growing network of so-called soviets, or elected councils. They represented factory workers, soldiers, and peasants. In addition, in St Petersburg, political parties opposed to the Provisional Government assembled to form the Soviet of Workers' and Peasants' Deputies. The key question for the moment was: which way would this dual-power situation sway? Which side would prevail? It was a turning point in Russian history.

Political forces supporting the Provisional Government were against monarchy. They stood for liberal reforms and a new social-democratic government. Three major political parties supported the Provisional Government. They differed in many details, but all wanted to secure a legitimate transition from the monarchy to the Constituent Assembly. Among the most powerful opponents of the Provisional Government was the left wing of the Russian Social Democratic Labor Party. Members of this wing were frequently called **Bolsheviks.** This name later became associated with the Communist Party of the Soviet Union. The Bolsheviks did not want gradual transition and a parliamentary republic. They wanted to usurp all the power through the Soviets. Unlike most of their political opponents, including parties on the left, Bolsheviks wanted to end the war, nationalize land, and hand over factories to workers. Using these ideas as political slogans, they generated support across the country and received majorities in the Moscow and Petrograd Soviets. Yet, by all accounts, this support was not substantial enough to win a majority in national elections.

The Bolshevik leader, Vladimir Lenin (1870–1924), insisted on a strategy to usurp political power in Russia without waiting for a national election. It was a favorite communist tactic, applied later in many revolts throughout the 20th century: win political power by any means, conduct radical reforms quickly, and let history judge later. Many communists were driven by the desire to establish a fair society and by the wish to destroy the old social world and its institutions (Brown, 2009).

The events of October and November 1917

An opportunity for a revolt came to Lenin on November 7 (Russia used an old calendar system at that time; in most sources the revolt is called the October Revolution because it took place on October 25). The Bolsheviks were in control of an armed workers' militia and could enforce their decisions. They also formed a Revolutionary Committee in St Petersburg and began to rapidly take over key government centers, post offices, bridges, and train stations. The Provisional Government officials were arrested. The Bolsheviks wanted to seize power before the opening of the All-Russian Congress of the Soviets.

The Congress approved the removal of the Provisional Government and issued three decrees of historic significance. The Decree on Peace called on all the nations at war to start peace negotiations. The Decree on Land confiscated all private land and nationalized all natural resources in Russia. Finally, the Declaration of the Rights of the Peoples of Russia announced the end of ethnic discrimination and gave minority groups the right to secede from Russia. The Congress also established the Council of People's Commissars, the highest executive body, with legislative functions. The first chairman of the Council was Lenin. Officially, these were provisional measures until the Constituent Assembly was elected. However, the Bolsheviks and allied parties had different plans. First they boycotted the Assembly in 1918, then they dissolved it. Right after the revolution, the new government began to issue decrees that radically changed the political, social, and economic foundations of the Russian state (see Table 2.1).

The core ideology of the government and the Bolsheviks, as the ruling party, was Marxism, a set of theoretical principles formulated by the German philosopher and economist Karl Marx (1818–1883). Applied to politics, Marxism claimed that capitalism was a fundamentally unjust form of production reinforced by an oppressive political regime. Working people are main producers of value. Therefore, they should become the true owners of resources, capture political power, and establish a new political and social system of universal equality called communism. In the 20th century and later, Marxism became a major ideological foundation for many communist, socialist, and social-democratic movements around the world.

Vladimir Lenin, the leader of the Bolshevik party and head of the new

Table 2.1   *Major decrees of the new Russian Government in 1917–18*

Issue	Policies and measures
Private land	All private lands were confiscated and the country's natural resources nationalized.
Banks	Nationalization of all private banks in Russia. Annulment of the state's debt obligations. Private accounts were confiscated.
Factories	First, workers were mandated to manage factories; then all the factories were nationalized. Fixed wages appeared along with an eight-hour workday.
Private Property	All private real estate in cities and towns, and Church property and assets were nationalized.
Foreign debt	All foreign debts were annulled and repudiated.
Political power	Criminalization of any claims on political power of any group other than a soviet.
Courts	A new system of elected judges began to function along with special revolutionary tribunals.
Family	Civil unions were established. All forms of inheritance related to private property and assets were abolished.
Military	The control of all military policies and operations was seized by the new government. All military ranks were abolished. All commanders had to be elected by popular vote.

Russian state, was a diehard Marxist. Addressing the issues of global poverty, injustice, and war, he believed that the main cause of these social problems was **imperialism**, which is the final stage of world capitalism (Lenin, 1916/1969). By liberating the oppressed, he wrote, the world's working class, called the **proletariat**, would simultaneously destroy the roots of injustice and war. A new world could be established through revolutionary violence against oppressive governments. Lenin justified dictatorship of one party as a tool to crush domestic resistance and build a new society.

The Bolshevik party assumed the role of the only representative of the working class and peasantry. The party adopted a hammer and sickle as its motif, on the red flag and coat of arms of the new state. All symbols of the old regime, including the Russian traditional tricolor flag established early in the 18th century, were abolished. (Russians restored the tricolor as the national flag in the 1990s.) By July 1918 the Bolshevik government issued the first Russian constitution, legitimizing the dictatorship of the "city and rural proletariat and poor peasantry" with the goal of eliminating the capitalist regime in the country. Thus the ruling party established an early legal precedent for its unlimited power, which lasted for more than 70 years.

The development of the Soviet state

The first 28 years of the development of the Soviet state can be divided into several periods. The first was dominated by the Russian civil war. In the second, this was followed by almost a 20-year period of reconstruction and rebuilding which ended with the Second Word War. In the third period, the invention of the atomic bomb after the war and changes in foreign policy made the country one of two most important players in global affairs. In just three decades after the end of the Civil War, Russia would become a superpower.

The civil war

The 1917 Revolution was a significant and traumatic event for the entire country. Millions of people accepted the rapid changes and began to participate in the creation of a new state. Others chose passive resistance. It has been estimated that 2 million people emigrated from Russia during that period (Sabennikova, 2002). Many others took arms against the new regime. A devastating civil war started in 1918 and lasted until 1923.

The war had several interconnected causes. Millions of people lost their property, possessions, and savings in 1917. The government established a rampant confiscatory policy. Peasants had to surrender large portions of their harvests and stock to representatives of the government. The scope and depth of the radical reforms affected all the key players in Russian politics. Most political parties were left out of power, which immediately created political tensions. The peace treaty signed with Germany was humiliating. Attempting to consolidate power, the new government launched a policy that became known as the red terror, establishing revolutionary tribunals and conducting executions. All these and other reasons caused people to resist, and this resistance rapidly grew into violent confrontation. The nation became divided into two large camps. **The Reds** supported the communist government and the general course of its reforms. **The Whites** opposed it. They had many internal differences, but were unified by the desire to end Bolshevik power. Russia had lived through many internal conflicts before, but this one was particularly monumental.

By the end of the civil war, the new Russian state had lost the territories of Finland, Estonia, Latvia, Lithuania, and Poland, which became independent states. Portions of Ukraine, Belarus, Moldova, Armenia, and some territories in the Far East were occupied by neighboring states. About 25 million people had died since 1914. Production levels had plummeted 80 percent; agricultural output had dropped 40 percent compared with the pre-First World War period. Scores of people became unemployed. Inflation was rampant and food shortages constant (Erlichman, 2004).

This was the sad legacy of the First World War and the civil war. Nevertheless, the country had a functional centralized government which had finally established control over the vast territory. Under these conditions, the state of the Soviet Union was officially formed on 30 December 1922.

Vladimir Lenin (1870–1924)

Vladimir Ilyich Lenin (his original last name was Ulyanov; Lenin was a pseudonym) was the first leader of the new Russian state and the Soviet Union. His government tenure was short. He suffered a series of strokes as early as in 1922, and died in 1924 at the age of 53. During his period in power, from 1917, he won practically unlimited power within the ruling party and government. How did he become a leader of such magnitude?

Lenin was born into an educated family from the provincial city of Simbirsk, located on the Volga River in the heart of Russia. His older brother, Alexander, was convicted and executed for his participation in an anti-government plot. In his student days and after obtaining a law degree, Lenin too participated in illegal political activities, for which he was arrested and sentenced. In 1900, he left Russia for Europe (although he returned briefly to Russia in 1905–07). There he worked on theoretical publications and began to put together a new political party. After the February Revolution he returned to Russia permanently. In a remarkably short period, he and his associates managed to assemble a large and efficient network protected by armed units. These units played a crucial role in the October Revolution of 1917. Lenin was personally involved in the creation of a new communist state. He supported extremely violent methods to implement his policies.

For almost 60 years after his death, the Soviet Union's official propaganda promoted an image of Lenin as a benevolent, intelligent, and caring individual with saint-like personal qualities. He became a symbol of the Soviet state. He was admired by millions of people in the Soviet Union and globally. Every Soviet city and town had a major street or square named after Lenin.

Lenin's opponents portrayed a different picture. To them, he was a brutal, shifty, and selfish individual driven by jealousy and vengeance (Solzhenitsyn, 1976; Avtorkhanov, 1990). Today, the Communist Party of the Russian Federation continues to glorify his name and his deeds, considering him one of the greatest political leaders of Russia, the founding father of the Soviet Union. Opinion polls show a mixed picture of support and rejection.

Map 3   *The Soviet Union, showing its 15 republics*

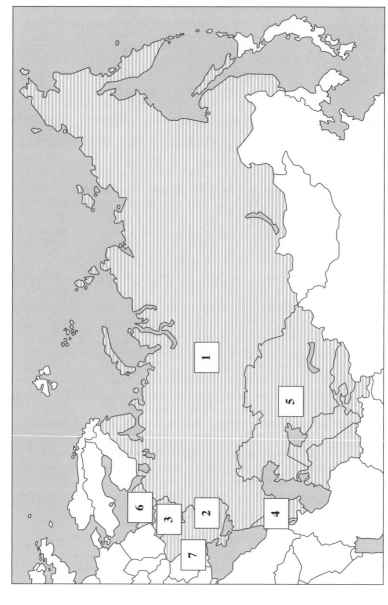

In 1922, the Russian (1), Ukrainian (2), Belorussian (3), and Caucasus Republics (4) formed a new Soviet state. Over the years, the number of the republics grew to 15. Notice that republics such as Georgia, Armenia, and Azerbaijan did not have that status until 1936. Asian republics (5) received their status in the 1920s and 1930s. Estonia, Latvia, and Lithuania (6) became Soviet republics in 1940 as the result of Soviet occupation. Moldova (7) became a republic in 1940 after Romania surrendered a portion of its territory to the Soviet Union.

Industrialization

In 1922, the Russian, Ukrainian, Belorussian, and Caucasus republics formed a new Soviet state. Over the years, the number of the republics grew to 15. Many smaller autonomous republics (with limited rights) were also created within the Soviet Union. In 1923, most of the central institutions of executive power were set up. They were called commissariats (but were later renamed ministries). The new constitution of 1924 declared the Union of Soviet Socialist Republics (USSR) a federation of states. On paper, each state had the right to leave the federation. Each member-state also had the right to conduct its own educational, welfare, and labor policies. In reality, independence for these states was out of question and Moscow controlled local policies. The supreme legislative power belonged to the all-Union Congress of Soviets, with a Central Executive Committee remaining in charge between sessions of the Congress. The Council of People's Commissars possessed the executive power. The Constitution underlined the superior political rights of the working class, and denied voting rights to some categories of former private property owners as well as the clergy. The constitution officially proclaimed Moscow as the capital of the Soviet Union. The headquarters of Soviet leaders and many other government institutions was a large fortified complex at the heart of Moscow called the Kremlin, and the term "the Kremlin" usually refers to the national government from this period onwards.

An urgent task was to restore the economy, stimulate trade, and improve the worsening living standards of the population. As a start, in 1921 the government introduced a policy of economic liberalization called the **New Economic Policy**. This policy halted the massive and excessive confiscations of grain and stock in the countryside, and established a more moderate policy of taxation. By 1925, agricultural output surpassed the output of Czarist Russia (Orlov et al., 2008). The right to own private property, which had been abolished in 1918, was partially restored. Now people could own, sell, or lease bakeries, repair shops, restaurants, retail stores, and even small factories. The government abolished the mandatory labor duty for city residents and allowed foreign investments in the economy. The monetary reform of 1922 reduced inflation. By 1926 the government no longer needed to ration food in cities and towns. The living standards of most Russian citizens were improving.

After 1925 the government began to implement a policy of rapid and massive **industrialization**. According to the communist doctrine, the strength of a state is determined by the size and quality of its heavy industries. Therefore, the prime targets of the Soviet industrialization were heavy industries and the manufacturing of machinery. The changes demanded rapid development of the coal and oil industries, metallurgy, road construction, and the extraction of natural resources. The Soviet economy began to switch to a highly centralized system of administration. Owned by the government, factories and plants became part of a sophisticated network administered by a centralized system of planning, production, distribution, and management. From the 1920s until the late 1980s, big cities and small towns were run by a centralized bureaucratic machine that was in charge of every aspect of planning and development (Ruble, 1990).

It was believed that economic planning was the key to economic success. The Soviet Union in 1929 introduced a new system of economic management based on five-year plans. These plans were prepared in Moscow, and contained detailed targets for production. Managers on all levels became responsible for the realization of the plans. Although the very ambitious targets of the first five-year plans were not fulfilled, over a very short period the Soviet Union developed an advanced industrial sector capable of competing with leading economic powers including the United Kingdom, Germany, and the United States.

Agricultural policies

In 1927, the 15th Congress of the Communist Party proclaimed a new policy, by which peasants were to be organized on a massive scale into **collective farms** whose members shared property and land. Local committees of the party received instructions about the importance of this reorganization. In 1930, Moscow decided to accelerate the development of agricultural collectives, and established quotas for each region, with the purpose of achieving total collectivization by 1932. The official policy was to "liquidate" wealthy peasants as a social class. Although officially membership of collective farms was voluntary, in reality the process of collectivization turned violent and often deadly. Most peasants who did not want to join were forced to do so. The economically successful suffered the most. Based on new laws, the government imprisoned or forcibly relocated millions of well-to-do peasants and their families. Hundreds of thousands perished. Their property was confiscated and given to the collective farms. The Kremlin suppressed all negative information about collectivization. There were incidents of mass starvation in the 1930s in the Ukraine, the Northern Caucasus, and some other regions (Shlapentokh et al., 2008: 58), but practically no reports of them emerged in Soviet newspapers.

The collectivization campaign set the foundation for Soviet agriculture for many years to come. Its negative consequences are still felt today in Russian villages. The government introduced mandatory quotas for harvests and established extremely low prices for agricultural products, and this significantly reduced the peasants' incentive to produce

(Conquest, 1986). The process also enabled the government to establish almost total control over the peasantry. Most importantly, the collectivization process was an act of **genocide**: it involved the purposeful extermination of people based on their social identity. That there was genocide in this period continues to be disputed by some officials and historians today in Russia. Although they accept that many peasants died, they argue that the deaths were the accidental result of the policy being carried out to excess in many places.

By the end of the 1930s, more than 90 percent of Soviet peasants lived and worked on collective farms (in which land and property were leased by the farm collective, which had obligations to the government) or soviet farms (in which land and property belonged to the government and the farm members were state employees).

Government bureaucracy

Both industrialization and collectivization required substantial support from the state. The government in Moscow needed to develop a new bureaucratic system capable of functioning in a new social and economic environment. It did so, and put the Communist Party at the center of it.

The Communist Party played a major role in all areas of economic and political life in the Soviet Union. The highest power in the party belonged to the Party Congresses, which were called regularly, usually once every few years. Between these meetings, an elected Central Committee was in charge. The Central Committee controlled numerous departments, each in control of a particular sector of the economy, area of social life, or policy. A few of the most powerful people comprised the managing body of the party, which was called different names at different times. The most recent was the Politburo (political bureau). In the regions, the party established regional committees (or republican committees in ethnic republics) for managing the party organizations in factories, schools, offices, and the armed forces.

The party established an official internal policy called **democratic centralism**. It was based on three key principles which were laid down early on in the Communist Party Regulations. The first was mandatory elections in all party organizations on all levels. The second was mandatory obedience to the majority in every organization, and the third principle underlined mandatory acceptance of the decisions of higher party organizations by its lower structures. The party regulations prohibited any factions or internal opposition.

Gradually, the core principles of party control of the government were established. The Communist Party installed its members in practically all important government positions and on all levels. There was no area of social and economic life free of party control. Despite the declared principles of democratic rule, most party leaders could not be elected without the consent of higher leadership. Within the party, organizations at lower levels could not criticize the decisions of their superiors. The media had to follow instructions from local or state officials.

Political repression

To increase its grip on power, the government established a vast system of internal intelligence, security, and persecution. From an ideological standpoint, the focus on internal security was based on the mistaken assumption that in a growing socialist state, there would inevitably be an intensifying domestic political struggle. In the late 1920s and especially in the 1930s, the government launched a massive campaign against "enemies of the state" (the official label used in propaganda). The party itself underwent several "cleansing campaigns." As a result, many prominent party leaders, factory managers, military commanders, and thousands of regular members were expelled from the party, imprisoned, or executed.

The cleansing campaigns did not spare non-party members. People were arrested, taken for interrogation, and never went back to their homes and families. Officials were often given quotas: told how many people they should find and arrest. Faced with threats against both themselves and their families, many signed forced "confessions" to crimes they had never committed. Many innocent people were found guilty on the basis of fabricated allegations. Some were executed, and many others were sent to labor camps (that is, prisons usually in remote areas, where they were forced to undertake hard labor). The government continued to maintain that these were necessary defensive measures against the growing number of enemies of the Soviet Union. The state-controlled press were not permitted to report on the state-sponsored violence, including most criminal prosecutions, imprisonments, mass deportations, and confiscations. Although historians both inside and outside Russia differ in their estimates of how many people were persecuted in the Soviet Union during this period, most believe that millions of people were victims (Shlapentokh et al., 2008).

What was the logic behind this policy of repression against Soviets themselves? Josef Stalin, who succeeded Lenin as the national leader, seems to have had several reasons. He used violence as a political tool, to rid the party of noncompliant members and unify its ranks. The terror policy was also a means of eliminating political opponents, both real and imagined. Many people believed the propaganda that the country was riddled with enemies who sought to destroy it, and the population rallied around the Kremlin and Stalin in particular. It is also quite possible that Stalin's personality—he was probably prone to unfounded suspicion and other paranoid ideas—played a part in his political decisions.

Political mobilization

To boost its support among ordinary people, the government sponsored many mass organizations to support the Communist Party and the Soviet government. Young people joined several youth leagues, the largest of which was called the Komsomol (translated literally as the Communist Union of the Young). There were several defense-oriented organizations, and party-controlled labor unions. Many people joined these organizations enthusiastically, while others simply had no other choice. Public schools and mass organizations began to serve as active promoters of communism. Many Soviet people supported the system wholeheartedly. They refused to see any deficiencies in their country, and believed that it was wrong for people to criticize the regime, which many of them had grown to love.

Atheism was an official policy of the Communist Party. Any public forms of religious expression were prohibited. Church property was confiscated, and priests were harassed, imprisoned, or executed. The government criminalized the production and distribution of religious literature. Under orders from Moscow, authorities across Russia began to demolish churches or convert them, for example into warehouses or swimming pools. The Soviet government declared war on organized religion. Only in the 1940s did the government permit some churches to open and their services to be restored. Stalin believed he needed the support of what remained of the Orthodox Church, provided it was loyal to his government, to encourage the country's war efforts.

In 1936 a new constitution declared the creation of a socialist society in the Soviet Union. According to this document, the country had completed its transition from capitalism to socialism. A union between the working class and the peasantry became, according to this document, the social foundation of the state, which was seen as exercising the dictatorship of the proletariat (Constitution, 1936). Such constitutional declarations strengthened the legitimacy of the Communist Party. They also solidified the authority of its leader. The 1930s was the time of tremendous consolidation of power in the hands of Josef Stalin.

The Great Patriotic War

By the end of the 1930s the Soviet Union was a highly industrialized state with a educated multi-ethnic population. Russia dominated it economically and politically. The legal foundation of the government was a one-party

Josef Stalin (1878–1953)

Lenin did not leave an official heir, but Josef Stalin, who had become general secretary of the Communist Party in 1922, gradually consolidated his position as the new leader of the Soviet Union. Although Lenin had been skeptical about Stalin's ability to head the party and the state, Stalin managed to sustain and strengthen his position, which he kept until 1953. What was his role in history?

As with Lenin, the name "Stalin" was a pseudonym. Josif Jugashvili (his real name) was born in the town of Gori in Georgia. Ethnically Georgian, Stalin spoke Russian fluently but with a heavy accent. He began his political activities early in life. In 1905, he met Lenin and they began to collaborate. Stalin became a member of the Central Committee of the Russian Social Democratic Labor Party in 1912. At the same time he began contributing to *Pravda*, the newly created party newspaper. Between his initial appointment in 1917 and his inheritance of the party leadership in 1927, Stalin occupied many posts in the party. His power remained unchallenged from the late 1920s until his death in 1953.

Stalin initiated the policies of industrialization and collectivization. He also directed the massive and coordinated policy of intimidation and terror against his own people. During the war against Germany (1941–45), Stalin strategically revived Russian nationalism and directed the effort to defend the Russian homeland against the invading enemy. Like Lenin, by leading the country through times of great peril and hardship, he solidified his position in the Russian collective consciousness as father of the nation. Supporters of Stalin's repressive actions often suggest that he had very little choice but to resort to harsh policies in a country as large as the Soviet Union. Political violence was necessary to overcome the difficulties of the transitional period. Opponents of Stalin's policies strongly disagree. They portray him as a classic tyrant: that is, someone who rules without law, whose power is virtually unrestrained, and whose ambitions are unchecked (Haslam and Reicher, 2007).

Even today, there is no strong consensus about Stalin's role in Soviet history. Most Russians in surveys say that they think his impact was negative. However, there are many others who associate Stalin's name with the super-powerful and unified state that the Soviet Union used to be, and who continue to find justifications for, and even support, the repressive policies he carried out.

political system. Stalin began to turn away from the Soviet Union's initial policies of international self-isolation. For example, the Kremlin sanctioned hundreds of volunteers to fight on the side of the left-wing government in Spain during the Spanish Civil War (1936–39). Moscow was involved in a military confrontation with Japan in 1938, and attacked Finland in 1939 and seized some of its territories. Stalin also sought and reached a political agreement with the increasingly powerful Nazi

Germany. After signing the Soviet–German pact in 1939, Russia moved troops into Estonia, Lithuania, Latvia, and portions of western Belarus and Ukraine. Using support from friendly communist leaders in the Baltic countries, the Soviet Union seized these territories. Supporters of these actions insist that this was a unification based on mutual agreement. Critics argue that the actions were illegal and immoral. Yet others maintain that although Russia's policies toward the Baltic States and Poland were questionable, they were necessary in order to protect the Soviet Union's security.

Unfortunately, the Soviet Union came to the major military confrontation of its history unprepared. In the 1930s the strength of the Red Army was built up, and there was an expansion of the military bureaucracy. However, Stalin removed and persecuted many top military commanders in 1937. This seemingly inexplicable political move seriously disrupted the country's defense policies and the process of modernization of the military. Although Stalin thought that a confrontation with Germany would be inevitable, he did not believe that it would start in the summer of 1941, when the army had still not been prepared to fight a war of this magnitude.

On June 22, 1941, Germany began military actions against the Soviet Union. This led to the most devastating war in the history of Russia. The German plan was for the Soviet Union to be destroyed militarily, occupied, broken into pieces, and converted into several vassal states. But the Soviet Union resisted fiercely, and things did not go according to this plan.

By the end of 1941 the Soviet Union had mobilized more than 14 million people between the ages of 18 and 61. Despite the mobilization of all available Soviet resources to try to prevent them, German troops reached Moscow and St Petersburg (which had been renamed Leningrad, though it resumed its original name in the final year of the Soviet Union) in the fall of 1941. The situation was critical, and the central government prepared for evacuation. However this never took place. Although the Soviet troops pushed the German armies back, by that winter Leningrad had been encircled by them and was under siege.

The siege of the city lasted for more than two years, and cost 1 million Russian lives, more than the combined total of British and US losses during the Second World War. In 1942, German troops pushed back in the southern part of Russia, captured several strategic regions in the Caucasus region and reached the major city of Stalingrad (as it was then called: formerly Tsaritsyn, it was renamed Volgograd in 1961). The Soviet Army defended the city in a historic battle, then began a full-scale counter-offensive in 1943, winning a decisive battle near the city of Kursk. In 1944 the army, aided by the British and American troops of the Second Front in Western Europe, began a decisive push. They ended the war in Europe in May 1945 by capturing Berlin.

For the Soviets, the victory was bittersweet. The whole European part of the Soviet Union was ruined and the country's resources exhausted. The country had lost about 26 million people, including about 11 million military casualties (Krivosheev, 2001). Yet the Second World War is widely considered today as one of the most glorious times in Russian history. Regardless of their political orientation, Russians are proud of the victory their troops helped to win. The many battles they fought, including those for Moscow, St Petersburg, Stalingrad, and Kursk, are glorified in the media and mass culture. Opinions vary, however, about many important details, and particularly the role of Stalin in the victory against Germany. His decisive role is as indisputable as it is controversial. He is credited as the supreme commander but criticized for making significant mistakes not just in the preparations (including the execution of commanders) but also in the conduct of the war, which contributed to the very heavy casualties.

On the whole, most Soviet people felt that the victory over Germany was a triumph not only for Russia but also for the Soviet system. They accept the view that was promoted in the Soviet Union, that the Soviet system acted as the defender of humankind against aggressors. The Soviet Union, in their view, also unified its many ethnic groups, who all fought shoulder-to-shoulder against the enemy. Nationalistic feelings grew: the war awakened Russian national self-identity (Grossman, 1970). Russians to this day are very sensitive about any evaluations of the Second World War that play down the role of the Soviet Union in ending the Nazi regime in Germany. Most Russians continue to emphasize the defeat of Germany as the main outcome of that war. They tend to give less weight to Stalin's mistakes and the aggressive nature of the Soviet Union's foreign policy after 1945.

Russians speak their mind ...

... On the Soviet occupation of Europe in 1945. Percentage of Russians saying that in 1945 the Soviet Army, after liberating Central Europe, established communist regimes there: 11. Percentage considering the actions of the Soviet Army as an act of "liberation": 77 percent.

Source: WCIOM (2009b).

The Soviet Union during the Cold War

After 1945, the Soviet Union emerged as a substantially weakened yet victorious nation, unified around its ruler. Although the leaders in Moscow, Washington, and London had established very productive relations during the war, in 1945 they failed to create the conditions for lasting good relations. The period from the end of the war to the late 1980s is known as the **Cold War**. This describes the global state of tension (though not outright warfare) between the Soviet Union and its closest allies on the one hand, and the United States with its allies, on the other.

There were several causes of this bitter division. From an ideological standpoint, the United States and the Soviet Union were examples of different types of political system, and both claimed that the other's system was inhumane and dangerous. The Soviet ideology maintained a belief in the inevitability of a conflict between communism and imperialism. Anticommunism was an official policy in Washington. By August 1949 the Soviet Union had become a nuclear power, after the United States had developed (and used) its nuclear capabilities in 1945. The emerging nuclear competition brought fear and distrust to both countries. Personal factors also contributed to the tension. Stalin, for example, became increasingly fearful about a nuclear conflict with the west, and even believed that it was inevitable (Zubok, 2007).

For almost the entire second half of the 20th century, both countries engaged in an endless global competition. Mutual suspicions and fears drove the defense and security policies of both nations, and the build-up of arms in the "arms race" drained national resources. Russia became a major international player, and tried to counter any real or perceived advance of the United States and its allies, in almost every part of the world. The Soviet Union joined China and North Korea in their fight against troops from the United States and the United Nations in South Korea in 1950–53. In a similar way, Moscow sent instructors, military aircraft, weapons, food, and money to the Vietnamese forces fighting against the United States during the Vietnam War in the 1960s and early 1970s. The Soviet government sponsored communist parties in their attempts to win or retain power in countries in Central Europe. Moscow crushed anti-Communist revolts in Hungary in 1956 and in Czechoslovakia in 1968. The Soviets openly supported Fidel Castro in Cuba, and placed nuclear missiles there in 1962, causing one of the most significant nuclear crises in history. In 1979 the Soviet military entered Afghanistan, and remained in the country for the next eight years. Moscow provided supplies and either openly or secretly participated in violent conflicts in Guatemala, Palestine, Angola, Mozambique, Ethiopia, and many other countries.

The post-war reconstruction

Back in the 1940s, the Soviet Union needed to recover from the post-war economic crisis. Most attention was given to heavy industries, many of which had been transferred temporarily during the war to eastern parts of Russia. The authorities continued to use semi-military policies. In some places, people who skipped work or underperformed were treated as criminals. The Kremlin continued to publish reports about hidden enemies, saboteurs, and foreign agents. In the countryside, because there was an acute shortage of laborers most small collective farms were reorganized and incorporated into larger collective or state farms. The number of these farms fell to 94,000, three times fewer than before the war (Orlov et al., 2008).

The economic situation began to improve in the late 1940s. The food rationing that had been introduced during the war was gradually eased, then abandoned. Monetary reform took place in 1947. State-controlled retail prices went down. Local governments began to restore ruined cities and towns, build new apartments, and distribute them for free among the neediest. However, there remained a housing shortage, and the lack of good-quality affordable housing is still a problem today.

The thaw

Stalin's death in 1953 was an agonizing event for the entire nation. He had been the country's supreme leader for more than 25 years. His name was commonly associated with his country's most spectacular achievements, including the victory in the war and the post-war reconstruction. Many people, particularly those who lived in large cities, genuinely believed that the political repressions that had taken place under Stalin's watch had been necessary. Some of them did not accept that innocent people had been persecuted, but believed all the victims had been criminals, saboteurs, wreckers, or spies (Davies, 1997). Others accepted that there had been massive abuses of power, but believed that Stalin had been unaware of all that was being done in his name. See Table 2.2.

However, a new and powerful political doctrine emerged in the middle of 1950s and shattered some of the pro-Stalinist beliefs. A new political leader,

Table 2.2   *The views of Russians today on Stalin*

Percentage agreeing with the following statements:	
Stalinist repressions were the right thing to do	2
Under Stalin, the country was moving in the right direction	37
The country under Stalin was moving in the wrong direction	48
Most victims of the repressions were innocent	51

Source: WCIOM (2008).

Nikita Khrushchev (1894–1971), came to power in the Kremlin, assuming the posts of the General Secretary of the Communist Party and Chair of the Council of Ministers. A down-to-earth, energetic, accessible, and outspoken leader, he was a direct contrast to Stalin, who had seldom appeared in public and remained in many ways a mysterious figure. But personality was not the only difference between Khrushchev and Stalin: Khrushchev was a pragmatic and populist leader. He sincerely believed in communist ideas, but he also believed that the country needed to change its direction.

One of Khrushchev's major decisions was a daring attempt to demolish the "personality cult" that had grown up around his predecessor. At the 20th Congress of the Communist Party in 1956, Khrushchev delivered a secret speech in which he described Stalin's methods as serious violations of "true" communist methods of management, which were supposed to be transparent and democratic. The report mentioned the mass repressions and human right violations that had taken place in the Stalin era. Khrushchev stopped short of calling Stalin's behavior criminal, but the signal was clear. Soon Stalin's statues began to disappear from offices and city squares. Stalin's embalmed body was removed from the mausoleum near the Kremlin where it had been placed next to Lenin's body (which is still on show there today) and buried in a grave by the Kremlin wall. Khrushchev's new policies called for openness and collegiality in decisions.

People could now speak freely without fear of being interrogated or arrested. The ability to learn from past mistakes was largely attributed to the socialist system's capability for self-improvement. The party was returning to the "normal" course of life and work: no repressions, no political witch-hunt, and no new personality cult. Foreign policy was changing. A new concept of coexistence with the capitalist world emerged. By the end of the 1950s, the quality of life had improved substantially for most citizens. By the early 1960s, television had become affordable for many Soviet families. Technology also brought opportunities to listen to foreign radio (although this was not formally encouraged). The government began to allow some trusted people to travel abroad (which had been forbidden formerly), and opened up limited opportunities to participate in foreign student and professional exchanges, especially with socialist countries. All these developments helped people acquire a more realistic image of their life and society. So Khrushchev's ascension to power and the implementation of new policies created an atmosphere of hopeful anticipation of change (Zubok, 2009).

The stagnation period

However, many senior Communist leaders were unhappy with Khrushchev's hectic leadership style and reckless decisions, and they voted him out of power in 1964. Under the next three leaders, Leonid Brezhnev (1906–1982), Yuri Andropov (1914–1984), and Konstantin Chernenko (1911–1985) (who all remained in power till their deaths), the country's economic development slowed down and liberal political reforms did not take place.

Overall, the Soviet Union remained a socialist country with a complicated system of internal control (Simanov, 2009). According to the Soviet governing doctrine, all economic decisions were made in Moscow by government planning and managing organs. Production targets were determined for each enterprise. Factory managers and regional party bosses were under tremendous pressure to fulfill these targets (Stephen, 1991: 36).

The governments in the 1970s and 1980s suppressed and marginalized most intellectual opposition. Censorship was strengthened and remained effective. Most people had only limited access to western countries (through infrequent tourism) and the western media. There were only rare instances of mass resistance to the regime. Public acceptance of the system and private unhappiness with it were the norm. Most Soviet people showed formal support for the government and its leadership, no matter who occupied the highest offices in the Kremlin. However, the 1970s was also a time when the prestige of official ideology and labor ethics were in decline. Mass cynicism (a mixture of skepticism and fake enthusiasm) spread steadily. The period from the late 1970s to the middle of the 1980s was a time of widespread political apathy in the Soviet Union. The events of 1985 and the political ascendance of Mikhail Gorbachev (discussed in Chapter 3) brought this phase to a close, and changed the country forever.

Critical thinking about Russia's history

To begin, search Google images for "Red Square." This is the center of Moscow, the area outside the Kremlin. What kind of associations do the images produce in your mind? Some will think mostly of a beautiful yet eclectic architectural assembly. For other people, the very name "Red Square" automatically conjures up associations with a brutal political regime of the past. To many others, Red Square is associated with stability, inspiration, and hope. Whose perceptions are more accurate and whose are misleading?

Perhaps that is the wrong question: for people almost always disagree how to interpret history and how to apply its lessons to today's developments, and very different viewpoints can all have their own validity. Equally, they can be all open to critical thought and reconsideration. Let's consider some examples.

The imperial-moralistic tradition

According to this view, Russia's might, influence, and success have always been associated with a strong, authoritarian power that was capable of consolidating the country. In contrast, all decisions and policies that caused disunity in Russia were harmful to the country, and caused significant problems to its population. The early periods of disunity among Russian dukes caused their major economic and military weakness and their ultimate inability to resist the Mongol invaders. The great dukes of Moscow managed to overcome the state of disunity. They expelled foreign rulers, escaped dependency, and built the foundations for the rapid economic and social development of the country.

To supporters of the imperial-moralistic view, the main lessons of Russia's history are clear. Continuously over hundreds of years, Russia has been surrounded by hostile neighbors. In the context of these tense conditions, the only way for Russia to survive as a nation and state is for it to consolidate its resources in the hands of a strong central authority. This authority needs to pursue policies that will preserve unity and ensure the state's survival. A unified Russian state (and by extension, Russian Empire) is an example of strength and stability. People taking this viewpoint accept that none of the authoritarian rulers of Russia have been perfect, but they believe that in spite of the alleged (and real) violations of human rights, these rulers pursued the policies that were necessary to keep the country unified and enable it to become a great power (Fillipov, 2009).

We will see later in the book how this view has shaped Russia's official policies. In particular, there are several key arguments or assumptions that underpin it, and many Russians today accept them.

First, as Russia's history proves it, Russia must remain united territorially and politically. Unity is the only way for it to survive and prosper.

Second, because of its size and diversity, Russia is not necessarily "ready" for democracy along the liberal, West European or North American lines. History shows that only a strong power in the Kremlin is capable of keeping Russia unified and "working."

Third, although there have been antidemocratic polices and abuses of power, critics tend to judge these too harshly. These policies were necessary because they helped Russia reach a higher goal of national unity.

Fourth, as long as Russia remains strong and unified, it will be surrounded by powerful enemies who oppose the country and its "sovereign" democracy. In fact, in the late 1980s only 13 percent of Russians believed that Russia had enemies. Twenty years later, the number went up, and today it reaches 70 percent in some polls (Gudkov, 2008b).

Supporters of the **critical-liberal** view reject these major assumptions of the imperial-moralistic tradition. They argue that Russia has not necessarily always been surrounded by hostile neighbors throughout its history. Authoritarianism is not the only reasonable way to govern. In fact, history suggests that a democratic path of development provides better conditions for a country, its people, and its relations with other states. They claim that concentration of power and resources in one location was harmful to the country's economic and political development. For example, Russia's victory in the Second World War is not a demonstration of the efficiency of the authoritarian system. It was the effort of millions of people who, in fact, won the war (Karatsuba, Kurukin, and Sokolov, 2006; Sokolov, 2008).

Russians speak their mind ...

... On Russian historic figures. *Which Russian historic figures draw most approval or sympathy today?*
Percentage of Russians evaluating Lenin positively: 40.
Percentage seeing Lenin negatively: 30.
Percentage of Russians evaluating Stalin positively: 28.
Percentage seeing Stalin negatively: 48.

Source: WCIOM (2008).

The "unique experience" models

Unlike the supporters and opponents of the imperial-moralistic tradition, who focus on what should happen in Russia today on the basis of its "good" and "bad" historic experiences, supporters of other models emphasize one particular aspect of Russia's past and try to explain its history from that point of view.

For example, supporters of the **Eurasian model** of Russia's development set forth two main propositions. First, Russian history is unique and its experience cannot be assessed by models applicable to other countries. Second, Russia's true destiny lies in preserving its natural Eurasian roots and avoiding the temptation to imitate western models of government and culture (Gumilev, 2004). The "Eurasians" tend to dismiss the positive impact of western experiences on Russia, and claim that Russia is capable of creating its own statehood without foreign, western influence (Orlov et al., 2008).

Others argue that certain Russian policies can be explained not by ideologies but by the circumstances surrounding Russia. For example, Russia grew in size and expanded because it could. It could be viewed as an aggressive and expansionist state, but in fact its policies were determined by Russia's unique geographic position, under which the policy of expansionism was a natural one (Aslund and Kuchins, 2009).

The Sovietologists

At least two major schools of thought regarding the Soviet Union were developed by **Sovietologists**, the name that used to be given to foreign specialists studying the Soviet Union. The first is the totalitarian school, which emphasized the abusive and authoritarian nature of the Soviet system. The other is the revisionist school, which has largely presented the Soviet Union as a "normal" society, one among many with similar features. The totalitarian theorists, as a rule, overestimated the Soviet regime's strength, stability, and its threats. They also miscalculated the Soviet people's disaffection with the Communist regime. Revisionists, on the other hand, while giving many important insights about gradual changes within the Soviet regime, were sometimes too eager (for ideological or political reasons) to portray the Soviet Union as a society not much different from any other country. While theorists of the totalitarian school condemned the Soviet regime, the revisionists were inclined to treat it in a rather accepting way (Shlapentokh et al., 2008).

For example, supporters of the totalitarian school of thought saw Russia as an exclusively authoritarian country. Overall, the Russian people have had very little exposure to democratic institutions, democratic traditions, and basic individual liberties over the course of the country's history. Whereas some democratic elements of self-government existed in various forms, and elements of collectivism have become major attributes of Russian culture, authoritarianism was and continues to be the backbone of the Russian civilization. The state was responsible for every aspect of life (Levinson, 2008). This stance of understanding the Soviet Union as a totalitarian society was supported by many scholars, including Hannah Arendt (1951) and Zbigniew Brzezinski (1966).

Prominent historians such as Richard Pipes (1984) have argued that socialist ideas did not in fact play an important role in Soviet history, seeing them only as a thin cover for Russo-centric authoritarianism. Pipes also disregarded the socialist nature of the 1917 October "coup" and a number of political developments that followed, and downgraded the significance of Marxist ideology in the belief systems of the original Russian revolutionaries. Socialist ideology, in his view, was only a convenient rationalization for power-thirsty Bolsheviks to grab control of the country. Another prominent author, Robert Tucker (1961), saw the regime that emerged under Lenin and Stalin as a type of neo-czarist order that labeled itself socialist. He considered the developments that took place in the 1930s as a setback in the direction of the Russian imperial order, and

saw the later Soviet policies as attempts to overcome the country's historical backwardness (Tucker, 1990). Overall, prominent totalitarianists have
portrayed the Soviet Union as a system rooted in prerevolutionary Russian
authoritative traditions.

Many critics of these views, particularly from the political liberal wing,
argued that some historians, and political scientists, who wanted to
emphasize the gloomiest features of Russia and the Soviet regime, most
likely exaggerated their facts because of their anti-Soviet and anti-communist ideological motivation (Fitzpatrick, 1986). After the success of the
Soviet Union in economic, space, and military fields, many scholars began
to claim that the Soviet socialism was a social system that had a number of
advantages over free-market capitalism. Some, like Walt Rostow (1967),
believed that the Soviet Union was just one of many modern industrial
societies. Others suggested that the Soviet experience could become a
model for developing countries in Africa or Asia, especially those that had
freed themselves from colonialism. These critics mostly dismissed reports
about troubling events in Russia, such as political oppression, as research
inaccuracies, deliberate lies, or right-wing propaganda. They emphasized
the welfare nature of the Russian state. They underlined, for example, that
in the Soviet Union, women were given paid leave before and after child-
birth, and the government had established a nationwide system of daycare
centers and kindergartens for preschoolers. Affordable 24 and 48-day
summer camps for children of all ages were very popular among Soviet
families. Soviet people did not have to pay for tuition for their children
because the government subsidized college education.

Conclusion

A history of any country sometimes looks like a parade of names. Russians
are proud of their heroes. They praise Duke Vladimir for baptizing Russia
and Alexander Nevsky for defending the land from the Teutonic knights.
They recognize Peter the Great for building a strong empire, and Field
Marshal Kutuzov for defeating Napoleon of France. They glorify Marshall
Zhukov for winning the Great Patriotic War in 1945, and are proud of
Yuri Gagarin for being the first person in space in 1961.

In other cases people are well known but their value is controversial.
Was Ivan the Terrible a great statesman conducting brutal policies or a
mentally unstable villain? Lenin, seen as a saint-like figure for three generations in the Soviet Union, now appears to many people as a dangerous
dictator. The events of the fall of 1917 are called by different names by
those who saw it as positive and those who saw it as negative and illegitimate: one person's Great October Socialist Revolution is another's

October revolt. Should Stalin be praised for building a powerful nuclear state, or should he receive condemnation because of the millions of innocent people who died because of his policies? Did Khrushchev strengthen the country by revealing Stalin's abuses of power, or did he weaken the economy and plant the seeds of doubt in the minds of many Russian people?

History teaches us different lessons. Russian politicians often interpret and use these lessons to justify their policies today, as we will see in the following chapters.

Chapter 3

The Soviet Transformation, 1985–91

Why the reforms were necessary
The beginning of the transformation
Perestroika and glasnost
Unintended consequences
Critical thinking about the Soviet transformation
Conclusion

> *We are experiencing a revolution, perestroika is a revolution.*
> Andrei Sakharov (1921–1989), nuclear physicist,
> human rights activist, and politician

> *Above all we have to admit that the collapse of the Soviet Union was the biggest geopolitical catastrophe of the 20th century.*
> Vladimir Putin, president of Russia, 2005

"Who lives well in Russia?" A celebrated Russian poet and critic, Nikolai Nekrasov (1821–1878), posed this illustrious question in his unfinished poem, studied in every school of the Soviet Union. The school curriculum required all Russian literature teachers not only to analyze Nekrasov's beautiful rhyme and metaphor, but also to remind eighth-graders about the injustices of tsarist Russia, where everybody had to endure a miserable, unhappy life. Socialism was supposed to be different, better. According to official textbooks, newspapers, and posters, life in the Soviet Union was great. Why were most people ultimately unhappy with the authorities and the situation in the country?

The beginning of the transformation

By the early 1980s, the whole of Soviet society had seemingly reached a point of economic and moral stagnation (Hosking, 1992). Most people were disappointed with the quality of their lives and disenchanted with socialism (Shlapentokh, Shiraev, and Carroll, 2008). There were several major sources of this dissatisfaction.

Mounting problems

First, the country was experiencing serious *economic problems*. The Soviet economy was struggling. The growth rate of GNP declined steadily through the Brezhnev years in power (1963–82), from 4.7 percent per year in the middle of the 1960s to 2.0 percent in the early 1980s. Significant slowdowns continued in industrial production, agricultural output, labor productivity, capital formation, investment, and per-capita income (Hewett, 1988: 52). Gigantic state subsidies to industries and agriculture and growing military spending put a tightening noose on the country's financial system. Many experts today agree that by the early 1980s the government in Moscow could not address many basic socioeconomic needs of the population (Gaidar, 2007). Key consumer products were absent from retail stores, while others were in very short supply: in big cities, for example, people could buy only three kinds of cheese and one kind of butter. Instant coffee was a rarity. It was next to impossible to find disposable diapers, toilet paper, and many kinds of first-aid medications. The country was far behind the west in average living standards (Shiraev and Zubok, 2000).

Second, the increasing economic failure went hand-in-hand with massive *social problems*. Bureaucracy and corruption at all levels exemplified the enormous organizational inefficiency. Bribery became an everyday norm: people paid money illegally to state employees to avoid a traffic ticket, obtain a pair of German shoes, or fix a leaking faucet. Soviet society was turning into an undeclared caste system. On the one hand, there was a small but powerful circle of people with status, perks, and limited privileges. These were party bureaucrats, government officials, and people with direct access to the state-run and corrupt distribution of goods and services. On the other side, there were the working poor with no assets and low income. In the middle, there was the majority: people with jobs but no investments and very little financial savings.

Third, *social apathy* was widespread. In the absence of real political competition within a one-party system, voting was mostly a theatrical act staged by the governments and silently accepted by most people (Bahry and Silver, 1990: 837–8). People in two successive generations began to recognize that, in reality, American, Swedish, and West German living standards were much higher, and that the gap between the Soviet Union and most western countries was too wide. Most people at that time believed that the wealth disparity between the Soviet Union and the west was because of the inefficiency of the socialist system. They also believed that the socialist system, in theory, was reparable (Gorbachev and Mlynar, 1994).

Overall, in the 1980s, the Soviet Union lived in a state of suspended belief in possible change. Very few people, however, including the most ardent but silent critics of the regime, believed that the change would come as rapidly as it did, or be as radical as it was (Shiraev and Bastrykin, 1988).

The rise of Mikhail Gorbachev

Within a short period, two top party leaders died: first Yuri Andropov (1914–1984), then Konstantin Chernenko (1911–1985). They were buried, according to tradition, behind the Lenin Mausoleum near the Kremlin Wall in front of Red Square. In March 1985 the sixth general secretary of the Communist Party, 54-year-old Mikhail Gorbachev, made a brief televised address to the people. Despite his relatively young age, Gorbachev was not a novice in the Soviet system. He had spent nearly 30 years in the ranks of the party bureaucracy, gradually moving to the highest position. His arrival

Mikhail Gorbachev

Mikhail Gorbachev was born in 1931 near Stavropol, in a southern region of Russia. His town was under German occupation for several months. After finishing high school he studied at the prestigious Moscow State University, from which he graduated in 1955 with a law degree (in the Soviet Union this was a five-year undergraduate degree). Almost immediately after graduation he received a political appointment in a regional Youth Communist League in Stavropol. Later he occupied a number of different party posts, moving gradually up to the position of first secretary of the Stavropol Region Party Committee in 1970. It was a prestigious appointment: he was in charge of one of the largest agricultural regions of the Soviet Union. His official position put him on the shortlist of candidates for appointment to the highest ranks of the party. In 1978, he was transferred to Moscow and elected secretary of the Central Committee of the Communist Party in charge of agriculture. In 1984, as a Politburo member, he was responsible for the party ideology (control of the media, publishing, creative arts, youth organizations, and so on), which also brought him to an informal second position within the hierarchy. After Chernenko's death in 1985, Gorbachev became general secretary, and kept this position until 1991. He was also elected chairman of the Supreme Soviet (parliament) in 1989 and then president of the Soviet Union (elected in 1990 by the members of parliament, according to the Constitution). After his resignation in 1991, he continued to be an influential commentator, writer, and a public figure known for his generous charitable work.

there meant the beginning of a new and final stage of the Soviet Union (Kort, 2006).

When Gorbachev took power in March 1985, he did not wait long to initiate changes. But what exactly were they? Very few people, including Gorbachev himself, knew how to move forward (Gorbachev, 1985). Moreover, he believed in socialism and thought it could be reformed. Most people in the Soviet Union shared his point of view (Shlapentokh et al., 2009).

Attempts to revive the old system

Once in power Gorbachev made it clear that he was a dedicated Marxist. He compared the early attempts at reform in 1985 to Lenin's revolution started 70 years ago. Gorbachev's picture appeared frequently on official posters with Lenin's profile in the background. Gorbachev himself used historical examples to link the proposed reforms with the country's glorious past. He regularly mentioned Lenin's New Economic Policy of the 1920s (see Chapter 2) as a blueprint for his own economic plans. In fact, it is common for government leaders conducting reforms based on an ideology to claim that their new policy is "in line" with the established ideological (as in China) or religious (as in Iran) tradition.

Gorbachev suggested several major improvements. First, he wanted to make factory management more efficient. Second, he sought to introduce incentives in the workplace so that people could make more money by working harder or being innovative. Finally, he hoped to decentralize economic decision making to some degree. Socialism would be preserved but a limited market economy with a flexible price system was a possibility. But what was a market economy? According to the recollections of Anatoly Sobchak, a prominent professor and future mayor of St Petersburg, the term was confusing to people who had never practiced it (Sobchak, 1992).

Despite these uncertainties, Gorbachev won broad support among the elites and ordinary people alike. His support came largely from three groups. Party officials, factory managers, and military commanders saw Gorbachev as a leader who could revive the declining economy and consolidate more power in the institutions of the Communist Party. Most ordinary people saw him as an energetic leader who could punish bureaucrats and thieves and make the entire country work efficiently. Finally, many critics of the communist regime thought that Gorbachev would allow some long-awaited political changes in the country.

It was supposed to be a safe transition: Gorbachev wanted to make changes within the socialist system without altering its foundations.

Early steps

A new term, "socialist entrepreneurship," appeared frequently in news-paper editorials. For the Kremlin, it meant an ideologically correct blend of socialism with elements of the free market (the government of China uses the term "market socialism" to label the similar economic reforms there today). Factory managers received instructions to embrace a new kind of socialist entrepreneurship and produce more of everything, of higher quality. However, these instructions contained little substance except for proposals for more government control. For example, to address the low quality of industrial production, in 1986 the government established a new institution of federal inspection, which had previously only been carried out in top-secret defense industries. The federal author-ities could now monitor the quality of all manufactured products and reject those of low quality. Yet the new inspection system was grossly inef-fective: manufacturers pressured federal inspectors not to reject their products. The entire bureaucratic system of the country tried to resist any innovation.

Some reforms led to unfortunate blunders. As an illustration, in May 1985 the Kremlin launched a new anti-alcohol policy. Excessive drinking was (and remains today) a serious social problem. Tens of millions of work days were missed every year as a result of drinking. The number of alcohol-related traumas and deaths had grown, overcrowded rehabilitation facilities could not provide decent treatment, and millions of families suffered. The new anti-alcohol campaign limited the production of hard liquor, beer, and wine. Cities and towns began to limit alcohol sales by establishing shorter hours of operation for state-run liquor stores. The government prohibited drinking in the workplace. Unfortunately, the reform did not bring the expected results. Long lines to buy alcohol appeared on the streets of every city. Many families began to hoard wine and vodka as assets for barter. Day laborers customarily accepted vodka as a payment for their work. Facing limited production and rationing, some people turned to "moonshine" (illegally produced alcoholic drinks) and surrogates. Most saw the anti-alcohol reform as another government flop, poorly planned and badly executed.

There were serious mistakes in other areas. Even though Gorbachev promised honesty and transparency in all areas of Soviet life, he and his advisers did not always follow what they preached. One of the worse examples of such inconsistency was the reaction of Moscow's officials to the nuclear power plant incident at Chernobyl in 1986. Although the accident had caused substantial loss of life and threatened the lives and health of millions of people in the areas adjacent to Chernobyl, Gorbachev was slow to allow the state-owned news organizations to disclose this information. In the eyes of ordinary people this procrastination was a typical example of the same old policy of suppression of politically damaging information.

Gorbachev knew of these and other mistakes. Before long he realized that a few superficial measures could not revive the sluggish economy or eliminate bureaucracy. The country needed a massive reform in all areas of its political, social, and economic life. The deep and sweeping changes initiated by Gorbachev and his close supporters received the famous labels **perestroika** and **glasnost**.

Perestroika and glasnost

In the Russian language *perestroika* means "restructuring" and *glasnost* means "openness." These two key words relate to the process of massive reforms undertaken in the second half of the 1980s and commonly associated with Mikhail Gorbachev, their initiator. What were the key elements of the reforms? We will look at domestic changes first and then examine Soviet foreign policy.

Opening up

Perestroika and glasnost were the names given to policies of massive restructuring in political and economic areas. These policies greatly changed people's access to information. Perhaps the earliest and real change that most people felt after 1985 was the rapid weakening and disappearance of political censorship.

In a series of dramatic moves, many previously prohibited books and movies were released to the public. Among them were works by writers such as Alexander Solzhenitsyn, Vasily Aksyonov, and Anatoly Rybakov. In December 1986, Gorbachev personally ordered the release of Andrei Sakharov, a renowned physicist, Nobel Prize winner and critic of the communist regime, from his internal exile in the city of Gorky. In October 1987, Gorbachev became the first Soviet leader to publicly denounce Stalin (as was mentioned in Chapter 2, Khrushchev did so 30 years earlier but only through party channels). Gorbachev called Stalin's crimes "enormous and unforgivable" (Doder and Branson, 1990: 183). He appointed a commission to review the purge trials of the 1930s, when numerous innocent citizens were falsely accused and executed. Gorbachev called these trials a "gross violation of socialist legality" (Taubman, 1987: 1).

Russians speak their mind ...

... **On Stalin**. Percentage of Russians in 2008 saying that Stalin played a positive role in Russia's history: 39. Percentage of Russians saying that Stalin played a negative role: 38.

Source: Levada (2008).

Web

On the book website you can access reviews (in both English and Russian) of literary works by Alexander Solzhenitsyn, Vasily Aksyonov, Anatoly Rybakov, and other authors whose works were prohibited in the Soviet Union prior to glasnost.

The middle of 1980s was a time of rapid political enlightenment. Newspapers began to publish unflattering facts about the Soviet Union's past, including government persecution of citizens for political reasons. With most restrictions against grassroots movements lifted, scores of people joined new social and professional organizations. People for the first time tested their personal freedom. Increasingly often, officials allowed public gatherings and demonstrations.

Changes in the media

Newspapers and weekly magazines played a crucial role in the reforms. Weakening political censorship did not mean that all publications immediately changed their content and tone. As often happens in history, it took a few brave individuals—producers, editors, and journalists—to accept responsibility and take the initiative (Korotich, 2000). At first, most articles critical of socialism were relatively "soft." However, by 1988, most printed media were involved in a relentless campaign of criticizing socialism as a system. Moscow publications such as the daily *Komsomolskaya Pravda* and weekly *Ogonyok*, *Argumenty i Facty*, and *Literaturnaya Gazeta* led a daring charge.

Television was changing too. In the mid-1980s the Soviet Union had basically one government-owned major network called Central Television. It was responsible for broadcasting all across the country. Outside Moscow, in addition to the programs generated in the capital and distributed through the network, people had access to one or two local government-controlled networks. With the loosening of the party control over programming, television professionals were allowed to produce almost anything they wanted. The late 1980s was the time of a genuine outburst of new entertainment programs, concerts, and game shows. Most popular were late-evening live talk shows. Their hosts discussed the most interesting topics of the day and answered phonecalls. The viewers liked these unrehearsed and innovative programs for their spontaneity and honesty. Gorbachev and his close advisers mainly supported such innovations.

Reforming the Communist Party

Gorbachev also tried to reform the party. First, he hoped to prompt discussions within the local party organizations. Competition and open debate within their ranks were a clear break from tradition. The Communist Party Regulations, a sacred rule book for generations of Soviet communists, specifically prohibited any factions within the party (see Chapter 2). The ban had also meant suppression of any open disagreement of regular members with party bosses. In 1988, however, dissent was allowed. These changes, as Gorbachev noted at a Politburo meeting on December 27, 1988, should have revitalized the Communist Party (Politburo Meeting transcript, 1988). However, many party members were unhappy with these changes. They believed that the party was taking a wrong turn.

Second, Gorbachev put through measures to introduce several democratic principles of government. He wanted to increase the power of local elected officials at the expense of the party committees (Gorbachev, 1996). It took almost two years to set up multi-candidate competitive elections for party officials, factory management, and local government bodies (Taubman, 1987). One of the most significant steps was the weakening of party control over economic issues. The Central Committee Secretariat, which was essentially in charge of industries, had to turn to internal, party-related problems.

In March 1990, Gorbachev assumed the newly established office of president, which enabled him to become free of direct party control. The intention was for him to hold the presidency for a five-year term, then the next time around the position would be filled through multi-candidate elections (Imse, 1990: 1). That same month the Communist Party reluctantly agreed to revoke Article 6 of the Soviet Constitution, which had enshrined the Communist Party as the "leading and guiding force" in Soviet life (Gorbachev, 1995a: 317). It was a formal yet significant political change. Most party hardliners were against this amendment. Their disagreement with the change was understandable. From that moment, the party lost its legal right to control elected bodies and other branches of government across the entire Soviet Union.

Case in point: The scope of the reforms

You should not form the impression that the Communist Party was an assembly of reactionary forces blindly opposing the reforms. People wanted to see the Soviet Union as a strong, efficient, and respected nation. The problem was that most party members did not agree how far and deep the reforms should go.

Here for example is a list of resolutions considered by the 19th All-Union Conference of the Communist Party, gathered in Moscow in summer 1988. It shows the scope and diversity of the problems the Communist Party was trying to address during the reform period:

On some urgent measures of practical realization of the political system's reforms.
On democratization of the Soviet Society and the political system's reforms.
On struggle against bureaucracy.
On relations among nationalities.
On glasnost.
On legal reforms.

As you can see, party officials tried to solve many massive problems at once, and make a difference in as many areas of life as possible. As history often shows, such rapid and massive political and social reforms can easily backfire and bring undesirable consequences.

Further political changes

In December 1988 a new law, On Elections of People's Deputies of the USSR, outlined a new type of parliamentary elections free from the party's control. The first elections of a newly created national parliament were held in March 1989.

In May 1989, the First Congress of People's Deputies gathered in Moscow. Although the selection of the delegates was not entirely democratic (they included delegates selected by official organizations such as labor unions, the Academy of Sciences, and the Communist Party), it was generally free and open. Honest, frequently raucous debates took place during the Congress's opening sessions. By June 1989 the delegates of the Congress had elected a new Soviet parliament. During the following year, people voted for regional and local soviets. The elections removed from office many conservative communists who had actively opposed the reforms. Now, pro-reform deputies constituted a majority of newly elected councils in Moscow, Leningrad, and many large cities.

After the crucial Article 6 of the Constitution of the USSR, guaranteeing the monopoly of the Communist Party on power, was amended in March

1990, almost overnight nascent political parties sprang up. Within six months some 250 parties had registered in Moscow; the relatively small republic of Georgia registered more than 160 parties. These new parties, however, were poorly organized, had sketchy ideological platforms, and had very little political influence (Glad and Shiraev, 1999).

The policies of glasnost had accelerated the development of political freedoms. Political reforms produced free elections. Yet in the economic sphere, the reforms were for the most part slow.

Economic reforms

As has been explained, the entire economic system in the Soviet Union was based on central planning. Federal offices in Moscow were in charge of all production decisions, quotas, delivery schedules, and prices. The state also controlled natural resources, manufacturing facilities, machinery, banks, stores, and commercial institutions (Kenez, 2006). A few small-scale economic measures were introduced during the first two years of perestroika. They involved easing the strict system of centralized management. On the local level, the government allowed limited forms of entrepreneurship. Many formerly illegal "black-market" activities became legal, such as buying wholesale and selling retail to make a profit. Some small-scale enterprises such as repair and tailor's shops passed into private hands despite the ambiguity of laws governing the privatization of property. Within days, scores of new businesses began to sell counterfeit Levi's jeans, Lacoste shirts, and many other locally produced products. State and private enterprises could now use cash instead of carrying out the traditional paper-based financial transactions.

One of the most significant legal changes took place on May 26, 1988. A new law allowed private enterprises to be set up. It let people form small private partnerships with collective property. The newly established economic cooperatives could keep their profits, both domestic and foreign. The federal monopoly on foreign trade, which was lifted on December 22, 1988 (by decision 1526 of the Council of Ministers) gave businesses a chance to bypass the federal government in international business deals. The law signaled a radical change. For years, citizens of the Soviet Union had been forbidden to own foreign currency. In 1988 private possession of dollars and other world currencies was finally legal. Almost immediately many people using interpersonal contacts began to exchange their rubles (although in insignificant amounts) for US dollars, German and Finnish marks, or other foreign currencies.

In publications and official documents appearing since 1988, these and other economic changes received the label **radical economic reform**. The word "radical" meant that the government had cancelled many existing

Soviet laws and regulations related to economy and trade. Companies could buy directly from one another. In Gorbachev's plans the state itself was to be a customer, although a preferred one (Doder and Branson, 1990: 239–40).

Unfortunately, the ongoing rapid changes brought the economy into deepening chaos. On the one hand, the state was the principal owner of factories, plants, natural resources, and agricultural land. The vast majority of people remained state employees. Most fundamentals of the socialist economic system remained in place. On the other hand, the Kremlin allowed and encouraged people to embrace the principles of the free market. In addition, the republics of the Soviet Union wanted more reforms: they hoped to establish their own independent economic policies (Brumberg, 1991: 53–4).

Weakening the federal system

At least two factors contributed to the weakening of the federal system during perestroika. The first one was the Kremlin's federal policies. The ongoing economic and political decentralization offered the regions more political power. The weakening of political censorship strengthened many local oppositional groups demanding more freedom.

The rapid growth of powerful nationalist movements in several Soviet republics was the other factor. These movements went through three stages of development. First, many such groups, such as the Sajudis in Lithuania, appeared as student, professional, or cultural organizations. Their initial goal was to assist with the ongoing political and socioeconomic reforms on a local level. Next, in 1988 and later, they began to pursue nationalistic goals, demanding more sovereignty for their republics. Finally, several such movements grew into strong political parties fighting for sovereignty. By 1990, the Kremlin had no effective political or administrative resources to suppress demands for national sovereignty.

From the very beginning of the reforms, Gorbachev and his followers had not planned to dismantle the Soviet Union as a sovereign state. A majority of Soviet people back in 1991 did not want the Soviet Union to collapse. The country held a national referendum in March 1991. The question on the ballot was, "Do you consider necessary the preservation of the Union of Soviet Socialist Republics as a renewed federation of equal sovereign republics in which the rights and freedom of an individual of any nationality will be fully guaranteed?" Of those who voted, 76 percent answered yes. Nevertheless, in a little less than nine months, the Soviet Union had disappeared as a country from the political map (Sakwa, 1999).

Changes in foreign policy

Gorbachev himself called his initiatives in foreign policy **new thinking**. He questioned some of the basic assumptions of international relations in the nuclear age. In particular, Gorbachev raised three important points.

First, he argued that the ongoing confrontation between the superpowers should stop immediately and without preconditions. Second, all nuclear countries, particularly the Soviet Union and the United States, should reduce their deadly arsenals to the minimum needed to guarantee mutual security and international stability. Third, the new world of the end of the 20th century should stop ideological competition and turn to what were described as the *universal values* of peace and cooperation in international relations. This was perhaps Gorbachev's central point: world leaders should change the way they thought about politics and global affairs (Gorbachev, 1985: 1). He was convinced that the world should and could function according to certain basic values of universal validity (Sheehy, 1990: 220).

The "new thinking" foreign policy led to progress in arms limitation talks with the United States. Top-level meetings between Gorbachev and US President Ronald Reagan in Geneva (1985), Reykjavik (1986), Washington (1987), and Moscow (1988), resulted in the signing of the Intermediate Nuclear Forces (INF) treaty. Significant forward movement

Case in point: GRIT versus spirals of insecurity

During the Cold War, advocates of nuclear disarmament, frustrated by the superpowers' inability to guarantee international security, argued that there should be a way to exit the cycle of mutual insecurity. They believed that an effective solution might be found if one of the competing nation-states would initiate a series of small goodwill steps toward its opponents. Such steps would not undermine security; seen as sincere intentions supported by policies, they might pave a way out of the spiral of insecurity. Small, incremental, and conciliatory steps represent the core concept of the model called gradual reduction of international tension (GRIT). This model was often criticized as a romantic dream of idealists until Soviet leader Mikhail Gorbachev implemented it in his foreign policy in 1987–89, and by doing so transformed the entire security doctrine of the Soviet Union. The ultimate result of GRIT was the end of the Cold War.

In today's world, politicians and the media frequently discuss the strengths and weaknesses of this approach to bilateral and international relations. Many questions don't have easy answers. For example, must a government negotiate with hostile political regimes? Should it approach dictators and alleged sponsors of international terrorism? Should it establish contacts with its ideological opponents? The example of GRIT shows that under particular circumstances, engagement in diplomacy can be more beneficial for international security than open confrontation.

on the limitation of intercontinental nuclear weapons was also achieved. Reagan and Gorbachev established open and informal personal communications, which helped to develop mutual trust (Chernyaev, 2000). Both leaders soon began to talk about burying the Cold War for good. The dismantling of the confrontation between the superpowers proceeded apace, in 1989 and later under the George H. W. Bush administration (1988–92).

Gorbachev took unilateral steps to implement his vision of a new world. By 1989, the Soviet Union withdrew its troops from Afghanistan, ending the deadly war that had resulted in almost 15,000 deaths and more than 50,000 serious injuries on the Soviet side. Moscow stopped supporting pro-communist insurgencies around the world. By 1990 the Warsaw Pact, the Soviet-led military and political coalition in Central Europe, fell apart while the Soviet troops remained in their barracks. East and West Germany were on the way toward unification.

Changes in the military

The Kremlin initiated several important changes in Soviet military organization. In December 1988 Gorbachev announced his plans for a unilateral reduction of 500,000 in the number of Soviet military personnel. Generals who disagreed were removed from their posts (Bunich, 1992: 260–2; Chernyaev, 1993: 163). The retirement of Sergei Akhromeyev as chief of the General Staff marked the removal from active duty of the last of the marshals of the Soviet Union (Odom, 1990: 58). The Kremlin no longer felt that it should deceive the west about the size of its military budget, and in May 1989 it revealed its "real" size. It was about four times larger than had previously been acknowledged (The State, 1989: 11).

Despite the continuing changes and some encouraging poll numbers, Gorbachev was facing growing criticism. Although most people believed that reforms were necessary, opinion differed about the scope and direction of the changes. On the one hand, many people believed that the reforms were slow and indecisive. On the other hand, there was a very powerful voice of the opposition demanding that the reforms be slowed down. The main argument of the opposition was that the changes had resulted in many negative consequences and were harmful to the country's economy and security.

Unintended consequences

In 1990, five years after Gorbachev introduced the reforms, the Politburo published an assessment of the situation in the country: "People are upset with lack of stability in the society. Crisis continues in the economy. There is a hard financial situation. [We see] the overall decline of discipline and order. Crime is flourishing" (*Materialy Politburo*, 1990). Despite the genuine efforts of the reformers in the Kremlin, the country was in a state of crisis.

Growing socioeconomic problems

Perestroika did not bring about rapid economic revival. Partial reforms did not work. By 1989 the new private sector was unable to obtain enough goods and supplies, since these remained under central control. Price reform did not occur, and there was rapid inflation which led to panic buying and excessive hoarding, which in turn contributed to the scarcity of consumer goods in stores (Medvedev, 1994: 39, 55). Wildcat strikes forced by economic hardships further undercut production. The old, centralized economic system was in disarray. Close advisors told Gorbachev that people were turning against the erratic economic reforms (Chernyaev, 1993).

By early 1990 nearly three-quarters of all respondents in a public opinion survey conducted by *Ogonyok* reported that they had experienced shortages of necessary food items "quite often" or "constantly" (Glad and Shiraev, 1999). In the 1970s, an average family spent about 50 percent of its income on food. By the 1990s, this number was close to 90 percent (Shiraev, 1999b: 114).

Uncertainty and frustrations

Bereft of guidance from the Kremlin, many local party officials expressed confusion. They constantly asked for advice but the Kremlin's reply was that they should figure out everything themselves (Ligachev, 1996: 85). Glasnost, while it promoted freedom of speech, also produced many unintended consequences. The revelations in the media about Josef Stalin's crimes and the relentless criticisms of socialism contributed to the psychological state of pessimism among people. Many of them had become accustomed to relying on the government in everything, and they could not adapt to the growing economic uncertainties of perestroika.

Gorbachev soon became the target of popular frustrations. The results of a poll published in the popular weekly *Argumenty i Facty* in 1989 indicated that Gorbachev was not among the top ten most popular figures in the Supreme Soviet (Doder and Branson, 1990: 391). At the May Day ceremony (a major occasion in the Soviet Union, with large public gatherings and official rallies in all cities) in 1990, many people near the reviewing stand in Moscow jeered the government officials. They chanted and carried banners with the slogans, "Down with Gorbachev" and "72 Years to Nowhere" (referring to the years that had passed since the 1917

Revolution). By spring 1991, Gorbachev's approval ratings in the national polls had dropped to 14 percent (Brumberg, 1991: 54).

Criticisms of foreign policy

The majority of people in the Soviet Union supported the ending of the unpopular war in Afghanistan, but the growing conservative opposition was generally unhappy with Gorbachev's foreign policy. They accused him and his advisers of making several fatal blunders. These arguments are especially popular today among Russian foreign policy elites. There were three main points of criticism.

First, the critics maintained that Moscow had lost its strategic positions in Eastern Europe. They saw the disintegration of the Soviet empire in Eastern Europe—as Poland, Hungary, Czechoslovakia, East Germany, Bulgaria, and Romania overthrew their communist governments—as a defeat in the Cold War. Following the fall of the Berlin Wall in October 1989, East Germany was officially reunited with West Germany, creating a country firmly in the western camp, and the Warsaw Pact was disbanded. Yet the US-led rival NATO alliance remained intact. This situation effectively put the Soviet Union in a very vulnerable strategic position.

Second, Gorbachev was accused of abandoning most of Moscow's long-term allies, such as Cuba, Nicaragua, Vietnam, Ethiopia, and Angola. Such a policy weakened Soviet geopolitical positions (Katz, 1991). Critics maintained that Gorbachev was setting a dangerous precedent, which would move other countries further away politically from the Soviet Union (Dobrynin, 1995, 622–32).

Finally, it appeared that the ongoing negotiations with the United States had really taken the form of unilateral concessions to the west. The Soviet Union was about to lose its superpower status. Critics underlined that although the Cold War was ending, Moscow had had to pay an unfair price: the Soviets had lost their strategic allies around the world and accepted the global domination of the United States in the post-Cold War situation. Washington offered almost nothing in return.

A collapsing union

At home, calls for national self-determination became louder. On December 28, 1989, Lithuania registered the first openly noncommunist political party in the Soviet Union, and in Latvia politicians openly challenged Moscow's economic policies. In March 1990 the republics of Lithuania and Estonia declared formal independence. Latvia and Moldova followed. On June 12, 1990, the Supreme Soviet of the Russian Federation issued an official declaration on Russia's sovereignty.

Finally, at a highly secret meeting at a nature reserve in Belarus on December 8, 1991, Russian Federation President Boris Yeltsin, and the leaders of the Ukraine and Belarus, delivered the death blow to the Soviet Union. A loose confederation called the Commonwealth of Independent States was created in its place.

The awakening of the opposition

Although by 1991 two-thirds of the important decision makers at all levels of the Communist Party, and the entire membership of the Politburo, had been replaced by people seemingly loyal to Gorbachev (Chernyaev, 1993: 63; Boldin, 1994: 293), a new opposition to the reforms grew up. The main source of the dissent was in the ranks of the military, the national security apparatus, and among conservative Communist Party members. They used the free press to launch attacks against Gorbachev and the reforms. The Orthodox Church pressured Gorbachev from a nationalist position. In December 1990, the Russian Patriarch (the supreme head of the Church), Aleksy II, joined several nationalists in a letter published in the pro-communist daily *Sovetskaya Rossiya*, demanding that Gorbachev declare a state of emergency and save the country from anti-socialist, pro-western forces that, it was claimed, represented a threat to religious Orthodoxy.

In light of the growing criticism, the Kremlin agreed to strengthen the powers of the military, police, and security forces. In 1989, the military cracked down on peaceful public protests in the Republic of Georgia. A presidential decree established a joint army–police patrol for enforcement of law and order on the streets. Another decree ordered security forces and the military to enter any establishment suspected of speculative activities and inspect their financial records. As a culmination of the growing crack-down, in early January 1991, federal troops in Vilnius and Riga used force to repress secessionist public demonstrations (Glad and Shiraev, 1999).

The opposition groups in the parliament continued to assail Gorbachev and his policies. At the same time, a strong opposition movement grew within the ranks of the reformers.

Democratic opposition

This reformist opposition movement was called **democratic opposition**. It was led informally by a widely popular leader and future president, Boris Yeltsin. To some degree, this movement was influenced by a personal battle between Gorbachev and Yeltsin. The new opposition was in favor of the reforms in general. Their concern was with the pace and scope of the changes. Yeltsin and his followers gathered strong support across Russia and in other republics of the Soviet Union. The opposition accepted the label "democratic" because it was largely an anticommunist and pro-democracy movement, supporting western-style political and individual freedoms. What did this group oppose?

First, the democratic opposition was concerned with the growing negative reaction in the country against the reforms. The rapid strengthening of antireform forces was an indicator that the reforms could be reversed as soon as Gorbachev was dismissed from power or yielded under pressure from his opponents. The democratic opposition, on the other hand, found support among Russia's liberal intelligentsia, educated professionals, college students, and a substantial proportion of the working class. The opposition believed that in order to overcome the crisis and succeed economically and politically, the country should isolate the most conservative political forces or remove them from power.

Second, the "democrats" (a popular name attached to the democratic opposition) saw the solution of the country's problems in a rapid accelera-tion of the reforms and an unconditional break with the communist past. They supported Gorbachev's foreign policy and wanted, in general, to model their country's future after a western example, the most convenient of which was the United States. This appeared to be a country resembling the Soviet Union in terms of its size and multi-ethnic composition.

Third, the democratic opposition supported national pro-independence parties in the republics. The "democrats" did not oppose the idea that ethnic republics could eventually form independent states. After 1988, many supporters of the democratic opposition in Russia began to wear tricolor lapel pins (in blue, white, and red—the colors of the Russian state flag before 1917) as a symbolic gesture of support for Russia's indepen-dence from the Soviet Union. They believed that Russia, as a sovereign country, would defend liberal democracy, the free market, and pursue a peaceful foreign policy.

This popular political group became a real political force, allowing people to exercise their political rights outside the traditional institutions of power. Many talented women joined the movement and quickly become influential. Historically, the Soviet system had claimed to encourage women's participation in politics, but this official policy was a sham: women appointed to political offices were expected to be loyal guardians of the Communist Party and its social policies. The democratic opposition gave women a real chance for political action. One of the brightest stars of the movement was Galina Starovoitova (1946–1998), a sociologist from St Petersburg elected to the Soviet parliament in 1989. She was a dedicated supporter of liberal democracy, national determination of the Soviet republics, and individual rights.

The democratic opposition's political platform won widespread public support. Yeltsin and his popular followers like Starovoitova appeared a viable alternative to the old regime. At the same time, Gorbachev's power was weakening. These two developments convinced the conservative forces within the party and government to act quickly, protect their positions, and try to avoid the looming demolition of the Soviet Union.

The August 1991 coup

In a private meeting with Gorbachev in late July, Boris Yeltsin, president of the Russian Federation, insisted that several senior officials in the government would have to be replaced after the signing of the Union Treaty—a recently proposed legal foundation for the new and decentralized Soviet Union, keeping its 15 republics. This conversation, secretly taped by security agents, alerted several high-ranking leaders and convinced them to take action (Gorbachev, 1996: 643). In addition, Yeltsin vowed that the Russian government would execute its policy of taking direct control of all the natural resources in Russia as soon as the Union Treaty was signed and a new Soviet Union was formed. Those who continued to hope that the Soviet Union might be preserved began to realize that the end of the old state was near.

In August 1991, a group of senior government officials, including Gennadii Yanaev (Soviet vice president), Dmitry Yazov (minister of defense), Boris Pugo (minister of the interior), and Vladimir Kryuchkov (head of the KGB, the federal security agency), attempted to remove Gorbachev from power and declare a state of emergency in the entire Soviet Union. The plotters formed a State Emergency Committee in an attempt to legalize their actions. Ultimately, they planned the suspension of certain laws and immediate political changes. The plotters were pursuing several interconnected goals.

Most urgently, they wanted to stop the process of disintegration of the Soviet Union, and discontinue the negotiations related to the Union Treaty. The coup organizers believed that the proposed treaty would eventually end the Soviet Union.

Next, they wanted to maintain order and guarantee stability in the country by introducing several restrictive measures including temporary limitations on individual and political freedoms. The measures included restrictions on free speech, a temporary ban on Soviet citizens traveling abroad, and limitations on demonstrations and strikes.

Finally, they wanted to revise the Kremlin's foreign policy to make sure that security interests of the country were not harmed in the new international environment. Ultimately, they wanted to keep the status of the Soviet Union as a viable world superpower.

Gorbachev was arrested at his summer residence in Crimea (today this is a territory of Ukraine) on August 19. His communications with Moscow were cut. The plotters announced on national television, which they now controlled, that Gorbachev had resigned (in fact he had not) and the State Emergency Committee was in charge. In some cities, local police chiefs, military commanders, and Communist leaders began to form so-called rescue committees usurping executive power. Immediately, local executive decrees in several regions suspended most civil freedoms.

However, political support for the coup was insignificant. By the end of the second day of the putsch, only a few local governments had supported it. In Moscow, Boris Yeltsin and the government of the Russian Federation defied the orders of the coup leaders. Yeltsin called their actions illegal. Many people went out on the streets to build barricades and protect local governments opposing the coup. Anticoup demonstrations took place in the largest Russian cities, Leningrad and Moscow. Most military commanders refused to use force against unarmed people. Overall, the indecisiveness of the plot organizers, the strong resistance of Boris Yeltsin and his government, and public demonstrations caused the coup leaders to retreat and surrender.

The failed August coup d'état accelerated the pace of political change and fragmentation in the country, and this led to its formal breaking-up four months later. The fragmentation of the Soviet Union did however leave most Russian government institutions intact. Boris Yeltsin occupied the Russian presidency. He had been elected in June 1991 in a popular ballot with 57.3 percent of the vote against five challengers. The Russian parliament—the Congress of People's Deputies—had been elected earlier, in March 1990. Although the majority of deputies to the Congress represented the Communist Party, they were generally reform-minded.

The word "romantic" which is often used in reference to this stage of the Soviet transition reflects the widespread elation and high expectations with which many Russian citizens greeted the political, economic, and social realms following the August 1991 coup and the break-up of the Soviet Union later that year. The success of the popular resistance to the coup helped to create a sense of empowerment and optimism in many Russians, which lasted for some time (Gibson, 1996).

Russians speak their mind ...

... On Russia after the August 1991 coup. Percentage of people in Russia who believed in 2008 that their country had been moving in the right direction after the Yeltsin's August 1991 victory against the coup: 33. Percentage who believed that the country began to move in the wrong direction: 40.

Source: Levada (2008a).

Figure 3.1   *The reforms of 1985–91: a summary*

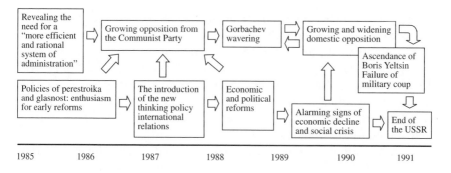

A summary: the reforms of 1985–91

In a nutshell, perestroika and glasnost represented a political program aimed at the reformation of the institutional, economic, and political systems of the Soviet Union. In 1985, the leaders of the reforms wanted to make the economy more efficient and the political system less authoritarian. They did not envision and were not ready for the sweeping changes that engulfed society and lead to the collapse of the powerful state in 1991. See Figure 3.1.

Critical thinking about the Soviet transformation

The peaceful ending of the Cold War was a remarkable event. Yet it continues to present a considerable intellectual challenge to many experts working in the fields of political science, history, foreign policy, national and international security.

Back in the early 1980s, the most common assumption among professional analysts in the United States and Western Europe was that the upcoming decade would be the most dangerous period since the Second World War. The pessimistic expectations were quite reasonable: the US military build-up under Ronald Reagan and the continuing Soviet decline were expected to generate a series of violent outbursts over the globe that could have led to a global war. Yet in 1987–88, the feelings of fear and insecurity were melting like snow under the sun.

Why did the reforms take place? Why did they end up with the collapse of an apparently strong state? Why did the Cold War end so rapidly? Various theories and assumptions attempt to explain the reasons for the reforms and their results (Strayer, 1998). We will distinguish theories emphasizing three groups of factors influencing the Soviet transformation between 1985 and 1991: international, domestic, and individual.

International factors: the Cold War pressures

A few experts including government officials and academics in the early 1990s were quick to claim that the stunning end of the Cold War was, in fact, a victory of the United States. According to this view, called **triumphalist**, the Soviet Union lost the Cold War because of the policies of President Ronald Reagan and in particular his tough foreign policy course, aiming at the amplification of American strength and pressuring Moscow on all fronts. Several US and western policies in the late 1980s further contributed to this outcome.

First, Washington refused to pursue a rapid disarmament and thus exhausted the Soviet economic resources and finances, a substantial portion of which were given to national defense. The announcement of the US Strategic Defense Initiative (SDI, also known as "Star Wars"), was the final straw that pushed the Soviets to seek ways to compromise with Washington.

Second, the United States had contributed to a military deadlock in Afghanistan by supporting the Islamic opposition (the mujahedeen) and other anti-Soviet forces there. The Soviet leaders understood that they could not win that highly unpopular war, yet they did not know how to end it quickly. As a result, Soviet resources had been draining there for a long time.

Third, by supporting Solidarity (an oppositional, anticommunist political movement in Poland) and other similar movements in Eastern Europe, the west further complicated the geopolitical status of the Soviet Union and contributed to the loss of its political prestige among its allies.

Fourth, by encouraging Saudi Arabia and other oil-exporting countries to reduce oil prices, the west reduced the Soviet Union's national oil revenue.

Finally, by waging a war of ideas, and by constant ideological pressure on Soviet leaders, the west undercut the Soviet ideological power bases, undermined the communists' confidence in themselves, and forced them into policies of retrieval and surrender. Soviet leaders did not have a choice but to throw in the political towel, ending their futile resistance.

This triumphalist point of view continues to find support. Some of the arguments make sense. In fact the Soviet economy, exhausted by the enormous military expenditures it maintained during the Cold War, was both inefficient and expensive to run (Gaidar, 2007). Fear of the United States was a powerful motivational factor forcing the Soviet leadership to seek ways to find a solution to ease the strenuous arms race. Therefore, as some argue, the Gorbachev reforms attempted to save the economy of the Soviet Union. However, most analysts consider that although western policies were important, they were not the decisive factor in the Soviet collapse (Zubok, 2007).

International factors: imperial overstretch

Other experts maintain that the pursuit for greater power brought the Soviet Union to a condition of acute economic and political exhaustion, a state known in comparative politics and international relations as imperial overstretch (Adomeit, 1998). From this point of view, like imperial Britain or France, the Soviet Union was doing too much and in too many places, and this caused its ultimate collapse.

In addition, the Soviet economy was oriented toward military production and failed to overhaul itself to satisfy the growing consumerist appetites of Soviet society. Although the profits from oil exports temporarily offset the continuing Soviet decline during the 1980s, the Soviet Union finally overstretched its power and exhausted its resources (Zubok, 2007). Ultimately, it could not survive as a state despite its enormous military power, and considerable economic and technological resources.

Domestic economic and political factors

Many specialists emphasize the importance of specific domestic factors that influenced the reforms and caused the end of the Soviet Union. With its resources exhausted, the Soviet system needed serious reform to survive. Unfortunately, the foundations of the system were too fragile to support any rapid improvement. As the result, the system imploded under its own weight in 1991 (Kotkin, 2008). Economists and political scientists emphasize different factors contributing to the collapse. Economists underline the fundamental domestic economic factors that caused the country to disintegrate (Gaidar, 2007). Political scientists refer to the colossal organizational problems that plagued the Soviet Union and stalled the proposed reforms. The country did not have a system of social and political institutions that could have carried the weight of the changes (Bauman, 1994: 15).

Other experts emphasize the strength of the nationalist forces in the republics. By the late 1980s, facing significant economic difficulties, Boris Yeltsin and the emerging new leadership in the republics began to define their strategies in nationalistic terms: they believed they all would be better off economically, and politically better able to guarantee their joint security and prosperity, without the vast bureaucracy of the Soviet Union. Boris Yeltsin and other nationalist-minded Russian politicians successfully challenged Gorbachev and won. Gorbachev enjoyed enormous international support for his new vision of international security. Yet at the same time, his power platform at home collapsed as a result of the unsuccessful domestic reforms. In the end, the state began to disintegrate under the blows of ethnic separatist movements and equally strong democratic forces.

Domestic factors: the elites

Another school of thought is based on the argument that perestroika was a practical result of an idealistic vision of a small group of party officials. The Soviet regime, although it badly needed reform, had sufficient resources to resist external pressures and maintain its self-sufficiency for a relatively long period. The crucial changes began not only because of economic problems, power struggles, and external pressures, but also because of the generational change taking place in the Soviet leadership and its inability to preserve the system (Glad and Shiraev, 1999; Kotz, 1997).

There is another point of view today that claims the reforms of the late 1980s were the result of a power struggle among different groups of Soviet and Russian elites (Simanov, 2009). National elites in the republics (including Russia) finally prevailed and won the competition, with the leaders attempting to prevent the dissolution of the Soviet Union. Other groups, witnessing the disintegration of the old planned economic system and the weakening of the old state power, quickly found their own political roles in the process of reforms. In fact, the failed reforms of Gorbachev cleared the way for a massive privatization of property in the early 1990s, when the governing elites gained access to state resources and enriched themselves (Cohen, 2001).

Individual factors: the Gorbachev–Yeltsin struggle

Political psychologists suggest that the personal style of Mikhail Gorbachev, his management skills, weaknesses, and idiosyncrasies significantly influenced the initiation, development, and eventual collapse of the reforms. His early collaboration and later rivalry with Boris Yeltsin made the most significant impact on the eventual disintegration of the state. Most experts agree that Yeltsin represented a more radical, uncompromising, and impatient wing of the reformers. In the process, he was confronting an increasingly inconsistent, hesitant, and even conservative Gorbachev. Their cooperation and rivalry can be described through four periods. The early phase was Yeltsin's initiation into the elite party structures. For a short period, at the beginning of the transition, Gorbachev needed Yeltsin to target the most conservative elements of the party. As long as all the institutions in the Soviet Union—the Communist Party, the bureaucracy, the security apparatus, and the military—retained their monopoly on power, Yeltsin too needed Gorbachev for political protection.

At first, Yeltsin played the role of a populist winning support and challenging the Soviet bureaucracy. However, when he began to openly accuse Gorbachev of slowing the reforms down, he was dismissed from his powerful party positions. Yeltsin remained in Moscow but occupied a relatively low-key ministerial position. During the second period of their political relations, Gorbachev ignored Yeltsin. However, as an articulate critic of communism, Yeltsin gradually gained popular support across the Soviet Union.

The third period—an open political rivalry and bitter confrontation—began after Yeltsin had returned to power by winning a popular election to the presidency of the Russian Republic in 1991. Yeltsin won a powerful popular mandate, which Gorbachev had never obtained because he never stood in a free democratic election (something he later regretted).

The final period of political competition between Gorbachev and Yeltsin began after the August coup of 1991. Eventually, Gorbachev accepted a secondary role as president of the increasingly weakened Soviet Union. On a personal level, according to his close confidants, Gorbachev was very ambivalent about, and sometimes bitter toward, Yeltsin. He would talk about his rival for hours, constantly thinking about and giving interpretations of his words and actions (Chernyaev, 1993: 218). (See Table 3.1.)

Table 3.1   *Gorbachev and Yeltsin compared*

Issues	Mikhail Gorbachev	Boris Yeltsin
Nationality, background	Russian, peasantry, southern Russia Born in 1931	Russian, working class, Ural region. Born in 1931
Education	Law degree and a second degree in agricultural management	A college degree in engineering
Party background	Moved up through party hierarchies	Moved up through managerial and party hierarchies
Attitude to Marxism	Belief in the possibility of reforming Marxism-Leninism	Growing disenchantment with Marxism-Leninism
Leadership skills	Collectivist with elements of authoritarianism	Collectivist with elements of authoritarianism
Intellectual and personal skills assessed by critics	Highly developed intellectual skills; lack of empathy and emotional closeness; difficulty in forming friendships	Average intellectual skills; strong empathetic abilities; recklessness; openness and straightforwardness

Conclusion

Any type of radical reform in any country tends to bring quite contradictory and conflicting results. It is rarely appropriate to judge reforms as either absolutely successful or totally disastrous. A clear triumph in one area of reform may be accompanied by a failure in others. As critical thinkers, let us put the main outcomes of the Soviet transformation into two categories.

On the plus side, the people of the Soviet Union had obtained political freedom by the late 1980s. Censorship was gradually eliminated and freedom of speech guaranteed. People could finally travel overseas with their own foreign currency and without exit visas. The one-party political system was gone. Limited private property became legal and small private businesses flourished. In the global context, the Cold War was over. Moscow and Washington agreed to destroy thousands of nuclear warheads. Russia and 14 new countries won their independence.

On the other hand, the reforms of the 1980s caused a profound crisis in the all spheres of life. Sharp social inequality and polarization emerged. Inflation skyrocketed. Food shortages became common by the end of 1989. Crime flourished. Lawlessness was rampant. In many regions violence broke out, taking thousands of lives and bringing destruction and despair to hundreds of thousands of people in the North Caucasus region, Chechnya, Ossetia, Armenia, Azerbaijan, Moldova, Abkhazia, Georgia, and several regions in Central Asia. Once peaceful, the Soviet Union now faced many ethnic conflicts on its territory.

> **Russians speak their mind ...**
>
> ... **Missing the Soviet Union.** Percentage of Russians in 2008 saying that they regretted the dissolution of the Soviet Union in 1991: 60.
>
> Source: Levada (2008b).

As you can see, the transformation of 1985–91 was an ambivalent process, full of contradictions, uncertainties, and questionable outcomes. Many contemporary Russian policies, as we will examine later in the book, reflect the results of this historic process that took place in the 1980s.

The second lesson is that any massive and rapid transformation of a country is a perilous enterprise. Many experts and some state leaders (in China, for example) support this argument. Although comparative studies show that in some countries rapid reforms can be successful, very few states have successfully undergone such a dramatic transformation, so rapidly and in all spheres of life, including the economic, political, ideological, and spiritual, as did the Soviet Union (Strayer, 1998). The Soviet Union did not have a powerful foreign sponsor and received no massive foreign aid, as did many European countries accepting Marshall Plan aid from the United States in the late 1940s. Moscow received relatively little help from the international community during the toughest transitional period. If such support had been given, we might have seen a different geopolitical situation, in which the Soviet Union would probably have continued to exist as a state (Tetlock, Lebow, and Perker, 2006).

The third lesson refers to the personal role of Mikhail Gorbachev. Gorbachev's motivation and personal qualities were crucial to the introduction of the reforms. Of the greatest importance were his belief that the Soviet system could be reformed and his rejection of violence to achieve his ambitious political goals. His case reveals the crucial role of a leader designing domestic and foreign policies. Very few times in history (President Woodrow Wilson can be mentioned here as an example) has the leader of a great power renounced the old rules of foreign policy in favor of a sweeping idealist agenda based on non-violence, cooperation, and interdependence (Levesque, 1997). Most probably, the Cold War confrontation would have continued today and the world would have been a more dangerous place if the Soviet Union had had a different political leader in the 1980s.

Part II

Institutions and Elections

The Executive Branch

The Constitution is a special agreement between the state on the one hand and its citizens, on the other.
Dmitry Medvedev, President of Russia, 2009

Article 3 of the Constitution of the Russian Federation states that the only source of power in Russia is its people. The printed words are clear and simple: No person or group may usurp power in Russia. The Constitution also says that people exercise their power directly or through the state and local government institutions. How close are these official declarations to reality? Who has most power in Russia, and who makes most important executive decisions there today?

Key developments

The executive branch of government in today's Russia is the paramount power. Although, as we will see later, the judicial and legislative branches are constitutionally independent, the executive branch is in almost total control in practically all areas of social life, business, and politics. To understand the nature of the executive power in Russia, we have to examine briefly some key events of the 1990s and 2000s that have largely shaped the executive branch of the government today. Several developments were of particular significance.

First, there was a peaceful transformation of executive power in Russia at the end of 1991 when the former Soviet Union disappeared from the map and the new Russian state emerged. Russia as a state preserved practically all the major government institutions left from the Soviet period.

The second key development was the constitutional crisis of the fall of 1993 and the adoption of a new Constitution by the end of that year. The Constitution provided the legal foundation for the major principles of functioning of the Russian government. The adoption of the Constitution was instrumental in the process of building a very strong executive and relatively weak legislative and judiciary branches.

The powerful office of president was able to exercise its significant power during the 1996 presidential elections, which was the third key event related to the discussion of Russia's executive branch. These elections allowed Boris Yeltsin and the elites supporting him to stop the generally popular communist opposition from taking over.

The fourth key development was the resignation of President Yeltsin in 1999. It paved the way for an uninterrupted transition of power and the rapid ascendance of the next Russian leader, Vladimir Putin, who significantly increased the strength of the executive branch.

Finally, the presidential elections of 2008 and the election of Putin's personally chosen successor, Dmitry Medvedev, reaffirmed the 1999 mechanism of power transition. Both presidents introduced specific legal reforms as constitutional amendments that have further consolidated the executive power in the president's hands and increased the power of the federal government in Moscow.

The adoption of the Constitution

Russia's government has a very strong executive branch. In comparison, many countries that underwent democratic transition in the 1990s, such as Poland, Ukraine, or Slovakia, produced strong parliamentary systems with a relatively weak centralized power compared with Russia. Why did Russia turn out this way?

One of the answers is found in the Constitution of the Russian Federation. The very way it was created is remarkable. Although the Constitution was adopted at the end of 1993, the preparations had begun almost four years earlier. The initial drafts appeared in 1990 when Russia was still a part of the Soviet Union. In June of that year the Constitutional Commission began its work. Boris Yeltsin was its chair, as president of the Russian Federation. The first draft emerged in November 1990. It received only lukewarm support from the parliament, so work on the draft continued. The second draft was ready a year later, in 1991. By the spring of 1992 the Constitution was still not ready to be debated in parliament. The leadership of the Congress of People's Deputies believed that the version presented to them was not satisfactory. As a result, the tensions between the legislative branch and President Yeltsin grew: he wanted the Constitution adopted as soon as possible, while the majority in the legislature, including its leadership and its chair, Ruslan Khasbulatov, wanted to delay.

Several factors contributed to these tensions. The uncertainty of the political and economic situation in Russia gave various political forces seemingly great opportunities. Many political groups competed for influence and an opportunity to drive through a favorable constitution. This led to an intensifying political struggle in Moscow, and especially within the Russian parliament. Moreover, the office of the president at that time did not have any efficient parliamentary strategy. The president and his closest advisers did not have enough political skills to deal with the parliament, bargain with different political groups within it, or make valuable tactical concessions. Unlike today in Russia, the president in 1993 faced a generally unfriendly parliament. These developments caused significant delays in the process of the Constitution's adoption.

The conflict

The disagreement between Yeltsin and the parliament grew into a rivalry that ended with violent conflict. The leaders of the parliament, which had been elected in the Soviet times, wanted to have a constitution that would guarantee a strong parliamentary republic. They argued that Yeltsin's draft diminished the power of the legislature and the people it was supposed to represent (Khasbulatov, 2008). Yeltsin, on the other hand, expected to build a strong presidential republic with a weak legislature. Next, Yeltsin wanted to develop a new economy based on the major principles of economic liberalism and private property. His opponents preferred government regulation and opposed policies of economic liberalization (Filatov, 2008). They hoped for a larger state share in major enterprises. Personal factors played a role too. Pushing for the adoption of his version of the Constitution, Yeltsin constantly attempted to bypass the parliament and diminish its procedural powers. His team tried to invent new legal procedures to make sure that his version of the Constitution was passed (see the Case in point). The animosity between the president and the leadership of the Supreme Soviet intensified.

The conflict between these two sides was not only about procedural issues. It was a fierce struggle between the old and new political forces in the country, a confrontation about the future of Russia and its political institutions. Overall, it was a critical struggle for power. On one side, there was Yeltsin with the support of political forces that were fed up with communism. They needed a strong presidential power to exercise their reforms. Among key Yeltsin supporters were the former acting prime minister Yegor Gaidar, Sergei Shakhrai, and Anatoly Chubais. On the other side, there was the parliamentary majority. It drew together dissimilar political forces

Case in point: The legal battle for the 1993 Constitution

The road to the new Constitution of Russia was very difficult for President Yeltsin. First, he overcame at least two major all-out legal battles in two months. In March 1993, Yeltsin as president narrowly survived an impeachment procedure in the Supreme Soviet of the Russian Federation. The reason for the impeachment vote was his alleged signing of an illegitimate law diminishing parliamentary powers in Russia. A question about Yeltsin's leadership and the course of his reform was posed during the April 25, 1993 national referendum. A majority of people (59 percent) expressed their trust in the president. A slightly smaller majority (53 percent) supported Yeltsin's and his government's "social-economic policy." Less than half (49.5 percent) supported earlier presidential elections. More than two-thirds (67 percent) of people supported earlier parliamentary elections. The April referendum was not a decisive triumph for President Yeltsin and his supporters, but it was a victory for them.

Legally, for the Supreme Soviet to adopt a new constitution it needed to be approved by two-thirds of the elected deputies. To avoid the possibility that his draft of the Constitution would not gain this support, and to give it more public legitimacy, Yeltsin created a Constitutional Council, with members selected from a large sample of social groups. In September he fired his vice president, Alexander Rutskoy, who became an ardent critic of Yeltsin and supporter of the parliament. Although the existing laws did not allow the president to fire his vice president, Yeltsin did so anyway. The parliament appealed against this decision and accused Yeltsin of violating the law. In September, to undermine the power of the parliament, Yeltsin issued a special presidential decree about constitutional reform in Russia. The decree ordered a gradual dismantling of the parliament over the fall and called for new parliamentary elections (the Duma elections) in December. The decree began with the dramatic statement: "The political situation that has developed in the Russian Federation is a threat to the national and societal security of the country." It clearly identified the Supreme Soviet of the Russian Federation as a "political obstacle that prevents the people from deciding its own fate" (Presidential Decree, 1993). However, the Constitutional Court declared the actions of the president unconstitutional and the parliament impeached him on September 23. The parliament also passed power to Vice-President Rutskoy. Yeltsin ignored this decision and called any other decision of the Supreme Soviet illegitimate. The legislature called on people of Russia to ignore Yeltsin's orders.

united by their opposition to Yeltsin. They did not support his rapid plunge into capitalism. Besides Khasbulatov, the opposition included the vice president, Alexander Rutskoy, and many regional leaders.

In the fall of 1993, the government in Russia was facing a serious political crisis. Tensions in Moscow grew rapidly. On October 3 and 4 sporadic but deadly violence spread across the city. Supporters of the parliament captured the Office of the Mayor and stormed the Central Television Center. However, Yeltsin was able to rely on the military, which gained control over the city. After a military assault with tanks and machine guns on the parliament building (which CNN broadcast live), the members of the Supreme Soviet and its leaders were arrested. All those arrested were pardoned a few months later.

On October 9, Yeltsin ordered the ending of the activities of all soviets at all levels in Russia, and on November 10 a new draft of the Constitution was published. Yeltsin then proceeded rapidly to hold a national referendum, and on December 12 this gave its approval of the Constitution, with 58 percent of those voting in favor. Yeltsin and his supporters had won a historic victory. On the same day, people voted for the delegates to a new Russian parliament, a two-chamber institution including the Duma and a Federation Council (Yeltsin, 1994).

Russians speak their mind ...

... **On the events in Moscow in October 1991.** Percentage of Russians in 2008 saying that Yeltsin's actions were right: 9. Percentage saying parliament's actions were right: 11. Percentage who felt both or neither side was right, or it was hard to tell: 80.

Source: Levada (2008c).

The president of the Russian Federation

The new Constitution of the Russian Federation identified both the rights and responsibilities of the president. Yeltsin's aides who drafted the Constitution had to rely on their knowledge of other countries and a very short history of Russian presidency. The position of the president was established in 1991 as the result of a referendum of the citizens of the Russian Federation, then a part of the Soviet Union. Yeltsin was elected the first president of the Russian Soviet Federal Socialist Republic on June 12, 1991. The Constitution of the Russian Federation of 1993 significantly changed the functioning of the presidency. Since 1993, in succession to Yeltsin, Russia has had two presidents: Vladimir Putin and Dmitry Medvedev.

As the head of state in Russia, the president has vast powers and responsibilities compared with those granted to the president in many other countries with a similar political system. Some duties are common to almost all constitutions in countries where there is a president. According to the

Constitution, the president is the guarantor and protector of the rights and liberties of Russian citizens. He (in the text of the Constitution the president is always described as "he," not "she") defines domestic and foreign policy. The president is elected to the office for six years. An amendment to the Constitution adopted in 2008 extended the term of the president from four to six years after 2012, and the term of the State Duma from four to five years. The elections are direct. Any citizen of Russia aged more than 35, who has lived in the country for more than ten years, has the right to run for the presidency. No one can occupy the office of president for more than two consecutive terms. The president can be impeached if it is felt he has failed to adhere to the Constitution. There is a complicated procedure for impeachment by the legislative branch of the Russian Federation: first the State Duma petitions the Federation Council, then the Council carries out the impeachment hearings.

Russians speak their mind ...

... On the president's power. Percentage of Russians in 2008 supporting the constitutional amendment to increase the tenure of the president from four to six years: 60. Opinions were divided about the Duma. Percentage supporting a one-year extension: 41; percentage opposing it: 42.

Source: Levada (2008d).

Basic functions

The president has to perform several functions. As *head of state* he has to protect the Constitution, the sovereignty and territorial integrity of Russia. Presidents also coordinate the functioning of various federal institutions and represent Russia internationally. The president is also the *chief executive officer* of the state. One of his major responsibilities is to outline both domestic and foreign policy. The president is the *commander-in-chief* of the armed forces of the Russian Federation. In the event of actual or potential aggression against the country, the president may impose martial law, a temporary system of administration of justice under the control of the military. This system may be established on the whole territory of Russia or only in one or several areas. The president also appoints a prime minister (the accurate translation is chair of the Government of the Russian Federation) with the consent of the State Duma (the lower chamber of the Russian parliament: see Chapter 5). This rule means that the Duma must vote and approve the candidacy. The president also appoints ministers, and has the right to be present and serve as a chair during the Government of the Russian Federation's meetings.

Vladimir Putin and Dmitry Medvedev

Vladimir Putin served as president from 2000 to 2008. Dmitry Medvedev was elected to succeed him in 2008. There are strong similarities in the lives of both men. Both were born in Leningrad (now St Petersburg). Both attended Leningrad (St Petersburg) State University Law School (a five-year program). Both took early steps in government service, working for the office of the mayor of St Petersburg. The mayor, Anatoly Sobchak, was at one time a professor at St Petersburg University Law School.

In Moscow, both Putin and Medvedev served in the administration of the president (Putin was working for Yeltsin; Medvedev served in Putin's administration). Before becoming president, neither of them had been elected to any public office by popular vote. Neither had had any experience in the judiciary.

Both men are married with children. Both speak at least one foreign language. Medvedev is 13 years the younger, and has had experience of working in private business. Putin, on the other hand, has had a rich experience of serving as a KGB officer. Putin was a member of the Communist Party of the Soviet Union, while Medvedev is the first head of the Russian state since 1917 who has never been a member of the Communist Party.

In terms of their personalities, Putin is dominant and straightforward. Medvedev is conscientious and diligent. Surveys show that Russian people recognize five major features in Medvedev: his relative youth, his intelligence, action, purposefulness, and sense of tact (WCIOM, 2008a).

Photo 1   *St Petersburg State University, alma mater of Presidents Dmitry Medvedev and Vladimir Putin*

Table 4.1   *Comparing two presidents of Russia*

Point of comparison	Vladimir Putin	Dmitry Medvedev
Birth year and birthplace	1952, Leningrad	1965, Leningrad
University education	Leningrad State University, Law	Leningrad State University, Law
Communist Party of the Soviet Union	Was a member	Never been a member
Business experience	None	Legal work, private companies. Director of Gazprom.
State security experience	KGB officer	None
Elected legislative positions	None	None
Work in the judiciary	None	None
Local government	Office of Mayor, St Petersburg, deputy mayor	Office of Mayor, St Petersburg, advisor
Federal government	Administration of the President	Administration of the President
	Federal Security Council	Deputy prime minister
	Prime minister	
Family status	Married, children	Married, one child
Favorite sports	Wrestling, skiing	Swimming
Favorite music	Rock	Rock
Foreign language	German	English
Religion	Russian Orthodox	Russian Orthodox
Personality	Tough, straightforward, sharp	Conscientious, diligent, virtuous

The president is also the *chief legislator*. He introduces bills (drafts of laws) to the Duma. The president signs bills passed by the Duma into law. In addition, as a chief legislator, the president can issue his own executive orders, which are mandatory within the territory of the Russian Federation. Presidents have the right to grant political asylum to individuals seeking it, and to issue a pardon or show clemency to (that is, reduce the sentence of) convicted criminals. The president has legal immunity: while he is in office the law protects him against prosecution or other legal claims. However, the immunity is not absolute. Article 93 of the Constitution establishes the procedures necessary to impeach a sitting president. Legally, the upper chamber of the legislature has the right to impeach, but it must receive supporting decisions from the upper courts of the Russian Federation (the Supreme Court and the Constitutional Court; see Chapter 6 for details).

In the event of the president's illness or incapability, the chair of the Government of the Russian Federation (see later in this chapter) takes over and becomes a provisional president. In this case, the provisional president may not dissolve the legislature (the Duma), call a national referendum, or amend the Constitution. According to the Constitution, as the *chief diplomat*, the president appoints ambassadors, interacts with ambassadors from other states, and has the authority to sign international agreements on behalf of the Russian Federation.

In summary, according to the Constitution, Russian presidents assume a superior position in the structure of the government. The president exercises both executive and legislative powers. Presidents can exercise judicial powers as well. For example, they can make legal decisions and resolve conflicts between the federal and regional governments (Nikonov, 2003: 23).

Obviously, one person cannot perform all these executive and legislative functions alone. As in other countries, Russian presidents as the highest executive officers rely on a vast government bureaucracy. Among the most important institutions are the Government of the Russian Federation (the Cabinet of Ministers), the Presidential Administration, and the Security Council of the Russian Federation.

The presidential administration (the executive office)

The key functions of the administration are mostly legislative and oversight-related. In terms of legislative functions, the administration is responsible for the preparation of legislative initiatives for the Duma's consideration. The second function is to monitor the implementation of federal legislation and the president's directives. The third function is coordination and communication with government and non-government organizations within Russia and abroad. Formally, the president is in charge of the administration. However, there is also a formal manager or head of the administration (chief of staff) who coordinates day-to-day work. Based on the 2004 Presidential Decree, the chief of staff has two deputies. The administration employs approximately 2000 people, and has several designated offices, including the press secretary, head of protocol, aides and advisers to the president, the president's representatives in state offices, the president's representative on the European Human Rights Commission, and 12 heads of different departments of the administration. The Office of Management takes care of financial and other technical issues. Seven president's representatives in the federal districts are also part of the administration. An important part of the administration is the Security Council.

The Presidential Executive Office is located in Moscow, and has offices in a number of buildings inside the Kremlin and in the vicinity of *Staraya Square* (which name is sometimes used to refer to it) and Ilyinka Street, former headquarters of the Central Committee of the Communist Party of the Soviet Union.

The Security Council of the Russian Federation

The Security Council is a constitutional establishment that advises and assists the president on questions related to the overall security of the country and the protection of Russian citizens' interests from internal and external threats. The Constitution includes the most fundamental provisions justifying the activities of the Security Council. There is also a 1992 law, "On Security," which details the responsibilities of this agency. The president is responsible for the appointment of permanent and provisional members of the Council according to the law. The Council has a secretary who is responsible for its daily operations. The secretary answers directly to the president. It is a powerful position, and was occupied in 1999 by the future President Putin. Among the permanent members of the Council are the most senior officials of the Russian government, including the prime minister, foreign and defense ministers, and the director of the Federal Security Service. Among the official responsibilities of the council are the identification of threats against Russia and Russian interests, the design and preparation of basic strategies related to national security, and the design of federal programs to implement these strategies.

The Security Council develops a general strategy for Russia's national security (Strategy, 2009). In its current form, the strategy covers the period until 2020 (see Chapter 13 for a more detailed description). The Council also prepares recommendations to the president about specific security policies. It makes collective decisions about extraordinary situations that could have significant and catastrophic consequences on Russian territory. The council makes recommendations to the president about whether or not he should declare a state of emergency across the whole of Russia's territory or in some regions. It advises the president about the effectiveness of the existing federal institutions responsible for security and the necessity of creating new ones.

Web

To learn more about the structure of the administration and to read updates, visit www.kremlin.ru and click on the English version.

The Government of the Russian Federation

According to the Constitution, the Government (Cabinet of Ministers) is a collective body exercising its power over the entire territory of Russia. The Cabinet consists of the chair of the government (prime minister), the deputies, and federal ministers. The president appoints the prime minister with the approval of the Duma. In theory, the Duma can refuse the nomination at least three times. After the third refusal, the president must dissolve the Duma and call new legislative elections. The Government (the Cabinet) must resign as soon as a new president is elected. Russian prime ministers are granted substantial legal powers. In case of disagreements and tensions with the Duma, the prime minister can petition the president to dissolve the Duma and call for new elections. This has never happened to date, however.

Main responsibilities

Overall, the Government of the Russian Federation is responsible for the planning of and control over the federal financial policy. One of its major tasks is preparing the federal budget. After the budget is approved by the lower house of the legislature (the Duma), the government is responsible for the budget execution. In addition, the Cabinet also manages the Russian Federation's federal property.

Besides planning and executing foreign and defense policies, the government has to prepare and carry out centralized federal policies in the fields of public education, health care, science, culture, social services, and environmental protection. It is also in charge of law enforcement, protection of the private property of Russian citizens, and the investigation and prevention of crime.

The executive branch of the Russian Federation can be described as functioning on three levels. The first level is **federal ministries**. Their prime responsibility is to conduct federal policy in specific areas such as foreign policy, domestic security, defense, health care, education, finance, and agriculture. The second level is comprised of **federal services**. They exercise and control the implementation of specific policies. For example, there are institutions such as the Anti-Monopoly Federal Service, the Customs Federal Service, the Federal Service of Federal Statistics, the Labor and Employment Service, and the Patent and Trade Service. **Federal agencies** comprise the third level. Their responsibility is to provide specific federal services. For example, there are federal agencies responsible for tourism, archives, forestry, railroads, and water resources.

Web

For a complete list of ministries, services, and agencies see the book's website.

The president directs the work of several ministries, federal services, and agencies in accordance with the Constitution. Among them are the key ministries of the Interior, Defense, Justice, Foreign Affairs, and also the Ministry of Civil Defense and Emergency Services. The prime minister manages the activities of other ministries and a wide range of federal institutions. Similar ministries, departments, and institutions function in many other countries. In Russia, the ministries include Agriculture, Finance, Transport, Energy, and Economic Development. Other ministries are less common internationally, but counterparts still exist in other countries. For example, the Ministry of Education and Science has the prime function of handling policies in all educational areas (including, to some degree, college education) and coordinating policies in support of scientific research across the country. The Ministry of Culture carries out federal polices in support of the arts, including literature, visual arts, performing arts, museums, archives, libraries, and some other areas. The Ministry of Sports, Tourism, and Youth Policy conducts policies in support of amateur sports, and a wide range of youth-related initiatives. By the time you read these pages, some Russian ministries might have been dissolved and some new ones might have appeared (See Table 4.2).

When President Putin's second presidential term was about to expire, he announced his support for Dmitry Medvedev as a presidential candidate and agreed to serve as chair of the government (prime minister) if Medvedev were elected in 2008. After Medvedev took office as president, he needed to deal with the common belief that Putin was still in total

Table 4.2   *Ministries of the Russian Federation*

Ministries under control of the president of the Russian Federation	Interior; Defense; Justice; Foreign Affairs; Civil Defense and Emergency Services.
Ministries under control of the prime minister (chair of the government)	Health and Social Services; Education and Science; Natural Resources and Ecology; Culture; Manufacturing and Trade; Regional Development; Communication and Mass Media; Agriculture; Transport; Finance; Energy; Sports, Tourism, and Youth Policy; Economic Development.

control of the country. Medvedev, commonly seen as Putin's hand-picked successor, tried to dispel the assumption that his high position was a political maneuver to give Putin a chance to return to the presidency in 2012. Meanwhile, Putin remained the most powerful politician in Russia (Osborn, 2009).

Russians speak their mind ...

... **Putin or Medvedev?** In whose hands is the real power in Russia today? Percentage of Russians naming Prime Minister Putin: 30. Percentage naming President Medvedev: 12. Percentage saying "both": 48.

Source: Levada (2009b).

The executive power of the government is based on the Constitution. We should not forget that the Constitution is a living document. It can be amended according to Articles 134 through 137. Several major developments took place between 1996 and the end of the first decade of the 21st century that provided favorable conditions for the further consolidation and strengthening of the executive power in the country.

The subjects of the Russian Federation

This term refers to specially recognized territorial units within the established federal state. The definitions of these units are fairly complicated, and the exact number of the subjects has changed several times. According to the Constitution (Article 65), the Russian Federation consists of republics, regions (known as *oblasts*), special regions (known as *kraj*), two cities with special federal status (Moscow and St Petersburg), and autonomous regions. Both republics and autonomous regions have this status because substantial proportions of their population are of non-Russian ethnic origin. In fact, these regions have ethnic autonomy within Russia. One autonomous region (the Jewish Autonomous Region) is based on a religious principle (although in Russia, Jews are defined as an ethnic group). With some exceptions, the oblasts are based on historic administrative divisions, dating from the time of the Soviet Union or even earlier. Each kraj must include at least one autonomous (that is, ethnic) region.

In 1991 there were 55 geographically defined regions, 20 ethnically based republics, and 11 ethnic districts.

Russia as a federal state

The Russian Federation is called a *federation* because it is a union of many self-governing subjects. The subjects' rights to make decisions are limited by the Constitution and applicable laws. For example, a subject of the Russian Federation may not send ambassadors to other states, issue its own currency, or form its own army, navy, or air force. However, the subjects may have their own constitutions provided they do not contradict the Constitution of the Russian Federation. As we will examine in detail in the next chapter, the highest legislative body of the Russian Federation is a two-chamber parliament called the Federal Assembly. It consists of the Federation Council and the State Duma. The Federation Council contains two representatives from each subject of the federation. The State Duma is elected according to different principles. The Russian Federation is also a *republic* because its major federal institutions of power are electable by the people. There are term limits related to each office (with small exceptions concerning some legal offices). The length of the presidential term is now six years; members of the State Duma are elected for a period of five years.

Discussing Russia as a federal stare, Russian leaders and scholars often emphasize that Russia is a **legal state**. In English, the best way of translating this is to say that it is based on the *rule of law*. This term gained popularity in the 1980s during the Gorbachev reforms. It is used to emphasize the importance of the law in comparison with ideological doctrines or political interests. People and politicians are equal before the law. Their rights are recognized and upheld in courts. However, there is a difference between defining a legal state on paper and implementing the rule of law in practice. A key consequence of concentrating political power in the executive branch is lack of transparency and rampant corruption. Unfortunately, these have become defining features of the Russian political system (Welu and Muchnik, 2009).

The subjects of the Federation have equal rights before the federal government. In addition, each subject may reach an agreement with the federal government regarding the way executive power is shared between them. The Constitution does not provide specific rules about how the regions should organize their governments. In other words, it does not say which specific governmental structures should be established. Typically, every regional government contains the three traditional branches: executive, judicial, and legislative. A common feature is that in all subjects of the Russian Federation the legislative organs must be re-elected at least every four years. Another common feature is that most senior executives in each subject are elected by local parliaments based on the recommendation of the president of Russia. We discuss this controversial issue later.

Regional authorities exercise a wide range of responsibilities not covered by the federal government. In most cases they do not need permission from Moscow to build roads, factories, hire and fire local officials, or allocate funds for various social projects. The interaction between federal and regional powers is frequently ambiguous. On the one hand, federal authorities have not yet put together a cohesive and uniform strategy to manage the regions. On the other hand, the Constitution itself gives federal authorities in Moscow a wide range of responsibilities on the regional level. This over-centralized nature of executive power in Russia unnecessary reduces the capabilities of the regions. This lack of regional power also leads many regional leaders to seek special economic and political privileges. In other words, under contemporary conditions, those regional leaders with personal ties and good contacts in Moscow are often able to bring special benefits to their regions.

The early evolution of the federal system (1991–2000)

Back in 1991, the president of the Russian Federation established by executive order a new system according to which he, as president, would appoint the heads of the regional administrations and autonomous republics. In turn, according to that system, the appointed heads of administrations were to appoint the heads of city governments and other smaller administrative units (Presidential Decree, 1991). The goals that President Yeltsin pursued at that time included getting rid of the previous party-controlled government structure, changing people in key leadership positions, and establishing a new system of democratic government. By 1992, most regions had established new administrations. In 1995 Yeltsin issued an executive order allowing regional leaders to be elected, not appointed from Moscow. By the end of 1996 elections had taken place in almost all regions of Russia, and a new elected leadership was in place. This was an important step toward democracy, praised by democratic forces in Russia and overseas. It was a sign that the Kremlin was gradually giving political power away to the regions. Moscow indeed intended to decentralize many elements of central power.

Contemporary Russian critics, however, complain that Yeltsin's decision weakened federal government and its ability to manage efficiently. Typically they argue that the regions received too much power and too much independence in the mid-1990s. Many of them soon started to resist the decisions of the federal government (Isaev and Baranov, 2009). Moreover, each subject of the federation sent two representatives—their head of administration and chair of legislature—to the Federation Council (the upper chamber of the parliament). This, according to critics, gave the regions too much power in the federal legislature. In addition, many power-sharing treaties between the Kremlin and the subjects which were signed around 1994 created confusion (Hughes, 1996: 40). These treaties meant that not all the Russian Federation's subjects had equal relationships with the center or equal rights (Treisman, 1996). In other words, Moscow was losing control over the regions.

The consolidation of executive power

The presidential elections of 1996 and the transition of power from Boris Yeltsin to Vladimir Putin in 2000 played a special role in Russia's recent history. The 1996 elections are discussed in some detail in Chapter 7 in the context of the Russian electoral system. The significance of the events of 2000 is that the world witnessed a very smooth transition of presidential power in Russia. Why was this transition significant?

After the 1996 presidential elections

The victory of the incumbent president, Boris Yeltsin, in 1996 allowed him to preserve the major institutions of executive power in the hands of basically the same elite groups that had ruled the country since 1992. Not only did Yeltsin retain power, he also marginalized the opposition from the right (nationalist forces) and from the left (mainly the Communist Party and its allies).

However, by the summer of 1999, Yeltsin was losing popularity and support across the country. The economic and financial situation in the country was worsening. Illness and other personal factors, including alcohol-related problems, meant that Yeltsin was notoriously inefficient in the office. Under pressure, on August 9, Yeltsin sacked his entire government and named a new acting premier, Vladimir Putin. Yeltsin also named Putin as his choice to succeed him as president. Less than five months later, on

December 31, Yeltsin, brushing away tears and pleading forgiveness, announced that he was resigning in favor of Putin, who became acting president (Sigelman and Shiraev, 2002).

In essence, the next president of Russia has been hand-picked by the former president. In remarkably short order, Putin was transformed from an obscure functionary into the most powerful man in the country. He came from within the government system. He was part of it, and promised to preserve it by consolidating more power in the president's hands. Putin first relied mainly on Yeltsin's Kremlin insiders. After becoming acting president he began to build his own team of political players (Boxer and Hale, 2000: 2).

Strengthening the executive branch

After being elected in 2000, President Putin began to act fast. He persuaded people it was necessary to reform the Constitution by drawing attention to the many weaknesses of a decentralized system of management in a country of Russia's size. There were several specific reasons for reform.

First, the president and his aides were increasingly dissatisfied with the Kremlin's ability to coordinate and manage federal policies. Throughout the 1990s the regions of Russia had received significant material and financial resources. About 60 percent of the federal budget was under the control of the regions (Gelman, 2006). Regional leaders, encouraged by local businesses and political groups, were constantly creating legal obstacles and barriers to reduce their dependency on Moscow. It was also clear that some of these legal obstacles were in contradiction to federal law.

The second reason was the complexity caused by the multiple bilateral agreements between regions and the federal government. Again, in many cases these agreements contradicted existing federal laws. The third reason was the rapid growth of local business, political, and ethnic elites, who were becoming increasingly powerful. Putin and his team saw this as a threat to the executive power of the Kremlin and the federal government. Putin wanted to restore Moscow's authority.

From the spring of 2000 onwards, President Putin began to build and strengthen Russia's "**power vertical**" (or "vertical power"—the term frequently used in Putin's speeches and in the media after 2000). There is no really satisfactory English translation of this term. In general, it stands for a strong hierarchy in the power system, a kind of line of subordination. In the eyes of Putin's supporters, this term stands for an efficient system of management from top to bottom. Critics say that the "power vertical" stands for an unprecedented strengthening and consolidation of Moscow's power and the weakening of Russia's regions. Before we study the essence of these debates, we must briefly examine the structure of Russia as a federal state.

Federal districts

In 2000 Putin created a set of new federal districts. This was a significant change in the structure of the entire government. A comparison might be a US president announcing that he was setting up five major regions in the United States, combining the states into Atlantic, Pacific, Southern, Midwestern, and Northern blocs. In Russia there were seven of these new administrative units: the North-Western, Central, Southern, Near-Volga, Ural, Siberian, and Far-Eastern (see Map 4). The argument behind this was that the 1991 system was too complex to administer, with too many disparate subjects, and the proposed simplification would make it more manageable.

A representative of the president was appointed for each of the districts. The main task of the representative is to coordinate policies in the region so that they are in agreement with federal policies. As you might expect, the appointment of seven federal "tsars" to the regions almost immediately put them in competition with governors and other regional leaders. The main question here was who had more power and authority to determine policies in the regions. In reality, the Kremlin won. In a few years the representatives, drawing on their direct support from the Kremlin, had gained significant power over governors, and even over federal ministers and other agencies (Isaev and Baranov, 2009).

Map 4   *Russia's federal districts*

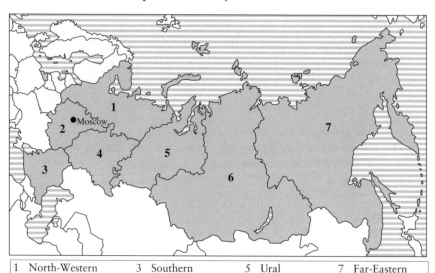

1	North-Western	3	Southern	5	Ural	7	Far-Eastern
2	Central	4	Near-Volga	6	Siberian		

The reorganization of the Federation Council

Although this reorganization referred to the legislative branch of government, the change also had a profound effect on regional executive power. Before 2000, governors and chairs of local legislatures automatically became members of the upper chamber of the Russian parliament. Putin discontinued this practice. This decision was not particularly popular and caused significant criticism across Russia. Why did Putin decide to proceed with this reform? There was growing belief in the Kremlin that the governors were gaining too much power as executive officers and legislators, working their way into the institutions of power in Moscow. In an attempt to preserve some democratic principles of collegiality, a State Council (*Gosudarstvennyj Soviet*) was set up as a forum for the governors. This was broadly similar to a council established by Tsar Alexander I (1777–1825). As in the 19th century, the 21st-century Russian State Council does not have significant power to influence important decisions made in the Kremlin. The Council is convened approximately four times a year. Between the sessions, there is a temporary committee of seven governors whose members are regularly cycled to avoid a concentration of power among a few individuals.

In addition to building the "power vertical," the Kremlin annulled most individual treaties between the federal government and the regions. The president also created the rights for his office to dismiss governors who are under criminal indictment, and to dismiss local legislatures should they not follow some types of legal instruction from the courts. In this new system, there were also regional executive officials who were responsible for the implementation of federal laws and other decisions passed down from Moscow.

Russians speak their mind ...

... **On the election of governors.** Percentage of Russians in 2008 supporting the idea that in Russia, governors of the subjects of the Federation should be elected rather than appointed by President: 63. Percentage opposing this idea: 19.

Source: Levada (2008d).

The political reforms of 2004

Further reforms took place in 2004. These had been in the planning stage for some time. Then on September 1 there was an act of terrorism in the town of Beslan in the south of Russia, in which many people including

Case in point: Does reform make the system more democratic?

In yet another proposal for reform, a new procedure for the appointment of top officials in the regions of the Russian Federation is being tested. Under this system the political party that receives the greatest number of votes in an election to the regional parliament is then entitled to propose three candidates for the post of regional governor to the president of Russia. The president considers the nominations and notifies the party of his decision within 30 days. You can check on the website whether this system has been adopted.

children were taken hostage, and a large number were killed and wounded when the "siege" was ended by force. The federal government brought in the reforms in response to this situation. It had caused much uncertainty and anxiety, and in this atmosphere Russian public opinion was generally supportive of strengthening federal power and weakening the power of local authorities. The most substantial reform was a fundamental change in the way local authorities and governors were selected. In future, the president suggested candidates for local governor and top executive officer posts, and the local legislatures then had the opportunity to approve them. In reality, the reform meant in the eyes of many observers that the Kremlin appointed governors.

The second change affected the electoral system, and eventually executive power. It was proposed that the country should have only all-state parties. The only political parties were allowed were ones that operated across the Federation, and single-subject parties were not permitted. Elections to the State Duma were to be based on proportional representation and party ballots. Special criteria were established for a political party to obtain its "all-state" status (see Chapter 7). To stimulate a dialogue between federal authorities and ordinary people, a special institution, a Community Chamber, was set up. Prominent Russian individuals were appointed to this and given the role of conveying public opinion to the president, keeping him informed about ordinary people's views of his policies. The Chamber remains an institution with mostly symbolic powers.

An expanding bureaucratic machine

During the Soviet Union era, the party bureaucracy was relatively small: it comprised just 0.1 percent of the total population. By 2000, the government bureaucracy had grown to three times as many people, although the total population of Russia was then only 50 percent of the population of the former Soviet Union (Isaev and Baranov, 2009).

The Communist Party of the Soviet Union had a special quota-based policy of diversity, intended to ensure that there was sufficient representation of various special groups in central and local government. These included women, peasants, workers, students, non-Russian minorities, and scientists. This practice was abandoned in the 1990s under President Yeltsin. Yeltsin surrounded himself with mostly young academics and other professionals such as economists, lawyers, and people with scholarly degrees. (Under General Secretary Leonid Brezhnev, in the 1970s, most people in the senior political elites had college degrees in engineering, construction, agricultural fields, and defense.) In contrast, President Putin selected many of his high-ranked federal officials from the military and the security services. Supporters of Putin's policies maintained that such a shift was inevitable, and was welcomed by most people in Russia. In their view, people's main demand was for strong and experienced officials in the Kremlin. Critics maintained that the change sent out an alarming signal: Russia was slowly being transformed into a police state.

The proportion of women in the federal bureaucracy went down significantly after the late 1980s. The regional elites—governors, legislature chairs, and other senior officials—were about ten years younger than their counterparts in the early 1980s. The average age of members of Duma is higher than it was in the Soviet Parliament 30 years ago, because communist officials maintained a high proportion of younger representatives in the state legislature (which did not have much real power). Studies conducted in Russia show that a substantial proportion of powerful federal officials—such as the mayor of St Petersburg, Valentina Matvienko, and Moscow's mayor, Yury Luzhkov—began their careers in the government or in the Communist Party and Komsomol back in the Soviet Union (Granovskij, 2004). A substantial proportion of the top

Case in point: Demographics of the government bureaucracy

It is interesting to consider the demographic changes over time in the characteristics of people in leadership roles in the regions. The average age of regional leaders in the Soviet Union in the 1980s was 59. During the Gorbachev period (1985–2000) it fell to 52. Under Boris Yeltsin in the 1990s it fell still further to an average of 49. After eight years of the Putin administration (2000–08), the average age had increased to 54. More than half of the regional elite had been Soviet officials in the 1980s or even earlier (Kryshtanovskaya, 2005).

federal elites came from Putin's birthplace, St Petersburg. Most political leaders in democratic countries tend to rely on familiar advisers, consultants, and friends, including many from their own home town or region. US presidents typically also create a cabinet staffed with close associates and previous employees.

Local government

Article 12 of the Constitution establishes local self-governance. In other words, the Constitution recognizes the ability of local authorities to manage a wide range of affairs in small villages and towns all across Russia. Local governments are not part of the system of federal government or of the governments of the subjects of the Federation. Individuals in charge of local government are either directly elected by local citizens or appointed under local legislation. Representative legislative institutions in larger towns are elected directly, not through party lists; there are none for towns and villages with a population of less than 5000. In these cases, local authorities are required to call regular meetings so that people can ask questions, make requests, and discuss issues of their choosing. Federal and regional authorities can delegate certain powers to local governments, including decisions on property rights and responsibilities.

In reality, however, local governments have very little power. According to a Freedom House report, Russia's entire system of local government lacks independence from regional and federal authorities (Freedom House, 2009). Local officers do not make decisions on most legal issues, which have to be decided at higher levels. For many years now, local governments have had to cope with power shifting to the regional centers. Local authorities often face chronic budgetary problems. In most cases, they have little capacity to collect taxes without seeking approval from the center. There were some attempts at recentralization of local power in the 1990s, but these were insufficient and unsuccessful (Lankina, 2004: 35). Corruption continues to be a serious problem.

Critical thinking about the executive branch

One of the ways to analyze the executive branch is over time, considering its evolution. We will begin with a brief discussion of this process and the changes it produced. Over the first 20 years of the Russian Federation, more power was concentrated in the Kremlin and less power remained in other government branches. Another method of analysis is to discuss executive power and the political system that has been developed in Russia. These debates are concerned primarily with the question, is

Russia democratic? In most modern political theories of western origin, representative democracy is associated with people's liberties (individual, economic, and political) and their equal access to power. Russian officials and their scholarly supporters interpret democracy differently.

Executive power: three stages of evolution

From a chronological perspective, we can identify three developmental stages in the transformation of executive power in Russia. In the first stage, during perestroika in the late 1980s, an eclectic group of politicians emerged. They gained their status because of their proximity to Boris Yeltsin or his most trusted political associates. Except for Yeltsin himself, they mostly had little previous political experience and no association with the highest echelons of the Communist Party. In 1991, the Communist Party of the Soviet Union was outlawed, and this significantly undermined the ability of many former communists to advance their political careers in Russia. The prime goal of the new elite was to eliminate opposition and defeat those who opposed the radical reforms. The struggle between the Yeltsin camp and the opposition was unexpectedly difficult, and resulted in the 1993 Constitution. To consolidate his victory over the defeated yet still powerful elites, Yeltsin and his team needed a strong legal foundation, and the Constitution provided that. Former chair of the Supreme Soviet of the Russia Federation Ruslan Khasbulatov and other critics believe that the Constitution of 1993 was the result of a direct plot to take the power away from the parliament (and the opposition in general) and keep it exclusively in the President's office (Khasbulatov, 2008).

In the second stage, another powerful group of political elites took shape in the mid-1990s. The main feature of this group was their association with big business and the existing political leadership (Gatman-Golutvina, 2000). After the rapid denationalization of property in the early 1990s, significant portions of the national wealth were in private possession, including coal mines, factories, oil fields, banks, and communications firms. A few individuals, often described as oligarchs, acquired substantial wealth.

With significant assets and tens of billions of dollars in their hands, these new elites moved to expand their power from the economic to the political sphere (read more about the "oligarchs" in Chapter 10). Many industrial, oil, and banking magnates gained significant political influence by providing generous financial support for various federal programs, paying off federal debts, and even financing election campaigns, including the presidential race of 1996. The oligarchs were interested in the decentralization of power. In the late 1990s, some regions received more power and freedom from Moscow than others

(Barner-Barry, 1999). A weak central power should have revealed new opportunities for business, trade, and finance. Feeling secure in their current role, federal officials in the late 1990s gradually gave away some of their political power (Kryshtanovskaya, 2005: 235).

In the third stage, Boris Yeltsin resigned in the wake of a serious financial crisis and amidst a continuing weakening of the federal government. Vladimir Putin's ascent to power created a new type of political elite. This new class of individuals had enjoyed few of the most lucrative benefits from the political reforms of the 1990s. In his quest to consolidate executive power, Putin decided to rely on the people he trusted most: his former partners and the most reliable and trustworthy cluster of officials from the military and security services. It was no great surprise that his team prevailed (Greenberg, 2008). To knock political power out of the hands of the oligarchs, Putin and his close supporters needed a new system of federal government, which was centralized and authoritarian in some ways. The 2000s under Presidents Putin and Medvedev were the years of the strengthening of the "power vertical" and an increase in federal control over Russia's regions (McFaul and Stoner-Weiss, 2008).

Authoritarian transitions

Most experts consider these transitions to indicate a continuous strengthening of an **authoritarian system** (Stoner-Weiss, 2006a). A political system is authoritarian if it has several distinct characteristics. It is nondemocratic and based on the rule of individuals, not necessarily the rule of law. It has meaningless or rigged elections. It tolerates or initiates attacks against political opposition. The system also restricts civil liberties and has a weak civil society (Brownlee, 2007). Based on these criteria, the Russian government has all the features of an authoritarian system (White, 2008). In fact, from a comparative perspective, presidential systems of government in countries going through political transition frequently produce authoritarian outcomes (Fish, 2005), especially if the country has a weak political opposition (Åslund, 2007: 285). The Russian political and social system can look to critics like a system of political, military, and financial obligations between powerful lords and obedient vassals (Shlapentokh and Woods, 2007). In sum, most commentators agree that the system under Putin and Medvedev is not democratic. Russian analysts for the most part disagree.

A "sovereign democracy"

Russian officials describe their political system as a "sovereign democracy": that is, a democratic system with unique Russian features (see

Chapter 1). About 40 percent of people in Russia believe that their country is building a democratic society (Dubin, 2008a). Many experts refer to Russia as a transitional society, which is essentially democratic but has not yet chosen a particular model of political and economic development (Gaidar, 2002, 2007). Presidential aides argue that, in general terms, Russian sovereign democracy is no different from European or any other democracy of the western type (Surkov, 2006). Others see Russia as an essentially free country with a wide range of freedoms (Zaslavskaya, 2004). They claim that western experts often overlook the uniqueness of the Russian democratic model.

Russians generally acknowledge the superior power of the executive branch of their government. However, in their view, three common arguments justify this superiority. First, a strong executive branch is necessary to correct the mistakes of the 1990s, when the central power was eroded to an extent that threatened the integrity of the state. Second, this system finds public support. Almost half of all Russians approve of the concentration of power in the hands of one person, and just 20 percent reject this (Dubin, 2008a). Third, the existing system is an attempt at efficient management (Isaev and Baranov, 2009). Attempts to bring in foreign models of democratic governance and apply them in the Russian context have been ineffective. Western models rely on the ability of people to self-govern and regulate their relations without a powerful authority. Russian people cannot self-govern yet. As a result, models that have been successful in America or Germany tend to fail in Russia.

Most importantly, Russian leaders continue to argue that the main accomplishment of Russia's political system is economic security for its people (Medvedev, 2009a). The government cannot guarantee improvements in all areas of life. Economic security is what people hope for, and finally, it is what they have received. This vision finds significant support across the country: many people want to see trains arrive on time, roads paved, or merchandise be delivered, regardless of how much or how little freedom people are allowed to have.

Russians speak their mind ...

... On trust. Percentage of Russians considering Putin trustworthy: 48. Percentage considering Medvedev trustworthy: 36.

Source: Levada (2009c).

Conclusion

Overall, most observers see Russia as a transitional system with strong authoritarian tendencies. Many believe that too much authority has been given to the president and his close associates (Nikonov, 2003: 9–11). Yet assessments of Russia's executive power vary. In Russia, loyal government supporters insist that this is the only appropriate system given Russia's conditions and historic experiences. Most other commentators are more pessimistic, emphasizing the strength of the authoritarian system and the diminishing amounts of freedom. Only a few believe that the authoritarian tendencies will lessen over time, and that the strong executive will be eventually replaced by more democratic government institutions (Remington, 2001; Shevtsova, 2005). It will require time and patience. Certainly, Russia will need plenty of them.

Chapter 5

The Legislative Branch

Key developments
The State Duma
The Federation Council
Critical thinking about the legislative branch
Conclusion

> *An obedient Duma is a myth, which is better dispelled by [our]*
> *work on the 2006 budget.*
> Boris Gryzlov, chair of the Russian Duma, 2005

There is a **separation of powers** in the Russian Federation, guaranteed by Article 10 of the Constitution. The article states that the power of the state in Russia is divided among three independent branches: the executive, legislative, and judiciary. The highest legislative body of the Russian Federation, according to the Constitution, is a parliament called the Federal Assembly. It consists of two chambers, the Federation Council and the State Duma. To understand better how the legislative system works, we will first examine several important developments in the short history of the contemporary Russian legislative branch. These developments have shaped the current state of Russia's legislative process and its relations with the executive branch. Then we take a look at the structure and functioning of the State Duma and the Federation Council. A critical-thinking review of the Russian legislative branch will, as usual, conclude the chapter.

It is important to keep in mind, even before you examine the critical thinking part of the chapter, that there is a difference between what is written in formal documents and the actual reality of Russia. We could probably say the same about many countries. In Russia this difference is substantial. In theory and on paper, the legislative branch of the government is powerful. In reality, the current legislature has little political power in relation to the executive.

Key developments

Several events that took place after 1991 have had a crucial impact on the development of the Russian government's legislative branch today. Among them were the events of the fall of 1993 (the October government crisis discussed in Chapter 4), the creation of the new Constitution, five parliamentary elections between 1993 and 2007, and the legislative reforms of 2004 and 2008. Over a period of just two decades, Russia has produced a stable legislative system. The system is based on democratic principles. However, it is somewhat different from legislative systems in the United States, the United Kingdom, and many other democracies. The Russian legislature today is essentially a rubber stamp for the powerful executive branch. While earlier elections in 1993 and 1995 allowed for some strong parliamentary opposition, the most recent elections guaranteed total victory for the ruling pro-Kremlin party.

The 1993 elections

The top legislative body in Russia between 1991 and 1993 was called the Supreme Soviet. It was the legislature elected in 1990 by the Congress of People's Deputies. The credentials of the Congress, if it continued its existence, would have expired in 1995. The first chair of the Supreme Soviet was Boris Yeltsin (May 29, 1990–July 10, 1991). After Yeltsin was elected president of Russia, this important role belonged to Ruslan Khasbulatov, a prominent economist who served for almost two years, from October 29, 1991 to October 4, 1993. As was outlined earlier in the book, after the inauguration of the Russian Federation as an independent state, the highest legislative and executive institutions clashed continuously (see Chapter 4). An escalating war of words and legal resolutions grew into an open conflict. Moscow in early October looked like a city under siege. President Boris Yeltsin brought in tanks to shell the parliament building. In the end, the executive branch won the military and political battle, and Yeltsin consolidated his power in the country. The violent struggle between the executive and legislative branches had resulted in the dismissal of the Supreme Soviet and its chair, Khasbulatov, rapid adoption of the Constitution on terms favorable to Yeltsin, and the parliamentary elections of December 1993.

These elections brought a somewhat unexpected success to political forces opposed to Yeltsin. Most probably, the violent actions against the parliament had mobilized those who were unhappy with Yeltzin's authoritarian methods. In particular, the Liberal Democratic Party, led by the flamboyant and blunt Vladimir Zhirinovsky, gained 23 percent of the electoral votes, the best result of all the participating political parties that year.

Zhirinovsky's and his party's strong performance in 1993 provided at least three important lessons. First, portions of the electorate, if they are unhappy with the executive, can elect a legislative branch that will be in opposition to the executive. In fact this happens regularly in countries such

Vladimir Zhirinovsky

Zhirinovsky is a prominent politician and parliamentarian, born in 1946 in Kazakhstan, a republic in the Soviet Union. He received college degrees in foreign languages and law. In addition, he earned an advanced degree in philosophy (the topic of his dissertation was *The Past, Present, and Future of the Russian Nation*). Zhirinovsky is one of the founders of the Liberal Democratic Party, and became its chair in 1990. This was one of the first parties registered in the Soviet Union. He was elected to the State Duma consistently after 1993, and served as a faction leader and (by rule) deputy chair of the Duma. Politically, he has been in constant but constructive opposition to the government, which has allowed him to get modest public support and eventually the votes necessary to win elections. He is known mostly for his flamboyant style, extreme nationalist statements, and anti-western views in foreign policy. He supports authoritarian methods of government, and appeals primarily to disaffected voters.

as the United States and France. Second, unlike in Paris or Washington, the victory of the opposition in the Duma elections did not significantly affect the policies of the executive branch in the Kremlin: the new Russian Constitution, the adoption of which had been pushed through by the executive branch, had designed a relatively weak legislature (Zorkaya, 2004). Third, the elections of 1993 demonstrated that Russia at that time, despite the existence of dangerous authoritarian trends, was adopting all the major features of the democratic political process, including the free competition of ideas, a multi-party system, and a relative transparency of electoral results (Bruter, 1994).

The 1995 elections

According to the Constitution, elections to the Duma, one of the two chambers of the Federal Assembly, are carried out according to special federal laws. The Constitution does not specify the frequency of elections or other details, it simply establishes the number of delegates in the Federation Council (two from each subject of the Federation) and the exact number of deputies for the Duma: 450. The elections of 1995, according to the law, were held two years after the first Duma elections. The law established a four-year period between parliamentary elections in the future.

The electoral system was complicated. Half of the deputies were elected according to party lists: each political party received a number of seats in the Duma that was in proportion to the number of votes cast for it. The minimum threshold (below which the party would not receive any seats) was established at 5 percent. Such barriers are common in other countries, and serve primarily to prevent very small parties from getting seats. The other half of the Duma's deputies was elected in what are known as "one seat," or more commonly "**one mandate**," districts: several candidates run for each seat and the one gaining the largest number of votes wins. The Federation Council was specified as consisting of the heads of the executive and legislative branches of each and every subject of the Federation, so there were no direct competitive elections for this second chamber of the Federal Assembly.

In 1995, the electoral rules allowed many small parties to participate. Because of this situation, one of the most efficient ways to win seats in the Duma was to form a political party and run a national campaign promoting the party's candidates. After 1995, politicians aspiring for political offices and government officials realized how important it was to establish a strong and organized political party in order to win seats in the Duma. They also realized that the chances of a party's succeeding in this would be improved if there were fewer competing parties.

The parliamentary elections of 1999 and 2003

The number of parties and political blocs participating in the elections decreased over this period. In 1999 there were 28, down from 43 four years earlier. In 2003, the number of competing parties was 23. One major reason for this fall was that small parties had realized it was very difficult for them to overcome the minimum threshold and win seats in the Duma. They chose instead to seek other ways to gain political power, or merged to form larger parties. The elections also revealed that when the electoral system is untested, elections may turn into a competition of groups trying to outsmart one another by taking advantage of the quirks in the legal rules and regulations. For example, by 1999 it had become clear that one successful tactic was for a group of people with significant financial support to form a political party a few months before the Duma elections. Its primary aim was to win its backers representation according to the list system (Bruter, 1999). Once this had been achieved, the party as an organization was no longer important.

The reform of 2005

Because the Constitution does not specify how to organize the Duma elections, this is done through federal laws. A new law of May 18, 2005 called *On Elections of the Deputies of the State Duma of the Federal Assembly of the Russian Federation* significantly changed the electoral procedures. One of the most significant changes was that it removed the one-mandate districts. A new party-list proportional representation system emerged, according to which all the parliamentary seats were allocated to the parties in proportion to the number of votes they received. This was a move by the Kremlin to diminish the electoral strength of local political forces in the provinces. Now the power to elect candidates was given to national parties and their Moscow headquarters.

Russians speak their mind ...

... On one-mandate districts. Percentage of Russians in 2009 wanting to return to one-mandate districts during Duma elections: 42. Those against: 18. Those with no opinion: 40.

Source: Levada (2009d).

The 2005 law also took care of the loophole that had become apparent in the 1990s laws, and was designed to prevent the creation of electoral groups or party coalitions whose sole purpose was to win seats in the Duma. Political parties now faced a more difficult organizational challenge. To receive approval from the federal government to nominate candidates for an election, a party had to meet a number of criteria. One of the most important requirements was that it must have at least 50,000 members. As a result, the Justice Ministry responsible for implementing this regulation registered only 15 political parties, down from 23 during the 2003 Duma elections. Strong parties with a long history of political battles, such as the Communist Party and the Liberal Democratic Party, had no difficulty in meeting these new requirements. Many smaller and less organized parties, however, were virtually eliminated. Another important change was an increase in the electoral threshold for gaining seats from 5 to 7 percent. Forecasters quickly calculated that a party would need to get from 5 to 7 million votes to win representation in the Duma.

The elections of 2007

These new amendments were implemented in the fifth Duma elections of 2007, which took place on December 2. Another significant change was that independent observers, except those appointed by the parties, were not allowed to monitor the elections. The Central Electoral Commission also significantly reduced the number of international observers (Levchenko, 2007). Although official sources in Russia considered the elections fair and legitimate, most oppositional parties in Russia and most international observers disagreed. They argued that the new electoral system under centralized federal control had given the ruling party, United Russia, a substantial advantage. Most critics also claimed that the decision of President Putin to run at the top of the United Russia party list was an attempt by the government to influence the elections. In the end, Putin's party received more than 64 percent of the popular vote. As might have been expected, supporters of the leading party argued that everything had been conducted according to the law.

The constitutional amendments of 2008

In the fall of 2008 President Medvedev, who had been elected earlier that year, suggested that it was necessary to modify the federal electoral system. His justification was that the complexity of the daily activities of the president and the members of the Duma required consistency and stability. The term of service for the president and the legislators was four years, but Medvedev argued that this was too short for efficient governance. He proposed several amendments to the Constitution, and these were discussed and adopted in a remarkably short period, even by Russia's legal standards.

On November 11, the president took the first step and sent a draft of a new constitutional amendment to the Duma. After two brief procedural delays, the Duma approved the amendments ten days later, with a majority of 392 voting for them and all the members of the Communist Party voting against. Five days later, the Federation Council also approved the amendments by 144 to 1. By three weeks later—December 16—two-thirds of the legislatures of the subjects of the Federation had also approved the amendments. This gave President Medvedev the constitutional right to sign the law to amend the Constitution. As a result, the presidential term was increased to six years, and in future deputies of the State Duma were to be elected to a five-year term.

The State Duma

Unlike in some countries which have centuries-old parliamentary traditions, Russia's democratic history is not very long. The first representative institution based on competitive elections was created only a little more than a hundred years ago, in 1906. It was called the State Duma. This parliament lasted until 1917. The word "duma" has two origins: it refers to both a council of people and a thinking process. Under Soviet rule, both the state and local legislatures, which were called soviets, were under the total control of the Communist Party despite the formal existence of elections. Boris Yeltsin and his supporters returned to the original term "Duma" in the Constitution of 1993, partly as a symbolic gesture of respect for tradition.

Structure of the Duma

The State Duma of the Russian Federation consists of 450 delegates. The Duma elections are called by the president according to the law, usually at the end of the designated year. After the constitutional amendments of 2008, members of the Duma are elected for a five-year term. (The First Duma was elected for two years; subsequent ones before this change had a four-year term.) The official voting age in Russia is 18, and the age limit for candidates for the Duma is a little higher at 21. By comparison, in the United States citizens must be 25 to run for Congress and 30 to be eligible to run for the Senate.

The members of the Duma gather in Moscow for regular meetings called sessions. After each election, the new members elect a chair and deputy chairs. These individuals preside over the sessions and supervise the internal rules of the chamber during sessions. To organize and manage its work on a daily basis and in different areas, the Duma creates committees and commissions, exercises parliamentary supervision over many issues within its jurisdiction, and holds parliamentary hearings (See Figure 5.1).

The chair and the chair's deputies are elected by secret ballot. The legislature itself can decide on the number of deputies elected. Usually, party factions in the Duma nominate one candidate for the chairmanship. However, any elected deputy can also run for the chairmanship. The winner must receive more than half of the votes (that is, 226 or more). The chair has a wide range of responsibilities. He or she has to moderate the sessions of the Duma, schedule hearings, and coordinate the activities of the executive staff. The chair represents the Duma in the country and overseas, and coordinates its parliamentary activities with other branches of the Russian government. The chair can distribute certain responsibilities among the deputies according to the law. In theory, the Duma may override any internal order or decision of the chair by voting to veto it.

The chair also directs the activities of the Council of the State Duma.

Figure 5.1 *Structure of the State Duma elected in 2007*

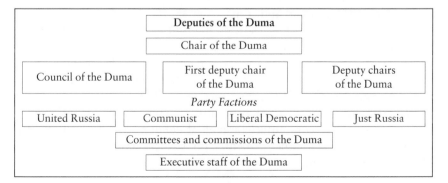

This institution comprises the chair and deputies, and conducts preliminary work on proposed legislation, and other organizational and procedural issues. Ranking members of the Duma have the right to attend its meetings and offer suggestions related to procedural questions (Organizational Procedures of the Duma, 1998).

The deputies of the State Duma organize **party factions**, which are defined by the law as an association of the deputies elected according to their party list. In other words, this is the group of elected representatives belonging to a party that received more than 7 percent of the votes and thus gained seats in the parliament. Each elected deputy can join only one party faction, and each one elects a head and deputies.

The Duma committees

According to the Constitution (Article 101), the State Duma forms parliamentary committees. Each committee works within a particular policy area. Committees have many functions, but mention of four will serve to illustrate their work:

- Committees submit their proposals and comments for a forthcoming session of the Duma.
- They discuss drafts of legislation (in other words, bills) and propose changes, if they think it necessary.
- They work on various assignments given to them by the Duma.
- Finally, they evaluate the implementation of the laws passed by the Duma.

There are more than 30 committees in the Duma, but the number is not fixed: it depends on the legislature's decisions. As an example, there are committees on labor and social policy, budget and taxes, energy, transportation, defense, foreign policy, science, culture, mass sporting activities (called in Russian "physical culture") and sports. The government sponsors amateur sports in Russia, which is why the Duma has a special committee on recreational and competitive sports.

In the Duma, as in most legislatures in the world, deputies are appointed to committees largely on the basis of their experience. For example, specialists in agriculture tend to serve on agriculture-related committees, and former army officers are likely to join the defense committee. The committee membership also reflects each faction's proportional size in the Duma, so if one political party has a majority in the Duma, it will also have a majority on every committee. Individual deputies can serve on several committees, and the number of people on each committee varies, but the 2007 law requires it to be between 12 and 35 (Duma, 2007).

The Duma can also establish special **parliamentary commissions** to address particular questions related to the work of the legislature, a policy issue, or the implementation of previous decisions of the Duma. These commissions are typically set up on a temporary basis.

The Constitution sets out the conditions under which the Duma can be dissolved, and the procedures for doing this. It can be dissolved by the president of the Russian Federation, but only under special circumstances (see Chapter 4). The president may not dissolve it within one year after its election, and it also cannot be dissolved in the period between its bringing accusations against the president and a decision being taken on them by the Federation Council. It also cannot be dissolved during any period of a state of emergency or martial law throughout the territory of the Russian Federation, or within six months of the expiration of the president's term of office. So far, no president has attempted to dissolve the Duma.

Russians speak their mind ...

... On the Duma. Respondents were asked which groups and which categories of society they would like to see representatives of in the Duma. (They could choose up to five.) Percentage of Russians choosing: economists: 45; lawyers: 42; scientists: 30; party leaders: 25; doctors: 21.

Source: WCIOM (2007).

Functioning of the Duma

The Constitution establishes the **jurisdiction** of the State Duma. Jurisdiction means the practical authority or specific rights given to a government institution or branch of power. It sets specific limitations on how much power the Duma can exercise. It also, in theory, prevents future arguments or even conflicts with other government institutions about who makes decisions and under which circumstances. In particular, the State Duma:

- approves the president's nomination for chair of the Government of the Russian Federation (prime minister)
- makes decisions on confidence in the Government of the Russian Federation
- appoints and can dismiss the chair of the Central Bank of the Russian Federation
- appoints and can dismiss the chair of the Accounting Chamber and half of its staff of auditors
- appoints and can dismiss the plenipotentiary for human rights acting in accordance with federal constitutional law

- can grant amnesties (in criminal cases)
- can bring charges against the president of the Russian Federation for his impeachment.

All deputies of the Duma have the right of **legislative initiative**. This term commonly refers to the ability or capacity of an individual or institution to introduce proposals with a view to their becoming law. In Russia, the deputies can introduce draft laws (bills) for consideration. The State Duma also adopts resolutions on the issues within its jurisdiction. To be passed, these resolutions must be adopted by a majority of the votes of all deputies in the legislature. There are some exceptions related to special types of votes for which the Constitution sets special conditions. A draft once adopted by the State Duma does not immediately become a law: it is then passed to the Federation Council for review within five days.

In some cases, the Duma and the executive branch must work together. For example, drafts on the introduction of new or abolition of old taxes, financial exemptions, federal loans, changes in the financial obligations of the state and other bills related to the federal budget may be introduced to the State Duma only with a corresponding resolution by the Government of the Russian Federation.

Case in point: The prime minister addresses the Duma

Prime Minister Vladimir Putin addressed the Duma on April 6, 2009. A special session was called for this purpose (this is a prerogative of the speaker). The premier spoke for 65 minutes; his formal statement contained 48 pages. In his report, Putin briefly described the work of his Cabinet during the previous year. However, he spent most of his time describing his plans to address the current global economic and financial crisis. Each parliamentary faction prepared three written questions to the premier. The answers were prepared in advance, and Putin answered only these written questions. Then the heads of the factions spoke. Communist Gennady Zyuganov demanded the resignation of several members of the Cabinet of Ministers. After these speeches, Putin made his concluding remarks and, speaking in general terms, used the metaphor "light at the end of the tunnel" to describe his cautiously optimistic view about the easing of the ongoing crisis. Putin was accompanied by a group of 25 of his executive associates and federal ministers. After they left, the Duma deputies began to discuss amendments to the federal budget to address the major additional concerns created by the ongoing crisis, and to approve the federal budget deficit.

Russians speak their mind

... **On Putin's speech in the Duma.** Percentage of Russians saying they did not pay any attention to the Putin speech: 54.

Source: WCIOM (2009c).

The Federation Council

Originally, the 1993 Constitution prescribed that every subject of the Russian Federation would send two representatives to the upper Chamber of the Federal Assembly, the Council of the Federation. One representative was to be sent from its executive and the other from its legislative branch. From 1995, the governors and speakers of regional legislatures joined the Council automatically. This practice was later discontinued and a new one established. Although the Federation Council was supposed to represent Russia's diverse regional interests in the federal legislature, most of the changes in the way it is assembled have helped the Kremlin's consolidation of power.

Structure of the Federation Council

At a glance, the structure of the Federation Council resembles the structure of the Duma, and indeed of many other legislature chambers in other countries. There are a chair, deputy chairs, heads of permanent committees, and executive staff. The members of the Federation Council elect the chair of the Federation Council and his or her deputies.

The chair and the deputies are responsible for organizational, strategic, and procedural questions relevant to the functioning of the Chamber. One of their prime responsibilities is to draw up agendas for the Council sessions, and submit proposed laws and other decisions to the members for discussion and voting. The chair presides over the sessions. He or she also coordinates the work of the committees. One of many ceremonial responsibilities is to administer an oath to newly appointed judges of the Constitutional Court and new prosecutors-general.

The chair is assisted by the Council of the Chamber. This is a collective organ designed to help in the preparation of documents for the sessions. It is a permanent institution which includes the chair, all the deputies, and the chairs of permanent committees of the Federation Council. Members of the Council make decisions collectively by majority vote. They are responsible for numerous procedural questions relating to the sessions, their duration, the list and order of presenters, number of guests or experts invited to testify, and so forth.

Figure 5.2   *Structure of the Federation Council*

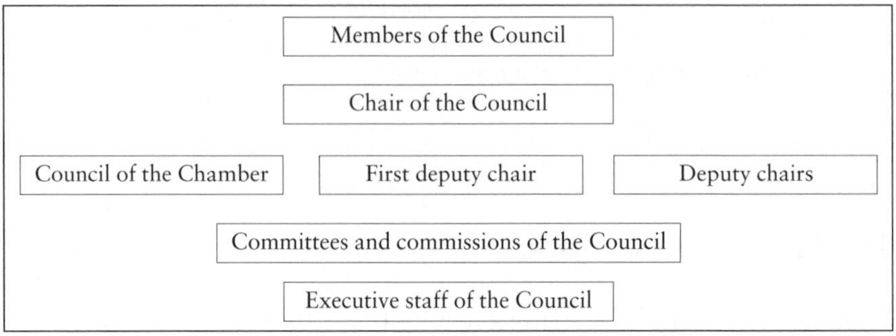

| Members of the Council |
| Chair of the Council |

| Council of the Chamber | First deputy chair | Deputy chairs |

| Committees and commissions of the Council |
| Executive staff of the Council |

Committees of the Federation Council

The Federation Council, like the State Duma, establishes committees and commissions, which are permanent and work along the lines of major government functions. Most committees of the Council resemble committees of the State Duma. Several of them reflect the differences in the functioning of these two chambers. For example, the Federation Council has a separate committee on order and organization of parliamentary work. There are also committees on regional politics and local self-management. All these committees are involved in parliamentary work related to discussion of new legislation, consideration of legislations (drafts of new laws) sent from the Duma, and supervision of the implementation of certain legislative decisions made in the past. Committees of the Federation Council may work closely with the Duma committees on drafts or legislative issues. There are also temporary commissions that can be assembled to address a specific legislative issue for a limited time. See Figure 5.2.

Membership of the Federation Council

The Constitution (Article 2) states that the Federation Council must have two representatives (Russians informally call them senators) from each subject of the Russian Federation, one from the legislature and the other from the executive branch. A 2004 Federal Law (no.160 FZ-3) details how the Council is assembled. The Council has 178 members (the number may vary based on the number of the subjects of the Federation). They can be either elected by regional legislatures or appointed by regional administrations.

The length of parliamentary service of the members of the Federal Council is not fixed, unlike that for the State Duma. Each senator continues to be a member for as long as is appropriate depending on the rules for membership that have been established by his or her subject body. For example, if there is an election to the subject legislature, the credentials of this senator will expire at the time of the election. A newly elected legislature is supposed to decide on a new senator (or may keep the old one).

Critics maintain that there are not democratic elections to the Federal Council, because in practice, most decisions on the appointment of senators are made in the Kremlin. It suggests candidates to governors or local legislatures who simply rubberstamp them. Not surprisingly, many senators disagree. They tend to argue that they have been elected by their local legislature in a democratic and fair manner.

Functioning

The Federation Council exercises parliamentary supervision over issues within its jurisdiction, and holds parliamentary hearings. The Council and its members have the right of legislative initiative. In other words, they can propose new laws or suggest amendments to existing ones.

The Federation Council must consider bills adopted by the Duma dealing with a number of specific issues and policies, including the federal budget, federal taxes and fees, and other financial and credit-related issues including printing money and issuing financial obligations. It is also required to consider laws that relate to the functioning of Russia as a state. This includes ratification and withdrawal from international treaties, issues about state borders and their protection, and war and peace issues.

The decrees of the Federation Council are adopted by a majority of all deputies to the Council. The sessions of the Federation Council are usually open to the public, but they can be closed if a special decision must be made. As in the case of the Duma, the Constitution defines the jurisdiction of the Federation Council. The jurisdiction is further explained in relevant laws, and includes several areas. For example, in the international field, the Council can make decisions about the use of the armed forces of the Russian Federation outside its territory. Domestically, it approves changes of borders between the subjects of the Russian Federation. The Council also approves the president's decrees on the introduction of martial law (giving the military the right to administer justice for a limited period) and a state of emergency (suspending certain government functions and in some cases particular civil liberties). The Council calls the elections for the president of the Russian Federation. This is a formal function, required to be performed every five years if a president serves a full term in office, or at other intervals in the case of a president's resignation or death. The Council may impeach the president. The Council is also responsible for the appointment of judges of the Constitutional Court of the Russian Federation, the Supreme Court of the Russian Federation, and the Supreme Court of Arbitration of the Russian Federation. Its jurisdiction includes the appointment to office and the removal from office of the prosecutor-general of the Russian Federation.

To exercise control over the federal budget, the Federation Council and the State Duma together appoint an Accounting Chamber, the membership and rules of order of which are determined by federal law.

If the Duma passes a bill but the Federation Council rejects it, the chambers may set up a conciliatory commission to try to resolve their differences. Once this has made recommendations, the bill is sent back to the Duma. If two-thirds of the Duma members vote for the bill again, it is passed regardless of what the Federation Council decides.

Deputies may not work full-time for other agencies of the federal government, or continue to receive a salary for any other activities except for teaching, research, and artistic work. Article 98 of the Constitution specifically acknowledges that the members of the Federal Assembly have legal immunity. They may not be arrested or searched, unless the law specifies otherwise, or if it is essential to do this immediately for other people's safety. The attorney general can petition for, and a Chamber can approve, cases involving the termination of the legal immunity of certain deputies.

The Duma and the Federation Council: Joint functions and procedures

The Federation Council and the State Duma normally meet separately, although the chambers may have joint sessions to listen to the addresses of the president of the Russian Federation, addresses of the Constitutional Court, or speeches of foreign leaders. A person may not serve in both chambers of the Federal Assembly simultaneously, and their members may not serve in local government at the same time.

How do the Russian legislature and executive power interact to pass federal laws? The procedure is quite complicated (see Figure 5.3). Within five days of a federal law being passed by the chambers, it is sent to the president of the Russian Federation for signing and publication. The President then has 14 days to sign it and make it available to the public via newspapers and/or the internet. The president can, however, veto any submitted law. In these circumstances the State Duma and the Federation Council reconsider it. If, during the second hearings, the federal law is approved in its earlier draft by a majority of not less than two-thirds of the total number of deputies of the Federation Council and the State Duma, the president's veto is overridden and he must sign it into law.

The legislative branch has the right to amend the Constitution, but the majorities required for this to be done are larger. Any amendment must be approved by at least 75 percent of the senators in the Federation Council, two-thirds of the members of the Duma, and two-thirds of local legislatures.

Figure 5.3 *Passing a federal law in Russia*

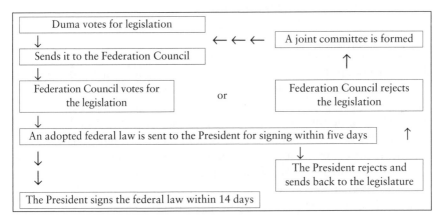

The Constitution can also be dissolved by a decision of an all-state constitutional (constitutive) assembly, which can be called and elected by the people of the Russian Federation for that purpose. (This is much what happened in 1918 when the Bolshevik Party had dissolved the first Constituent Assembly.)

Russia is a presidential republic. The president has significant executive and legislative powers. However, his powers are not unlimited. Not only does the Federal Council have the constitutional right to impeach a sitting president, according to Article 117 of the Constitution the State Duma also has the right to demand the resignation of the Government of the Russian Federation (the Cabinet of Ministers). A special procedure is set down for this too. If the Duma demands the government's resignation once, the president may or may not agree to satisfy the demand. If the Duma votes for resignation twice within three months, then the president must do one of two things: either dissolve the government or dissolve the Duma itself. In addition, the prime minister can initiate a confidence vote regarding the government in the Duma. If the outcome of this is a vote of no confidence, the president has the right to dissolve either the government or the Duma. In the 1990s, the Duma occasionally used these legal rules to influence Yeltsin's policies. Because of the strong pro-Kremlin majority in the Duma, such developments are very unlikely these days.

Critical thinking about the legislative branch

Although formally, the three government branches are independent and equal in Russia, as in many other states, in reality they are not necessarily all equally strong. As you learned in Chapter 4, Russia is a strong presidential republic with an exceptionally strong executive branch. As a consequence, the legislature in today's Russia is weak.

A weak legislative branch

Even at the outset, in 1993, the Constitution outlined a legislature that would not match the power of the executive branch. President Yeltsin wanted to have a political system in which the Kremlin would have a decisive voice and the final call on most important issues. Later in that decade however, the Duma began to gain strength and occasionally challenge the president: for example, it blocked the president's suggested candidate for prime minister in 1998. Yeltsin and his team continued efforts to weaken the legislature, and especially the power of the most dominant opposition in the 1990s—the Communist Party. They succeeded in this task. President Putin then weakened the legislature further by eliminating "one-mandate" districts and establishing party lists for the Duma elections.

The legislative electoral system

Many observers in Russia are unhappy with the new electoral system based on party lists. In the minds of these critics, this system is beneficial only for large and powerful parties. Under the system, even moderately strong parties that manage to overcome the difficult 7 percent barrier might get only a few seats in the parliament. A one-mandate electoral system, as was used for legislative elections in Russia back in the 1990s, is more democratic. Under this (one district–one member) system, two or more candidates run for a single seat in one geographical district, and the candidate who gets the most votes wins. Common sense suggests that a direct system is more free from the bureaucracy and deal-making associated with internal party politics. However, it also has drawbacks, as the experience of other countries shows. The United Kingdom, for example, uses a "first-past-the-post" system in which each geographic constituency elects one member of Parliament. (This is just one of several types of single-member constituency system, in which only one round of voting takes place and there is no redistribution of votes cast for losing candidates.) It tends to skew election results because small parties that gain significant numbers of votes across the country but top the poll in only a few, if any, constituencies, get little or no representation, and this discourages their supporters from continuing to vote for them. One of the two largest parties almost always wins enough seats to form a government.

Nevertheless, there is a significant difference between the Russian and British political systems. In the United Kingdom, one of the two large parties is to the left and the other is to the right of the political spectrum.

Either one of these two parties is generally expected to win a majority of votes. In Russia, there are two large political parties, the Communist Party and the Liberal Democratic Party, that historically stand in opposition to the ruling government. In a first-past-the-post system, between them they might win a majority of the seats in the Duma, while under the present system they win only a sizeable minority. (The United Russia party tends to win the majority of seats, as we will see later in Chapters 7 and 8.) With a majority, the opposition parties would have significantly more power, and this would change the dynamics of the political process. Although the Duma's power is no match for the power of the Kremlin, neither Putin nor Medvedev wants to engage in constant disputes and clashes with the legislature.

In fact, the party list electoral system is exactly what the executive branch wants to have for Russia's political system. The president now has enough power to influence elections and keep solid legislative support in the Duma and the Federation Council. The electoral reform of 2005 gave the executive a tool to skew elections in favor of the executive branch.

Many critical questions about the nature of the political process in Russia arose after the remarkably quick adoption of the amendments to the Constitution in 2008 (extending the lengths of times in office). In a positive sprint, within two months after the amendments had been suggested by President Medvedev, they had been fully adopted by both federal and regional legislatures. The opposition expressed serious concerns about the legality of such a "rush delivery" of a major constitutional issue. According to the law, they argued, there is a mandatory one-year period for discussions of proposed constitutional amendments before they can be adopted by regional legislatures. These arguments were ignored by the decision makers in the Kremlin.

Conclusion

Russia's legislature seems to have a solid legal foundation, but it would be misleading to believe that it is fully built. It is incomplete and even deficient because it is relatively ineffective and weak in comparison with the executive branch. In theory, the Duma must represent the will of the people. In reality, it represents the will of the parties and their central offices in Moscow. It is true that in other countries, political parties possess significant power. However, citizens of those states have significantly greater opportunities to affect the electoral process and elect candidates who oppose the ruling party. In Russia, the system is different. The elections are not necessarily free—note however that this view is angrily disputed by many Russian commentators—because the ruling authorities use federal resources to make sure that "acceptable" candidates win.

Historically, the Russian Duma was almost always in a vulnerable position: it was dependent on the will of the emperor of Russia early in the 20th century, and it is shaped by the political calculations of the president in the 21st century. Several times during the short history of post-communist Russia, the electoral rules for the Federal Assembly have been changed, and there is no guarantee that they will not change again in the near future. Yet most probably, the future of the Russian democratic state will depend on how much power the legislature can obtain or preserve. Russia must not fumble its chance for a free and democratic system.

Chapter 6

The Judicial Branch and Justice Administration

Key developments
The Constitutional Court of the Russian Federation
The Supreme Court
The Supreme Arbitration Court
The Russian Criminal Code
The Prosecutor's Office
The Ministry of Justice
Law enforcement: the Ministry for Internal Affairs
Critical thinking about Russia's judicial branch and justice administration
Conclusion

> *The Russian judiciary system is no longer a guardian of the electoral law. By creating an illusion of serving the law, it is in reality an obedient instrument of the executive power.*
> Garry Kasparov, former world chess champion
> and an opposition leader, 2008

The judiciary branch has been affected by the same course of important events as the executive and legislative branches since the inception of the Russian Federation as an independent state, including several legislative elections, especially in 1993, and presidential elections. Overall, the judiciary branch in Russia has not experienced dramatic changes or significant turnarounds over this period. Together with the system of justice administration, it is going through a steady, evolutionary development. However, despite steady changes that have taken place in the judiciary since the 1990s, it has not achieved full independence from the executive branch. The justice system—Russia's leaders talk about this openly—suffers from inefficiency, bureaucratic delays, and corruption. The problem is that the authorities have not found an efficient remedy for these problems. More transparency and independence could be a good start.

Key developments

Among the most significant developments have been the preservation and gradual modification of the federal court system and the trial system. The principal source of law in Russia is the Constitution. The Constitution states that justice in Russia is administered only by law courts. As in other countries, a **court of law** in Russia is supposed to establish the legality or otherwise of a certain action (which could be the behavior of an individual, a decision of an institution, or a government decree, for example), then pass a ruling. Judiciary power is exercised in four major areas: constitutional, civil, administrative, and criminal. The law courts in Russia constitute a hierarchy, with the higher courts having the right to overrule decisions of lower courts. The creation of special or extraordinary courts that do not follow the procedures of the ordinary court system is prohibited.

The secondary source of law is the system of codes: in other words, a selection of written laws related to specific areas. There are about 20 such codes, and their number can change (Legal Acts of the Russian Federation, 2009). Among them are the Criminal Code, which describes crimes and corresponding punishments, and the Civil Code, which regulates legal agreements, property rights, intellectual property rights, and so forth. There is also a Civil Procedural Code regulating court procedures in civil cases. Others include the Tax Code and the Land Code.

The federal court system

The Constitution identifies three federal legal bodies and outlines their basic responsibilities: the Constitutional Court of the Russian Federation,

Figure 6.1   *The federal court system of the Russian Federation*

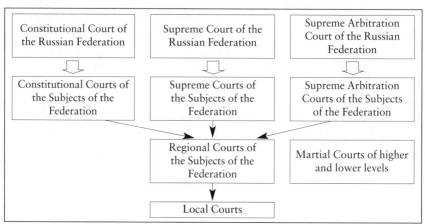

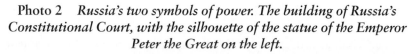

Photo 2   *Russia's two symbols of power. The building of Russia's Constitutional Court, with the silhouette of the statue of the Emperor Peter the Great on the left.*

the Supreme Court of the Russian Federation, and the Supreme Arbitration Court of the Russian Federation. These courts have the right of legislative initiative within their jurisdiction (see Figure 6.1).

A federal judge in Russia must be a Russian citizen, a minimum of 25 years old, holding a law degree. The Constitution adds another age restriction: an individual must spend at least five years in the legal profession before becoming a federal judge. Federal law may establish additional requirements for federal judges. Judges are independent in their decisions; they may not be suspended, replaced, or fired. They also possess immunity from criminal prosecution. However, federal laws also outline the conditions and grounds for exceptions to these rules. The president of the Russian Federation nominates judges to the Constitutional Court, Supreme Court, and the Supreme Arbitration Court, who are then appointed by the Federation Council. Judges of other federal courts are appointed according to federal law.

The trial system

The Constitution establishes that trials must be conducted on an adversarial and equal basis. According to Article 123 of the Constitution, all trials are open to the public. As in the United States and many other countries, criminal defendants in Russia have the right to appear in person at their trial (Benderskaya, 2008). Back in the Soviet Union, there were often court hearings in absentia, especially for the special tribunals and other courts assembled specifically to investigate political crimes at the request of senior

Communist Party officials. The law in Russia today lays down the limited circumstances in which there can be court hearings in absentia. For example, the Criminal Procedural Code allows a person accused of a crime (of low severity) to petition for the case to be considered without their being present.

Federal law (a law of July 27, 2006) also allows courts to hear cases of severe crimes in the absence of the accused if they are outside the territory of Russia, or refuse to appear in court, and are not being tried elsewhere for the crime. For example, the North-Caucasus district military court sentenced three military officers (who were absent during the trial) to lengthy prison sentences (11–14 years) for murders committed in Chechnya during the long-running military conflict in that area. In another high-profile trial on November 29, 2007, a court in Moscow tried entrepreneur and billionaire Boris Berezovsky for embezzlement, over the 1996–97 alleged theft of more than $200 million from Aeroflot, a major Russian airline. The verdict was guilty and he was sentenced in absentia to six years in prison (Trofimova, 2008).

Recently, the federal court trial system has begun to use jurors. Although there was a jury system in the Soviet Union, the jury members (usually two) directly served the court system and seldom challenged prosecutors and judges. The new system, the establishment of which is suggested but not mandated by the Constitution, was supposed to provide independence for the newly formed category of jurors (Federal Law of August 20, 2004). However, jury trials are used only in a small number of cases, mostly serious ones. Prosecutors tend not to like using juries, particularly because they often return "not guilty" verdicts. Overall, government officials are not especially eager to install this new jury trial system.

The Russian court system is very complex, and extremely busy. For example, in a single year, the courts heard more than 9 million civil cases, more than 5 million administrative cases, and 1,200,000 criminal cases (Lebedev, 2008).

How does the judicial system function, what problems does it face, and how does it interact with other branches of the government?

The Constitutional Court of the Russian Federation

The Constitutional Court of the Russian Federation was first elected by the Supreme Soviet of the Russian Federation in 1991. The major role of the court is to consider the constitutional legality of certain laws and policies of the Russian Federation. During the constitutional crisis of 1993, the chair of the Supreme Court participated in negotiations between the Office of the President and the parliament in attempts to mediate and resolve their disputes. Twice in 1993, the Constitutional Court ruled against President Boris Yeltsin and found his actions—including dismissal of the parliament—to be unconstitutional. These rulings led to impeachment procedures. On 21 September of that year, Yeltsin dismissed the Constitutional Court and suspended its activities. The legality of this action of the Russian president is still being debated. However, the court began its activities again in February 1995. From that moment, its work has been based on the new Constitution.

The court's functioning

The Constitution describes the major principles and prerogatives of the Constitutional Court. Its main function is to resolve cases involving the compliance of certain legal decisions, rulings, or treaties with the Constitution of the Russian Federation. For example, a presidential decree, a federal law, an international treaty, or a treaty signed between two subjects of the Federation could be challenged in the Constitutional Court. The Constitutional Court might consider, for example, a case in which one of the republics passed a law that might affect the jurisdiction of federal law enforcement within that republic. The court may also consider international treaties, but if only they have not entered into force.

The Court has the right to interpret the Constitution. However, to initiate the procedures, a special request must come from the president, the Federal Assembly, the Government of the Russian Federation, or legislatures of subjects of the Russian Federation. An essential function of the Constitutional Court is passing judgments to resolve disputes over jurisdiction. In other words, the court decides which federal or other government bodies have the right to make decisions, and under what circumstances. This is a typical function of most high courts in other countries. Another responsibility is reviewing the laws that might violate the constitutional rights and freedoms of citizens of Russia, on the basis of requests from other federal courts. The Court may also rule on the constitutionality of certain exceptional procedures, such as when the president of the Russian Federation is charged with state treason or other severe crimes. (This has never happened so far.)

The Constitutional Court consists of 19 judges, and has its permanent residence and its meetings in St. Petersburg. This is unusual because virtually all other federal agencies are located in Moscow. However, this recent relocation was partly motivated by the desire to keep the court away from possible political pressures in Moscow. The judges are divided into two chambers with equal legal powers, one containing ten and the other nine judges. Some decisions can be made within just one of the chambers; others must be made by all 19 judges together. In 2009 President Medvedev suggested that the chair of the Court should be nominated by the president and appointed by the Federation Council.

Court rulings

During its first 15 years of work, the court made approximately 300 rulings. Most of them considered the constitutionality of specific laws and rulings, and in approximately 15 percent of all cases the lower-court rulings were overturned. For example, in 1995 the Constitutional Court upheld the decision of the federal government to use military force in the breakaway province of Chechnya. In 1996, the Court struck down rulings restricting residency in several cities including Moscow. In 2005, the Court declared constitutional the decision of the president to appoint governors or chief executives for the subjects of the Russian Federation.

The Constitutional Court also reviews the constitutionality of certain enacted laws. Take, for example, the case decided in 2009 related to the federal law on mental health care. Based on an appeal from three Russian citizens, the Supreme Court decided that several articles of the Civil Procedural Code and the Federal Law On Psychiatric Help and Citizens' Rights Guarantees were unconstitutional. These provisions denied individuals the right to give testimony before a court that determined their mental capability. The old law also limited the right to appeal against the court's decisions. One substantial result of that decision is that now it is

---

Case in point: A case considered by the Constitutional Court

On April 20, 2009, the Constitutional Court announced its decision regarding Article 38 of the Federal Law On Military Duty and Military Service. This law establishes the duration of mandatory military service for Russian men (women are excluded from mandatory service). The Constitution also provides that no individual may be detained for more than 48 hours without a court decision. The plaintiff, Islam Kuashev, was serving in the military. During his service, he was indicted for a crime. As a result of this indictment, the military authorities detained Kuashev and kept him within a military base for six months after the official date of his discharge from the service. The plaintiff's lawyers claimed that these actions were unconstitutional, because they arbitrarily discriminated against an individual, and violated the principle of equal protection under the law.

The Court agreed with the plaintiffs and recognized the action of the military as unconstitutional.

Source: Constitutional Court of the Russian federation, Ruling on April 20, 2009: http:// www.ksrf.ru.

illegal to commit a person to a mental institution without their consent, unless there is a court decision allowing this to happen (Constitutional Court Decision, February 27, 2009).

Russians speak their mind ...

... On the Constitutional Court. Percentage of Russians admitting that they know very little or nothing about the activities of the Constitutional Court: 60.

Source: Levada (2009e).

The Supreme Court

The Supreme Court of the Russian Federation is the highest judiciary body for civil, criminal, administrative, and other matters. The Supreme Court has jurisdiction over several areas. For example, the Court can challenge any decision of the Duma or the Federation Council, a presidential decree, or a Cabinet decree. The Court conducts legal reviews of legislative initiatives (requests) from the subjects of the Federation to amend specific federal laws. The Court interprets certain provisions of federal laws or legal codes. The Court also issues recommendations about the applicability of certain laws. It can terminate a national political party, a national religious or other organization, or disagree with a decision of the Central Electoral Commission related to national elections. The court has jurisdiction over criminal cases filed against a federal judge or an elected member of the Federal Assembly.

The Supreme Court also reviews the decisions of lower courts, and considers appeals on cases from lower courts. For example, an appeal related to a case decided in St Petersburg might reach the Supreme Court, and one of its judges would decide either to accept the case for consideration or to decline it. The Court may either affirm or reverse the decision of a lower court. If it is reversed, the Supreme Court can either render its own resolution or decide that the case should be reheard in a lower court.

The Supreme Court's structure

Judges of the Supreme Court are nominated by the president of Russia and appointed by the Federation Council. In order to become a judge a citizen of Russia must be 35 or over, and have a legal qualification and at least ten years of service in the legal field. The Court consists of several boards or collective panels of judges issuing opinions about different categories of

Figure 6.2   *Structure of the Supreme Court of the Russian Federation*

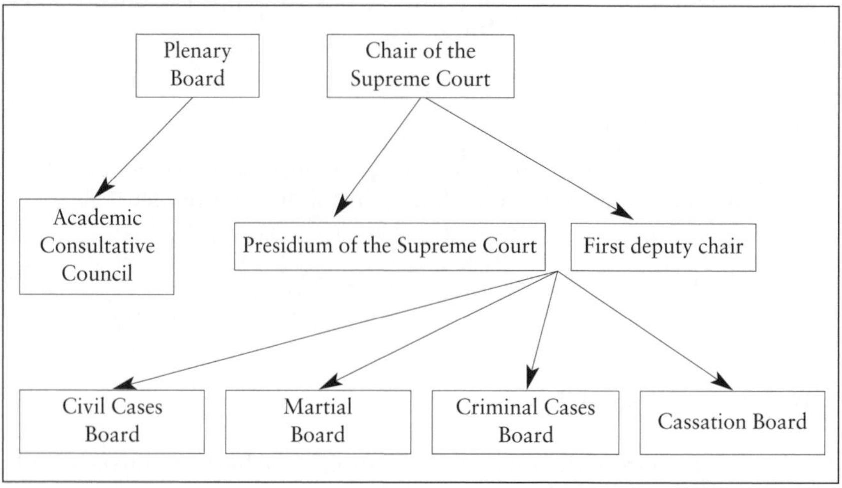

decisions. For example, the Civil Cases Board deals with civil, social, and labor-related cases. The Criminal Cases Board considers criminal cases, and the Martial Board deals with legal issues related to the Armed Forces. Appeals on the decisions of these boards are brought to the Cassation Board. The Supreme Court joins together for plenary sessions at least once every four months. All judges of the Supreme Court, the justice minister, and the prosecutor general of Russia must attend these sessions. The Supreme Court studies lower courts' decisions and issues recommendations on how to apply certain laws.

To ensure its work is efficient and to enable it to stay in touch with legal scholarship and practice, the Court has a special consultative body, the Academic Consultative Council. It consists of the Supreme Court judges, legal scholars, attorneys, and law enforcement professionals. The members of the Academic Consultative Council are elected in plenary sessions of the Supreme Court. The Presidium of the Supreme Court consists of 13 judges including the chair and deputy chairs (Federal Law, October 28, 1994), and performs coordinating functions and reviews cases. See Figure 6.2.

Court decisions

What kind of decisions does the Supreme Court make? Let us consider a few examples. In April 2008, the Supreme Court issued two decisions related to drivers and their automobiles. One decision stated that car insurance companies should pay out on claims from their customers regardless of the person who had been driving the damaged car, provided this person had been driving the vehicle lawfully. Another decision stated that owners of pay parking lots are financially responsible for cars stolen from their property (Kulikov, 2008). There are, of course, other types of decision. For example, in April 2009 the Supreme Court clarified to lower courts some issues regarding debts. A borrower is responsible for paying back a loan they take out from a bank, and should the borrower die before repaying the loan, the beneficiaries of their estate (their heirs) are responsible for paying back the debt (Kozlova, 2009). The Court also has the right to declare that any group is a terrorist organization (on the basis of evidence, of course) and ban this group on the territory of Russia.

The Supreme Arbitration Court

The Supreme Arbitration Court of the Russian Federation, according to the Constitution, is the highest judiciary body resolving economic disputes and other cases considered by lower arbitration courts. It also supervises the activities of all lower arbitration courts. Specifically, the Court decides on financial and other disputes among businesses and other organizations. It considers appeals related to certain legislative acts involving business and financial matters, as well as taxation and property disputes. Foreign citizens may submit appeals to the Court (Federal Law, April 25, 1995). For example, a foreign manufacturer of a chocolate candy brand sold in Russia filled a motion before the Court stating that several Russian candy manufacturers were violating its trademarks and producing similar candy without permission. The Court ruled in favor of the foreign plaintiff (Lavrov, 2009).

There are four levels of courts in the arbitration court system: 81 arbitration courts of the subjects of the Federation, appeal courts, ten federal district arbitration courts, and finally, the Supreme Arbitration Court. All judges of the Supreme Court of Arbitration including its chair are nominated by the president of Russia and appointed by the Federation Council. In order to become a judge a citizen of Russia must be aged 35 or over, and have legal education, and at least ten years of legal service.

The Russian Criminal Code

The Russian legal system is different from the US and many other legal systems in that it does not generally recognize judicial precedent as a source of criminal law. The main source of criminal law is the **Russian Criminal Code**. In general terms, a criminal code is a set of written laws related to criminal offenses and descriptions of punishments that should be imposed on convicted offenders. The Russian Criminal Code specifies the minimum and maximum penalty for each crime it describes. This includes monetary penalties, jail terms, and suspended sentences. The 1996 Criminal Code is the only legal definition of crimes and corresponding punishments on the territory of the Russian Federation.

The new Federal Code, which replaced a 35-year-old Soviet-era code, contains a complete list of crimes and related punishments. Comparing the old and new criminal codes, legal experts in Russia maintain that the new one is strongly oriented toward defending the rights and liberties of the individual, puts less emphasis on the interests of the state, and contains harsher penalties for severe crimes and lighter sentences for minor offenses (Krylova, 2000). Seventy new offences were included in the Code along with the elimination of 80 former types of crime, such as homosexuality, spreading anti-Soviet propaganda, and possession of foreign currency.

It is important to realize that Russia's criminal law is almost exclusively in the hands of the federal government. Local authorities and subjects of the Federation may not legislate on criminal law. For example if the Criminal Code suggests a sentence of three years in prison for a particular type of violent assault, a local legislature or a judge may not extend the punishment to seven years or drop it below three. Therefore, any change in the criminal law must become an amendment to the Criminal Code of the Russian Federation.

Structure of the Criminal Code

There are two parts of the Code, known as a general and a special part. The general part of the Code describes broad principles of criminal law and their applicability. It defines concepts such as crime, the suspect, guilt, conspiracy to commit crime, punishment and its types, and release from criminal responsibility. The special part has six sections and 19 chapters describing various crimes and punishments. There is no crime that is not indicated in the Criminal Code.

The Code classifies crimes into two categories. The first one is major offenses, such as rape, kidnapping, state treason, espionage, crimes against the justice system, and serious violent crimes such as murder. The second category consists of lesser offenses, such as offences against property and disorderly conduct in a public place. This distinction has been used historically in Russia to determine the type of correctional institutions to which convicted criminals are sent (Nikiforov, 1995).

The Criminal Code is applicable on the entire territory of Russia within its state borders, and within the 12-mile zone of its territorial waters (Federal Law, July 31, 1998). Russia follows international standards and also applies the law within its airspace, for up to 100 kilometers above the surface. The law is also applicable on the continental shelf of Russia

(Federal Law, November 30, 1995), and in special "zones of economic interest" within a 200-mile zone, established in international law (Federal Law, December 17, 1998). The law says that the government reserves the right to prohibit and prosecute activities in these such as creating foreign bases, unlawful drilling, or geological and other kinds of research (Komissarov, 2005).

The Criminal Code also applies to aircraft, piloted space ships, and sea and navy ships, under the flag of the Russian Federation regardless of their location. However, the law allows some exceptions related to crimes involving drug trafficking, safety, terrorism, and other offenses. Under certain conditions, the Russian Criminal Code applies to Russian citizens living or serving abroad. Foreign citizens in Russia may also be prosecuted according to the Code if their actions are considered harmful to Russia's interests or the interests of its citizens (Bastrykin and Naumov, 2007).

The Prosecutor's Office

The Constitution of Russia (Article 129) establishes the Prosecutor's Office of the Russian Federation. This is a single centralized system in which lower prosecutors are subordinated to higher prosecutors and the prosecutor-general of the Russian Federation heads the hierarchy. The prosecutor-general is appointed by the Federation Council, on the basis of a nomination by the president of the Russian Federation. Prosecutors of Subjects of the Russian Federation are appointed by the prosecutor-general after consultations with the Subjects. Other prosecutors are also typically appointed by the prosecutor-general.

Purpose of the Office

The major task of the Prosecutor's Office is to supervise compliance with the Constitution. A second task is to supervise the execution of laws within the territory of the Russian Federation. For example, the Office supervises the execution of any laws by federal executive authorities, legislative and executive bodies of the Subjects of the Russian Federation, local governments, military administration bodies, and governing bodies of private organizations. It also supervises the observance of human rights and freedoms.

The Office can prosecute any person within the scope of powers prescribed by the legislation of criminal procedure in the Russian Federation. It can challenge any court decisions, sentences, and rulings that are assumed to be contrary to the law. It also coordinates the crime-control activities of Russia's law enforcement agencies. The Prosecution Service of the Russian Federation can participate in law-making activities (Federal Law, January 17, 1992). The law allows the Office to cooperate with governments of other states on legal matters and crime control, and it can participate in the drafting of international treaties of the Russian Federation.

Structure

The Prosecutor General's office is located in Moscow, and coordinates the activities of numerous departments and institutions across the country. Overall, there are more than 30 departments responsible for specific areas of supervision: for example, Supervision over Execution of Economic Legislation, Supervision over Observance of Human Rights and Freedoms, and Supervision over Execution of Transport, Customs and Environmental Legislation. The Prosecutor General's office is in charge of the prosecutorial work in the seven federal districts. Its organizational structure is outlined in Figure 6.3.

The Prosecutor General's Office supervises the work of the chief military prosecutor, who is responsible for supervising of the execution of the law within the armed forces of the Russian Federation. It also supervises the Academy, a specialized research and educational institution within the Office. Specialized prosecutors' offices oversee the execution of the laws in special fields such as environmental protection, and in special institutions such as prisons, which are officially called "correctional institutions" in Russia. The attorney general is in charge of an Investigative Committee headed by the first deputy attorney general. Both the office and the position were created relatively recently.

Figure 6.3   *The organizational structure of the Prosecutor's Office of the Russian Federation*

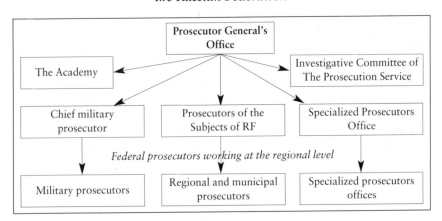

Case in point: The Investigative Committee of the Prosecutor's Office

Based on a presidential decree of 2007, this newly formed committee should help to separate the supervising and investigative functions of the Office. The Investigative Committee has both investigative and supervisory responsibilities. One of them is crime prevention, but its central function and task is the investigation of the most serious crimes. One of the Committee's responsibilities is to use federal resources to carry out effective investigations of sophisticated crimes that require expensive means of surveillance and great coordination between local and federal offices, which cannot be achieved on the regional level.

Several priorities have been identified for the Investigative Committee. The first is the investigation of "cold cases," or serious crimes that remain unsolved after some time. The second priority is the protection of the least socially protected categories, such as children, the elderly, and the poor. Crimes against women are given special attention too. The next priority is the investigation of corruption in federal and other government institutions. One of the most significant directions of investigation is fraud and embezzlement of federal funds (Bastrykin, 2008).

Russians speak their mind ...

... On the Investigative Committee. Percentage of Russians saying they knew nothing or very little about the work of the Investigative Committee of the Prosecutor's Office: 67.

Source: Levada (2009e).

The Ministry of Justice

According to a 2004 presidential decree, the Russian Federation Ministry of Justice is responsible for the realization of federal policy in several designated areas. In particular, these include the functioning of the courts, execution of criminal sentences, public defense services, and notary services, which perform a range of activities including registration of property, registration of political parties and religious organizations. The ministry coordinates the activities of several departments and services, including the Federal Registry, Federal Service of Implementation of Sentencing, and Federal Service of Court Marshals. The institution of federal marshals is generally responsible for the execution of the decisions issued by federal courts related to individuals, organizations, and their

Case in point: The Federal Service of Implementation of Sentencing

This federal service manages Russia's prison system. In 2009 Russia had 888,000 prison inmates, slightly less than 1 percent of its entire adult population (people over 14 years old). There were more than 68,000 women among the inmates. About 56 percent of the convicted criminals were not in work or education prior to their conviction, and 66 percent were repeat offenders. On average, about 300,000 people receive jail sentences every year (Lebedev, 2008). There are 12 special facilities in Russia to care for about 800 children of imprisoned women. To provide health care for the inmates, the government maintains 131 specialized hospitals including nine drug rehabilitation clinics. The prison system has 309 high schools for inmates, 334 vocational schools, and 464 religious establishments which provide facilities for services and prayer. The system has approximately 328,000 employees, so there is about one federal employee for every three inmates. The Federal Service of Implementation of Sentencing runs eight colleges that train specialists in the fields of law enforcement within the prison system, and more than 70 research facilities and educational centers. It provides regular training for its employees.

property. The Ministry also represents Russia in the European Court of Human Rights.

Law enforcement: the Ministry for Internal Affairs

The system of law enforcement in Russia is based on a hierarchical federal structure. The president is in charge of the Ministry for Internal Affairs. The minister is appointed by the president based on the recommendation of the chair of the government (the prime minister). The minister's deputies are also appointed by the president. Russian law enforcement units called "militia" have the responsibility for protecting life, physical health, rights and liberties, property, and the interests of the state and society from criminal and other unlawful infringements. The Ministry exercises its activities in several major areas: criminal law enforcement, public security and safety, and migration of citizens. It is also responsible for criminal investigation of offenses, traffic control, control over weapons on the territory of Russia, and protection of state property (source: Ministry for Internal Affairs).

The Ministry is also in charge of a section of the armed forces called Interior Ministry troops. Major tasks of the Interior Ministry troops include the protection of public order, the security of important federal facilities and shipments, defense of Russia in the event of a war, assistance to the Federal Border Patrol in protection of the country's borders, and anti-terrorist operations on the territory of Russia. During the escalation of conflict in Chechnya from 1994 to 1996 the Interior Ministry troops took part in major operations in that region. From 1999 throughout the first decade of the 21st century the troops have been participating in anti-terrorist operations across the entire North Caucasus region of Russia.

Russians speak their mind ...

... On civil rights. Percentage of Russians admitting that they have never heard of any human rights organization that would help them in the event of police mistreatment: 55.

Source: Levada (2009e).

Critical thinking about Russia's judicial branch and justice administration

Assessments of the first 20 years of the Russian legal system's development are largely concerned with the critics' views of the reforms in general and their attitude toward the Kremlin and Russian bureaucracy as a whole.

How independent is the system?

Most commentators outside Russia believe that, overall, the legal system is not independent. Although the Constitution establishes a free judiciary, in reality it is not free, critics insist. Some consider this a predictable development because the Constitution gives the executive branch powers that diminish the strength of the judiciary. Others disagree. Although the office of the president has the most power in Russia, the court system does not have to be dependent on the will of the Kremlin.

Supporters of the critical view try to find examples of how the Kremlin and other federal offices have attempted to regulate the judiciary and keep it under control through a well-managed system of promotions and appointments. One often-cited example is a 2009 proposal about the selection of the chair of the Constitutional Court. Under the existing system, the chair is elected by the judges. In the proposed new system, it will be the president who nominates the chair, then the Federation Council has to approve the candidacy. Critics maintain that this is a perfect example of how the executive is increasing its control over the judiciary (Golz, 2009).

Besides, it would be naïve to expect Putin and Medvedev to make an exception to their overall policy of power consolidation. Why should they exclude the judiciary (and law enforcement generally, by the same token) from the Kremlin's tight control?

The Kremlin dismisses these arguments. It points out that in the United States, for example, a similar system is in place: the president has the power to nominate judges to the Supreme Court. Second, it claims there is no evidence that the system of judicial nominations is unfair: in fact, the best and most qualified people receive nominations and the elimination process is transparent. Supporters of government polices offer numerous examples of the judiciary challenging the government and suspending rulings of the executive branch. For example, the Communist Party was banned by the Kremlin, but restored to functioning by the courts. The decision of the Constitutional Court rebuking the defense ministry (see page 140) is another example. The decision to move this court from Moscow to St Petersburg is also an indicator that the executive support the independence of the judiciary.

The system as an unfinished "work in progress"

Both critics and supporters of the system agree that the judiciary in Russia is still a developing system, and that it could not have evolved overnight from a Soviet-style legal system dominated by the Communist Party into one typical of a developed liberal democracy. The Russian legal system is in a state of transition. It has made significant advances: for example, the 1996 Criminal Code legalized a number of activities that were seen as crimes in the Soviet period, such as homosexuality, handling anti-Soviet propaganda, financial speculation (buying and reselling with the intention of making a profit), and the possession of foreign currency. As in the countries of the European Union, there is currently no death penalty in Russia: President Boris Yeltsin ordered its suspension in 1996, although it has not as yet formally been abolished. The system of criminal prosecution is quite selective in the administration of sentences. For example, between 1995 and in 2008, only 30–33 percent of those convicted received jail sentences. The remainder received fines or suspended sentences, or community service. Judges do not necessarily issue arrest warrants in every case. They sign only 90 percent of investigators' requests (Lebedev, 2008). These and many other facts are indicative of some ongoing changes in the Russian legal system, including law enforcement.

However, the lack of transparency is probably one of the biggest problems that the judiciary and law enforcement face today. Many ordinary people believe that the Russian legal system is unjust because of the lack of transparency. Despite the federal authorities' positive assessments, most people see the current situation differently. They believe that the judges and executive authorities in Moscow and the regions are part of a unified system in which the judges serve the interests of the executive. They point to some (admittedly, selectively chosen) high-profile cases which seem to justify this critical evaluation.

For example, a notorious 2002 case involved a highly publicized terrorist act in Moscow. A group of terrorists captured several hundred hostages during a musical performance, and after two days of negotiations had failed to free them, law enforcement forces used an unknown gas to knock out the terrorists so that they could safely storm the building. Unfortunately more than 170 hostages, including many children, died as a result of the operation—most of them apparently of gas poisoning. Despite numerous legal requests, the government refused to reveal the exact name of the gas used, citing national security concerns. The official cause of death of most hostages was never announced. The media and the public accused the government and the courts of a massive cover-up of the reckless decisions made during this operation.

Conclusion

The Russian legal system is a developing project which shows many features typical of a democratic structure, but also traces of the old communist system. The Constitution establishes the independence of the judiciary. The existing reality is different from the written statute, however. The strength of the executive branch and the circumstances of post-Soviet developments have impacted the judiciary and the whole legal system. It still lacks transparency and remains very vulnerable to the relentless attempts of the executive branch to interfere. This is probably what the Kremlin needs these days: a cooperative judiciary and convenient law enforcement to go along with Moscow's policies. Pro-government supporters in Russia do not openly deny that it is essential to have an independent and transparent judiciary. However, they insist that the problems it faces are inevitable in any state undergoing transition. One day, they suggest, Russia's legal system will be truly independent and transparent. Time will tell.

Part III

Political Behavior, Participation, and Communication

Chapter 7

Political Parties

Key developments
On Russian political terminology
Major political parties
Critical thinking about political parties
Conclusion

*As in most democratic nations, the leaders of the political strug-
gle will be parliamentary parties which periodically replace
each other in power.*
President Medvedev on the future of Russian democracy

*We have to understand that the "managed democracy" is not a
democracy but a dictatorship under which a multi-party system
is a farce.*
An anonymous entry on the blog http://student.km.ru

Things change. For more than 70 years, the Communist Party had a
monopoly on power in the Soviet Union. The party played a crucial role in
all spheres of Russian life. Any person attempting to form another party or
even discuss the possibilities of a multi-party system in Russia faced criminal charges. The transformation started in the late 1980s, and by the time
of the Soviet Union's implosion, numerous political parties already existed
in Russia. Today's federal laws regulate the functioning of political parties.
In theory, anyone can form a party and recruit members. However, the
Russian multi-party system is different from those existing in most democratic countries. Political parties in Russia have failed to develop in the way
they developed in other post-communist countries moving from authoritarianism to democracy. Most observers agree that they do not play an
crucial role in Russia's political life. Moreover, the executive branch was
able to create its own mass political party, a centralized network for unconditional support of the existing government and its policies. Things change.
However, the centralization and consolidation of political power remains
a signature style of Russian politics—at least for now.

This chapter is about Russian political parties. First, it deals with their
brief history, beginning during perestroika. Next, the chapter describes key

political parties, their ideology, and main activities. Finally, it provides a critical evaluation of Russia's multi-party system and the role of the executive power in partisan politics.

Key developments

By the late 1980s, during the last years of the Soviet Union, the country already had an emerging multi-party system. It was a new political phenomenon, a new social development, which most Russians promptly accepted. Although political resistance in the Soviet Union has a long history, Russia's multi-party system, in general terms, grew rapidly out of the open political opposition to Gorbachev and his policies of the late 1980s. Many of the early "oppositionists" were part of the ruling elite, who were already within the top echelons of the Communist Party and the government (see Chapter 3). Initially, two critical "camps" appeared within the opposition.

First, there were those who believed that the reforms had slowed down and perestroika as a policy was losing momentum and giving up its reformist agenda. Prominent leaders such as Boris Yeltsin, Eduard Shevardnadze, and Alexander Yakovlev represented this wing. On the other hand, there were those who opposed the reforms, considering them too radical and destructive. Party leaders such as Yegor Ligachev and Ivan Polozkov, among many others, belonged to that wing. The country appeared divided. There were considerable forces who demanded more reforms based on principles of liberal democracy and a free-market economy. They consolidated into various groups and movements to promote their political ideas. Others disagreed with the reformists and hoped only for a modest and cautious transformation. They began to form their own groups and organizations (Glad and Shiraev, 1999).

After the end of the Soviet Union, Russia's multi-party system developed in an atypical way. Typically, political parties in developing democracies tend to embrace people with similar political beliefs and interests. In democracies, like-minded politicians join political parties and combine forces to achieve their political goals (Hale, 2005: 1). In other words, developing political parties affect government. In Russia, it was government that was affecting and changing political parties.

The Russian multi-party system has developed in several stages: a discovery stage, a growth period, a consolidation phase, and a centralization period. The first stage was short: it lasted from the late 1980s to the early 1990s. It was an exciting period of trial and error, when people suddenly realized that they could form political parties without facing criminal penalties.

The first stage: discovery

Different views exist today on which party was the earliest. In many accounts, it was the Democratic Union, founded in 1988 by Valeria Novodvorskaya, who became its chair. This party stood for sweeping democratic reforms, government transparency, and free market policies. It was noticeably anti-communist. Another early party was the Democratic Party of Russia (Nikolai Travkin was its chair), promoting essentially similar views. In 1989 the Union of Constitutional Democrats emerged, with a platform of political liberalism. Its founders underlined a cross-generational link between themselves and a party of a similar name in the early 1900s. Another newly founded party, the Christian Democratic Union of Russia, promoted democracy but also emphasized the importance of fundamental human, Christian values. Russia's Peasants' Party was founded in 1990, representing, its founders believed, the interests of Russia's rural regions. An important event was the creation in 1989 of the Liberal Democratic Party, with Vladimir Zhirinovsky at its leader. Because of Zhirinovsky's sparkling character and his loud statements blasting government bureaucrats, he quickly became popular. In general, most political parties shared a similar feature: an anti-communist platform.

The second stage: growth

The second stage was marked by the rapid creation of many political parties in the new political climate of Russia, when the Communist Party was no longer in power. In the early 1990s, overall three political orientations began to emerge among the many political parties. Parties of so-called democratic opposition (see Chapter 3) pursued mainly western models of modernization: they worked for free-market economics and a wide range of political freedoms, coupled with social protection such as pension plans and unemployment benefits. The last issue was central in their programs, and made them different from President Yeltsin's policies oriented toward rapid market reform. The "democratic opposition" parties formed two loosely connected blocs or associations. The first was the Civil Union, with an emphasis on civil liberties and social partnership. The other was the Russian People's Assembly, which pursued strong centralized power and democratic liberties. These blocs did not last long (Isaev, 2008).

Many small parties of the political center pursued a relatively pragmatic agenda. They supported the Kremlin's general policy but emphasized the importance of a rapid reinforcement of political reforms by social and economic changes including land reform, substantial stimulus for the collapsing agricultural sector, constitutional reform, a minimum wage for workers, and more effective law enforcement. Several parties of the center-left formed the Commonwealth of the Left Democratic Forces, pursuing a social protection agenda and support of collective ownership of factories and banks. Among many in this grouping were the Labor Party, the Socialist Workers' Party, and the Federation of Independent Labor Unions of Russia. These parties and blocs maintained moderate views but remained critical of President Yeltsin's policies.

This was also the time of a rapid development of parties pursuing radical agendas. Nationalist groups were the largest, and the most vocal, but they were also disorganized. By the end of 1992 about 40 large and small nationalist parties had been formed (Isaev and Baranov, 2009: 274). They demanded a radical change of Russia's polices in favor of nationalization of industries, social protection, guaranteed jobs, and even the restoration of the Soviet Union. These ideas found significant support among many members of the parliament (which was dismissed in 1993). On the left, several relatively small pro-communist parties and blocs were active. They wanted a shift in polices toward a planned economy. They demanded massive welfare policies: policies that were, in fact, central to Gorbachev's reforms in 1985.

The Liberal Democratic Party (with its leader, Vladimir Zhirinovsky), which would play a significant role in the history of Russian elections, occupied a special place in the spectrum of political parties, embracing primarily a protest-based ideology and tactics that drew elements from right-wing nationalism, left-wing populism, and the centrists' acceptance of a free-market economy.

The third and fourth stages: consolidation and centralization

The third stage (roughly between 1995 and 2003) was characterized by the consolidation of smaller parties into large units, and the creation and

Case in point: The Communist Party on trial

One of the most remarkable cases heard by the Russian Constitutional Court during its early days was the case that determined the fate of the Communist Party. The hearings lasted for almost six months. The Court considered Yeltsin's 1991 presidential decree that had suspended the activities of the Communist Party. Yeltsin's decree came out right after the unsuccessful August revolt of 1991. Yeltsin then believed that it was the right time to strike against the Communist Party. The 1992 decision of the Court was reconciliatory. The Court ruled that the Constitution did not prohibit political activities, and that people had the right to form or join any political association. The Communist Party was officially back.

management of national parties and electoral blocs from "above" specifically for the purpose of winning parliamentary elections (see Chapter 5). The fourth stage began approximately in 2003, and was related to the inception and development of a single and powerful party called United Russia. This party maintains a clear pro-government course, and has a commanding majority in the Federal Assembly and other branches of the government (Ivanov, 2009). More discussion about these stages follows below.

On Russian political terminology

Before we describe the development of Russia's party system, it is necessary to explain several political terms that are important for understanding Russia's partisan politics.

"Left" and "right" distinctions

Most of us have at least a general sense, gained early in life, of what is meant by the political "left" and "right": the left represents liberal, and the right conservative, beliefs and policies. However, comparative political scientists warn that these broad and imprecise terms can easily lead to misperceptions, because there are tremendous variations in the way they are interpreted in different countries. In Russia, **the left** is typically associated with communist and socialist parties and groups, who promote a larger share of the government in the economy, the nationalization of key industries, and price control of most important products and services, including food, energy, and public transportation. The left support the welfare state, with a vast range of social benefits and services mobilized for the least protected categories of the population. The Russian left today acknowledge the necessity of a multi-party system (although this had been prohibited in the former Soviet Union, which was governed by the Communist Party), and they support basic political liberties. They also support higher taxes on the rich, and big spending programs in the fields of education, housing, and health care. The left are cautious about Russia's friendly relations with the west, and especially with the United States. They support a strong Russian military. They view the 1991 dissolution of the Soviet Union as a negative, even tragic, event because a new era of capitalism, the system that they oppose, has emerged.

The right, in a general sense, represents a wide range of views focused primarily on regaining Russia's strength as a state and a powerful force on a global scale. The right support the Russian welfare state, but their priorities are with a free market economy and wealth accumulation, which should provide social protection. The most distinguishing features of the right in Russia, however, are their nationalist attitudes, xenophobic views, and the desire to restore Russia's armed forces to the meaningful levels of the Cold War. The ideology of the Russian right embraces among other views monarchism, nationalism, racism, isolationism, populism, and anti-western xenophobia. Some confusion may occur from time to time if you read English or other translations from Russian sources: some reporters and commentators deliberately or unintentionally misuse the term "right" as value-laden in their articles and interviews, to portray someone in a negative light.

The term **"center"** describes a structure of attitudes and policies related to moderate actions and measures in the political, economic, security, and foreign policy fields. Centrists generally support the incumbent government in the Kremlin, and often identify themselves as moderates by criticizing both the right and the left. The centrists in Russia tend to support a moderate nationalistic platform, which is less radical than the views of the right and the left. In general, centrists support a bigger role for Russia in global affairs. For many people, however, centrism is a convenient label for a lack of particular political preferences.

The use of the terms **"liberal"** and **"conservative"** in today's Russia is also somewhat different from their use in the United States and the United Kingdom. It is probably inaccurate to equate Russian liberals with the left and conservatives with the right. In the classic textbook sense, *liberal* implies a range of views supporting basic political, economic, and personal freedoms. To be labeled a liberal in Russia today means that you support

---

Russians speak their mind ...

... On ideological values. Percentage of Russians supporting "traditional Russian values," including the strengthening of a powerful state and defense of the interests of the Russian people: 33.

Percentage of Russians supporting "left-wing, socialist ideas," including social justice, equality, and anti-globalism: 24.

Percentage of Russians supporting "right-wing, liberal ideas," including economic freedom, human rights, and coming closer to the west: 17.

Percentage supporting none of these choices: 26.

Note: Respondents could choose one of these three options. Please note that the use of these terms in Russia does not precisely match their use in the west, so it is no contradiction to espouse "right-wing, liberal ideas." See the explanation in the text.

Source: WCIOM (2008b).

predominantly western models of government, a free market economy, a free press, a transparent government, and independent courts. A typical Russian liberal is easy to recognize because they vehemently oppose authoritarianism.

A *conservative* in Russia generally supports the government's protection of social welfare, the idea of Russia's greatness as a world power, a mixed economy with a large portion of it being under government control, and relative tolerance of authoritarianism. In a brief summary, liberal and conservative individuals in Russia differ in their tolerance of authoritarianism, acceptance of free market principles, views of the west, views of Russia's role in the world, and overall evaluation of the Soviet Union as a social and political system.

Spectrum of attitudes

As has been noted earlier, traditional labels of the spectrum of political attitudes as liberal, moderate, and conservative do not fit well into the frame of Russian politics today. Russian conservative groups support the government's regulation of business, including the nationalization of large industries. They stand for substantial government support for the needy, higher capital gains taxes, and the urgent restoration of Russian military power. Most communists support these views as well. Russian liberal groups, on the other hand, tend to advocate free enterprise and less government intervention in the economy and business. Pro-socialist attitudes are more often identified in Russia as conservative. Many communists, on the other hand, do not want to be called "conservatives" and support modest social-democratic reforms. In the 1990s, some critics suggested that the most effective way of describing the differences in political views was to put supporters of communism on one side and anti-communists on the other (Lebed, 1996). Other authors distinguished between liberal-democratic views, pro-communist views, patriotic ideas (nationalism, populism), and "the undetermined" (Bruter, 1994).

In the late 1990s, a new category of political attitudes emerged: conditionally pro-government. People automatically supported candidates from the government offices so long as these individuals conducted policies guaranteeing economic security and social order. Other factors, such as civil liberties or political rights, became less important if the politician promised social benefits and safety. In fact, the relative weakness of Russian political parties can be explained partially by these conditionally pro-government attitudes of the population, who lean toward whatever political group occupies the highest offices in the Kremlin.

Major political parties

A 2001 federal law and several amendments (Federal Law, December 20, 2004) regulate political parties in Russia. According to the law, in order to be registered a political party must have no fewer than 50,000 registered members. However, this is only one of the conditions. A party must also have regional offices throughout the subjects of the Russian Federation, with no fewer than 500 members in each of half of the subjects and no fewer than 250 members in each of the remaining half. After 2009, the membership requirements will gradually be reduced, so there will be ongoing changes in the way political parties are organized (see the website).

Which are the major political parties in Russia today? What are their political programs and aspirations? How much power do they have today? What are the most probable forecasts about their future role in Russian politics?

United Russia

This has been the most powerful Russian party so far this century. The early beginnings of the party can be traced to 2001, when several parties and movements of the government-supporting political center unified their structures and programs and joined together as a single party. Boris Gryzlov, who later became the chair of the Duma, was elected the party leader in 2002. In 2003, the party took the name United Russia. The official position of pro-government commentators is that United Russia is a natural product of the growth and consolidation of several parties sharing similar views of democracy, stability, and the free market (Ivanov, 2009). Critics are unanimous in their assessment of United Russia as a convenient merger of several political groups that allows Vladimir Putin to maintain control of the government and neutralize potential opponents within Moscow's establishment (White, 2007: 21–53).

From the start, United Russia proclaimed that its purpose was to create a "presidential majority" and gain widespread popular support for presidential policies. By 2004, the party was the major political force in the country, with control over the state Duma. The party did not hide the fact that most of its official documents and statements endorsed Vladimir Putin, calling him the "national leader." Even the party's plan of political and economic activities is called the "Putin Plan." Putin became United Russia's chair in May 2008.

The Putin Plan (2007) describes the party's main policies up to 2012 and beyond. The program contains a mix of general statements and specific proposals. For example, among the general goals are to develop "Russia as a unique civilization," defend a common "cultural space" and historical customs, increase Russia's global economic competitiveness, provide a "new quality of life" for Russia's citizens, and support "social initiatives." More specific goals include wage and pension increases (up to 40 percent of a worker's monthly salary), helping the needy with affordable housing, and increasing the country's defense capabilities (United Russia, 2007).

In the economic sphere, United Russia supports a mixed economy with private and state-run sectors. It supports anti-monopoly measures, offers support for small businesses, and promises to reform the existing tax and tariff policies. The party endorses farm subsidies and supports the agrarian-industrial complex, a term commonly used in the Soviet Union to describe an economic infrastructure that coordinates industrial and agricultural production.

In the fields of defense and foreign policy, the party expects reciprocity in relations with foreign countries and fulfillment of international obligations. United Russia considers the fight against international terrorism a priority, and supports nuclear non-proliferation. The party underlines the importance of international cooperation over the environment, and supports the idea of global multi-polarity.

In the social sphere, the party intends to establish a new social security system with people investing in their own pension plans. Yearly inflation rates should be kept at a 5 percent level. The party promises to stop the decrease in Russia's population and stimulate birth rates. By 2012 the party promised to establish transparency in all areas of "public life." It also promised to conduct policies for the "moral development" of people in Russia.

One of the party's goals is to sponsor culture, the arts, and the performing arts. Special attention is paid to the promotion of the Russian language and literature. The party sees as a priority the formation of an "all-Russian civil identity" and common values for all ethnic groups populating Russia (while respecting the minorities' unique cultural features). It supports youth movements and organizations promoting patriotism, learning, and a healthy lifestyle. For example, a massive pro-Kremlin youth movement, Nashi (which means "ours") was organized in 2005 to support Putin and his policies. Although the movement considers itself independent, it clearly endorses Putin and his policies (http://www.nashi.su/). Many commentators see Nashi as the Kremlin's creation and a "junior wing" of United Russia (Hammerschlag, 2007).

The Liberal Democratic Party

The Liberal Democratic Party of Russia (LDPR) was formed in 1989 as a social-democratic group, and was officially registered as a political party in 1991. From its inception, the party has mainly been associated with

Case in point: Understanding the LDPR

To understand this party platform better, let's look at the issues that the party opposes.

First, it opposes the communist ideology. Communism has failed in the Soviet Union. Communism is a naïve utopia that promises equality and prosperity but never delivers them. No party can make people equal.

Second, the party opposes democratic ideology. Specifically, it claims that the West European and American models of a multi-party system, free competition, and a free press do not work in Russia. Russia should have its own model of government.

Third, the LDPR is against one-party control over the institutions of power. It argues that the biggest problem in contemporary Russian party politics is that United Russia was created "from above" by the Kremlin and for the Kremlin. This is unacceptable, because it leads to the executive branch forcing people to join its own party—exactly the way it was in the Soviet Union.

Vladimir Zhirinovsky (for a brief biography, see page 119) and his flamboyant style of behavior. Zhirinovsky possesses a wide range of credentials within the party.

The LDPR's official political platform is based on two pillars: liberalism and patriotism. The party claims its commitment to general liberal values. Patriotism, according to the party's program, refers to the strengthening of the Russian people's power. "The Russian people should fortify the whole country," states the official party's website. (The statement appears, of course, in Russian.) Liberalism is impossible without patriotism. A strong national state is a guarantor of liberal values and nonviolent solutions of political conflicts (LDPR, 2009).

What does the LDPR stand for? According to the party program, it supports strong presidential power, the three branches of government, and a one-chamber parliament (the Duma). At the same time, the party endorses the possibility of "a regime of personal power" during a transitional period (by which it probably means its leader, Zhirinovsky, taking power). The party also supports limiting the number of seats in the Duma that one party can have (to 40 percent). It wants the nationalistic principle, "what is good for the Russians should be good for the country" to be adopted. Russia should limit immigration and support all Russians living overseas.

In the fields of economic policies LDPR, like United Russia, supports a mixed economy. However, it believes the state should control defense, transport, oil and gas, communication, metal industries, and the extraction of mineral resources. The party also supports the nationalization of the alcohol, tobacco, and sugar industries. Whenever necessary, the government should regulate prices, interest rates, foreign trade, and employment. Specifically, the government should keep energy costs low, create jobs, and pay for pensions, unemployment benefits, and health care.

The party supports military service on a contractual basis (Russia currently has an obligatory military draft). It opposes the use of the Russian military overseas, and thinks Russia should switch its attention from the west to China, India, Iran, and Venezuela, and should never give away foreign aid for free. The party believes that the United States and West European countries are Russia's adversaries, and is against NATO expansion. However, it concedes that the United States could be a partner in anti-terrorist and disarmament policies.

The LDPR supports the unification of the former members of the Soviet Union into a new democratic state. Russia is the center of eastern Christian culture and civilization. The party states that "there will be the time when we will regain all our territories, and all Russians will live calmly, knowing that they have a Russian flag over their heads. But to achieve this, there is a need to have a Big Master—tough and predictable, strong and purpose-driven" (LDPR Program).

Case in point: LDPR policies

During the economic crisis at the end of the first decade of the 21st century, the LDPR proposed specific policies to combat the emerging problems:

- Register the foreign assets of all Russian companies.
- Prohibit the purchase of foreign securities and assets by Russian firms.
- Investigate and overhaul Russian commerce and trade with foreign countries.
- Get rid of intermediary companies that keep prices high.
- Reorient the Russian economy toward manufacturing.
- Overhaul domestic trade and establish caps on retail profits at 20 percent of the wholesale price.
- Establish price controls in the energy sector, and for agricultural products and food products.
- Reduce interest rates for bank loans (from 13 to 10 percent).
- Create jobs and reduce unemployment by giving the unemployed federal jobs including road construction.
- Allow people to build their own homes, and give them interest-free 20-year mortgages from the government.
- Give a 20 percent housing cost discount for each child in the family.
- A family with four children should be allowed to build its own house for free.

The program is filled with populist promises and declarations. Consider just a few of them. Women, by law, should work a shorter day than men. People who lost their savings during the 1990s should get them back. The government should provide free medications and pay for medical procedures for the retired. Mortgages with an interest rate of 2–3 percent should be granted for 30 to 50 years. The party promises, when in power, to cut the number of federal employees to a tenth of its existing level. See the Case in point box.

The party is vehemently against corruption and nepotism (an attractive position), defends the poor and the defenseless (another strong point), and picks on the government for any mistake or blunder it makes. LDPR frequently appears as a vocal critic of many government policies. It is an "anti-party" that always attracts a significant proportion of votes during parliamentary elections (Bruter, 1999). Nevertheless, in reality this party has never been a serious opposition to any government-backing legislative majority (Hale, 2005a). In fact, LDPR fills the convenient but largely symbolic role of an opposition party without real power.

The Communist Party

The Communist Party of the Russian Federation was formed in February 1993 and registered by the Ministry of Justice in March. Three important developments related to the party need to be considered.

First, President Yeltsin banned the Communist Party in 1991 after the August revolt. The Constitutional Court disagreed with the presidential decision and the party was officially restored (see page 158). Second, most members of the party previously belonged to the Communist Party of the Soviet Union. Third, the CPSU itself went through a painful period of transition and inner struggle between 1989 and 1991. The main disagreement was between the liberal and conservative wings of the party: one side wanted to reform the party, the other was willing to make small changes but insisted on keeping the basic ideology intact.

In 1992, the new Communist Party brought several pro-communist groups together. Gennady Zyuganov became chair of the party's Executive Committee. The party has more than 550,000 members (Isaev and Baranov, 2009: 269). In contrast, in the 1980s the Communist Party of the Soviet Union had almost 19 million members. According to the "old" party rules, they all had to be atheists. Recently, almost 30 percent of the party members say that they believe in God (Zyuganov, 2009).

Like the LDPR, the Communist Party opposes most of the Kremlin's policies. The party program calls these policies a "regression" which could cause a "national catastrophe" (CPRF, 2009). Russian communists believe, based on the party's platform, that the core struggle between capitalism and socialism is not over, and the world will move eventually toward socialism. There is a way out of the crisis. Two things must be accomplished: nationalization of economic production, and distribution of wealth according to each person's quantity and quality of labor. Three stages of reform are proposed: first, to reach stability; second, a transitional stage; and third, the establishment of true socialist principles of government and economy.

Specifically, the Communist Party supports the nationalization of all strategic industries. All the profits made by enterprises must be used at home, on domestic needs. All assets kept in foreign banks must be returned and invested in Russian banks. The government must establish price controls over essential products, and cap home utility bills (gas, water, and electricity) below 10 percent of family income. Being generally anti-big business, the party supports small and medium-sized private entrepreneurship.

In the social sphere, the party supports subsidies and discounts for the poor and free services for the needy. It supports limited censorship of the media to limit "kitsch and cynicism," provide wider access for all political forces to the media, and stop the media besmirching Russian history. The party's motto is "Russia, labor, people's power, and socialism."

In foreign policy, the Communist Party sees the United States and other leading world capitalist powers as major threats to societal progress and peace. The party opposes almost every foreign policy decision of the United States and its allies. It considers western policies to be imperialist, colonialist, and fundamentally unfair. Hoping to continue the old policy of the Soviet Union, the party supports parties and governments that conduct anti-American or anti-western foreign policy.

Just Russia

This party (another translation of the title is "Fair Russia") was formed in 2006 in a merger of three parties with center-left and left orientations. Several smaller parties with a similar orientation joined the Just Russia party later. This is the forth party in terms of representatives in the State Duma (37 seats after the 2007 elections), and its leader, Sergei Mironov, served as chair of the Federation Council of the Federal Assembly. He justified the creation of the party as an exercise in democracy, and claims the party's activities are a necessary way to keep the powerful United Russia and the government establishment in check (Mironov, 2009a). Critics maintain that this party is oppositional only in its name, and its activities are just a showcase to persuade the Russian people and world public opinion that the county has embraced an efficient multi-party system.

The party's key concern is the domestic agenda and vigorous welfare policies. Its motto reflects the party's main priorities: "Motherland, the Retirees, Life." The party's official goals are quite general, including equal rights and liberties for all people, solidarity among generations, patriotism, responsibility, democracy, the well-being of the family, and social security (Just Russia, 2007). The party also put forth several specific goals and projections. For example, it supports a new tax policy under which the rich would pay 30 percent of their earnings (almost twice as much as they currently pay) and the poor would pay nothing. It also supports higher taxes on companies involved in the extraction of natural resources (gas, oil, and ore, for example).

The party suggests an increase of cash payments to people who are 70 years of age (today the age limit is 80). To fight corruption, the party suggests a law to make corruption a form of treason, which would provide harsher penalties for officials found guilty of this crime. One specific proposal is that no citizen should wait more than 20 minutes for an appointment with a government official.

Overall this party generally advocates pro-government policies and criticizes the ruling authorities only for their alleged tactical mistakes, not strategic decisions. In 2007, 36 percent of Russians considered Just Russia a pro-government party. However, 41 percent could not identify the party political position at all (Levada Center, 2007a).

Other political parties

In addition to the four major parties described here (of course, their number might increase or decrease depending on the political situation and the results of the next Duma elections), a few smaller parties continue to function in Russia. One of the oldest is the *Jabloko (Apple) Party*, which between 1993 and 2003 had its own small faction in the Duma. Until 2008, the party's leader was Grigory Yavlinsky (born in 1952), a charismatic economist of the perestroika period and a well-known political leader of the 1990s. The party has always been in opposition to the government (it preferred to identify its position as a form of "democratic opposition"). It maintained a center-left position and was very critical of the Kremlin's violent approach to ethnic separatism in the southern province of Chechnya. According to its 2001 Program, the party's domestic goal is to build a society based on major democratic and liberal values, in contrast to authoritarian and anti-democratic trends that, from the party's view, are apparent in today's Russia. Since 2008, the political role of this party has substantially weakened.

Another party supporting a liberal democratic agenda is the *Union of the Right Forces*. It also represents the interests of the political opposition, endorsing individual freedoms, economic liberties, and the political openness typical of western-style democracies. The party's representatives have included many famous Russian politicians, the young and promising "stars" of the late stages of perestroika and the early stages of Yeltsin reforms. Among them were former acting prime minister Yegor Gaidar, former deputy prime minister Boris Nemtsov, and famous economists and public officials such as Anatoly Chubais and Irina Khakamada. Recently, this party changed its strategy and moved closer to the Kremlin. In 2008, chair Nikita Belykh left the party. He was offered a position as governor of the Kirov Region. This move prompted many commentators to assume that the government had begun to buy out the political opposition, and that opposition politicians were eagerly cooperating. Torn apart by disagreements, the party dissolved itself in 2008, but its remaining leaders and rank and file members are likely to revive the party or form a new one with a similar agenda (check the book website for updates).

Another group of oppositional parties appears under the label of *The Other Russia*, which as such began its activities in 2006. The main goal of the movement (this is how its members prefer to be called) is to change the existing political regime in Russia by peaceful, legal means. The word "other" in the title indicates that this movement envisages a different government from the one existing in today's Russia. That, however, is where the common goals of the coalition's members end. The Other Russia coalition includes organizations and movements quite dissimilar in their goals and ideologies. For example, one member of the coalition is the Republican Party. Its main goal is to establish true democratic principles of government and to fight against the rampant corruption and bureaucratic power. Among a few somewhat abstract goals, including investing in "human capital" in Russia, the party aims at a radical reform of the military and security services, and giving more autonomy to Russian regions. At the same time, The Other Russia coalition is supported by the National Bolshevik Party (NBP). This organization was made illegal by court order. Many supporters of this group joined The Other Russia as unaffiliated individuals, not as members of their party. The ideological platform of NBP is communism. Despite their major disagreements about how Russia should develop in the future, The Other Russia and the NBP hope to accomplish their main task: to dismantle the existing regime.

The incompatibility of many groups within The Other Russia is obvious. There is a group called For Human Rights, which pursues protection of civil rights and offers free legal help for anyone who needs it. On the other hand, there is the Avant-Garde of the Red Youth, which is effectively a radical, communist, and neo-Stalinist group. Among the famous people whose names are associated with The Other Russia is Garry Kasparov, former world chess champion and an outspoken critic of the regime, who frequently publishes articles in major newspapers in the United States. Another is Eduard Limonov, a famous writer, public figure, and a leader of the illegal NBP.

As you can see, the development of political parties and the twists and turns of Russia's electoral procedures have proceeded side-by-side. One affected and changed the other. The process is far from complete, and changes take place frequently. Yet although we need to recognize the young "character" of the Russian political system, we can also come to several preliminary conclusions.

Russians speak their mind ...

... On freedom. Percentage of Russians saying that they have enough freedom: 56. Only 30 percent of Russians said the same in 1990. Percentage of Russians saying they don't have enough freedom: 18. Percentage saying that Russia has too much freedom: 20.

Source: Levada (2008e).

Critical thinking about political parties

Views of the party system in Russia tend to be subjective: they are colored by the personal views of the critical observer. However there is general agreement that Russia's multi-party system is weak and depends on the country's executive power. Differences emerge when observers try to explain or justify this system.

The developmental approach

Commentators within Russia's political establishment accept that Russia is imperfect and its political dynamics are not without problems. The transformational process is bound to be fraught with difficulties. The current party system is a natural reaction to the disarray of the 1990s, when many parties and individuals competed for parliamentary seats. Today's political consolidation and the existence of a strong leading party are the signs of growth and maturity in the system. Bringing representative government to a people accustomed to autocratic rule requires more than lifting the yoke of repression under which they have suffered. It is also necessary to build institutions for linking the people to the government, and develop respect for the rule of law. This process does not happen overnight. As President Medvedev put it, "Our political system is not yet fully developed. It must develop, and it must become more mature" (Medvedev, 2009a).

The worsening of the social and economic situation in the country in the 1990s gave rise to parties with radical left and right ideologies. Economic stability, on the other hand, was associated with popular support for the government, Presidents Putin and Medvedev, and parties of the center. It was natural for the ruling parties to make political adjustments and create political platforms that could help them win next time (Isaev and Baranov, 2009).

The authoritarian view

The Russian party system functions within an authoritarian political structure. Authoritarianism, as was explained in Chapter 4, is a form of government with a centralized and concentrated power structure and a relatively weak civil society. Individual leaders, and not necessarily elected organs, hold much of the power, and political freedoms are limited to some degree (Brownlee, 2007). In Russia, however—this view remains popular there—under certain conditions, authoritarian methods of government are the only viable option. Without authoritarian power in Moscow, the country might self-destruct. Many Russians say off the record that you can't even imagine how bad the situation could have been without a strong authoritarian power in the Kremlin.

Russian experts also maintain that the Russian people have been inclined historically to seek out strong men to give them the order they need. Their experience under a totalitarian regime compounded these problems (Gozman and Etkind, 1992). Others refer to the culturally inherited nostalgia for a strong and wise national leader (Grunt et al., 1996). Individuals who are uncertain about the future and disappointed with the present are apt to search for a strong guarantor of stability and order (Mikulski, 1995). Overall, as far as this argument goes, Russia is probably incapable of functioning without a "big brother" with a "big stick." Back in the 1990s, only 18 percent of people believed that the country needed a one-party system. By 2001, when the current party structure began to take shape, 27 percent had become one-party-system supporters (Zorkaya, 2004).

The nationalist platform

The main argument of supporters of this view is that whatever takes place, its value should be judged by how well it serves Russia's interests. The interests of Russia are often defined vaguely and inconsistently: among the most common are Russia's territorial security, possible expansion up to the borders of the former Soviet Union, absence of ethnic conflicts within its territory, and resistance to the west. It is argued that Russia needs a strong leader, and therefore electoral systems designed to produce a tough commander-in-chief are justifiable. Moreover, a highly competitive party system weakens the country. Russia needs a multi-party system but the parties must work in unison to ensure stability and steady development.

In fact, the authoritarian and nationalist views overlap. Opinion polls show that radical nationalist ideas, prejudice against minorities, and support for a "strong hand" in the Kremlin are correlated, and that all these tendencies get stronger when the economic situation in the country worsens (Gudkov, 2008a).

Populism

This term refers to political strategies that pursue the goal of mass support by appealing directly to most people's immediate needs. **Populism** is based on promises and corresponding actions designed to give people what they want. It is also associated with scare tactics and exaggerated threats, persuading people that their major values, assets, and the way of living are in danger (Albertazzi and McDonnell, 2008). If people are scared or uncertain about their future, they are likely to turn to politicians who offer simple answers to problems. As the history of Russia and scores of other countries shows, poverty and injustice always make ordinary people particularly susceptible to populism, and it has always been a policy of choice for both Soviet and Russian leaders. The lack of democratic principles of government also allows populist politicians to win sympathy and support. Because of all the uncertainties of today's life, many people in Russia look for simple answers, and trust politicians who promise everything, in large quantities. Populism is a common and convenient strategy for most political parties in Russia. The government maintains a similar strategy. That is why it is sometimes difficult to differentiate the policies of the different political parties.

The powerful elites view

From this point of view, the problem with political parties lies in the nature of political power in Russia. The country's federal and local leaders will always create a party system to pursue two major goals. One is to satisfy their own political interests, and the other is to gratify the interests of their sponsors: financiers and industrialists. Systematically, after the 1990s, Russian party formation was constantly undermined by the emergence of various substitutes. Some were regional electoral groups supporting the aspirations of local elites, mostly governors or industrialists. There were also national electoral political machines: "parties" specifically designed to win parliamentary elections. In effect, these "party substitutes" crowded genuine Russian political parties out of the electoral marketplace (Hale, 2005). The government's reform of the electoral system during the rule of President Putin was, in effect, an effort to strengthen a pro-government party, United Russia. The official establishment endorses democracy.

However, in reality everything is done to keep the system unchanged or consolidate more power in the hands of the Kremlin's incumbents (Trenin, 2006). For example, widespread populism in Russian politics is not ideological: it is pragmatic. It allows leaders to keep and increase their power (Manikhin, 2003). This view finds substantial support in Russia these days.

Conclusion

The 1993 Constitution created a very powerful executive branch of the Russian government. Perhaps it was natural that the members of this branch would seek to build and maintain an electoral system that would benefit the president. A multi-party system evolved in Russia, but its shape was determined by the will and decisions of the executive officers. However, a strong executive branch is not the only reason for a weak party system. The political transformations of the past 20 years were taking place within a relatively supportive political environment. Being unhappy with the difficulties of the Yeltsin's era, a solid majority of the Russian people developed a stable attitude of conditional support for the government. Many people expect the Kremlin to guarantee stability and provide basic benefits. In exchange, people agree to accept the type of government they have. The powerful financial and industrial elites, at least for the moment, do not need a strong multi-party system. In addition, many conservative and nationalist forces support the current system, which uses moderate populism to stay the course and generate support. As soon as the demand for strong political parties increases, the political "market" in Russia is likely to produce them. Their fate will depend, however, on the government response.

Chapter 8

Presidential and Parliamentary Elections

Key developments
Parliamentary elections
Presidential elections
Critical thinking about elections in Russia
Conclusion

> *Dictatorship is a system of external limitations. Democracy is a system of internal ones.*
>
> Boris Berezovsky, Russian politician and businessman,
> currently living in exile in the UK, 1996

Russia now has a new generation of voters born in 1992, right after the dissolution of the Soviet Union. Unlike their parents and grandparents back in the days of the communist state, the young can vote in presidential and parliamentary elections and use ballots with multiple names printed on them. But what else is different in today's Russian electoral system from the one that existed not long ago? How did the system develop through these past two decades?

In this chapter we discuss these and similar questions. Because the chapter gives special attention to the transformation of the electoral system, the section on key developments only outlines several major themes, which are discussed later.

Key developments

Russia's electoral system has a relatively short history. To better understand how the system works, several key developments on the past should be considered.

Early democratic elections

As was outlined in Chapter 2, in the late 18th century land and property owners in Russia received limited voting rights. They could nominate candidates and vote in a complicated ballot system to elect representatives to local legislative organs. This was an early case of limited democratic elections in an otherwise authoritarian state. Russia held its first national elections relatively late compared with the United States and most European countries. Only in 1905 did the emperor reluctantly agree to allow a wide range of political freedoms in Russia. As a result, political parties began to function. The reform also established a parliament elected by popular vote through a multi-stage process—the State Duma. The 1906 Duma elections were the first democratic elections in Russia's history. Many categories of people received voting rights, including peasants and workers. In the following 12-year period, Russian people participated in several national ballots. Every time the electoral rules were different. Only once did the Duma serve its full term, because the emperor kept dissolving the legislature when it continually challenged the executive power. After the communists seized power in Russia in the end of 1917, national and local elections for the most part were no longer free.

Elections in the Soviet Union

The Soviet Constitution gave the ruling Communist Party exclusive political power. It was in charge of local and national elections. The local party committees were responsible for selecting candidates for the soviets and submitting their names for approval by superior committees. Most party leaders on all levels were among these candidates. As a general rule, only one candidate's name appeared on the paper ballot given to a voter on election day. Officially, the ballot was secret and the voter could reject the candidate or write in any other name. However, because of the tight government control of elections, the real ballot count is unknown. According to publications in the party-controlled press, almost every candidate running for local and national parliamentary elections received 99 percent of the votes or higher. This electoral system was undemocratic because of unyielding government control and the absence of transparency.

Some elections in the Soviet Union resembled a competitive process. They usually took place on the local level or at the workplace, to elect foremen in working units, captains of sport teams, or leaders of small party or youth organizations. Such elections allowed multiple candidates, debates, and disagreements about small issues. Yet the core principles of the communist ideology were left out of the debates. Although these local elections resembled a democratic process, their outcomes were insignificant because the elected individuals had no real political power in their hands. All other elections were organized in such a way that only preselected and approved candidates were allowed to run and win.

The country moved gradually to semi-free elections in the late 1980s.

During perestroika, the Soviet people finally received an opportunity to nominate candidates freely, participate in electoral debates, and vote in multi-candidate elections. One of the results of free elections in most Soviet republics was new and independent legislatures which immediately started energetic and successful campaigns for their republic's independence.

The rapid formation and legalization of many parties and political organizations created a state of confusion among a significant portion of the electorate in the 1990s (see Chapter 2). Frequent national, regional, and local elections caused "electoral fatigue" in the general population. People wanted to see the results rather than endless campaigns, promises, and instability. The desire for political stability was an important subjective factor which affected the behavior of many Russian voters in the 1990s and later. People preferred to deal with fewer political parties which would do more and debate less.

Now we examine briefly the evolution of the electoral system since the early 1990s. Parliamentary elections are described first, then presidential campaigns and presidential elections are discussed. A critical thinking section summarizes the analysis of Russia's electoral system.

Parliamentary elections

According to federal law, the **Central Electoral Commission (CEC)**—a 15-member institution appointed by the president and the Federal Assembly—is in charge of organizing elections on the federal level. It is appointed for four years and responsible for both presidential and parliamentary races. The CEC has broad powers within its jurisdiction to conduct federal elections and supervise elections within the subjects of the Russian Federation (Churov, 2009).

The Kremlin's executive branch has played a crucial role in the way the electoral system developed. Elections in Russia during the past 20 years have transformed Russia's political environment and changed, both directly and indirectly, the structure and balance of political forces. The parliamentary elections of 1993, 1995, 1999, 2003, and 2007 have left a definite mark on Russia's political system and society in general.

The 1993 Duma elections

In 1993, Russian voters participated in their first free elections after the break-up of the Soviet Union. No political party was a clear favorite. No political group or candidate had received an open endorsement from the Kremlin.

Three large political groups emerged during the short race before the

December elections. The first one was pro-government and supported the president's policies of economic liberalization in general. The two other groups were in opposition. The communists and their supporters were against the policies of liberalization. Nationalists and populists also disagreed with the government but did not support the communists either. Overall, after the elections, the parties of the pro-government center formed a slim majority over two parties of the left, including the Communist Party and the Agrarian Union (115 seats), and the nationalist-populist Liberal Democratic Party (LDPR) (64 seats). The biggest electoral winner, in fact, was the populist LDPR (23 percent of the popular vote), which did not join any electoral bloc and appealed to nationalistic, disenchanted, and disgruntled voters disappointed with the worsening economic situation (Bruter, 1994). Pollsters also learned that Zhirinovsky's party performed stronger than the polls had anticipated (Ferguson, 1996: 44). The emerging multi-party system produced an eclectic parliament with no parties holding a decisive majority.

Two important lessons could be drawn after the 1993 elections. The first was that it was becoming clear that a well-organized political party could attract a large number of voters and win seats during a time of instability and economic difficulties. Second, it also became apparent that in order to win seats in the Duma, political candidates needed to pay very serious attention to setting up a political organization that would generate financial and logistical support. To win, a candidate needed to get the support of a strong "political machine," or party that would promote its candidates. Campaigning required money, a national network and infrastructure, scores of volunteers, and access to the media. As a result, by 1995, approximately 50 national political parties had emerged in Russia. Typically, each party gathered around it several smaller "sister" political groups. There were about 250 of these smaller organizations, representing a full spectrum of ideological and political orientations. As was mentioned in Chapter 7, these groups were largely party substitutes playing a clear role as legal organizational and financial structures assembled to win elections. Both the government and emerging business elites began to form parties to serve their interests.

The 1995 Duma elections

The Duma elections of 1995 demonstrated again that the composition of the new Russian legislature reflected the voters' disagreement with the course of the president's reforms. Many people rejected Yeltsin's economic policy of "shock therapy." This policy made some people extremely affluent but left scores of others in poverty. People were concerned about poor social protection, growing crime rates, and rampant corruption. The

Communists and the LDPR—the main opposition—wanted to direct voters' attention to several unfortunate outcomes of Yeltsin's policies: low wages, inflation, and high prices. The results were favorable to the Communist Party. Parties of the left bloc, including the Communists, gained strength (211 seats in the 450-seat Duma), parties of the center gained 154 seats, and the LDPR received 51 seats (there were also 34 independent deputies). The Communist Party and political groups close to it became the largest voting bloc in the Duma. It was probably the most organized and unified political party in Russia at that time.

The 1995 elections provided at least two major lessons, one procedural and the other political. From the procedural standpoint, the four parties that passed the required 5 percent barrier collected only 50.5 percent of the total ballots cast. Overall, 43 parties and electoral blocs competed, and 18 garnered at least 1 percent of the party list votes. This meant that almost half Russia's votes in 1995 were "wasted" on small parties that were unable to reach the minimum percentage of votes required to win a seat (Ferguson, 1996: 44). The winning parties did not mind this outcome, but for those that lost out, it was an indication that the electoral system was deficient.

Second, just as in 1993, the elections demonstrated again that only a well-organized and well-funded group of people was capable of winning a substantial number of seats in parliamentary elections under the voting system. Russia's political elites continued to create such groups for purely electoral purposes. The Kremlin also learned an important lesson. Although the legislative branch was relatively weak, according to the Constitution, an oppositional Duma could have presented a problem to the Kremlin. Therefore, after the ascendance to power of Vladimir Putin the central government began to manage the parliamentary elections, especially in 2003 and 2007, to increase the chances of producing results favorable to the Kremlin.

The elections of 1999, 2003, and 2007

The main strategy for every participating party in the election in the fall of 1999 was to form a nationwide electoral coalition and try to attract as many voters as possible. Two major political groups began to form powerful electoral coalitions—in Russian official terminology, "initiative groups." These groups began their campaign work just a few months before the elections.

The first was the Inter-Regional Movement Unity (nicknamed Bear), created in September 1999. The group backed the policies of Putin, then newly appointed as prime minister. This bloc won 23 percent of the votes. Later this movement grew into United Russia, the largest pro-government political party in the country, which received the largest share of the votes in the Duma elections in 2003, with more than 37 percent. The second movement founded in 1999 (which also later contributed to and partially merged into United Russia) was called Fatherland-All Russia. Its major participants were Evgeny Primakov, former prime minister, Yuri Luzhkov, mayor of Moscow, and Vladimir Yakovlev, mayor of St Petersburg. Formed in August, this bloc won 13 percent of the votes during the election four months later. The 1999 Duma elections reduced the power of the LDPR to only 14 deputies. The parties of the left overall received just 127 seats, so they lost almost 40 percent of the seats they had held after the 1995 elections.

In the 2003 elections Zhirinovsky's LDPR slightly improved its position, winning 35 seats. The left (now a coalition of the Communist Party and the electoral faction Motherland) received 89 seats, and the center, represented by the government-supporting parties, gained 303 seats. The 2007 Duma elections did not change much the distribution of Russia's political forces. The communists won 57 seats and the LDPR 40 seats, with the rest going to the newly formed pro-government party, United Russia, with support from the Just Russia party which received 38 seats.

That year was the beginning of a new period in the history of Russian elections and political parties. For the first time since the 1980s, Russia had a dominant and legitimate political party supported by the governing establishment and the voters. For people to associate themselves with United Russia—whether they were students, teachers, entrepreneurs, or officials—was a sign that they supported the government and the president. In many people's minds such an association was good for their professional career and social status.

Chapter 5 explained how a new party list proportional representation system was put in place for the 2007 elections. According to this system, political parties prepare lists of candidates for the upcoming election—naturally, with their leaders at the top of the list. Each party has to be operative right across the federation, and meet tough membership requirements. Voters then cast their ballots not for an individual, but for a party. After the election, parliamentary seats are allocated to each party in proportion to the number of votes it receives. In addition, unaffiliated candidates might be nominated by a political party. This means that parties can include on their lists people who are not actually members of the party. In theory, this policy allows political parties to better appeal to unaffiliated groups of voters.

Overall, these changes made it still more difficult for small parties to compete in the Duma elections. Many parties could not reach the 50,000-member requirement for registration. The bureaucratic system began to reject still other parties for different reasons: for example, some of their required

Table 8.1   *The number of parties winning seats in Duma elections, 1993 to 2007*

Year	1993	1995	1999	2003	2007
Parties	14	23	6	4	4

endorsement signatures were not accepted (this disqualified the Green Party and the People's Union, and a few others). Some parties were rejected (The Other Russia was an example) because the government categorized them as coalitions or movements rather than political parties.

Table 8.1 summarizes the number of political parties gaining seats in the Duma in elections from 1993 to 2007. Notice the decline after 1995. At the same time the "party of power" (United Russia) was going from strength to strength: in 2003 it won 223 of the 450 seats, and it increased its presence still further to 315 seats in 2007.

Russians speak their mind ...

... On voting for parties. If the election were held this Sunday, which party would you vote for? Percentage of Russians choosing United Russia: 55; Communist Party: 9; Liberal Democratic Party: 5.

Source: WCIOM (2009d).

Presidential elections

As the first Russian presidential campaign got underway before the 1996 elections, the nascent Russian party system was extremely fragmented, polarized, and volatile, with virtually every conceivable ideological perspective and societal interest being represented, along with the personal followings of various leaders. Conspicuously absent from any of these parties was President Boris Yeltsin, who sought to maintain a posture of being "above politics" and to avoid the stigma of party membership, as it was seen after 70 years of Communist Party rule. Three out of every four Russians did not identify with any of the parties vying for their support (White, Rose, and McAllister, 1996: 135).

The presidential election of 1996: Populism and fear

Just one year prior to the 1996 presidential elections, the Communist Party could hardly have hoped for a better outcome than its collective 30 percent of the left-leaning vote in the Duma elections (Stavrakis, 1996: 14). Vladimir Zhirinovsky's Liberal Democrats were placed second with 11 percent. With the presidential race slated just six months after the 1995 Duma elections, Yeltsin's prospects for re-election looked dim. In a nation in the throes of hyperinflation and mired in an unpopular war in the break-away republic of Chechnya, only 8 percent of those polled in January 1996 pronounced themselves "satisfied" or "mostly satisfied" with their life, and fewer than 1 percent considered the political situation "favorable" or the economic situation "good." Only 6 percent said they were planning to vote for Yeltsin (Treisman, 1996a), whose popularity had declined steadily since 1992 (White et al., 1996: 167–70). The threat of the Communist Party taking over the Kremlin was very real. Some of Yeltsin's close supporters believed that the only way he could stay in office would be to cancel the election (Korzhakov, 1997).

Popular disillusionment with the way things were in the country was accompanied by increasingly negative attitudes toward the government. By 1994 opinion polls showed that only 4 percent of Russians fully supported the actions of the Yeltsin government, and 31 percent believed that he should resign (ESP, 1994). In 1995, 60 percent of respondents to a poll agreed that the country's leaders had exhausted their potential and favored a change. Some even came to look at the past with a different eye. In July 1995, 80 percent of those surveyed in a national poll thought their rights were less protected under Yeltsin than they been under Brezhnev (Vox Populi, 1995). Sixty-five percent thought Russians' opinion of the government was worse than it had been in the former USSR (Grunt et al., 1996; Wyman, 1997: 125–7).

Although the predictions were gloomy for Yeltsin, he made a strong and surprising comeback. In the first-round ballot on June 16 he received 35 percent of the vote. The early favorite Zyuganov, representing the Communist Party, made it into the run-off with 32 percent. The other candidates (including Zhirinovsky with 6 percent) were eliminated (Treisman, 1996b: 64). According to exit polls of both first-round and run-off voters, economic issues were foremost in voters' minds, followed at a considerable distance by the war in Chechnya and concern about crime and corruption (Mitofsky, 1996).

This first round was followed by a series of political maneuvers. For example General Lebed, one of the first-round candidates, popular because of his anti-corruption message, was appointed secretary of the Security Council, a move most observers saw as likely to bring votes to Yeltsin, and there was a relentless anticommunist campaign in the media. In the July 3 run-off Yeltsin won 54 percent to Zyuganov's 40 percent, with 6 percent rejecting both candidates (Valenty and Shiraev, 2001).

There were several reasons for Yeltsin's win, including bitter memories of communist rule, his aggressive campaign maneuvering, Zyuganov's poor strategy, the pro-Yeltsin media onslaught, and Yeltsin's relentless populist promises and pork-barrel programs for the regions (McFaul, 1997). The opposition to Yeltsin was uncoordinated during the 1990s (Abalkin, 1995: 30), and this became its major problem during the election year. In very general terms, fear of a Zyuganov victory and the Communists' return to office was a serious factor which helped Yeltsin and his team to win the elections. It was a near-classic example of a negative campaign, when a candidate wins not because people are enthusiastic about him, but because he portrays his opponent as a real threat to the country (Sigelman and Shiraev, 2002). Yeltsin and his supporting elites believed they were justified in conducting a smear campaign against his opponent because it was so important to prevent a Communist takeover.

After Yeltsin won, official sources in the Kremlin maintained that the elections had been tough but fair. His opponents, including other groups as well as the Communist Party, maintained that the Yeltsin team had used a range of illegal methods: pressure on the media to provide unfavorable coverage of the Communists, illegal financial operations, and even direct electoral fraud. The leadership in the Kremlin ignored these allegations, but it must have brought it home to them how difficult it was to manage a successful presidential campaign without the organized infrastructure of a loyal, pro-government national party.

The presidential election of 2000: Managing from the top

By the summer of 1999, the public was anxiously anticipating Yeltsin's departure, and nine out of ten Russians, according to the polls, considered the domestic political situation "tense" or "explosive." On August 9, Yeltsin fired his entire government and named his newly appointed acting premier, Vladimir Putin, as his choice to succeed him as president. On December 31 Yeltsin announced that he was resigning in favor of Putin, who became acting president. Yeltsin's resignation and premature exit from the political scene had the effects of moving the presidential election, which had been scheduled for June, up to March 26, and of immediately establishing Putin as the overwhelming front-runner.

The sudden resignation threw his opponents into near-total disarray, and brought Putin to office in an atmosphere of high hopes. In remarkably short order, Putin had been transformed from an obscure functionary into the most popular politician in the country. According to a nationwide survey conducted in January, Putin enjoyed a remarkable 79 percent approval of his performance in office. This was widely regarded as a sure sign that he would be elected in March, and numerous poll results bore out that indication. In polls by national organizations after Putin succeeded

Yeltsin in office, none of his potential or actual rivals ever came closer than 25 points behind him (Sigelman and Shiraev, 2002).

All of this marked a truly extraordinary turnaround from the situation of midsummer 1999, when it had been widely anticipated that the ailing Yeltsin's departure would produce a chaotic power vacuum. This did not happen. Many attributed Putin's victory to the dramatic turnaround in public support for the Chechen war. It was a very unpopular conflict, but Putin was able to present it to the public as Russia's ultimate struggle for survival against barbaric terrorists. He won widespread public approval for his strong stand. In the absence of an effective opposition, and aided by the three-month advancement of the election calendar occasioned by Yeltsin's resignation, Putin managed to elbow aside the other reformist and centrist candidates in the first round, and redefine the election as "a referendum on hopes about the future rather than on his own performance during the previous five years" (Treisman, 1996a: 3). It then effectively became a confrontation between dissatisfaction with the status quo and fear of the Communists' return.

Several potential candidates dropped out of the race in the fall of 1999. This left only Zyuganov as a major challenger to Putin. Although Zyuganov could count on the Communist hard core, his prospects for appealing more broadly than that were insignificant. Public enthusiasm about Putin's leadership waned as time passed, but Putin managed to hold on to majority support, carrying 52.5 percent of the votes cast on March 26, 2000. Zyuganov trailed with 29.4 percent, and no other candidate polled significantly.

The 2008 elections

As was mentioned earlier, presidential elections are supervised by the CEC, which bases its decisions on federal law (in this case, a Federal Law of January 10, 2003). The Federation Council set the date for the next presidential elections (which had to be on a Sunday, within 90 and 100 days after the official announcement, which followed the date-setting) as March 2, 2008. This gave candidates just about four months to campaign. In comparison, in the United States the earliest primaries and caucuses begin in January, about ten months prior to the presidential elections.

According to the law, officially registered political parties can nominate presidential candidates in Russia, and individuals can also nominate themselves. About 30 people expressed their desire to run in 2008. However, only six people overcame the difficult, requirements-filled nomination process (see the Case in point box). Among the candidates were Dmitry Medvedev (first deputy premier), Gennady Zyuganov (leader of the Communist Party), Vladimir Zhirinovsky (leader of the LDPR), Boris

Case in point: A tale of a presidential candidate

Garry Kasparov, former world chess champion and leader of the United Civil Front, believed he was treated unfairly by officials who thwarted his attempts to register as a presidential candidate for the 2008 elections. To become a presidential candidate in Russia, it is necessary to call an official meeting of a so-called initiative group, a group of endorsers. This group must consist of a minimum of 500 people who are eligible to vote (people may not count children, for example, as endorsers). After this meeting, the CEC gives the candidate permission to start collecting signatures nationwide in support of their bid. There must be 2 million of these, including no more than 50,000 from any one subject of the Federation (Federal Law, January 10, 2003). After the signatures have been submitted, the CEC verifies them and registers the candidate. Parties with deputies in the Duma do not have to collect signatures for their presidential candidates. In Kasparov's case, the deadline for collecting the signatures was January 16, 2008. However, Kasparov hit an obstacle during an earlier stage of the process. To hold a 500-person meeting, he had to rent a large hall in Moscow. This apparently became a big problem: there was suddenly no available facility for holding this size of meeting at such short notice. Kasparov claimed the government had created this technical obstacle on purpose to get rid of an "inconvenient" candidate. Critics disagreed, saying that Kasparov had not had much chance of wining anyway, and had used this incident simply to draw attention to himself.

Source: Lenta (2007a: 12).

Nemtsov (Union of the Right Forces), Andrei Bogdanov (leader of the Democratic Party), and Mikhail Kasyanov (ex-premier and leader of the People's Democratic Union). The list shrank after Nemtsov decided not to participate in December. Next, the Central Electoral Commission disqualified Kasyanov for technical reasons in January (the government found 13 percent of invalid signatures in the petitions submitted on his behalf). From the start, Medvedev was a clear front-runner.

Medvedev had the support of at least four major parties including United Russia. Most importantly, he had an official endorsement from the incumbent president. Putin in turn received an offer from Medvedev (which was supported by the United Russia party) to become prime minister in 2008 should Medvedev win the March elections. Putin agreed to accept the nomination (Lenta, 2007). Opinion polls showed a lead for Medvedev as early as December, and his substantial support (60–70 percent) did not diminish during the winter. Medvedev refused to debate any of his official opponents on television, a typical strategy of most front-runners in presidential elections. His campaign involved travel into Russia's regions and staged televised meetings with local officials who were loyal to him.

Federal elections in Russia are funded by the government. In addition, each candidate has the right to solicit and accept private funds. As expected, Medvedev drew more campaign donations than other candidates: he received 188 million rubles (about $7 million), compared with Zhirinovsky's 160 million and Zyuganov's 53 million. However, unlike his opponents, who spent almost all their funds, Medvedev spent just 15 percent of his campaign fund (Raikov, 2008). Critics maintained that he could afford to save the money because the government controlled all the media and he did not need to outspend his opponents, who urgently needed national exposure, in order to get coverage. Medvedev supporters argued back that their candidate's electoral program was very appealing in the first place, and people had no need of endless reminders about his candidacy to be prompted to vote for him. In the end, a very predictable campaign ended on March 2. According to the official results, Medvedev won with 70.3 percent of the votes cast. Zyuganov drew 17.7 percent of the vote, Zhirinovsky received 9.3 percent, and Andrei Bogdanov received 1.3 percent. Dmitry Medvedev duly became the third president of the Russian Federation.

Russians speak their mind …

… **On elections.** Percentage of Russians believing that Vladimir Putin has preserved his influence on Russia's political life after leaving the presidency: 87.

Source: Levada (2009c).

… **On electoral violations.** Percentage of Russians in 2007 believing that fraud and manipulation are possible during parliamentary elections: 69.

Source: Levchenko (2007).

Case in point: Russian electoral turnout

In 1991, Boris Yeltsin was elected president in an election in which 75 percent of the population voted, the largest proportion in Russia's history. During the first round of the 1996 elections about 70 percent of those eligible to vote came to the polling stations. The average turnout during almost two decades of elections has been approximately 66–7 percent. The number is higher for presidential elections and lower, about 60 percent, for parliamentary elections. The lowest turnout was 55.6 percent for the Duma elections in 2003.

Source: WCIOM-RBK (2008).

Critical thinking about elections in Russia

As in every developing democracy, the Russian electoral system has been undergoing evolution. The type, format, and frequency of elections are determined everywhere by historic contexts and specific circumstances. In the United Kingdom, for example, there are no presidential elections because there is an unelected, largely ceremonial head of state. In the United States, the federal authorities do not establish a special electoral commission to monitor federal and state elections. In Lebanon, there is a special system known as confessionalism, which is designed to ensure that Christians and Muslims both have a share of power.

Russian democratic elections have long roots but a relatively short history. Most comments about elections in Russia after Putin's ascendance to power in 1999 are concerned about one key question: how free are these elections? There are substantial disagreements between Russia's official point of view and many independent commentators' opinions.

It is true that elections in Russia are far from being perfect, but as the government and experts who support it argue, they are generally democratic and free. People are allowed to express their opinions in any way they want, and cast their votes for any candidate. Others disagree with this rosy opinion, and underline that elections in Russia have become increasingly undemocratic because the ruling elites were able to impose an electoral system that, in fact, puts serious limitations on a competitive political process.

Russian elections are democratic

Many Russian commentators and some analysts outside Russia suggest that overall, Russian parliamentary and presidential elections are no different from many similar elections taking place in democratic countries all over the world. It is true that international observers in the 1990s were critical of the clearly pro-government media coverage of Russian elections, and scores of procedural improprieties giving advantage to pro-Kremlin candidates. However, in the end these observers have given all Russian elections relatively high marks. For example, the Organization for Security and Cooperation in Europe (OSCE) analyzed the 1993 and 1995 Duma elections and called them free and fair. Other elections received positive evaluations for their apparent transparency and accuracy. The main conclusion of the supporters of this point of view is that Russian elections have consistently met accepted international standards (Shleifer and Treisman, 2004).

Russian government officials and many commentators suggest that most of the criticism about Russian elections is caused by a generally negative perception of Russia's leadership. From this point of view, violations of electoral laws take place in every country. In many elections, including the 2000 presidential elections in the United States, the results are controversial and end up being reviewed by a court, which has almost never been the case in Russia. Like everywhere in the world, there are government supporters and opponents, but the Russian government allows all of them to participate in elections if they are officially registered. There is a legitimate multi-party system in Russia today, and it is not a sign of anything wrong if one party becomes more popular than the others. For example, in Japan the Liberal Democratic Party was dominant for decades, and faced little opposition until 2009. As in other countries, newspapers and television in Russia have their preferences and freely endorse political candidates. Overall, these and similar arguments support the view that Russia is a "sovereign democracy" with a democratic electoral system (Churov, 2009a). However, other observers disagree with these assessments of Russian elections.

Elections are problematic

Critics focus on specific violations taking place in Russia which, they argue, affect the entire electoral system. These violations are not random mistakes or the inevitable setbacks of a young, developing democracy. They represent deliberate attempts to control the elections by authoritarian means (McFaul and Stoner-Weiss, 2008: 72). Russia's ruling elites were able to establish a political system that is amenable to their interests, and now they are making sure that the electoral system will produce results in favor of the Kremlin each and every time. Several points of criticism are among most important.

First, it is argued that the Kremlin does everything possible to create a favorable political atmosphere for the functioning of pro-establishment political parties. These parties, such as United Russia and Just Russia, receive support from powerful government officials and are in a good position to win elections. On the other hand, only a few opposition political parties are allowed to win seats in parliamentary elections. Critics claim that both the Communist Party and Zhirinovsky's LDPR are oppositional Duma forces only in name, because they conveniently accept their subordinate roles and prefer not to challenge the established majority between the elections (Trenin, 2006). One of many mechanisms to reduce competition is the process of official party registration. This procedure excludes many parties from elections and political competition, as we saw in Chapter 7. The other mechanism is party lists. This electoral practice can easily prevent small parties from winning representation in the Duma.

Second, it is also argued that the media in Russia, especially television, are under the commercial and administrative control of the government (McFaul and Stoner-Weiss, 2008: 70). As a result, pro-government parties and candidates receive practically unlimited airtime and very positive coverage during electoral campaigns. In contrast, the political opposition these days has very limited access to television, the most popular medium in Russia in the early 21st century. This practice inevitably influences political campaigns and ultimately the results of elections.

Internal factors

Other critical assessments of Russian elections are less concerned about the question of whether they are free. Their main purpose is rather to find tendencies in electoral outcomes and the way the elites manage elections in Russia. We will illustrate these assessments with just two examples.

The 1996, 2000, and 2008 elections showed the importance of the incumbency factor in Russian politics. Yeltsin appointed Putin in 1999, and Putin won the election in 2000. Similarly, Putin appointed his successor in 2007, and Medvedev easily won his election several months later. In the United States, in comparison, vice presidents running for the White House are not that successful. Over the past 50 years, four incumbent US vice presidents have run for the presidency and only one succeeded: George Bush in 1988. Unlike Putin in 2008, President Yeltsin in 1999 was very unpopular. Yet Putin, his appointed and virtually unknown successor, won by a landslide several months later. One possible explanation for this takes us to the second important factor that probably affects electoral outcomes in Russia: the individual personality of political leaders. In difficult times, an apparent strongman becomes a front-runner because people facing insecurity tend to rally round the leader.

Other studies focus on the political processes that take place in Russia and determine the outcome of elections. Some experts argue that Russian elections, like those in many other countries, generally reflect political battles among powerful business interests. For example, Boris Yeltsin in the 1990s represented a powerful group of magnates who had amassed their fortunes during the early years of his government. These powerful business interests did everything possible to keep Yeltsin in power and to help produce favorable outcomes in elections. In today's Russia, one reason the elections are not necessarily free is that the business elites around Putin and Medvedev are pursuing the consolidation of their resources, and are therefore very much interested in preserving their power in the Kremlin and the Federal Assembly. Political power is needed to win business battles (Treisman, 2008: 10).

Conclusion

Although Russia as a country has a history of elections, very few of them in the past were democratic. On the surface Russian elections of the past 20 years have been based on a multi-party system and voters have enjoyed basic political liberties, but many questions remain about the true nature of elections in Russia. Supporters of the official model of "sovereign democracy" which is popular in Russia maintain that elections are free and democratic, and comparable with elections in most other democratic countries. Some commentators suggest further that Russia's electoral system today is a "work in progress," as are many other social and political institutions in the country. They say that Russia should continue to go through a difficult process of reforms before it establishes a viable, democratic electoral system. However, most critical observers within Russia and outside the country tend to disagree. They consider the Russian electoral system to be tainted by authoritarianism. The ruling elites increasingly often ignore democratic principles and use elections to further consolidate their own power. There is a hope that Russia will make its elections more democratic and free. Otherwise, contrary what the Kremlin leaders think, more people will see them as the elected authoritarian group they have come to resemble.

Chapter 9

Political Communications and Mobilization

Key developments
The media today
Strategies of political communication and mobilization
Critical thinking about political communication and mobilization
Conclusion

> *We should not think of the Internet as potentially the most dangerous criminal environment compared with others. The Internet is not an absolute evil.*
> President Medvedev in an interview for *Novaya Gazeta*, 2009

Flipping through Russian television channels during primetime, you might find a historic documentary, the latest international news updates, episodes of *The Simpsons* with a Russian soundtrack, a Russian gangster thriller, or a soccer game from the English Premier League. Article 29 of the Constitution of the Russian Federation guarantees every person freedom of "thought and speech." The basic law also guarantees Russian citizens the right to express their opinions and beliefs by lawful means. The Constitution declares the freedom of the press. It explicitly prohibits censorship. How are these important constitutional guarantees implemented in Russia? Where do Russian people get information related to government and politics, and how do they use it?

This chapter deals with **political communication**: the general ways in which information related to politics and government is distributed in Russia. Attention is given to common means of communication including television, radio, newspapers, and the internet. The chapter provides a brief overview of the existing media, their ownership and major political agendas. It also deals with **political mobilization**, or ways to preserve or change the existing political system. Both the government and the opposition use political mobilization to achieve their goals. Mass media are a powerful tool to promote a political agenda, and this is why we discuss political communication and mobilization in the same chapter. As usual, a critical thinking section compares several competing views about the functioning of the media and their roles in contemporary Russia.

190

Key developments

Although new technology is constantly increasing people's access to information, governments at all times try to limit or control that access, especially if the information relates to political power. The media have therefore played, and continue to play, a very important role in every country's political process.

The Soviet period

In the Soviet Union, the Communist Party exercised total control of the country's mass media. The central and regional party committees supervised and managed newspapers, radio, and television. The government played a **gatekeeping** role, determining which information was allowed or recommended for publication and which was not. One of the general criteria determining suitability for publication was agreement with party policies and Marxist–Leninist ideology. Gatekeeping is a special form of **political censorship**: the restrictive practice of reviewing and determining what is allowed to be published or broadcast, based on ideological or political considerations. Until the 1980s, the vast majority of Soviet citizens lived on a strict informational diet: any printed or transmitted information that could have undermined the power of the Communist Party and its main ideological doctrines was carefully censored out.

Political censorship was part of political mobilization in the Soviet Union. Censorship noticeably affected individual political behavior and mass participation: both ordinary people and media professionals were aware what information it was permissible to publish and discuss. They also knew what was prohibited. For example, newspaper editors were not allowed to publish critical information about domestic and foreign policy, the failing policies of friendly communist regimes, the accomplishments of free-market capitalism, or human rights violations in the Soviet Union. Nor did reporters and editors dare to print information related to the Communist Party leaders' health or their personal life, including their marital problems, hobbies, and so on.

Gorbachev's policies of glasnost in the mid-1980s (see Chapter 3) first limited and then eliminated political censorship. For the first time in more than 70 years, people received access to uncensored news, reports, and analyses. At least two key fundamental questions or dilemmas about freedom of speech were debated across the country in political circles in the late 1980s and early 1990s . The first question was, can freedom of speech be unlimited? The second question was about ownership. Who should have the right to own a newspaper or radio station, and determine what information it publishes or broadcasts?

Crucial changes

Many people in Russia supported the new political atmosphere of freedom in the country and rejected political restrictions on free speech. However, scores of others believed that criticism and negativism—which had been dominating Russian newspapers and airwaves since the late 1980s—should have reasonable limits. They maintained that for the sake of social stability, some restrictions on speech might be imposed.

Because the government no longer legally controlled the media, fierce battles began among various individuals and business groups for the ownership of existing and newly emerging media. The process of consolidation of private media ownership continued under President Yeltsin. Gradually, up to the mid-1990s, the most significant newspapers, radio and television stations came into private hands. Supporters of the free market argued that the privatization was a natural process based on the principles of supply and demand. Their critics disagreed. Their argument was that the Russian media were coming under the control of a few individuals who used their ownership to increase their political power. This argument found substantial support from the newly elected president, Vladimir Putin. He realized that if it lost control of the media, the government would weaken its gatekeeping and political mobilization capacities. Unless this trend changed, the Kremlin would not be able to communicate effectively with the public, and would lose a crucial channel of political mobilization, especially during elections.

In the first decade of the 21st century, the government in Moscow undertook a massive and sustained effort to put the media under federal financial control. These policies found substantial support in Russia, where public resentment against monopolies and the super-rich has always been strong. Many Russians continued to believe that mass media should to some degree be regulated and controlled by central authority. In 2001, 57 percent of Russians said that Russian media need government censorship (Public Opinion Foundation, March 22).

Because the government did not have the legal means to seize newspapers, television and radio stations, one of the most suitable ways to regain control was by buying out their existing owners. The prime target was television. Gradually, the government gained financial control over the most powerful television networks. Over a relatively short period, most significant broadcast outlets moved from private hands into the control—through a variety of financial and business institutions—of the federal government. In effect this was **nationalization**, or the process of taking an industry or assets into public ownership. President Putin and supporters of this policy argued that the new state ownership would not mean censorship, because that is unconstitutional. Therefore, according to the official position, any claims about the government's censorship of the media are unfounded. This view finds support among many Russian scholars (Alekseeva et al., 2008). To critics, the virtual nationalization of the media in Russia was another example of the antidemocratic policies of the Kremlin, a continuation of the consistent effort by the federal government to expand its political, financial, and economic power in the country (Pipes, 2007).

During the process of nationalization of the television networks, two former media tycoons, Boris Berezovsky and Vladimir Gusinsky, emigrated from Russia, fearing that they faced criminal prosecution (see also Chapter 10). When President Putin came to power in 1999, the three most powerful television networks were privately owned. Within a few years, the Kremlin controlled all three, plus several others. Today, the federal government either owns or has commanding shares in all major Russian television networks and two national radio networks. Although the government owns only two of the 16 newspapers with a national circulation, it controls 60 percent of stock in regional and local papers (Voroshilov, 2009; Lipman, 2008). The government continues its attempts to expand its financial control over printed and online media (McFaul and Stoner-Weiss: 2008, 70).

The media today

In this section of the chapter we look at the major Russian media, including television, newspapers, radio, and the internet, and their general role in political communication in the country.

Television networks

A television network is a communication enterprise. It consists of a company responsible for producing programs, such as news reports, talk shows, or discussions. The company then distributes its programming through airwaves or cable to local stations called affiliates. In return for receiving daily programming, these local stations share with the programming company the revenues collected for commercials or user fees. There are, of course, other business arrangements, but this is the typical set-up in Russia.

Table 9.1 lists the most influential television networks in Russia. The viewing figures were provided by the companies themselves.

Financial power gives the Kremlin, both directly and indirectly, the ability to manage the networks' general policies. Although the law specifically prohibits owners from interfering in matters related to news content, it is

Table 9.1   *Leading Russian television networks:*
viewing figures and ownership

TV network and location	Number of viewers	Ownership
Pervyj Kanal (The First Channel) Moscow	98.8 percent of population	Joint stock company; 51 percent belongs to the federal government
Rossyia (Russia) Moscow	117 million	Federal government
TV Centr (TV Center) Moscow	91 million	Government of Moscow
NTV Moscow	120 million	Gazprombank (controlled by the federal government).

Source: viewing figures provided by the companies.

difficult to believe that such interference does not exist. In Russia, as well as in many other countries in which the government owns the media, control can be exercised in a number of ways without using evident censorship.

The first way is **agenda setting**, the process by which the owner determines what type of information will be seen as news at any time, and what will not. For example, during the major debate in the United States about the health care system in 2009, major Russian networks aired reports about cases of insurance fraud, denial of service, and the prohibitive cost of medical insurance in the United States. Because the media criticism of US policies corresponded with the general critical tone of the Kremlin in dealing with the United States, it was never likely that Russian television would provide positive coverage of the US health care system. During the 2009 elections in Iran, Russian television provided mostly critical views of the anti-government demonstrations in Tehran, tending to side with the ruling clerics and justify their violent actions against the opposition who disagreed with the results of the elections. When television reports discuss Iran's nuclear program, they tend not to focus on the potential nuclear weapons threat. Instead, Russian television emphasizes the importance of productive economic relations between Moscow and Tehran. This pro-government coverage of Iranian policies corresponds with the generally positive tone of the Kremlin in dealing with Tehran.

The second way to exercise control is **framing**. This is deliberate interpretation of events and polices from a particular standpoint or in certain contexts. Thus, after Barack Obama was elected president of the United States in 2008, major television networks echoed the view of the Russian government and expressed cautious but positive opinions about him. It was emphasized that only US policies, not promises, would help to improve US–Russian relations. For the most part, Obama's forthcoming presidency was framed as a defeat for the policies of the former President Bush, which Russia had criticized relentlessly (Shiraev, 2008).

Table 9.2 offers some examples of how Russian television networks use agenda-setting and framing in their coverage of international events. It should be clear that there are obvious trends in the coverage.

In sum, the television networks tend to report and analyze international

Table 9.2   *Russian television's coverage of selected international events*

Events and polices	Coverage in Russia
Events in Iraq and Afghanistan	Russian government maintains a negative view of US involvement in both countries. Russian network coverage is mostly critical of US policies. Emphasis is put on US casualties and the difficulties that people in Iraq and Afghanistan are currently experiencing.
Iranian nuclear program	The Russian official position is that the Iranian nuclear program does not represent an immediate military threat. Most reports deal with cooperation between Iran and Russia, and also focus on Western countries' critical position toward Iran.
The war in Georgia in 2008	In contrast to most of the world's media, Russian television journalists and commentators took a belligerent, anti-Georgian position. Almost every report about Georgia was critical and accused this country of genocide. The atrocities committed by the Russian side were totally neglected.
US presidential elections in 2008	Both Russian government and television networks adopted a neutral position toward the US elections. Yet the general tone was critical of former President Bush.
Iranian elections 2009	Unlike the coverage in Europe and North America, there was almost no criticism of the Iranian government's violent actions against mass demonstrations in Tehran.
Death of Michael Jackson	Russian networks provided detailed and generally positive coverage of Michael Jackson's life.
Sport news and events: NBA and NHL	Russian people watch basketball and hockey games played in North America. American football and baseball are rarely shown on Russian television because people show little interest toward these games.

events in a way that is in agreement with the basic polices of the government. When the government does not have an official position —this relates primarily to sports and entertainment—the coverage is determined largely by the preferences and demands of the market.

Newspapers

There are several types of owners of today's most popular Russian papers. The federal government is one of them. For example, *Krasnaya Zvezda* (Red Star) is the official daily paper of the Ministry of Defense. All military bases, military institutions, and installations have to subscribe to this paper. The materials in it are addressed primarily to men and women serving in the armed forces or working for the military in some capacity. The paper is also known for its patriotic tone and a strong pro-government attitude.

Political parties own newspapers as well. One of the most popular remains *Pravda* (Truth), once the official daily paper of the Central Committee of the Communist Party of the Soviet Union. Today, *Pravda* continues to express the views of the Russian left. Although a majority of its readers belongs to an older generation, the paper boasts a growing young readership base. *Pravda* remains consistently critical of the Kremlin's leadership and its policies. It maintains a clearly antiwestern and anti-American approach in its coverage of international affairs. Another newspaper, *Sovetskaya Rossiya* (Soviet Russia), is similar to *Pravda* in its reporting of domestic and international events. Like *Pravda*, this newspaper has a clear pro-communist orientation. It calls itself "an independent people's paper," and remains very critical of the free market, big business, social inequality, and the policies of most western countries.

There are also independent newspapers such as *Izvestia* (News). This was once the official paper of the Soviet legislature; now *Izvestia* is under private ownership. Its publications are designed for the political center, and are fairly pro-government. The most popular daily newspaper remains *Kommersant*. This publication focuses on domestic and international events, and pays special attention to business and finance matters. Among the most popular weekly papers is *Argumenty i Facty* (Arguments and Facts), which claims sales close to 3 million copies per week. It is a private informational, analytical, and entertainment paper remaining largely within Russia's political center.

Novaya Gazeta (New Paper), which is printed in Moscow, has been the strongest critic of government policies in Russia to date. This newspaper's orientation is liberal democratic. It is privately owned and operated. One of its owners is former Soviet President Mikhail Gorbachev. The paper criticizes authoritarian trends in Russian government policies. Compared with other newspapers, it is significantly less supportive of Moscow's

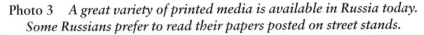

Photo 3   *A great variety of printed media is available in Russia today.
Some Russians prefer to read their papers posted on street stands.*

confrontational foreign policy. It is also more willing than the other papers
to interview people who oppose the Kremlin leaders and experts. The
paper's popularity in Moscow was one of the reasons that President
Medvedev decided to arrange for an interview with *Novaya Gazeta* in
2009. In this now famous interview, Medvedev talked about the necessity
for free media in the country (Medvedev, 2009a). This paper sells about
170,000 copies in Moscow and about 570,000 across Russia (smi.ru,
2009).

Most papers in Russia are not under the government's financial control.
Critics argue, nevertheless, that most of the existing newspapers are
managed by entrepreneurs loyal to the Kremlin who have an impact on
editorial policies. Self-censorship has become a general practice.

Radio

As in other countries, Russian radio is heavily entertainment-oriented.
Music programs dominate the radio waves, but there are also many information programs and politics-oriented talk shows. The federal government
owns several radio networks, such as *Mayak* (Lighthouse) and *Radio Rossii*
(Radio Russia). The Moscow city government owns a leading information-
oriented station, *Govorit Moskwa* (Moscow is Speaking). Among several

noteworthy developments of recent years has been a deliberate attempt to reduce the power of foreign information sources in Russia. For example, for several years the US federally funded network *Radio Svoboda* (Radio Freedom) was able to broadcast its materials through almost 60 radio stations located in many areas of Russia. Since 2006, Radio Freedom has only been allowed to broadcast from Moscow. The authorities claim that decision was prompted by the company's violation of business regulations. The company management disagree, and believe it is nothing more than political censorship. The restrictive measures were a response to the station's critical approach to the government and its policies.

> **Russians speak their mind ...**
>
> **... On the media.** Percentage of Russians trusting major television networks in Russia: 70. Percentage trusting major newspapers: 50.
>
> Source: WCIOM (2008e).

New media

Because of Russia's vast territory, it is important for a radio network to have local stations that can rebroadcast its signals. This need for local affiliates creates an opportunity for the government to impose legal restrictions on broadcasting companies. However, with the development of satellite radio and the internet, the authorities have fewer restrictive options. Therefore, some of the new media based on digital and satellite technologies have become not just a real business challenge to traditional media such as newspapers, television, and conventional radio, but also a political challenge to the government's ability to control broadcasting. Digital newspapers, news outlets, and blogs remain practically unregulated in Russia. As in every country, they are instant sources of various opinions and extremely diverse political ideas.

For example, on various Russian independent blogs it is very easy to find both supportive and very critical information about the Russian government, its policies, and its political leaders. Critics from the left sometimes praise the government for its populist policies but blast it for policies supporting the free market and big business. Oil and gas companies are under constant criticism. In contrast, other authors and commentators publish nationalistic and openly racist materials about Russia's weak immigration policies, and the necessity to beef up national security and conduct a more decisive foreign policy. From their side, liberal critics blast Moscow's authoritarian policies. They ridicule the Kremlin's confrontational approach in relations with other countries. To get some

Case in point: The televised embarrassment of a tycoon

In May 2009, millions of Russian viewers saw a rare moment: former President and current Prime Minister Putin was shown being visibly angry during an impromptu meeting involving scores of government officials surrounded by television cameras. Putin had just arrived in a small town near St Petersburg after hearing the news that local workers had blocked a major highway. They were demonstrating against the recent closure of their factory. The factory owner—Russian billionaire business tycoon Oleg Deripaska—argued that the factory was not profitable. Putin remained undaunted. "Where is the social responsibility of business?" he asked. In his typical manner, which stresses almost every word, he continued, "I think you have kept thousands of people hostage to your ambitions, unprofessionalism, and maybe simple greed. This should not have happened" (Rb.ru, 2009). Then Putin offered the viewers something even more spectacular. "Come here," he said to Deripaska. "Sign here." The owner went through more public humiliation when he was forced to sign an affidavit committing himself to reopening the factory. "Give me the pen back"—with these unceremonious words Putin ended the procedure. Detailed video reports of this incident were immediately aired in news briefs all over Russia.

A few minutes later, scores of blogs posted the clip so people could watch it and post a comment. Three types of comments emerged almost immediately. Most postings were supportive of Putin's harsh actions. The commentators were very critical of Deripaska and other owners of big enterprises. Some commentators wrote that they wished the government would take over all big businesses. Other comments were more balanced but still defended Putin's actions. They argued that government intrusion into private business happens everywhere in the world. Some even cited US policies. Several other comments expressed disagreement and even irritation with the actions of the prime minister, and his rude treatment of a businessman and private citizen.

Unlike some other countries such as China or Iran, Russia does not censor the web. The internet today is a fine source of uncensored public opinion, and a resource of information about a country where most traditional information outlets are under government control.

sense of this coverage, see the book's website and visit some Russian sites and blogs in English and Russian.

Russians speak their mind ...

... **On computers and the web.** Percentage of Russians who said they don't have a personal computer at home: 67. Percentage of Russians who use the internet almost daily: 16. Percentage of Russians who never use the internet: 67.

Source: Levada (2009f).

A quick review of entries on Russian blogs shows that people today are seemingly free to look at any information they want, and most importantly, make any comments they wish. Endorsements as well as criticisms of Putin or Medvedev are common and frequent in Russia.

It is important to emphasize that most authors of official websites reveal their names, and they do not necessarily face any consequences if they are critical of the government. For example, in 2009, a group of four Russian scholars and commentators published a very critical editorial in the *Washington Post* (Gudkov et al., 2009). The article was translated and posted in many Russian blogs (see, for example, http://www.inosmi.ru/translation/249794.html). The authors portrayed the Russian political system as deeply undemocratic, and warned the White House not to make the mistake of developing unconditional friendly relations with Moscow while turning a blind eye to Russia's expansionism and disrespect for civil liberties. In many authoritarian countries this would have led to immediate action against the authors, but this did not happen. One of the reasons is that (as the box shows) the internet is not as popular and widespread as other media, and most Russians still get their knowledge and information through newspapers and television. The experience of other countries such as China suggests that when the internet becomes popular and accessible to many citizens, the government might step in to apply censorship.

Despite the possibilities open to it, the Kremlin has generally rejected expensive Soviet-style censorship and adopted different strategies of political communication and mobilization. These strategies are inexpensive and apparently efficient; let us now look at them.

Strategies of political communication and mobilization

In the former Soviet Union, the Communist Party used the skills of hundreds of thousands of professionals to implement massive censorship in the field of political communications, including both mass media and personal contacts. The government's goal was to limit the average person's access to information that went against the ruling communist ideology. For example, until the late 1980s it severely restricted the ability of Soviet citizens to travel outside the country, especially to capitalist states. The few lucky tourists who visited France, Italy, or Egypt were not allowed to bring back books critical of the Soviet regime or possess foreign magazines such as *Newsweek* or the *Economist*. The government undertook significant efforts to block the signals from foreign radio stations on Soviet territory. Its strategy was to prevent any form of political expression outside the allowed pro-government forms.

From the 1990s the government's role in political mobilization was changing. There are at least two distinct periods in this process. Initially, during the years of Yeltsin's presidency until 2000, the central government in Moscow appeared to pay little attention to political mobilization. Only during crucial elections, like the dramatic presidential campaign in 1996, did Yeltsin's political team turn to the media for support to defeat the surging communists (see Chapter 8). Moreover, the Kremlin had little power over the private media, which were then owned by a few financial and business groups. The situation changed after Putin's ascendance to power. By reacquiring power over television networks and limiting the possibilities for political dissent, the central government generally regained important tools for political mobilization. The strategies of political mobilization today are quite different from those in the Soviet Union. In summary:

- The Kremlin and its loyal regional governments follow the Constitution and allow a wide range of political freedoms, including freedom of the press.
- However, the government pays serious attention to some topics, and above all, it attempts to limit information that could be used to strengthen the opposition.
- Russian authorities also work constantly to try to damp down political opposition or strong popular dissent.
- The Kremlin has created its own proactive and effective mobilization policy, by promoting patriotism, loyalty, hard work, and moral values—all associated with major government policies.

Let us consider these points in some detail.

What the government ignores

In Russia, people can openly criticize the government and even Moscow's top leaders. For example, most newspapers and television networks practice **muckraking**: investigative efforts to expose examples of excessive bureaucracy, negligence, or corruption among business executives or government officials. Journalists and commentators reveal unpleasant facts and offer critical opinions about the work of private enterprises and government institutions. Their criticisms are often harsh and justifiable.

Unlike in the Soviet Union, today's Russian media publish reports about natural disasters, accidents, wrecks, and violent crimes (similar to what people see daily on the television in any free country). With the notable exception of information about ethnic conflicts on Russian territory, most reports about news events seem to be uncensored and appear without

Photo 4   *Western performers appear frequently on the Russian stage. This poster announces a Britney Spears summer concert*

delay. The government allows reporters and commentators to publish and openly discuss any information related to the health and personal life of senior government officials.

The government does not censor popular literature. Private companies publish a wide range of fiction and non-fiction books, and Russian bookstores are filled with new items. The spectrum of political views expressed in these books is striking. Some books promote Russian nationalism. Others are packed with anti-immigrant statements. Some paperbacks are very critical of Russia's past. Others promote religion as a source of stability, prosperity, and national rebirth. Yet others mock and denigrate the current political regime in Moscow. Books by authors such as Vladimir Sorokin and Zakhar Prilepin, in which the authors portray Russia and its leaders in a very critical way, are national bestsellers. These and other writers publish interviews on the web in which they make disparaging remarks about the government, its leaders, and their policies (Sorokin, 2004).

These are some examples of political tolerance in Russia. In contrast, there are issues to which the government pays special attention, where its actions lead to widespread criticism from independent observers.

Sensitive issues

One such sensitive topic is the possibility of organized mass movements acting in opposition to the government. Although public rallies are legal in Russia, unless they support the government, their organizers are not normally given permission to demonstrate in city centers, and are directed to places that are generally away from the public eye. These tactics also give the authorities an excuse to arrest demonstrators who, they claim, violate the rules and disrupt public order. State-controlled television rarely covers any mass protests against government policies, and when coverage is unavoidable, the protesters are labeled as nothing more than an angry mob of fanatics who hate their own country. People can only learn about such demonstrations on the web, and as we have seen, most Russians do not yet have access to it.

These policies aimed at preventing mass protest rallies, and suppressing news coverage when they do take place, were in part influenced by the mass protests in Georgia, Ukraine, and other countries earlier in the 2000s, which led to a relatively peaceful but significant transformation of these countries' political regimes. These events were known as "colored revolutions" because the protesters wore a particular color—orange in Ukraine—as a symbol of their movement. The government was understandably anxious to prevent similar unrest in Russia, which from its viewpoint could have posed a serious threat to the state. It is important to mention that such protest groups do not generally receive overwhelming

---

Case in point: In defense of the Constitution

On August 31, 2009, a group of Muscovites attempted to organize a public rally in the center of Moscow in defense of Article 31 of the Russian Constitution, which says, "Citizens of the Russian Federation shall have the right to gather peacefully, without weapons, and to hold meetings, rallies, demonstrations, marches and pickets." Television was silent about the event, but twitters and blogs gave a vivid account of what happened. As soon as a crowd began to gather, dozens of uniformed police officers arrived on the scene. The crowd was peaceful, but most of the organizers were immediately surrounded by police. One person, Roman Dobrokhotov, began to sing the Beatles song *Yellow Submarine* in English. On the videos you can clearly hear warnings to the crowd over the police loudspeakers, then you can see the arrest of several people including the singer. A few people chanted "Russia without Putin!" and "Down with the police state!" Overall, about 40 people were detained.

Source blogs: http://vorobieva.livejournal.com/
http://community.livejournal.com/ru_opposition/1643949.html

support from the Russian public. Yet the authorities are particularly nervous about any publicly expressed form of political opposition.

Other sensitive topics are Russia's armed struggle against separatists in Chechnya and Northern Caucasus, and its military actions in the Georgia region. Official information from these places is carefully filtered. Journalists are expected to provide information uncritical of the government's actions. Foreign journalists' options are strictly limited. Human right groups, especially from other countries, are pressured and their activities are restricted. One of the most dramatic events associated with the media coverage of the conflict in Chechnya was the murder of Anna Politkovskaya, a reporter from *Novaya Gazeta*. She was famous for her critical views of Russia's policies, and reporting on human rights violations in the region and around the country. Some of her work was published after her death (Politkovskaya, 2008). The chapter on security policies returns to this subject to discuss how the Russian government uses information from the zones of tension to advance its security policies.

Elbowing out the opposition is not the only strategy in political communication and mobilization. Since the early 2000s, the Russian authorities have been deliberately proactive in their attempts to mobilize government supporters and demobilize the opposition without using oppressive techniques.

What the government promotes

One of the major strategies of mobilization is the promotion of pro-government groups, or movements supporting the president and his policies. An example is the *Nashi* movement (see Chapter 7). Officially called the Youth Democratic Antifascist Movement, its goal is to make Russia "a global leader of the 21st century." Its manifesto proclaims that Russia is a "historic and geographic center of the contemporary world" and a country that always resisted hegemony "either of Nazi Germany or the United States." Its goal is the creation of a "free, just, and united society" (http://www.nashi.su). From the beginning, the movement received generous support from the government, including very sympathetic coverage on television. Nashi's public rallies take place in places where the opposition is not allowed. As a sign of the Kremlin's support of the movement, Nashi's leader Vasily Jakemenko (born in 1971) became head of the federal agency in charge of youth affairs. More recently Nashi has become actively engaged in numerous social ventures, including environmental initiatives, care for the disabled, and educational and science-related projects.

The government has actively adopted the strategy of coopting mass social or political movements driven by public disagreement with policies. On page 169 it was described how the Union of the Right Forces went from an influential political party to virtual collapse after its leader was invited to become governor of a large region. Similar tactics are being used with smaller groups, such as a popular internet-based social protest movement to allow Russian people to buy and use right-hand-drive Japanese cars. Without resorting to police raids or censorship, the authorities gradually incorporated its leaders into government structures as advisers and experts on traffic rules. In this and similar cases, grassroots groups that become popular are typically outmaneuvered and outspent by the authorities (Fossato, Lloyd, and Verkhovsky, 2008). Other less significant groups are simply ignored.

Finally, the government is actively engaged in mobilizing people around several key ideas which it hopes will act as national unifiers. At least three basic strategic ideas about Russia as a state and its leadership are constantly recycled in the public statements of government officials and echoed by the state-owned media. The first is that democracy of the western type is not necessarily the best fit for Russia. Next, Russia is destined for a special, unique, and positive role in history. Third, Russia is surrounded by hostile powers that are working to undermine its sovereignty and stability. And fourth, there was a turning point in Russian history associated with the leadership of Vladimir Putin and his followers (Isaev and Baranov, 2009: 190–6).

The failures of the free market to secure economic stability, and the inability of the fragile democratic system to produce an efficient government in the 1990s, led many people in Russia to believe that democracy in its liberal-democratic, western form was not suited well to Russia. An economic upturn in the 2000s (caused primarily by the high cost of energy resources exported from Russia) gave the government some assurance that people will not worry too much about the deficiencies of democracy in Russia provided the country enjoys economic stability and security (Medvedev, 2009a). To further strengthen the idea about Russia's sovereign democracy and the country's "special path" in history, a new foreign policy doctrine was introduced (see Chapter 12 on foreign policy). This official set of guidelines was based on an assumption that Russia has to survive in a very unfriendly environment dominated by the United States. From the late 1990s, most international developments were covered by the Russian media through the prism of a confrontation between virtuous Russia and the "mean-spirited" rest of the world. Russian people were led to believe that that their country's economic rebirth was unwelcome to the west. However, many Russians believe the Russia of Putin and Medvedev is new and confident, and a force to be reckoned with.

These ideas become sources for the agenda setting and framing of the reported news in the government-controlled media. They are also supported by many Russians. Communists and nationalists, for example, despite their disagreements on social policies, find the national idea appealing and useful for political mobilization purposes. In contrast, the promotion of liberal democracy and criticism of authoritarian methods of government are either marginalized or severely restricted. The managers of the media continue to play their gatekeeping role by excluding information that does not conform with Kremlin policies.

Russians speak their mind ...

... On trust in the media. Percentage of Russians expressing their trust in: Central television: 70; National newspapers: 50; National radio: 44; The internet: 23.

Source: WCIOM (2009f).

Critical thinking about political communication and mobilization

Is the Russian media actually free? Can people in Russia today exercise freedom of speech? What kind of restrictions do they face? Several views exist about the status of basic civil liberties in Russia, including freedom of speech and freedom of the press. There are also both supportive and critical views about the relationship between Russian media and government, and their role in political mobilization.

From the mainstream point of view, which is largely supported within the country, the Russian media are free and independent. The most important point of comparison here is other countries' experience and their policies about their national media. Although Russia's experiences with political freedoms are not perfect, the country is gradually improving its democratic system. What happens in Russia is no different from other states in similar historic contexts. Most experts, however, including both domestic and international commentators, maintain that the media in Russia are not free, and freedom of speech faces serious problems in a generally undemocratic environment. The government decides which freedoms are to be protected and which are not. The general atmosphere of self-imposed censorship contributes to the realization of these government policies.

Russia is like any other country

Many Russian political commentators maintain that the media in Russia today are generally independent and free. If there are some problems, they are no different from other countries' problems. The following arguments are used.

Everywhere in the world, journalists and editors are salaried employees. They frequently express their own views. In other cases, they collect information, select events and facts, and write reports to accommodate the views of the owners of the medium. Russian journalists are no different in this from their British, German, and Japanese colleagues: they work for companies and often represent the views of a professional establishment. In Russia, this establishment happens to be close to the government. Therefore, the media can serve a very important political mobilization role, which is needed to consolidate the entire society and pull Russia out of economic and social backwardness.

Like in every country, broadcast networks and printed publications have their own political, ideological, and cultural preferences. In the United States, the major television networks are commonly considered more liberal than conservative; they frequently side with Democratic administrations and serve as sources of political mobilization for a relatively liberal part of America's society. Talk radio, on the other hand, is for the most part a tool for the political mobilization of conservatives. In a similar fashion, Russian television supports Russian political leaders and their domestic and foreign policies. The internet, in contrast, provides many examples of political dissent.

In response to criticism about persecution of Russian journalists, pro-government supporters argue that in other countries too journalists are pressured, and expected to report "politically correct" stories. In the United States, they argue, broadcasters frequently lose their jobs for saying "inappropriate" things on the air.

The Russian leaders, Putin and Medvedev, are often criticized for holding "staged" press conferences with preselected questions. However, this too is common behavior elsewhere. Other world leaders, including American presidents, routinely organize discussions, "town hall meetings," and press conferences, in which the questioners and their questions are specially selected in advance.

Finally, the supportive argument goes, in every country journalists must obey the law on what may or may not be printed, aired, or posed. Most countries impose limitations on the use of swearing and profane words. Other common restrictions relate to decency, privacy, and state secrets. Russia is no exception. The law, for example, tries to prevent deliberate slander or libel. The Constitution only allows the publication of information that has been obtained legally. It also prohibits people from publishing state secrets (see Chapter 13 on Russia's security policies). Journalists admittedly face legal restrictions on coverage of the events in Russia's zones of conflict, such as Chechnya and Ossetia, but then, virtually all countries impose similar restrictions in the event of war.

Case in point: Street propaganda and the law

A key argument of the supporters of the existing practices in Russia is that in any country, speech that violates existing law should be restricted. Both federal and local laws put restrictions on public speech. Consider a 2009 case, for example. A local committee of the Communist Party in the regional city of Voronezh paid to install several billboards in the city which proclaimed, "130-year anniversary of Stalin's birth. Victory will be ours." The federal authorities, however, disagreed with the message. They ordered the billboards to be removed, arguing that their text violated the legal requirements for billboards, that their messages must either serve a commercial purpose or further charitable or community-oriented goals.

Source: Lyskov (2009).

The media are not as free as they are in other states

Some experts accept that Russia's media are not truly free. There are indeed violations of basic rights and freedoms. However, the kinds of occurrence that are seen in Russia are very common in many countries undergoing similar processes of political transition. These countries typically have strong executive power and very weak social institutions, and there are often conflicts between journalists and the authorities. Bribery and corruption are often difficult to control, and they definitely undermine freedom of speech. Journalists in Russia can face severe penalties if they do something that upsets the authorities, including loss of their jobs or even criminal prosecutions that could put them in jail, but this is also true in many other countries, including Turkey, Belarus, Hungary, Mexico, and South Korea. There are sometimes unfortunate incidents which involve excessive use of authoritarian methods of government, but this again is all but inevitable in countries at this stage of democracy. Supporters of this view argue that Russia has been singled out unfairly. It is harshly criticized mostly because of its visibility and the important role it plays international affairs (Shleifer and Treisman, 2004).

The media are not free

Most international and some Russian independent observers argue that the Russian media for the most part are not free. Because of the government control, only political figures loyal to the Kremlin have access to the major media on a regular basis. During political campaigns, opposition leaders have very limited airtime. Journalists expressing disagreement with the government face serious consequences, including harassment, intimidation, and unemployment. Intimidation of reporters is common, especially of foreign journalists who provide critical coverage of Russia's military or security policies.

Its financial control over the media gives the government power over what appears on the air. This happens in violation of the Constitution. The annual reports of Freedom House, a nongovernment organization studying civil liberties globally (see Chapter 1), have assessed Russia's mass media as "not free." Russia ranks as one of the most dangerous places in the world to be a journalist, behind only Iraq and Colombia. The international organization Reporters Without Borders reported that 21 journalists were murdered in Russia between 2000 and 2008, including Anna Politkovskaya, a very well-known investigative journalist (McFaul and Stoner-Weiss, 2008: 70).

In summary, freedom of speech in Russia is limited. Mass media, and especially television, the most accessible medium in Russia, are under government control. As a result, most Russian people cannot receive objective information about events in their country and in the world. This lack of truthful and diverse information is detrimental to the functioning of a democratic society, which is what Russian leaders claim to be building.

Creative authoritarianism

From this standpoint, freedom of speech is commonly practiced in Russia and the media in Russia are generally free. However, note the words "commonly" and "generally." Freedom of speech and freedom of the press are selective in Russia. Unfortunately, most people consider this state of affairs normal, and many support the government's approach to political speech. This governmental policy is called innovative or *creative authoritarianism* (Shlapentokh, 2000). We look below are how some of its basic elements relate to the media and free speech.

First, the government allows people to exercise their freedom of speech in the forms and methods most available to them. As mentioned earlier, critical reports about government's policies and public officials do appear in the media, especially on the web. In fact, the internet has become a hub of critical information about Russian domestic and foreign policies. Caricatures and videos ridiculing political leaders are frequent. Books critical of the current regime are sold freely (in the Soviet times their authors would have been jailed or expelled from the country). However, because only a small proportion of Russian people have regular access to the web, it does not have the mass impact of television.

Second, unlike in the Soviet days, the ruling authorities now appear absolutely unconcerned about critical articles in digital and print media including journals and books. Officials have found a remarkably clever way of dealing with such information: they simply ignore it. In the past, during communism, enormous resources were dedicated to suppressing free speech. Today it is not necessary. Because television—the most powerful medium—is in the government's hands, other media are allowed to criticize the government within certain limits. In any case, it is not necessary to impose censorship because reporters and editors themselves try to stay in line and not challenge the established system.

This happens because the government has established an atmosphere of **self-censorship**: that is, people tend to censor their own work because of fear, deference, or a pragmatic judgment that toeing the government line will best serve their interests. Building the political and economic conditions for self-censorship is the third element of creative authoritarianism. The economic boom triggered by high oil and gas prices means that economic factors have become a powerful stimulus. Journalists who please the authorities and have great connections can lay claim to good salaries, benefits, and promotions. They feel they are reporting fairly, but they consciously avoid potential problems with the authorities, and become part of the establishment (Voroshilov, 2009; Lipman, 2008). Particularly because there is not a viable opposition, most journalists prefer to support the status quo. Of course, there are still people inside the political and intellectual establishments who publicly challenge the regime, but their numbers are insignificant, they are kept in media obscurity, and they fall well short of providing a powerful source of political mobilization.

Conclusion

In sum, analytical articles, columns, interviews, and reports on Russian policies and its political leadership appear daily in the Russian media. An author or commentator can in theory pass any judgment about the government and aim their criticism at specific policies and officials if they choose. The government also allows empirical studies of public opinion and their subsequent publication and discussion.

However, it is important to appreciate the roles that the mass media actually play in practice in today's Russia. Most of Russia's commercial television is now under the government's control. It functions under a very strong presidency, in a country with a weak political party system and fragile independent civil society (Stoner-Weiss, 2006a). Television provides generally positive coverage of the Kremlin policies, and restricts opposition access to the airwaves. Because of the political climate and self-censorship, many independent newspaper editors also choose loyalty to the government over confrontation with it. Only the internet remains a free medium, where an uncontrolled exchange of ideas is taking place, but this is perhaps partly because of its limited spread to date and its relative insignificance. Under these circumstances, the government can easily mobilize support, demobilize the opposition, and maintain the main gatekeeping role in the political process.

Part IV

Russian Policies

Chapter 10

Economic and Business Policies

Key developments
Government regulation of the economy
Economic strategies
Critical thinking about Russia's economic policies
Conclusion

> *A point of view that the state should increase its presence in the economy is Neanderthal. Neanderthals have died out and this ideology must die too.*
>
> German Gref, federal minister, 2008

In 1992 Russia was free, independent, and broke. Its economy was in disarray. It retained almost all the birthmarks of the Soviet period. Major industries were under state control. Although they were free from obligations to fulfill government plans (such plans no longer existed), they had serious problems in finding resources and customers. The major task for the Yeltsin administration was to put aside the legacy of the Soviet-style economy and implement reforms. But what kind of reforms did Russia need? The arguments about the most appropriate economic policies for Russia in the post-communist era began at that time. They continue today. Russia, like every country on the planet, is in constant search for the optimal way to manage its economy, finances, and employment.

Key developments

Several key developments of the past 20 years have made a decisive impact on Russia's economy and economic policies. There are three overlapping periods in this process. The first one began in the early 1990s. It was a time of rapid privatization of government assets, the introduction of radical market principles of economy and commerce, and deregulation of many branches of the Russian economy. The second period, lasting until the end of the 20th century, involved the rapid consolidation, with the government's blessings, of economic and financial assets in the hands of several large companies and individuals. The third period, which continues today, is marked by the government's attempts to redistribute some resources, reorganize the economy, and create an efficient economic and financial system. The start of this period was also associated with high oil prices, which contributed to Russia's relative financial stability but created other unexpected problems. The crisis of 2008–09 was a serious test of the survivability of the Russian economic system and its economic policies.

Let us now consider some key economic and political developments that gradually shaped the Russian economy today.

The reforms of the early 1990s

In their attempts to reform Russia's economy, Yeltsin and a close group of his advisers chose a strategy of economic liberalism. It was based on three key policies. First, the government encouraged people to privatize property previously owned by the state. Second, the federal government was no longer responsible for establishing and controlling prices. Third, the government gave up its obligation to ensure full employment, which had been guaranteed in the Soviet Union. The main assumption of the reformers was that after a few painful months of these changes, called **shock therapy**, the privatized industries and businesses of all kinds would start to produce. Production would in turn stimulate commerce. Then the recovering economy and commerce would stimulate the banking system. Finally, the growing tax revenues would allow the government to invest in certain areas of business and assist the most disadvantaged groups of the Russian population, including retirees and children. Privatization was also a political maneuver to consolidate and distribute power among the supporters of the free market. Unfortunately, the reality did not meet even the modest expectations of the economic reforms' architects (Gaidar, 2002, 2007).

In the economic sphere, the effects of shock therapy were severe. The privatization program became bogged down in bureaucracy and fraud. Inflation soared to 3000 percent in 1992 and another 900 percent in 1993, and gross domestic product (GDP) fell by more than 40 percent in the period between 1991 and 1993, while industrial production dropped 43 percent. Hyperinflation especially hit people on fixed incomes. By 1993 some 31 percent of the Russian population was below the poverty line. During the 1991–96 period GDP fell some 52 percent and industrial production was down 60 percent—twice the impact of the Great Depression in the United States (Shlapentokh and Shiraev, 2002). GDP per capita in Russia by 1996 was approximately US$5,000, twice as much as in China, about the same as in Brazil, but four times lower than in most developed countries. From 1992 to 1995, GDP went down 49 percent, real income went down 29 percent, and inflation was at 650 percent (*Argumenty i Facty*, #27, July 1996).

To stimulate private investment and generate confidence in the population, the government introduced state vouchers or stock guarantees. This new policy stated that every citizen was about to own a share of the property of the Russian Federation. In an ideal scenario, people were supposed to invest their vouchers in industries and commerce. They would become instant shareholders and owners, ready to receive benefits from their investments. However, the public was largely uninformed about how to invest their vouchers. Meanwhile, well-placed figures in government and industry used their insider positions to obtain large blocks of stocks in the most potentially profitable industries. The reforms helped the new elites to consolidate their resources and strengthen their power in the country. Yet the reforms did not improve the overall economic situation (Åslund, 2007).

Russians speak their mind ...

... On who to blame for the economic disaster. Polls taken in the early 1990s showed that a majority of people identified two main groups responsible for the poor state of their country's economy: government and criminal organizations.

Source: Shiraev (1999b).

The crisis of 1998

The Russian government turned to bonds and foreign borrowing to rescue its budget. This policy worked until global oil prices began to collapse in 1997. This has a devastating impact on Russia's financial system. In August 1998 the government, being essentially bankrupt, drastically devalued the ruble (the Russian currency) to reduce its domestic obligations, then announced it would not pay billions of dollars in outstanding loans to Russian and international lenders (McFaul and Stoner-Weiss, 2008: 79).

The financial crisis of the late 1990s was a global one. However, the crisis in Russia was different from the situation in some industrial nations in Southeast Asia, such as Korea, Singapore, and Japan. The principal difference was that most Russians did not have sizable monetary savings. Therefore, the consequences of the crisis were dire because they affected people's wages, on which they relied to buy daily essentials. Virtually everyone lost approximately three-quarters of their monthly salary. People with bank accounts saw them virtually disappear. As an illustration, between 1990 and 1997, Russian GDP dropped by nearly 50 percent according to the estimates (Rosstat, 1997). The World Bank estimated Russian GNP per capita in 1996 at US$4,500, comparable to Egypt's $4,200 and behind developing countries such as Colombia ($6,000) and

Thailand ($8,800) (World Bank, 1997). Opinion polls showed that more than two-thirds of people were afraid of looming impoverishment (Shiraev, 1999a).

The economic collapse resulted in the inability of the government to sustain social policies. Government support for education, culture and the arts, science, pensions, housing, youth programs, and health care dwindled. At the same time, the profits of most oil, gas, and aluminum corporations (now in private hands) grew between five and 36 times (Shleifer and Treisman, 2004).

The economic growth of the 2000s

Russia started the 1990s as a decayed, centralized economy, but was transformed into a market by ten years later (Shleifer and Treisman, 2004). In the late 1990s the economy began to show improvements. Several factors contributed to the upward development.

First, Russia's currency devaluation reduced imports and spurred Russian exports, which together with the fiscal austerity that the government practiced in this period, pushed economic growth in the late 1990s (McFaul and Stoner-Weiss, 2008).

Second, the country had a new president, Vladimir Putin, who was deeply involved in economic policymaking. He supported a policy based on free market principles but with significant government regulation of key industries. Capital gains and personal income taxes remained low in order to attract new investments and stimulate business.

Third, under Putin, social polices became more predictable. In turn, these policies became possible because of the changing financial situation in the Russian markets. Most importantly, Russia had achieved financial stability. Inflation remained modest and the Russian economy began to grow at a steady pace of around 6–7 percent annually.

The improvements also took place partly because of an increased cash flow to the state budget as a result of high prices for crude oil and natural gas. Prices first began to go up in 1998, and have continued to increase since 2002, approaching US$100 a barrel (McFaul and Stoner-Weiss, 2008: 80). The government was able to balance the budget, create a budget surplus, and establish a special reserve fund based on the surplus.

The crisis of 2008–09

The global financial crisis that began in 2008 has affected Russia in many ways, and its long-term effects are significant. However, the government has demonstrated its ability to make fiscal decisions, stimulate the banking system, and assign "stimulus packages" to industries to avert catastrophic developments. Although the Russian stock market crashed in 2008, various stimulus packages sustained it in 2009 and shortly after. Although several government programs had to be eliminated because there was a significant shortage of tax revenues, the government continued to pay salaries, pensions, and stipends to tens of millions of state employees, students, and retirees.

Russians speak their mind ...

... **On the 2009 crisis.** Percentage of Russians who though that the government did not do enough to address the crisis: 66.

Source: Levada (2009g).

Government regulation of the economy

Several government agencies are directly involved in Russia's economy. Their goal is to exercise policies and conduct legal regulation of a wide range of economic activities. There are ministries under the direct control of the federal government of the Russian Federation, as well as federal committees and federal services. Table 10.1 lists the ministries and their main functions. Ministries are typically in charge of several industrial branches or services such as agriculture, transport, or energy sectors. There are also ministries in charge of direct investments in Russia's regions and the management of natural resources.

Federal services are involved in specific areas of regulation. They exercise and primarily control the execution of specific policies (see Chapter 4). For example, the Federal Service for Labor and Employment "controls and supervises," according to the law, policies in the areas of employment and labor. It is also in charge of providing federal assistance in cases of unemployment, labor migration, and certain labor disputes. Federal agencies provide specific federal services. For example, the Federal Atomic Agency is in charge of directing the atomic industry of the Russian Federation, including research, production and protection of nuclear products. The Federal Space Agency provides federal services to manage federal property related to space exploration. It also coordinates research and exploration of space for peaceful purposes. In addition, Roskosmos (this is how the agency is commonly called in Russia) is in charge of projects in the rocket industry in both defense and civilian spheres. There are special agencies in charge of state border customs, tariffs (taxes on foreign products), anti-trust activities, and so forth.

Table 10.1   *A sample list of ministries of the Russian Federation involved in regulation of the economy and resources*

Ministry	Policy and regulatory decisions in the areas of:
Finance	Unified financial policy and organization of finances on the territory of the Russian Federation.
Natural Resources	Study, use, reproduction, and protection of Russia's natural resources.
Industry and Trade	The civil and defense industries, as well as aviation technology development, technical standardization and metrology, and foreign trade activities.
Energy	The fuel and energy industries including electric energy, oil, gas, coal, and renewable sources.
Regional Development	Social and economic development of the regions (subjects of the Russian Federation) and municipal units.
Agriculture	The agrarian-industrial complex, sustainable development of agricultural territories, as well as study, protection, reproduction, and use of animals designated for hunting.
Transport	Civil aviation, the use of airspace, aerial search and rescue, rivers, railroads, automobiles, city electric (subway) systems, industrial transportation, and road services.

The Finance Ministry

One of the most important ministries is the Finance Ministry. It has 17 types of major function, including policy and regulatory decisions in the fields of the federal budget, federal taxes, insurance and banking industries, federal debt, precious metals, customs fees, and anti-terrorist financial operations. The Finance Ministry manages the collection of federal taxes and is in charge of special stabilizing funds.

The Stabilization Fund was created out of a portion of the federal budget to stabilize the economy in the event of economic or financial problems. If global prices for oil are above a "base price" of US$27 per barrel, the government transfers the surplus money into the fund. The size of the fund is also set as a proportion of GDP, which ranges between approximately 4 and 7 percent every year. If the price falls below the base, no money is transferred into the fund. The fund may be used to stabilize the budget in the event of lower tax revenues in the future, as well as to finance additional social programs.

The executive branch, not the Duma, manages the Stabilization Fund. Typically, the assets of the fund are secured in foreign reserves (45 percent in US dollars, 45 percent in euros, and 10 percent in pounds Sterling) or in foreign securities (for example, US Treasury bonds). There is also another important federal fund. The National Prosperity Fund (or National Well-Being Plan) is used to co-finance optional pension saving plans for Russian citizens and stabilize the Pension Fund of the Russian Federation.

The Finance Ministry publishes monthly updates (you can check them online) about the size of each fund on its website. In 2008–09; the average size of the Reserve Fund was over US$100 billion. The size of the Fund of National Prosperity rose from US$32 billion to US$86 billion.

Web

The size of the National Stabilization Fund is published monthly by the Ministry of Finances of the Russian Federation: http://www1.minfin.ru/ru/nationalwealthfund/

Taxation and tax policies

Taxes are collected in Russia based on the Tax Code and other laws. Russia had a progressive individual tax policy before 2001, with tax rates ranging from 12 to 45 percent of yearly income. The Kremlin considered this system unsatisfactory, and Russia then established a policy of an annual flat rate for individual income tax. With some exceptions, it is 13 percent, which is significantly lower than in most developed countries including the United States and United Kingdom. Nonresidents pay income tax at a 30 percent rate. In some cases, foreign residents can avoid double taxation or lower their taxes if there is a dual-taxation agreement between Russia and their home country. Like many states, Russian tax laws grant tax deductions based on the size of a family (the more children a family has, the less tax it pays), charitable contributions, and other conditions. There are also capital gains taxes and other payments, tolls, and duties paid by businesses. For example, on average private oil companies in Russia pay US$27–30 in federal taxes for every barrel of oil sold (Nemtsov, 2008).

There are three types of taxes: federal, regional, and municipal (see Table 10.2). The government tax policy is more pragmatic than ideological. Opposition parties on the left (see Chapter 7) argue for a more progressive tax policy (with higher levels of tax on higher income) and a more active role for the government in wealth redistribution. The federal government's goal, however, is to maintain financial and economic stability and adjust tax policies to the changing conditions of national and global markets. Overall the government maintains a predominantly liberal approach to taxation, based on the assumption that lower taxation should

Table 10.2   *Russia's taxes: different types and examples*

Type of taxation	Examples of taxation
Federal. Established by the federal government.	Individual, corporate profits, and financial gains taxes. Unified Social Tax (mandatory payments to social security funds). Customs taxes (on foreign products brought to Russia). Taxes on the use of natural resources. Taxes on domestic animals and pets. Environmental taxes (to support forests and water resources). Federal licensing fees. Taxes on special products (alcohol, liquor, beer, tobacco, natural gas, gasoline, motor oil, etc.).
Regional. Established by subjects of the Russian Federation.	Property tax for organizations and individuals. Roads tax (repair and maintenance of roads). Transportation tax (for most kinds of vehicles). Sales taxes. Regional licensing fees.
Local. Established by local governments.	Tax on land in private possession. Tax on individual property. Tax on advertisements. Inheritance and gifts taxes. Local licensing fees.

stimulate economic production and trade, and thus bring more revenue to the federal budget. The high oil and gas prices of much of the 2000s provided confidence to the supporters of this approach. However, the global financial turmoil that started in 2008 has affected Russia's tax revenues, and the tax system might change in the near future to compensate for the losses (Trunin, 2009). See the book website for updates.

Economic strategies

After massive economic reforms and the turmoil of the 1990s, Russia's main priority under Presidents Putin and Medvedev was to provide all the necessary conditions for steady growth of the economy. Economic stability and concomitant social stability are two most important strategic goals of the government. Therefore, Russia's economic policies, as you might expect, attempt to create favorable conditions for pursuing these goals. For example, maintaining Russia's currency, the ruble, at an exchange rate which makes it cheap compared to the euro and dollar allowed Russia to have a competitive advantage: the cheaper the ruble is, the easier it is to sell Russian products overseas. On the other hand, foreign products in Russia become more expensive.

Principles of economic policies

There is no uniform view in Russia of the most appropriate economic policies needed for a country of this size. Overall, the Duma's opposition factions (including the Communist Party and the Liberal Democrats) maintain an ideological view. Although they support private property, disagreements exist between them and the government about the share of the government's role in key industries. The two opposition parties are in favor of a larger government share in business and finance. The crisis of 2008–09 gave the critics additional arguments in favor of their position.

United Russia, along with the president and prime minister, maintains a more pragmatic approach and formally defends liberal economic policies with an emphasis on private business. In many statements, both Putin and Medvedev have insisted that "state capitalism" or government ownership and management of companies is not the way Russia plans to develop its economy. The opposition disagrees, and considers these statements misleading. Critics on the left complain about "selling out" Russia's resources and businesses into private hands. Other critics complain about the government's surreptitious but constantly increasing presence in business through small regulations, licensing, and other rules that make private business less free. The Kremlin does not challenge critics on these issues, and points out that the government has to play a certain role in regulatory economic policies.

For example, one of Russia's economic priorities is the strengthening of government participation via investments in and regulation of several key industries. The priorities are the airplane and shipbuilding industries, atomic energy, defense industries, and nanotechnologies. These sectors will receive the most substantial government investments in the near future (United Russia, 2007). The strategic goal is to make Russia a global leader in technological development.

The energy sector

Exports of Russia's natural resources have been the main source of foreign revenues for the government. Russia is pursuing a clear policy of getting maximum profit out of its natural resources. The money from these sales allows the government to pursue social programs and stabilize the ruble,

Case in point: The 2009 "Gas War" crisis

Ukraine is one of the biggest purchasers of Russian natural gas, and is also on the route of a gas pipeline through which Russia delivers 25 percent of the European Union's gas supply. In 2009, Russia raised the price of gas from US$179 to US$250 for 1,000 cubic meters. Ukraine claimed that the new price was unwarranted and excessive, and refused to pay it. Russia in response cut off the entire supply of gas to and through Ukraine. This was a particular problem because any lengthy interruption in gas delivery could have meant that several countries in Central Europe would be without a major source of heating in winter. The European Union accused Russia of power games. Russia claimed that the action was legitimate, and the country to blame was Ukraine, which had allegedly been stealing some of the gas going through its territory from Russia to Europe.

The conflict was perceived entirely differently in Moscow and in European capitals. The west believed that this action was Russia's way of getting back at the government of Ukraine for its openly pro-western policies. Russia wanted to remind the world of its power to affect policies. The Kremlin denied this interpretation, and claimed it was all a matter of business: getting the price it wanted for its resources. As a result of these problems, the European Union began to seek alternative ways of delivering gas to its consumers.

which means above all low inflation and higher living standards. In a very straightforward way, Russia is interested in keeping oil and gas prices high and prolonging the world's dependence on imported energy resources. However, without massive financial investments Russia is not capable of maintaining high levels of production. Therefore, foreign companies are allowed to participate in the Russian natural resource sector. However, the government tends to maintain control of a large portion of the oil and gas industries.

One of Russia's priorities for the second decade of the century is to invest in alternative sources of energy. Russia anticipates a global decline in demand for oil and gas as a result of growing environmental concerns and the increasing use of new sources of energy. Therefore, Russia's official policy is to seek opportunities to become a producer of new forms of energy (Shakkum, 2006).

Agricultural policies

If you drive as little as 50 miles from the flashy streets of Moscow or St Petersburg you will see a different Russia. For many years, Soviet and then Russian officials tried to boost the country's agriculture and improve the living conditions in Russian villages. However, the social and political experimentations of the past 100 years devastated the land and most of the people living there. Although political freedom and social changes after 1991 have transformed Russian villages, the state of Russia's agriculture is one of the main and most challenging problems in the country. Among the biggest obstacles is demographics: the aging population and migration out of the countryside have depleted the rural population. Russia has almost 9.5 percent of global agricultural land but lacks farmers to work on it. The second problem is the need for massive investments to change the country-side's infrastructure and make the work of the farmer rewarding and attractive. Substantial and speedy improvements in the agricultural sector have been among the highest priorities of the ruling party and the president (United Russia, 2007).

A substantial change took place in the early 2000s when a major land reform was implemented. The new Russian Land Codex (2001) allowed private ownership of land for the first time since 1917, when all land had been confiscated from its owners. Russian citizens can now buy, sell, rent, or lease land based on market prices. There are limits: no one can own more than 10 percent of the land within one municipal jurisdiction. The priority to purchase was given to the people who already live on agricultural lands, which had been the property of the government. Approximately 46 million acres of agricultural land was allocated to almost 13 million people.

The problems continue, however. From 20 to 40 percent of agricultural lands are not in use, although they have been in the past. The land tax, a main source of revenue for the municipal governments, did not generate the expected revenue. Many peasants sell their land unwillingly or are incapable of developing it. The process of buying and selling is complicated, long (it can take up to a year), and requires a great deal of documentation, all of which stimulates fraud and corruption (Chetverikov, 2009).

To revive the agricultural sector, the government launched a massive stimulus program under the umbrella of the National Priority Projects (see Chapter 11). The ambitious **National Agrarian-Industrial Complex Project** is pursuing three major goals: development of stock farms, financial and other support for small farms, and assistance in housing construction in the countryside. Specifically, the government will assist farmers by providing 8–10-year credit terms, assistance with leasing programs, and eliminating or reducing tariffs on foreign-made machinery and equipment necessary in agriculture.

Foreign cooperation

Two views exist about Russia's interaction with foreign companies. The first view is liberal-economic, and based on an assumption that economic freedom is the vehicle of economic development. Despite Russia's great potential, with fine natural resources and a skilled work force, the country needs massive foreign investment to boost industrial development. To become a global competitor is to become a global participant. Therefore, Russia must attract foreign investments and businesses.

The other view favors economic **protectionism**, or a policy of restraining foreign trade and limiting foreign investments. The main claim of protectionists in Russia (as well as in other countries) is that the government must protect its own country's producers and consumers first, before caring about global developments and long-term international projects. There are ideological protectionists in Russia, such as the Communists, who believe that foreign cooperation is harmful to Russia. In their opinion, foreign companies want to destroy Russia's economic potential. There are also non-ideological protectionists who insist that protectionism is only a temporary policy necessary to increase Russia's competitiveness, protect the job market, and provide stability. After these goals are achieved, Russia may become a more active global partner (Shakkum, 2006).

The privatization policies of the 1990s resulted in the creation of a large social class of property owners. The right to own private property—one of the major rights denied by the communist ideology—is acknowledged by all

Photo 5   *Since 1990, more than 100 McDonald's restaurants have opened in Russia, serving about 200,000 customers daily*

political parties and groups in Russia today. Pro-small business policies are a priority of the government. The government and the opposition make clear statements about the necessity to support, protect, and develop small businesses, their owners, and employees. Opinions differ, however, about big corporations and their owners, who in Russia are known as "the oligarchs."

Politics and big business

In the middle of the 1990s, the government began to sell its shares in major companies across Russia (we discuss different views of the reasons for this sell-off in the critical thinking section). It was a time of business and financial consolidation. Smaller companies merged into bigger ones or were pushed out of business. During the 1990s, several powerful financial and industrial magnates gained significant political power and influence.

The financial crisis of 1998 destroyed some private financial corporations in Russia but cleared the way for others, especially those with the government's backing. They consolidated and expanded their resources and assets. A constantly increasing demand for natural resources drove prices up, which was helpful to the Russian businesses and economy. A period of economic stability followed. During that period, the first Russian billionaires emerged. In 2000, no Russian citizen could claim that they were worth US$1 billion. Since 2001, that situation has changed, and Russian industrial and financial magnates began to appear on "top 100", "top 400" and other financial lists and reports. The number of billionaires in Russia has however fallen from 101 to 49 during the financial crisis of 2008 and 2009 (see Table 10.3).

The Kremlin's policy toward the super-rich magnates and financiers is inconsistent and contradictory. On the one hand, all three Russian presidents have acknowledged the importance of big business in the Russian economy, and underlined the necessity to develop Russia's global competitiveness. On the other hand, there is a common perception that the government shows favoritism toward some of the magnates but not others. Several of the most prominent and most powerful business leaders of the 1990s, including Boris Berezovsky, Vladimir Gusinsky, and Mikhail Khodorkovsky, have been

Table 10.3   *Estimated numbers of billionaires in Russia, 2004–09*

2000	2001	2002	2003	2004	2005	2006	2007	2008	2009
0	8	7	25	24	39	50	61	101	49

Sources: http://www.finansmag.ru/90892; *Forbes Magazine*.

Case in point: The fate of Mikhail Khodorkovsky

Mikhail Khodorkovsky, one of the most successful Russian businessmen in the 1990s and early 2000s, is a representative of a new wave of Russian entrepreneurs not associated with most powerful government elites in the Soviet Union. He started his business activities in the late 1980s and turned to finance in 1990. A year's successful career in business propelled him to the status of an adviser to the prime minister. He also served as a deputy minister of fuel and energy of the Russian Federation. In 1995 he financed the purchase of 45 percent of shares of the Yukos oil company. He became its vice president in 1996 after expanding his ownership of the company. His business and profits grew. By 2000, Khodorkovsky had become one of the richest entrepreneurs in Russia. Although he did not criticize Putin publicly, he was openly against the authoritarian system that he believed was forming in Russia. He supported the opposition: both the liberal-democratic group, including the Yabloko party, and the Communist Party.

On October 23, 2003, Khodorkovsky was arrested and led away from his private plane after landing in the city of Novosibirsk. He was immediately brought to Moscow for investigation and trial. The formal charges were illegal operations with the company's stock, embezzlement, and fraud. Khodorkovsky and his business partner were sentenced to seven years in prison (Rodionov, 2007). In 2007 the General Prosecutor's Office brought new charges against Khodorkovsky: this time they involved theft and money laundering.

Opinions about the Khodorkovsky case vary. One group of commentators supports the government's position and maintains that Khodorkovsky was a felon who has received a justified sentence. About 19 percent of Russians believe that he ought to remain in prison where he belongs.

From another standpoint, the case was prompted by business motives, and was about redistribution of wealth: somebody in the government has made money out of this case. About 66 percent of Russians believed that the case benefited a small group of government and business officials.

A third view is political. Khodorkovsky was a growing challenge to Putin. With his oil money, he could effectively place his own candidates in the Duma, and could then have challenged the "main office" in the Kremlin. In fact, about 35 percent of Russians believe that the Kremlin was unhappy with Khodorkovsky's political aspirations.

A different point of view is based on an assumption that the case was orchestrated to set an example. Khodorkovsky most probably was no different from any other successful entrepreneur (this view is shared by 49 percent of Russians). His mistake was that he dared to challenge the system and the president. As a result, the Kremlin decided to show everyone what could happen to a big businessman if he did not get along with the politicians (Panyushkin, 2006).

Source of polling data: Levada (2009h).

accused of various illegalities. Two of these three have escaped prosecution and had to seek legal protection abroad (they also deny the charges). The case of Mikhail Khodorkovsky is special because he is the first Russian billionaire who has been given a lengthy prison sentence on multiple charges of business and financial violations.

Web

Information from groups in support of Khodorkovsky can be accessed at: http://khodorkovsky.ru/

Critical thinking about Russia's economic policies

When Gorbachev first introduced glasnost and perestroika in the Soviet Union, he had enthusiastic supporters across the country (Smith, 1990: 6). But with the break-up of the old regime and the political and economic turmoil of the transition period, a profound disillusionment grew up about free market reforms. Over time, as problems were mounting, the leaders in the Kremlin had to face difficult questions. What should be Russia's economic policy for years to come? Which direction should the country choose? Should it be a special version of free market capitalism with open competition and few government regulations? Or should it be a kind of capitalism with a vast social protection and economic and financial guarantees to individuals and businesses?

Profound disagreements began to emerge back in the 1990s. These continue to be very divisive issues today. Just like people in Washington, London, and Tokyo, people in Russia have a variety of opinions about the extent of the government's role in economic and financial policies. One side in such debates is leaning toward economic liberalism, while the opposite side defends government regulation.

A liberal or illiberal economy?

Supporters of economic liberalism believe that an open-market economy is best for any national economy: under these conditions, both labor and natural resources are used most efficiently. An open market encourages innovation. State intervention in business tends to become permanent, according to the liberal approach, and throttle civil society and free economic entrepreneurship. This view was openly expressed by Vladimir Putin, who even criticized state intervention in rescuing falling banks and businesses during the economic crisis of 2009 (Putin, 2009).

Russian political leaders of the early 1990s were overall economic liberals, believing in the power of free market to unleash healthy competition, coupled with individual responsibility and discipline. It was widely believed that private ownership alone was a strong motivational force that could transform both the individual and society. However, the country lacked three basic conditions necessary for the successful development of free market policies. From the economic standpoint, the country had a very weak infrastructure. From the legal standpoint, Russia had very few laws capable of regulating the new type of business and societal relations. From the psychological standpoint, the vast majority of people had no positive experience of free entrepreneurship. The young Russian capitalism could not produce a miracle. To the contrary, the free market transitions pushed the country to the edge.

In the middle of the 1990s, the government in Moscow faced serious budget shortages. The Kremlin needed money urgently and in large quantities. One of the ways to solve the problem was to cut social programs and increase taxes. However, this could have had serious consequences and affected social and political stability. Under those conditions, Yeltsin would definitely have lost the 1996 elections. The government chose a different way. To earn cash, the Kremlin initiated a massive sell-off of government shares in key companies across Russia. Yeltsin's advisers also believed that in order to avoid the Communists' return to power in 1996, the Kremlin should create a large and powerful group of big property owners. These new business elites would become a backbone, a social base of the government, and would prevent all attempts by the Communists to regain power (Gaidar, 2002).

However, despite these massive transfers of assets and resources into private hands, Russia was struggling with its ability to embrace truly democratic forms of government. The problem did not necessarily lie with Russian leaders' inability or unwillingness to promote democratic methods of government. The problem is embedded in Russia's political and economic situation, in Russian cultural customs, and in the way most Russians learn how to do business or complete a sale.

Today, government officials and the media do not hide the fact that corruption and theft remain major social problems. About ten years ago Russia did not have enough legal rules to support business. Today such rules exist, but unfortunately they are often not followed or not properly enforced. Informal contacts frequently substitute legal rules of conducting business (Ledeneva, 2006). Under these conditions, the government established what are often described as illiberal, proscriptive policies, based on the ability of the executive authority to make decisions. For that matter, Russia has embraced illiberal economic policies, a mixture of authoritarian methods of government coupled with the acceptance of free market principles—but only when it is convenient.

Russians speak their mind ...

... **On corruption.** Percentage of Russians who believe that corruption is "undefeatable": 58. Percentage of Russians who believe that the government and the people together could overcome corruption: 37.

Source: WCIOM (2009g).

As some commentators say, Russian big business promises to support the government and sponsor its policies; in exchange, the government supports the free market (Levinson, 2008a).

State capitalism?

Do illiberal policies mean that Russia is reverting to state capitalism? **State capitalism** is the way of organizing the economy in which federal government controls a large proportion of the economy and plays an important managing role, as a kind of chief executive officer. In other words, the government becomes the biggest shareholder in key businesses. There are different opinions on this matter. Mikhail Kasyanov, a former prime minister and now a leader of the opposition, claims that since the early 2000s Russia has been moving in the wrong direction, trying to restore a Soviet-style economy and many elements of state capitalism. However, both presidents, Putin and Medvedev, continued to claim publicly that state capitalism is not their choice. The Communist Party, on the other hand, constantly accuses the Kremlin of deregulation policies and support of private businesses.

Whose argument is more accurate? It is hard to say, but it is interesting to consider Table 10.4, which lists ten of the most successful and powerful Russian companies, leaders in their sphere of business: they include oil, gas, metals, communications, and transportation companies. Most of these are joint stock companies. They trade publicly and accept foreign ownership of portions of their stock. Five of them are under either complete or partial government control (the size of the government's share varies).

Future developments

Several questions remain. What will be the direction of current and future changes? Will government increase its control over the country's economy? Or will the government let the market determine the future?

On the one hand, many supporters maintain that state capitalism is the only choice for Russia. There are several arguments in support of this view.

Table 10.4 *Some top Russian companies, their functions and ownership*

Company	Main function	Ownership
Gazprom	Extraction and delivery of natural gas	Joint stock company. Government has a controlling share.
Lukoil	Extraction and delivery of oil and oil products	Joint stock company. Multiple owners including foreigners.
Gazpromneft	Extraction and delivery of oil, gas, and oil products	Joint stock company. Gazprom owns a controlling share.
Norilsk Nickel	Mining and smelting operations; production of nickel, cobalt, copper, platinum, gold, and other metals	Joint stock company. Multiple owners including foreigners.
Basic Element	Aluminum production, management, military production, insurance, construction, etc.	Single owner (Oleg Deripaska).
AFK Sistema	Telecommunications, retail, advertisement.	Joint stock company. Multiple owners including foreigners.
Aeroflot	Largest Russian airline company	Joint stock company. Government has a controlling share.
Avtovaz	Car manufacturing	Joint stock company. Multiple owners including foreigners.
Mosenergo	Energy supplier	Joint stock company. Multiple stock ownership. Largest shareholders are Gazprom and the Moscow Government.
OZhD Russian Railroads	Railroad transport services	Federal Government.

Sources: *Expert Weekly*; Information provided by the companies.

First, supporters of state capitalism refer to the positive economic experiences in countries such as China and Singapore: if capitalism works there in authoritarian political climates, it can work in Russia as well.

Second, they point out the mistakes of the 1990s when Russia was overly reliant on free market principles. As a result, Russia did not invest in production and manufacturing. A substantial portion of capital moved into the banking system because of seemingly lucrative possibilities in that sphere. Consequently, Russia entered the 21st century with an underdeveloped manufacturing sector (Shakkum, 2006).

Third, many experts believe that top Russian officials have both the political and personal motivation to keep most businesses under control. There are two ways to exercise this control. The first is government ownership. Choosing this path, the Kremlin will gradually increase its ownership, and its regulatory role, in both private businesses and the national economy. But why does the Kremlin need to control the economy? In fact, the Kremlin is likely to gain politically if it invests in and increases its control over industries. This populist course of action constantly finds substantial support among the Russian population. Many people in Russia, like elsewhere in the world, believe that government should play a bigger role in economic issues. This attitude was further reinforced in Russia during the economic crisis of the end of the first decade of the century: in times of crisis many people are looking for the safety and security of the government rather than the risk and variety of capitalism.

These arguments in favor of state capitalism find support among many economic experts and scientists who openly endorse the government's investments in several economic and social areas. One is social security: pension plans, unemployment benefits, medical care, and education. Another is technology, especially those areas that are unlikely to produce a profit within five to seven years (Shakkum, 2006). The third area is heavy industries responsible for military and defense production. Fighting corruption is another problem, which cannot be solved or even addressed without the government's persistent intervention. And finally, the government can also stimulate investment in areas of relatively low profitability such as machine manufacturing (Greenberg, 2008).

A second way of controlling the economy and big businesses is to use authoritarian methods of pressure and manipulation. This is again essentially an illiberal economic policy. It involves a mixture of two strategies: relying on free market principles, and making personal interventions. The government rewards those big businesses and their owners who are loyal to the authorities, or at least become manageable. In contrast, the government punishes those entrepreneurs who appear to threaten the established status quo. One of the major government weapons here is the country's legal system. Using legal and other officially authorized tools, the Kremlin can threaten, bargain with, or punish any big business. The supporters of this view may use the example referring to Russia's oligarchs: some of them remained loyal to the Kremlin and thus were allowed to stay in business. Others, however, were forced out of the country or prosecuted (see Case in point). As you can see, the government does uses selective "prosecution and reward" policies to manage big business. Of the five most powerful Russian entrepreneurs who emerged back in the 1990s, two, Abramovich and Potanin, remain on good terms with the Kremlin. Three others, Gusinsky, Berezovsky, and Khodorkovsky, have had problems. As the result, the first two had to leave the country to avoid charges against them; the Khodorkovsky case was discussed on page 228.

Case in point: The oligarchs

These are among the most prominent Russian business and financial magnates who emerged in the 1990s.

Vladimir Gusinsky, born in 1952, created the first independent television network in Russia, and also set the course for professional and objective television news coverage in Russia. The emergence of NTV+, an offshoot from his NTV channel, was a groundbreaking event for Russian media. NTV+ was the first satellite channel ever to broadcast in the former USSR. He has lived outside Russia since 2001.

Boris Berezovsky, born in 1946, made his fortune importing Mercedes cars into Russia in the 1990s and setting himself up as an intermediary distributing cars made by Russia's Avtovaz. He was a co-owner of the Sibneft oil company and became the main shareholder in the country's top television channel, ORT. He used television to help Boris Yeltsin in the 1996 presidential elections. He served as a deputy secretary of the Security Council of Russia. He has lived in Great Britain since 2001. Criminal charges have been filed against him in Russia for an alleged financial fraud.

Mikhail Khodorkovsky, born in 1963, created and expanded a financial business in the early 1990s. He owned one of the biggest oil companies in Russia and the world, and was arrested and prosecuted for financial fraud and embezzlement.

Roman Abramovich, born in 1966, created or gained control of several companies in manufacturing, trade, and the oil business. He gained control over Sibneft, one of the most powerful oil companies in the world, and had good access to Boris Yeltsin and his family. Allegedly, he was the chief sponsor of Yeltsin's presidential campaign of 1996. He has been governor of Chukotka, a subject of the Russian Federation. In early 2000, he moved to the United Kingdom.

Vladimir Potanin, born in 1961, is a banker, owner of several companies, and media mogul. He served as first deputy chair of the Russian Government (Cabinet of Ministers). He remains active in business, and still lives in Russia.

Other critics underline the ineffectiveness of illiberal systems. One of the problems of illiberal economic policy is that its main focus is to distribute and redistribute wealth without paying attention to actual management and planning. These critics are not necessarily defending free market principles, and contrasting them with heavy government regulations. Their point is that any state regulation tends to be harmful for business (Gusev, 2003). Moreover, for many years, Russia's economy has relied heavily on oil and gas. Russia's fortunes and the legacies of its leaders have been dependent on the fluctuating prices for these resources. Russia's addiction to natural resources persists, and its political-economic system is still driven by the imperative of distributing the wealth from the country's natural resources (Gaddy and Ickes, 2009).

Supporters of the free market approach reject massive government intervention in principle. To them, state capitalism is a giant monopoly. Furthermore, facing no competition, it is inseparable from three social sins: corruption, mismanagement, and inflation. The type of Russian capitalism that is being built, some commentators complain, resembles similar authoritarian forms in Latin America and in Asia, where governments allow private enterprise but limit political liberties (Nemtsov, 2002; Bolshakov, 2004). State-run businesses have little incentive to take business risks, try new methods, and grow. Federal bureaucrats have no responsibility for what they are doing, beyond their fear of losing their lucrative jobs. Gazprom, for example, the biggest Russian gas company, has not increased its production of gas in the 2000s (Nemtsov, 2008). Because of the lack of competition, in 2009 Russians began to pay more for a gallon of gasoline than Americans did.

Negative experiences

One of the reasons that there is a deep-seated ambivalence toward free market principles is the country's negative experience with economic reforms. Leading world economic powers like the United States, Japan, the United Kingdom, and Germany have been developing their free market economies for decades, learning and changing economic policies in the process. Russia's experience is brief: just a little more than two decades. In critical times, people look for someone to blame for their difficulties. In Russia, during the difficult economic reforms of the 1990s, the obvious scapegoats were the new democratic leaders under Yeltsin, and foreign economists, mainly from the United States, who were giving advice about the free market and promising a fast turnaround (Khasbulatov, 2008). The reforms did not produce the immediate positive results that had been expected, and that negative experience resulted in many people's skeptical views of the free market.

Conclusion

In the late 1990s Russia ended a decade of economic uncertainty. Early in the 21st century, Russia led by Vladimir Putin has overcome the economic difficulties of the past and moved into a new period of steady economic growth. Several factors, including high energy prices, relatively low taxes, and general stability in the country, have contributed to a healthy economy. The biggest problems remain: a heavy emphasis on energy resources, relatively weak manufacturing, huge bureaucracy, and widespread corruption. Russia continues to look for its own unique way of economic development, and sways between two choices: the free market, and government regulation. It is not yet clear how things will develop over time, but it looks as if a regulated free market supported by illiberal policies appears the most attractive choice to the Kremlin.

Chapter 11

Social Policies: Health, Education, and Housing

Key developments
Government institutions
The National Priority Projects
Critical thinking about social policies
Conclusion

> *Russia will finally stop being a country of the poor. The popu-*
> *lation decline will be stopped.*
> 2007 electoral platform of the ruling United Russia party

Democratic countries tend to develop their social policies gradually, as a result of a comprehensive political debate. Russia is debating too: which type of social policy to choose? Current priorities and specific problems can change the course of the debates rapidly. However, certain tendencies and trends in Russia's social policies have already appeared.

In this chapter, we look at the very short history of some basic Russian social policies related to health care, education, housing, and social security. The legacy of the Soviet Union has played a significant role in the way Russia handles its social policies today. There is a paradox. On the one hand, the government proclaims the principle of individual responsibility: every citizen must be accountable for their future, and the quality of social services depends on a person's contribution to society. On the other hand, there is a very strong and deep-seated belief in Russia that the government must play a major role in the distribution of social services.

Several key developments in the last 20 years will help us better understand this paradox.

Key developments

Under the old Soviet system, in theory, every citizen had equal access to health care, education, housing, and a wide range of social services such as cheap public transport. The Soviet state was a welfare state: the federal and local governments provided virtually every social service in every area of

237

life, from an individual's birth to their very last days. On the basic level, the vast majority of Soviet citizens lived under a system that guaranteed at least some social protection and minimally decent living standards: there was almost no homelessness, unemployment, or chronic starvation in the country after the early 1950s. In simple terms, the government guaranteed a roof under everyone's head, a job, and the right to get basic medical help (Shlapentokh and Woods, 2007). It must be mentioned, however, that the quality of such services in most cases was very low.

One of the major developments of the 1990s after the elimination of the Soviet welfare system was the rapid worsening of already limited social services. The old institutions, such as clinics and schools, remained in place. Yet the economic crisis had nearly emptied the federal budget. The government simply did not have enough resources to maintain a comprehensive welfare state. According to official reports, more than one-third of Russia's total population dropped below the poverty line in the 1990s. In most parts of Russia, people waited for several months to receive their wages and pensions (see Chapter 10). Many medical facilities could not offer even the simplest medical procedures such as vaccinations (National Projects, 2009). The official position of Russian government today is that many serious policy mistakes of the 1990s have caused significant problems in education, health care, housing, and pension systems. One of President Putin's urgent priorities in the early 2000s was to revive social policies. However, he claimed that he had inherited a difficult legacy.

Health problems and population decline

By the early 21st century, the overall health and demographic situation in Russia was gloomy. The mortality rates from heart-related problems were three times as high as in North America and Western Europe. Tuberculosis deaths in Russia were about triple the World Health Organization's definition of an epidemic (50 cases per 100,000 people). About 24,000 Russians died of tuberculosis yearly compared with 650 people in the United States. Average alcohol consumption per capita remained among the highest in the world. Alcohol abuse was a major contributor to serious physical and mental problems. About 1 million people in Russia have been diagnosed with HIV or AIDS (Feshbach, 2008).

Health problems contributed to Russia's steady population decline. Life expectancy rates today remain low, especially for Russian men, who on average are expected to live to 61 years, compared with 74 for women, which is seven to ten years lower than in most developed countries. If this trend continues, almost half of today's 16-year-old young men will not live to see their 60th birthday. Globally, Russia rates below more than 100 countries with higher life expectancy rates. Russia's low birth rates

Table 11.1   *Number of children per family in the Soviet Union and Russia*

1959	1970	1980	1990	2000	2009
2.6	2.0	1.9	1.9	1.2	1.4

Source: Rosstat (2009).

contribute to depopulation as well. More people die in Russia each year (16 per 1000 people) than are born (10 per 1000). In 2008, for example, about 280,000 children were born in Russia and 343,000 people died (Rosstat, 2009). On average, a Russian family has only 1.4 children. To sustain its population, a country should have a minimum of 2.1 children per family. As you can see from Table 11.1, Russia is far below that level. The birthrates have declined significantly since the 1950s, with only a small increase by the end of 2009.

In 2004 Russia had approximately 144 million people. By 2008 the number had declined to 142 million, and it continued to decline through 2009. This is despite a relatively large influx of immigrants: almost 287,000 people came to Russia legally in 2008 alone. More than 20 percent of all people are above retirement age, and the number is increasing. The dwindling population and serious health problems affect the economy. The Federal Labor Service reports that the average age of factory workers in Russia is 53–54. Most vacancies in Russia are for factory jobs. The rural population keeps declining too: many young people move into cities to seek better opportunities. How did the government address these and other social issues and problems?

Health care

The Soviet health care system was federally sponsored but community-based. A resident of a city or town was legally assigned to a local "polyclinic," an outpatient facility bringing together several health specialists under one roof. Scores of community doctors would visit patients in their homes when they become sick. Local hospitals took care of inpatient services. Regional government-run health departments reported to the Health Ministry in Moscow. Overall, the government was capable of monitoring the health of most citizens, fighting infectious diseases, and providing most basic medical procedures.

Life expectancy in the Soviet Union had reached 70 years by the 1970s. The relative effectiveness of the Soviet health care system in the first half of the 20th century was due in part to its low cost. However, after the 1970s, when national health care required massive investments in new diagnostic technologies and treatment methods, the disadvantages of the Soviet social and economic system became obvious. Although the services were free, the waits were long and many procedures or medications were not available. As a result, corruption was rampant (Yakobson, 2009).

After the dissolution of the Soviet Union, 1991 and 1993 federal laws reintroduced a government-sponsored health care system but allowed private options. Most doctors, nurses, and medical technicians remained government employees, with only some joining private clinics and hospitals. The most serious problem of the Russian health care system remained consistent over time: shortages. According to Russian official statistics, the country in 2008 had 50 doctors, and 110 nurses and technicians, to each 10,000 people. However, these numbers mean that less than 60 percent of vacancies for doctors were filled. More than 30 percent of all practicing physicians had not received top-up training for more than five years: training is simply unavailable to them. About two-thirds of motor vehicles used in health care had significant problems because of age or overuse. The government could only finance 30 percent of the technologically advanced medical procedures requested by doctors for their patients (National Projects, 2009).

One of most serious problems that Russia faces is significant alcohol consumption and resulting alcoholism. As a medical and social problem, this is a major contributor to many other health problems in Russia. Some public officials, including the chair of the Federation Council, consider alcoholism a problem related to national security, and have called for government control of the manufacturing and distribution of alcoholic beverages (Mironov, 2009).

Pensions

In the Soviet Union, for many years there was a federal retirement policy according to which every individual was entitled to a federal pension based on their employment history. The retirement age was 55 for women and 60 for men. Local pension offices distributed cash to retired citizens on a monthly basis. In Russia after 1991, the government continued to guarantee pensions. However, the decision was made to create a more effective financial system that would allow better management of payments to Russia's senior citizens. In the late 1990s, the Pension Fund of the Russian Federation was established. After a series of reforms over the past few years, senior citizens' monthly pensions are funded from three major sources: mandatory taxes, insured assets, and special savings. Both individuals and their employers contribute to the fund. This system is complicated, and might have changed by the time you read this (many other financial policies in Russia might undergo rapid changes as well). However, regardless of the technical details, it will probably continue to be based on the Kremlin's current core principle of stimulating a socially oriented market economy. Under this paradigm, social policies are expected to incorporate both government regulations and free market principles (National Projects, 2009).

A portion of the pension fund is guaranteed by the government, but other portions are invested in the market and managed by private firms. Moscow believes this policy can deliver benefits. It encourages people to save more money for their retirement using the private sector, confident that a sizeable portion of their retirement income is already guaranteed by the federal government. It also reduces the government commitment and bureaucratic issues, by decentralizing management of the pension fund. The government remains in charge of the base pension payments, however, whose size is determined under federal law. Between 2007 and 2010, the size of the minimum pension—determined entirely by the Kremlin—went up from approximately 1,700 rubles (approximately US $50) to 2,500 rubles per month (US $80).

Housing

In the Soviet Union, local governments were responsible for housing people. According to the law, every person was entitled to a place to live, but the government did not guarantee its quality. Despite this entitlement, there was a significant housing problem, which the Communist Party openly acknowledged. About one-third of the population at that time lived in substandard accommodation (for example, it was common for two adult children and their parents to live together in a one-bedroom apartment). Very few options existed for families except to rely on the government's goodwill. The problem was that the Soviet government did not have enough resources to solve the housing problem. The Yeltsin administration in the 1990s initiated a major change in housing policy: it rapidly denationalized and privatized property. For a small fee, people could purchase the apartments and houses they were currently living in. By 2004 almost 75 percent of housing facilities in Russia were in private hands. More than 90 percent of all construction companies became private.

Privatization did not resolve the housing problem, which continued through the 1990s and still exists today: there are millions of people in Russia living in overcrowded or poor-quality facilities. Although people can buy and sell property, a substantial portion of the Russian population are still not in a position to purchase their own housing. As a matter of social policy, local authorities maintain official waiting lists of families in need of better accommodation, and hoping to be allocated a federally subsidized apartment or house. Although the overall situation has improved, housing continues to be a serious social problem in Russia today. There are several reasons for this.

First, the volume of residential construction until recently was low. Companies preferred to build more expensive facilities because there was high demand from high-income individuals. The quality of low-priced apartments remained poor. Second, most people who needed to improve their living conditions could not afford an apartment or house. Up until 2010, Russia did not have a reliable system of long-term finance (that is, mortgages) for potential buyers. Only a few banks had developed financing plans, and the interest rates were typically about 25 percent annually for ten-year mortgages. Among those who found the situation most difficult were young people, the disabled, and retirees. The fact that most apartments and houses were purchased for cash had unfortunately created the conditions for fraud and corruption. Third, local authorities did not have effective legal mechanisms for allocating land for the construction of houses and apartments. As a result, according to national surveys in the early 2000s more than 60 percent of Russians were dissatisfied with their housing.

Russians speak their mind ...

... On leaving Russia. Percentage of Russians who answered "no" to the question whether they wanted to move abroad permanently: 80.

Source: Levada (2009j).

Education

Like almost every country in today's world, Russia has compulsory elementary and secondary education. Most children go to school at the age of six, and finish at 17, going through 11 grades in the process. Public education is mostly under the control of local governments, although it is funded from both federal and local budgets. The public school curriculum is generally uniform in Russia: federal institutions are responsible for establishing a standard list of classes and subjects that students must take over the entire course of education. Students in most schools do not choose which classes they want to take, they simply follow the set curriculum. After finishing ninth grade, students can choose whether to continue their studies in high school or enter a professional school, which offers secondary education plus training for a particular profession. High-school students also have the choice of going to college for two years, where they can earn an advanced degree in professions such as nursing, teaching, engineering, or management (this is broadly equivalent to US junior colleges). There are also high schools with a special focus on sports, music, or fine arts. Every kind of public education is free of charge.

Russian laws allow private schools. They are usually better equipped than public schools, and have fewer students per teacher. Tuition fees are very high, however. According to official statistics, more than 14.3 million Russian students are in public schools and only 71,000 attend private schools. Almost 800,000 enter professional schools each year (Rosstat, 2009).

Russians speak their mind ...

... On learning the theory of evolution at school. Percentage of Russians who think that both Charles Darwin's theory of evolution and creationism (the religious argument opposed to evolution) should be taught in Russian schools: 43.

Source: Levada (2009k).

Higher education

A student with a high school diploma or a professional school degree has the right to apply to study at an institution of higher education (which might be called a university, academy, or institute). There is normally a competitive admission process, so would-be students submit recommendation letters, scores for the standard federal exams, and other supporting information. As you might expect, some schools in Russia are more difficult to get into than others. Historically, among the most prestigious schools are Moscow State University and St Petersburg State University (the alma mater of presidents Putin and Medvedev).

In the Soviet Union, all institutions of higher education were under dual federal and local control. Moscow was responsible for budgetary and other strategic decisions; local authorities often took charge of hiring staff, directing research, and other issues. Nevertheless, most undergraduate and graduate schools in the Soviet Union had relative autonomy. This tradition continues today: the law guarantees autonomy to universities and other institutions of higher education. Schools are free to choose their teaching subjects, research programs, and methods of teaching (Federal Law, 1996). Some schools are under the federal government's authority, while other schools report to local governments. There are also private schools, which must be properly licensed to issue academic degrees to their graduates.

About 1.3 million people receive undergraduate degrees each year in Russia. Most students attend state schools and about 20 percent go to private colleges. Undergraduate and graduate education in public schools is free. College students may also receive grants from the government: their eligibility is based on their grades. Today, schools in Russia are allowed to establish pay-per-study plans to enroll additional students with exam grades too low for them to enter conventionally. There are about 68,000 foreign students attending Russian colleges. About a third come from the Commonwealth countries (Ukraine, Belarus, and Kazakhstan in particular). Law degrees and economics degrees are most popular these days: about 40 percent of all students pursue them. Almost a quarter of the population aged between 15 to 34 is engaged in education on either a full-time or part-time basis (Rosstat, 2009).

Government institutions

One of the most substantial innovations in social policies is that the government is giving up its role as the sole distributor of benefits and entitlements. Although the government allocates money, the distribution role is increasingly being assigned to independent institutions, such as funding bodies and local authorities.

Key ministries

Many federal ministries and agencies in the executive branch of the Russian government are responsible for the implementation of social policies. For example, the *Ministry of Health Care and Social Development* conducts federal polices and exercises regulatory functions in the fields of health care, consumer rights, labor policies, and a wide range of social policies. The ministry's 20 departments are responsible for federal strategies in areas such as new medical technologies, social protection, population health forecasts, and health insurance. The ministry is in also in charge of the Federal Pension Fund, and institutions responsible for the mandatory medical insurance, medical supervision, and others.

The *Ministry of Education and Science* carries out federal policy in the fields of secondary education and research. The ministry is charged with directing all elementary and secondary education in Russia, including professional schools. Research is coordinated through various federal programs, grants, exhibitions, and investigative centers. The ministry is also in charge of federal property used for research-related purposes.

Figure 11.1 *The structure of the Ministry of Sports, Tourism, and Youth Policy*

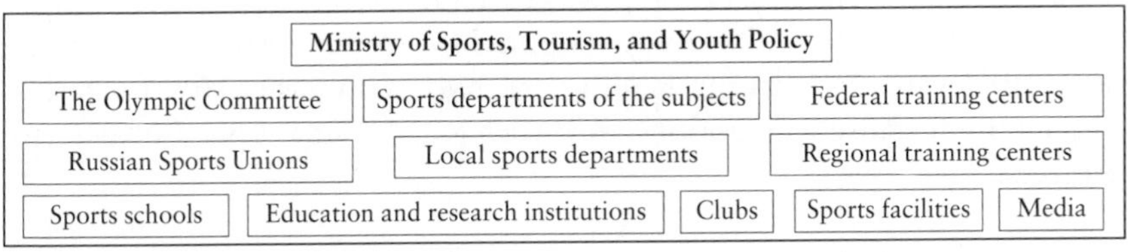

Ministry of Sports, Tourism, and Youth Policy		
The Olympic Committee	Sports departments of the subjects	Federal training centers
Russian Sports Unions	Local sports departments	Regional training centers
Sports schools	Education and research institutions	Clubs	Sports facilities	Media

The *Ministry of Sports, Tourism, and Youth Policy* has to coordinate federal programs related to sports and recreation. Together with local authorities, this ministry directs the activities of specialized sports schools and other sport-related facilities. Many children with potential athletic skills attend special sport schools for free, and compete in sports leagues and tournaments run by local leagues, state, or federal organizations. The ministry is also in charge of Russia's participation in the summer and winter Olympics, including the Special Olympics and Paralympics. See Figure 11.1.

Policy dilemmas

An important measure of any society's success is in its ability to provide effective social services for the young, the old, and the afflicted. In prosperous countries, education, health care, and welfare services are efficient and affordable. However, the debates in such countries continue: who should pay for these services? There are at least two major views. According to the first one, the government's responsibility is to build and protect favorable conditions for wealth creation. Wealth then translates into a wide range of social services and protective policies against unemployment, illness, or accidents. In short, wealth creation is the backbone of social policies. The opposite point of view is based on a different assumption: wealth created under free-market principles does not necessarily translate into effective social policies. Therefore, it should be every government's responsibility to take an active part in the social sphere. From this perspective, wealth redistribution through taxation, and not necessarily wealth creation alone, is the most effective way to address both real and potential social problems.

No matter how well the federal institutions function, they cannot change quickly the difficult situation that Russia was facing in the first decade of the century. Russian authorities have to manage a country with a declining population, low birth rates and life expectancy, significant housing problems, and scores of other social issues. There were two fundamental policy options to address this difficult situation. One option was to move forward slowly but steadily, in the hope that an improving economic situation and high oil and gas prices could bring additional financial resources in the future. Those resources would then be used to address the social problems. The other option was to act decisively and create a stimulus program which would serve as a boost for rapid improvements in the fields of housing, education, health care, and many other social services. The Kremlin chose this option, and introduced a new policy of priority projects.

The National Priority Projects

The Russian government's emphasis on significant improvements in social policies was implemented in the **National Priority Projects** (NPP) program, launched in 2005 with the endorsement and support of President Putin. NPP is a range of massive federal investments and new policies in the fields of health care, education, housing, and agriculture. The ultimate goal of these policies is to dramatically improve the living standards of Russian people in many spheres of their life, and make a major change to the country's declining demographic situation. Russia chose to launch this project in 2005 for four major reasons.

First, by 2005 Russia had accumulated enough resources to finance a massive social program. Very high gas and oil prices had generated extra profits for the Russian budget, so the government could make investments without running the risk of inflation. In simple terms, the Kremlin had enough money to sponsor an ambitious social plan. The second favorable condition was organizational. Because by 2005, the "power vertical" had been established and most leaders of the subjects of the Russian Federation had to be approved by the Kremlin, the government in Moscow had strengthen its ability to manage big social programs on the national level. In short, the Kremlin had accumulated substantial power. Third, in the context of political and financial stability, the government was able to move to a three-year cycle of planning, compared with a year-by-year system of planning in the 1990s. NPP required long-term planning, and this seemed possible: the price of oil was relatively stable, and most economists did not foresee the financial crisis that actually took place in 2008. Finally, this massive social program appeared to be the right thing to do: there was a growing consensus in society that one of the government's policy priorities must be the social sphere.

To coordinate the NPP, former President Putin decided to create and chair a special council comprised of government officials, public representatives, and professional experts. (President Medvedev is now in charge of it.)

The National Health Project

Of course, the government cannot make people healthy or order doctors to cure every patient. The goal of the National Health Project (NHP) was to create conditions under which the health care system could provide its best services in the prevention, diagnosis, and cure of illnesses. The Russian government builds its health care policy on several principles. The most important premise is that health care should be free for every Russian citizen, and the government should pledge its support for this constitutional guarantee. However, this does not mean that every citizen can receive any kind of medical help at any time. The government guarantees only basic medical care for existing conditions. Access to this basic care is equally available to everyone. Russians have to contribute to this basic type of health care through mandatory insurance (a form of taxation). A specialized federal institution manages the insurance-related funds. However, every individual has the right to pay for additional insurance plans, which provide more services and opportunities.

The ultimate goal of the NHP is to reduce the incidence of most illnesses and increase the recovery rates from major complaints. How does the government plan to achieve these ambitious goals? For the foreseeable future, one of the main priorities will be to guarantee the accessibility of health care. In other words, every individual should have easy access to health care outside major hospitals and emergency rooms. To achieve this goal, Russia is working to place more doctors and nurses directly in local communities. For example, the government planned several years ago to have almost 25,000 additional doctors, fully trained and certified to work in communities, including those working full-time on house calls. In addition, it is making substantial investment in purchasing modern equipment for diagnostic and treatment purposes. The wages of doctors and nurses are to be increased so that most of them will not need to seek additional part-time jobs, but will focus instead on their full-time obligations. The government also aims at reducing the patient waiting period for diagnostic procedures to one week.

Some promised benefits are substantial. For example, the medical system is intended to acquire more than 12,700 new vehicles for ambulance and other hospital services. The government will pay for continuing education for thousands of doctors. The plan also calls for reducing the number of fatalities related to car accidents. On average, more than 28,000 people die in car accidents in Russia every year. The plan calls for reducing this number to 25,000. Another target is for death rates related to cardiovascular illnesses to fall from 325 per 100,000 to 250. Despite the economic crisis, Russia has continued to increase its investment in health care (Putin, 2009).

Case in point: Support for families with children

The text of the 2007 Federal Law on Additional Measures of Federal Support for Families with Children is long, and filled with numerous and complicated legal details. However, the essence of the legislation is simple: a family with two children is to receive financial support from the government. Initially, this "mother's capital" or "family capital" sum was 250,000 rubles, which is slightly more than US$7,000 per family. The sum was later increased to more than 300,000 rubles due to inflation. Families eligible for the stimulus money can spend it in three areas: education of their children in Russia, improving living conditions, or investing in the family members' pension plans. (In other words, there are safeguards to ensure they spend it on core goods, and not on luxuries such as fancy clothes, flat-screen TVs, or jewelry.) There was originally a waiting period of three years after the birth of their second child before a family could spend or invest the money. However, a 2008 amendment to the law allows people to use the money toward their mortgages without a waiting period.

This stimulus plan pursued three main goals: to boost birth rates immediately, to help parents improve their housing conditions, and to reinvest some money in pension plans. It is too early to fully assess its results: they will probably become apparent around 2013–15. However, recently Russia's birth rate has gone up slightly, and the Kremlin expects this tendency to continue.

To fulfill these and many other obligations, the government planned to spend almost 350 billion rubles (US$10 billion) between 2007 and 2009, and make new investments after that period. These policies should improve the health situation, keep the labor force intact, and ultimately increase life expectancy in the country. Another radical measure related to demographic policies was to stimulate birth rates. The Kremlin announced a massive stimulus program for families with more than one child (see the Case in point box).

The National Education Project

Compared with health care, Russia's educational system was not in bad shape. Therefore, the goal of the new educational policy is to preserve its strengths and at the same time, substantially modernize it. The educational reform should transform the way children and young people are taught in Russia. Accessibility must remain a high priority, yet market needs must be incorporated too: Russia needs to invest in those educational areas that could produce professionals in the most competitive modern fields. Several approaches are being implemented.

First, the government seeks out, selects, and rewards individual educators, schools, school districts, and whole regions that are engaged in innovative and effective teaching methods. The government will support individual and collective efforts financially. As an example, every year 3000 schools in Russia each get 1 million ruble grants for their innovative programs.

Second, new educational methods will be ineffective if a school does not have material resources or unrestricted access to modern technologies. Thus the federal government will invest in classroom technologies, computers, and internet access. By the time you read this, all Russian schools should be online. To have access to global information is important, but a more basic problem is that many children in Russia find it hard simply to get to their schools, which are often located many miles from their homes. Thus, the government has announced a massive purchase program for school buses, especially for rural areas. Initially, the decision was made to send rural schools more than 3500 buses every year, so that by 2011 all Russian schools that need buses would have them. This is financed from both federal and regional budgets. The government has also launched experimental programs paying 500 million rubles a year to improve the quality of school meals.

Third, one of the keys to success is transparency of education. Schools have to form boards of supervisors or visitors, representatives of local community organizations who will help the school system to become more responsive to parents' requests and societal demands. The government has also started experimental pilot projects to examine ways to reduce administrative control over schools and give them more freedom to make daily decisions.

Fourth, the system of financial support of education needs to change and become more flexible. Schools should be allowed to receive most of their additional funding directly and not through the regional offices. Teachers should be paid for extra work based on the conditions of their work. For example, a teacher working as a class principal should receive an extra 12,000 rubles a year (about US$400). Overall, the plan is for more than 800,000 teachers and other specialists to receive increased salaries. Students who are champions at national and international science or technology fairs (more than 5000 people annually) are to receive cash rewards, of from 30,000 to 60,000 rubles each.

College education

Two major innovations have been proposed in this area. One is the creation of a new type of educational institutions: federal universities. The second innovation is the development of business schools linked to leading foreign universities and colleges, and issuing degrees acceptable in foreign countries. Two of these business schools are being developed today, one in

Moscow, the other in St Petersburg. The latter was created by a special government decree in 2006. It is planned that by 2015 these and several other business schools will have 1200 Russian and 600 foreign students enrolled. They will have an internationally diverse faculty to teach and carry out research. Up to 4000 managers and other professionals will attend short-term educational programs there each year.

Federal universities are relatively large educational and research institutions consolidated out of several existing universities and colleges, and funded by the federal government. The first two schools of this type, the Southern and the Siberian Federal Universities, have been in operation since 2006. The government plans to finance a number of experimental programs there, and create educational centers, research labs, and infrastructure in various fields of science and technology. Each school will have about 40,000 students and 8000 faculty members. If this model is successful (according to the government's plan, these two schools should be among the top 10 Russian schools by 2013), many other universities of similar structure should appear. Overall, 13.4 billion rubles of federal money was invested in these two universities between 2007 and 2009. President Medvedev suggested several sponsors for future federal universities: these include government institutions, the Russian Academy of Sciences, and private businesses.

In 2003, Russia entered the **Bologna Process**, an international initiative to develop a unified standard for academic degrees across Europe (it will involve four-year first degrees and two-year master's degrees, in a similar way to the US system). By 2007, Russia had adopted this two-level degree process.

The National Housing Project

According to government estimates, to solve the housing problem, Russia has to build another 1570 million square meters (one square meter is approximately 11 square feet) of living facilities: in other words, to add one half to the total of existing space in all houses and apartments (National Projects, 2009). The Russian government can no longer afford to provide public housing in the style of the Soviet Union. An ultimate goal of the federal housing project is to create conditions within the market economy that allow individuals with limited means to purchase their own housing, with or without government assistance. For example, by 2010, it is anticipated that at least one-third of Russians will be financially capable of buying real estate using various savings, loans, and credits. The official policy is that in a market economy, the government too should use market means. Four steps are planned.

First, a range of federal programs will provide the conditions to stimulate

> ## Case in point: Russia's demographic situation
>
> Will these new social policies improve the demographic situation? Could financial incentives and better living conditions affect the family in a positive way? Some of the numbers are encouraging, as Russian leaders point out (Putin, 2009a). Back in 2003, the divorce rate was much higher (there were 5.5 divorces and 7.7 marriages annually for each 1000 people) than in 2008 (4.8 divorces contrasted with 9 marriages). Birth rates went up slightly. Life expectancy went up, for men from 59 to 61 and for women from 72 to 74, in just a decade. Infant mortality went down to 10.2 (per 1000) from 11 in 2005. Maternal death also went down from 25.4 to 23.8 (per 1000).
>
> Source: Rosstat (2009).

banks to issue affordable mortgages. In particular, the interest rates on new mortgages should drop (with government assistance) to 8 percent. This will likely boost demand and create an additional supply of apartments and houses. Second, young families will receive special assistance in purchasing their living accommodation. It was planned that by 2010 more than 181,000 young families would improve their living conditions. Third, the Kremlin will create incentives for banks and local authorities to stimulate new construction projects. It will provide federal guarantees for some loans, which will reduce costs, risks, and eventually make these loans more affordable. Finally, several special categories of people, including orphans, military veterans, and the handicapped, will receive individual attention and financial help including loans and grants. The plan will also invest in housing construction for farmers across the country.

Critical thinking about social policies

Both support and criticisms of Russia's social policies come from ideological and pragmatic positions. Ideologues put their beliefs first and then assess policies from their favored point of view. Supporters of pragmatic assessment look at the current Russian social policies and then evaluate their effectiveness.

Ideology-driven opinions

There is serious criticism in the country of the Kremlin's current social policies, especially from the Communist Party and other communist and socialist organizations. Not surprisingly, ideologues on the left believe that all the highly publicized projects and improvements in social policies are just a smokescreen for the Kremlin's major policies supporting big business. Critics on the left also say that both Putin and Medvedev want the people to believe that the country is in "good hands." They want public opinion to remain on the Kremlin's side and help the government to win elections. The critics claim that since 1991, all the governments in the Kremlin had been conducting deliberate economic and social policies to promote inequality. In the eyes of the opposition, the shift toward denationalization and privatization of many industries including health care is another confirmation that the government's goal is to help corporations and big businesses grow stronger, and give them even more power in the country.

Most government supporters claim that the leftist opposition has criticized the social programs for political reasons: the opposition gets more support when the country's economic and social conditions get worse. In a way, the better the Russian people live, the fewer chances the communists and others have politically. Besides, there is no alternative to the current trend of social policies. People will continue to be dependent on the government to some extent, but this dependency must be reduced gradually—and this is exactly what has been happening in Russia during the tenure of Putin and Medvedev.

Other critics disagree: they believe that the current social policies will increase people's dependency on the government for many years to come. On paper, people use the free market to achieve at least some of their dreams: they can buy a house or achieve some financial security. In reality, these plans would be impossible to realize without constant government supervision and huge financial injections into the economy. Many critics of "big government" suggest that despite the Kremlin's claims to be giving people more freedom and incentive, the ultimate goal is to keep all the power in Moscow. Take, for example, the goal of the education reform to stimulate diversity in the methods of education. Private and state schools are in theory equal players in the process. However, some experts maintain that the government is not actually that interested in seeing competition from private schools. Moscow does not want to lose its control over the university system in general (Lukov, 2009).

Russians speak their mind ...

... On human rights. Percentage of Russians who, when asked, "Which human rights do think are most important?" chose "the right to receive free education, health care, and pension and disability benefits" : 68.

Source: Levada (2009a).

Pragmatic assessments

Historically, practically minded critics in Russia have been distrustful of governments' optimistic plans and rosy predictions of rapid improvements. Many skeptics in Russia, for example, compare the ambitious NPPs with the grandiose five-year plans for socioeconomic development in the Soviet Union (see Chapter 2), under which everything in the country's future was carefully planned and predicted. Approved during ostentatious Communist Party congresses, they spelled out many tons of steel the country would produce, how many apartments it would build, and how many liters of milk Soviet citizens would drink. Lots of people did not believe in these promises, and with some reason: many of the targets were not met.

Does this old communist tradition of planning continue in the 21st century? The federal government in Russia has promised to double pensions, deliver buses to rural schools, reduce the incidence of cardiovascular diseases, place federal universities among the top ten Russian schools, increase birth rates, and provide new loans to young families. These might sound like unrealistic promises of everything to everybody. Such bold plans and promises might seem to resemble electoral campaigns in North America and Western Europe, in which candidates often promise remarkable achievements and great benefits to voters. However, in Russia, the announced NPPs are not part of any political campaign. In addition, the government faces some risks: if these promises are not fulfilled, the gloomy social situation may become a substantial liability in forthcoming parliamentary or presidential elections.

Many Russians try to assess social policies from the standpoint of fairness: does the proposed plan benefit everyone equally, or does it bring advantages to one category of people and not to others? As you can anticipate, many elements of social policies can be criticized from this standpoint. For example, take the university system. Who should finance universities? The new reform openly endorses outcome-based financing: an educational institution that achieves good results will receive better funding. However, this strategy creates financial inequality: some schools will become rich while others will struggle. Next, the claim that the government will guarantee equal access to colleges will be impossible to fulfill. About 70 percent of people in Russia believe they do not have access to high-quality higher education (Lukov, 2009) People rightly believe that the rich and the privileged have better access today, but not ordinary people across the country.

The future of the pension system generates concerns too. For example, the goal of the ruling political party was to make everyone's pension correlate with their average salary before retirement (United Russia, 2007). So the more money you make, the bigger your pension will be. This logic most probably sounds reasonable to many observers. To many Russians, however, especially those with low-income jobs, it is fundamentally unfair. They argue that they have been working for 10, 20, even 40 years during which the state promised relatively similar pensions to everyone. Now most of the pot will go to high-income Russians and their lower-income compatriots will get less. Thus inequality becomes institutionalized, in their view.

Many people remain uneasy about involving the market in the pension system. As was explained on page 241, Russians have to contribute portions of their income to special savings funds that will be used for their future pensions. In theory, these contributions should grow over the years as the businesses in which they are invested generate profits. In reality, the pension fund lost almost 20 percent of its value in 2008 and 2009 because of high inflation and unfavorable stock market conditions (New Politics, 2009). Supporters of the market-based plan maintain that this is basically a problem of timing: the plan began to function during an economic and financial downturn. When the market starts to go up, the pension plan will accumulate money. To Russian critics, however, the current losses are what counts, and even if the market does go up again, this has shown that the investments are too risky, and therefore unacceptable.

Conclusion

It is difficult enough to change any country's social institutions, but it is a truly daunting task to transform a massive welfare system rooted deeply in Russian history, culture, and social beliefs. The Soviet Union provided guarantees for healthcare, education, and different forms of social security. It was only minimal support yet it was guaranteed. Today, Russia needs to take decisive steps and implement new policies to bring social policies up to the standards of an advanced European country, or it could abandon any ambitious hopes for improvements and move forward slowly. In reality the Kremlin has decided to move fast, but the actual progress in social policies is slow. The core of the government's approach is pursuit of welfare capitalism, a combination of market economic and financial principles, and massive government participation. This fits with Russia's leaders' prime goal of achieving a socially oriented market economy. Most probably this policy will work. But almost like in the Soviet times, the ambitious plans will be constantly corrected along the way to make them less ambitious, so they will create an impression of a continued success among the government supporters. We can only guess whether and how their opponents will respond.

Chapter 12

Foreign Policy

Key developments
Foreign policy institutions
Foreign policy concepts
Specific policies
Critical thinking about foreign policy
Conclusion

> *This is the world of one master, one ruler. And in the end this is harmful not only to all of those who are within that system, but also to the ruler, because it is destroying [the ruler] from within.*
> Vladimir Putin, 2007, referring to the United States

> *The main threat to our country, to our society, is the idea—that is being driven into the heads of the Russian people—of the existence of a foreign threat.*
> Leonid Radzihovsky, political commentator, 2009

On a typical chilly October morning in 1991, the edition of the major Soviet daily newspaper, *Izvestia*, that appeared in the news kiosks included an interview given by Andrei Kozyrev, the energetic young Russian foreign minister. In response to a question about Russia's future relationship with the west, and the United States in particular, Kozyrev predicted a strong, lasting alliance (Kozyrev, 1991). Seventeen years later, another foreign minister, Sergei Lavrov, speaking before a college audience in Moscow, blasted the United States for its foreign policy, and warned Washington and the west not to make a "historic mistake" in their tough approach toward Russia (Lavrov, 2008).

International alliances and foreign policies change with time. What were the reasons for such a significant change in Russian attitudes? Leaders in the Kremlin blame Washington and its European partners. The western leaders accuse Moscow of changing course. Of course, the true reasons are more complicated. Any country's foreign policy depends on many factors, both domestic and global. Under their influence, Russia has made significant changes in its foreign policy in the past 20 years. In this chapter we examine Russian foreign policy, its current goals, priorities, and decisions. As usual, we first look at key developments in the recent past. These events should help us understand better how Russia conducts its foreign policy.

Key developments

Foreign policy refers to a country's relations with other states and international organizations. In the USSR, policymaking had been the unquestioned purview of Communist Party elites, and Politburo members in particular. Perestroika in the 1980s marked the beginning of serious changes in Soviet foreign policymaking (Dobrynin, 1997).

Russian foreign policy since 1991 has developed in roughly three phases, which we can call accommodation, reorientation, and consolidation. During the early period of the young state, Russia played its role in global affairs by trying to be a key and accommodating partner of the United States and major European countries. As it turned out, however, Russian political elites provided only lukewarm support for the Yeltsin administration's western-oriented policies. Moreover, this support gradually waned (Malcolm, 1995: 26–8). A key turning point was in December 1995, when elections to the State Duma resulted in a large majority of seats going to opponents to "soft" foreign policy. Bowing to pressure from legislators, Yeltsin finally removed Kozyrev and replaced him with a reliable and "tough" individual, Evgeny Primakov—a move cheered by the opposition. Kozyrev's fall also signaled a new age in Russian foreign policy, which began to be shaped primarily by elite power struggles and the search for a new post-Cold War identity for Russia. This involved turning away from the pro-western foreign policy of the early 1990s (Shiraev and Zubok, 2000).

During the second period of reorientation, from 1996 to 2000, Russia began to reconsider its major foreign policy priorities. However, during this period Russian policy was mostly a reaction to international events. In essence, Russia had to be remade as a world actor in a new, post-Cold War world, and forging consensus on a new foreign policy was difficult. Not only was the domestic political context highly contentious, post-Soviet Russia was greatly weakened economically and militarily. Its leaders had to contend constantly with the fact that their country was no longer one of the world's superpowers.

After 2000, when President Putin took office, Russia began to rearrange its foreign policy. It was a stage of "consolidation," as Russian commentators try to portray it today. They refer to Russia's consistent behavior: looking for new useful alliances, strengthening the country's security, and challenging western policies on many issues (Morozov, 2004). Several specific international developments also affected Russia's new foreign policy. Among these events were the conflicts in the Balkans, the expansion of the North Atlantic Treaty Organization (NATO), the conflict around Caucasus, the struggle against international terrorism, the wars in Iraq and Afghanistan, and the status of treaties related to nuclear weapons. The way Russia responded to these problems reflects the evolution of its foreign policy. Let us review these developments.

The war in Bosnia

The civil war in the republics of the former Yugoslavia in the early 1990s, and the western response, provided the first serious point of disagreement between Russia and its western partners. The rising political opposition in Russia considered western pressure against Serbia and Serbian forces in Bosnia as a direct slap in the face to Russia, a historical ally of the Serbian people. Polls showed that a majority of Russians, along with many Russian senior officials, perceived western military intervention in Bosnia as an attempt to punish small Serbia and establish American control over the Balkans (Shiraev and Terrio, 2003). Washington again fell under serious criticism during the US-led NATO military campaign against Serbia in 1999. Russians were especially irritated by what they called the arrogant and irresponsible actions of the western powers against a small but sovereign country in the heart of Europe. This powerful anti-western mood crossed party lines. Even cautious moderate politicians began to issue statements against American and NATO policies. In the wake of the war in Serbia, by the end of the 1990s, opinion polls yielded a steady 60 percent national average of anti-western attitudes, which doubled the ten-year average for anti-western sentiment (Shiraev and Zubok, 2000).

The NATO expansion

After 1991, relations between Russia and the former socialist countries of Central Europe and the Baltic states remained stable but uneasy. The former Soviet satellites wanted to be part of a new, united Europe, defended by American power. In 1994–96 Poland, the Czech Republic, and Hungary gained membership of NATO. Washington supported the expansion of the alliance (Goldgeier, 1999). In 2004, Estonia, Latvia, Lithuania, Slovenia, Slovakia, Bulgaria, and Romania acquired full membership too. Russia, however, viewed NATO's westward expansion as a demonstration of disrespect to Russia's security concerns. Russia accused the United States of deliberately attempting to undermine the post-Cold War strategic balance in Europe. Russians did not understand why NATO forces should be introduced into countries from which Russia had removed its troops in the 1980s. For several years now, the Kremlin has considered any further expansion of NATO as a threat to Russia's national security and a rallying cry to mobilize Russia's nationalistic forces.

Counter-terrorism and Chechnya

In the 1990s Russia had its first series of tragic encounters with domestic terrorism. Waves of deadly attacks against the civilian population were launched by several separatist groups from the Chechen Republic, which lies in the Caucasus region in the southern part of Russia. The Chechen rebels (Russians commonly call them terrorists) claimed that their attacks were in response to Russia's brutal crackdown on the independence movement. Russia, on the other hand, considered Chechnya an inseparable part of Russia, and viewed the terrorist groups as a direct threat to Russia's security (see Chapter 13 on security policies). Moreover, Russia claimed that some foreign organizations and groups had sponsored the Chechen rebels in an attempt to create an Islamic state in the Caucasus region. This assertion by the Kremlin effectively framed the terrorist acts within Russia as an international problem, and not necessarily a purely domestic one.

The events of September 11, 2001 moved both Russia and the United States together in terms of their shared attitude to and policies against international terrorism. It was one of only a few issues over which both capitals have found significant common ground. Both Moscow and Washington began to consider certain forms of Islamic fundamentalism as dangerous to international security. Both countries agreed to collaborate in antiterrorist measures. American policymakers began to see the Chechen problem as Russia's attempt to struggle against international terrorism.

The wars in Afghanistan and Iraq

Russia's response to the US invasion in Afghanistan in 2001 was both emotional and pragmatic. Although President Putin first quickly confirmed his country's strong support of the United States, high-ranking officials in the Kremlin soon articulated the conditions under which Russia would participate in any international actions to support the United States. They clearly signaled that Russia was not giving the United States complete discretion in its actions. Moscow indicated that it would support Washington, but not on all occasions. The idea of direct military action in Afghanistan was unpopular in the Kremlin from the beginning. However, Russia cooperated with United States on intelligence issues, and did not object to America's pursuit of temporary military bases in Central Asia (in Uzbekistan and Kyrgyzstan).

Russia, however, was very displeased with the US invasion of Iraq in 2003. Moscow resisted US initiatives in the United Nations, and even appealed directly to France and several NATO countries, trying to prevent the war. Moscow, in fact, was one of the most vocal opponents of the war. It considered the conflict as a source of instability in the region south of Russia's border. It also viewed the US presence in the region as a form of aggression, expansionism, and neocolonialism.

Nuclear arms talks

Although nuclear security issues are addressed in more detail later in this chapter, it is important to mention the status of negotiations in the recent past between Russia and the United States concerning nuclear weapons, and their impact on Russia's foreign policy. Overall, Washington's decision in the early 2000s to walk away from the Anti-Ballistic Missile Treaty (which limited the ability of both countries to expand the arms race) became very unpopular in Russia. Although this strategic issue was understandable to a very few experts, the government and the media in Russia considered Bush's move to be unwise and dangerous. Most importantly, it evoked old Cold War concerns about the United States seeking unilateral advantages, such as new defense systems, at the expense of Russia, which would not be able immediately to match them.

The Georgia conflict

Georgia, with its capital in Tbilisi, is a former republic of the Soviet Union that is now an independent state. Unfortunately tensions between Georgia and Russia began to increase in the 1990s, and grew into open hostility in the first decade of the 21st century. From Russia's standpoint, Georgia has always attempted to distance itself from its northern neighbor. Moscow accused Tbilisi of deliberate attempts to turn to the European Union, NATO, and the United States, to the detriment of Russia. The Kremlin used Georgia's own problems with two areas with large ethnic populations—Ossetia and Abkhazia—as a source of pressure: Russia began to support ethnic separatists in these areas, which gave Georgia another reason to accuse Russia of anti-Georgian policies. The conflict culminated in summer 2008 in open war between Georgia and Russia. Russia occupied portions of Georgian territory and declared its support for the independence of Ossetia and Abkhazia.

One of the most remarkable issues related to the conflict is the significant difference between the way the conflict was portrayed in Russia and in most other countries. Russia categorically refused to call itself an aggressor, and accused Georgia of war crimes. However, a significant majority of the world's countries condemned the Russian attack on Georgia and did not recognize the independence of the two new states. The Kremlin tended to read this as the rest of the world failing to support Russia's actions simply because Russia had acted independently (Lavrov, 2008).

These and many other international developments provide some evidence about the pattern of Russian reactions in the past, the evolution of its foreign policy methods, and the Kremlin's reactions to other countries' foreign policy decisions.

Before looking at Russian foreign policy, its principles and goals, we will briefly look at the institutions responsible for this policy.

Foreign policy institutions

Perestroika marked the beginning of serious change in Soviet foreign policy institutions in the late 1980s. Most of the restructuring came after Russia gained independence in 1991.

A brief history

Facing immediate and potential domestic problems, President Yeltsin began efforts to keep decisive control over foreign policy. He deliberately enlarged the number of institutions involved in foreign policy in an effort to prevent any one person or institution from gaining power that might rival his own. A relative isolation of foreign policy from democratic control continued through the 2000s: the power remained concentrated in the executive branch. The dominance of the president in foreign policy-making was also formalized in the 1993 Constitution.

While the legislators gained some influence, an oligarchic style of decision making has, of course, long been favored by Russian elites. The public seemed largely content to let their political leaders handle Russia's external affairs.

The Ministry of Foreign Affairs

The Ministry of Foreign Affairs is the federal executive institution responsible for Russian foreign policy. The president is directly in charge of the ministry, which is regulated by established procedures and bylaws (Presidential Decree, January 26, 2007). The ministry's main tasks are to develop strategy in the field of international relations, suggest polices to the president, and exercise the country's foreign policy. Figure 12.1 shows its organizational structure.

The president of the Russian Federation appoints the minister of foreign

Figure 12.1 *Structure of the Ministry of Foreign Affairs*

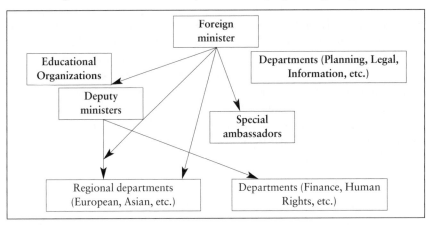

affairs after the chair of the government (that is, the prime minister) submits the name of a candidate. Russia's foreign ministers have vast responsibilities, ranging from signing treaties, negotiating with foreign countries, and coordinating the work of foreign missions, to managing key job appointments within the ministry, reporting to the president, and interacting with the media. Foreign ministers are usually members of Russia's Security Council.

The minister has eight deputies (the number can change) who are in charge of specific regions or areas of activities. As in similar institutions in other countries, the ministry has two categories of departments divided according to their function. There are 15 territorial departments coordinating activities in specific regions of the world or groups of countries. For example, there are four departments dealing with the former republics of the Soviet Union. There is a separate North American Department in charge of the United States and Canada, and a Latin American Department. In addition to the regional departments, there are 22 special departments coordinating particular policies within the ministry or abroad. The minister of foreign affairs, for example, personally manages five departments, including legal, planning, and information. The deputies coordinate territorial and special departments including the departments of International Organizations, Human Rights, Russians Abroad, and Archives. There are also four educational institutions attached to the Foreign Ministry, issuing college degrees in diplomacy and international relations, as well as a Language Institute for future diplomats, analysts, translators, and interpreters.

The ministry has to coordinate its policies with scores of other institutions, ministries, and agencies, including the Ministry of Defense and the Federal Security Service.

Foreign policy concepts

Russia's economic and financial weakness in the 1990s was a substantial factor affecting the country's international behavior. Russian officials became increasingly convinced at that time that most powerful countries had accepted a discriminatory policy of rejecting Russia's interests and treating Russia as a junior partner. This led, from Russia's view, to its isolation and a diminished international role. Many politicians and policy experts in Russia believed that the west was interested in weakening Russia further and even splitting it into several pieces.

The new concept under Putin

In the spring of 2000, a new concept of Russian foreign policy emerged. Commentators in Russia described its basic features in three words: predictability, consistency, and pragmatism (Morozov, 2004). Several key goals became a foundation for this new strategy. Among them were the strengthening of national security and a much bigger role in global affairs (Karaganov, 2007).

At that time Putin and his officials began to talk about the necessity for Russia to pursue its strategic national interests, the most essential strategic goal being to achieve security and well-being for its people. Specifically, it appeared that Russia needed global stability, long-lasting security of its borders, stability in neighboring regions, nuclear non-proliferation, and weakening of the domination of the United States, which was seen as a factor contributing to instability. How would Russia achieve these goals? Several possibilities emerged.

One of the most obvious goals was to develop bilateral relations with as many countries as practically possible. Russia under Yeltsin had neglected many important ties, but Putin now clearly wanted to restore them. Next, Russia had to strengthen existing international institutions such as the United Nations, and develop some alternative organizations. In relations with Washington, Moscow underlined the importance of parity and equality. One of the main doctrines promoted by the Kremlin in the 21st century has become the concept of a **multi-polar world** in which no country claims military and economic domination or takes advantage of its own strength at the expense of other countries. Instead, several states working through international organizations should form long-term peaceful alliances working for global security and economic prosperity. The pursuit of a multi-polar world—which is, in fact, a continuous attempt to reduce US influence in most parts of the world—has become Russia's dominant strategy in foreign policy (Concept, 2000a).

One of the first steps to implement the emerging new strategies was

Moscow's attempts to consolidate some of the former Soviet republics, now independent countries. The Commonwealth of Independent States (see Chapter 3) was a loose and inefficient alliance. Most countries preferred bilateral relations with one another without using the framework of the Commonwealth. Putin needed better ties with these countries for three reasons. First, Russia needed guarantees of stability near its own borders. Second, a more efficient alliance of states could have had significant and positive economic consequences for Russia and other countries. Third, more manageable and friendly neighbors could have allowed Russia to switch attention to other, more serious international problems.

But how could Russia consolidate these countries? Moscow chose a simple "carrot and stick" approach: a combination of incentives and sanctions. The countries willing to cooperate with Russia would receive maximum economic and political benefits. The countries unwilling to join would not. As a result, after 2000, Russia had to deal with at least two groups of former republics of the Soviet Union. Belarus, Kazakhstan, Armenia, Kyrgyzstan, and Tajikistan formed the first group. Other countries including Ukraine, Georgia, Moldova, Azerbaijan, and Uzbekistan were reluctant to move closer to Moscow. Uzbekistan later changed its position. The three Baltic republics, Estonia, Latvia, and Lithuania, were leaning clearly toward the west, and had no intention of considering any alliance with Russia. They were also members of NATO. These countries would witness a lengthy period of unenthusiastic relations and occasional tensions with Russia.

The next step was the creation of a system of collective security in Eurasia. The participating countries signed a treaty containing certain security and mutual protection guarantees, which in reality meant that Russia would now take on a more robust role in the affairs of the participating countries.

Continuation under Medvedev

The continuing strategy of Russian foreign policy under President Medvedev after 2008 incorporated the belief that Russia's role in international affairs had increased, and as a result the country had to assume even greater responsibility for global developments. According to the official strategy for foreign policy, Russia has to pursue several important goals (Concept, 2008): see Figure 12.2.

The first goal is national security and territorial integrity of the country. Next, Russia needs to create favorable external conditions for itself, which will also ensure its competitiveness in a globalizing world. Further, Russia should pursue a just and democratic world order based on collective decisions and international law. Russia is also interested in maintaining good

Figure 12.2   *Russian foreign policy under Putin and Medvedev*

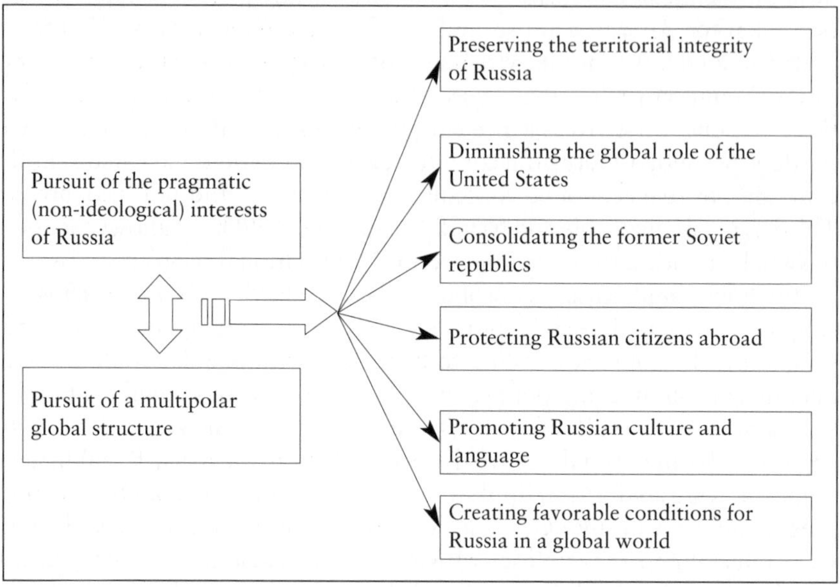

neighborly relations with bordering states, and it will seek to eliminate potential tensions and conflicts. Russia will protect the rights of Russian citizens and compatriots abroad. And finally, one of the goals of Russian foreign policy is the active promotion of Russian language, culture, and an overall positive image of a "socially oriented market economy" and an independent foreign policy (Concept, 2008).

Now let us look at specific Russian policies at the beginning of the second decade of the 21st century. We will consider three major areas: relations with the former Soviet republics, relations with the west, and policies related to China.

Specific policies

For many decades, relations among the republics within the Soviet Union were a domestic policy issue guided by the Communist Party. After 1991, this was no longer the case and Russia had to develop diplomatic relations with 14 independent states.

The former Soviet republics

Among the key priorities were relations with two Slavic nations on Russia's western and southwestern borders, Ukraine and Belarus. The relations between Russia and Belarus have remained friendly since 1991. The authoritarian government of Alexander Lukashenko in Minsk maintained a stable and relatively predictable pro-Moscow policy, despite several setbacks caused by occasional disagreements between the two states about economic and trade policies. Both countries maintain similar or comparable views on most international problems, including a critical view of NATO and some policies of the European Union. Both Russia and Belarus disagree with western criticism of Belarus's authoritarian domestic policies.

Besides Belarus, a friendly Ukraine is vital for Russia's strategic interests. Ukraine has access to the Black Sea, which is essential for the functioning of the Russian Navy in that region. By agreement the Russian Navy is still stationed in Sevastopol, a Ukrainian city on the Crimean peninsula. Close to a quarter of the total population of Ukraine are ethnically Russian, and in some regions about 50 percent of the population are Russian. Russia maintains the position that it cares about the rights and legitimate interests of the Russians living in Ukraine. Ukraine is one of largest buyers of Russian oil and gas. Growing trade and active economic cooperation between these two countries is essential to both of them, and

Map 5   *Russia and its 14 former republics*

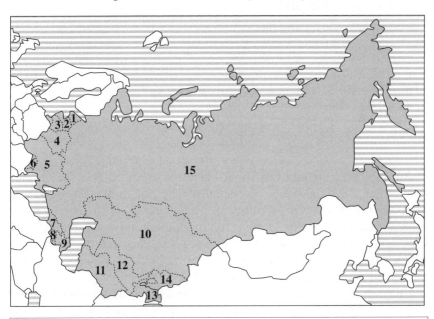

1 – Estonia	6 – Moldova	11 – Turkmenistan
2 – Latvia	7 – Georgia	12 – Uzbekistan
3 – Lithuania	8 – Armenia	13 – Tajikistan
4 – Belarus	9 – Azerbaijan	14 – Kirgizstan
5 – Ukraine	10 – Kazakhstan	15 – Russia

should always be a mutual priority, according to Russian politicians (Ivanov, 2001).

However, Russian relations with Ukraine remain "uneasy," as Moscow has officially admitted (Medvedev, 2009). Ukraine was reluctant to respond to Russia's call for a closer integration. Several key problems between the countries remain. The first one is economic. For several years Russia accused Ukraine of taking (stealing, in non-diplomatic language) substantial amounts of the natural gas that was delivered to Central Europe through gas pipelines that crossed Ukraine's territory. The second lingering problem is related to the Russian Navy. The official position of Ukraine is that Russia must eventually cease to have a naval base on Ukrainian territory. Russia insists in return that for the Russian Navy to leave Sevastopol would hurt Moscow's security interests. Russia also maintains that the Crimean peninsula has always been part of Russia. In an unfortunate turn of events, this territory was given to Ukraine by former Soviet Prime Minister Khrushchev about half a century ago. Overall, Russia is looking for a compromise in this problem and trying to legitimize its presence on the peninsula. Ukraine is not willing to agree.

Russians speak their mind ...

... On opinions about Ukraine. Percentage of Russians expressing a negative view about Ukraine: 62. Percentage expressive positive views: 29. In contrast, percentage of Ukrainians expressing positive views of Russia: 91. Percentage of Russians wanting to see both countries as independent and friendly states: 68. Percentage of Russians believing that Russia and Ukraine must unify: 23.

Source: Levada (2009l).

Another difficult point in Russia–Ukraine relations was the Orange Revolution, a massive public protest movement that took place in Ukraine in 2004–05. These events resulted in the election of a pro-western president, Victor Yushchenko. It is a common opinion in Russia, especially in pro-government circles, that the election of Yushchenko was planned and sponsored somewhere in the west, and that the western powers, probably the United States, played a very active role in the elections.

Chapter 10 discussed the "Gas War" and resulting tensions between Ukraine and Russia. Another significant obstacle between these two countries is the open question of whether Ukraine should become a member of NATO. Russia has maintained the position that it is also essential for Moscow's strategic interests that Ukraine does not join NATO. Although most Ukrainians, according to opinion polls, continue to reject NATO membership (Umland, 2008), Moscow believes that the Ukrainian government might ignore public opinion and seek to join.

Another key vector of Russia's foreign policy is its relations with some key Eurasian states, which are also former Soviet republics. Russia's key interests focus on several issues. The first and most important one is security. Russia is very much interested in having stability in these countries, which are predominantly Muslim (except for Georgia and Armenia). Therefore, the Kremlin prefers to support authoritarian regimes that guarantee security, rather than run a significant risk of supporting free elections and potentially sacrificing regional stability. For example, having a stable and secure Central Asia means to Russia a diminishing threat of international terrorism. Russia coordinates antiterrorist policies in the region, and provides security for the governments of the Central Asian region.

The second issue is energy resources. Azerbaijan's oil industry is clearly important, and there are potentially vast sources of natural gas in Turkmenistan and oil in Kazakhstan. Russia wants to make sure that it will play some role in the extraction and delivery of these resources. Moscow's goal is to prevent foreign countries from getting into these regions and offering economic and financial assistance to local governments in exchange for their loyalty.

Another important issue is drug trafficking. Probably more than half of all drug shipments to Europe go through Central Asia. Russia has a vital interest in cutting off the supply routes. No less important for the Kremlin is the status of the Russian-speaking population in these states, especially in Kazakhstan, which has a large proportion of ethnic Russians.

The relations between Russia and Georgia are one example of Russian failure to maintain stability on its borders and develop friendly ties with a former republic of the Soviet Union. The conflict between Russia and Georgia was briefly described early in this chapter. Moscow has been profoundly disappointed by the western and US reactions to the conflict, and continues to accuse Georgia of unfriendly politics. Regardless of different interpretations of the causes and results of the conflict, Russia has mishandled its relations with Georgia, and this failure has resulted in almost unanimous criticism and condemnation abroad. Russia came out of this conflict with a damaged international reputation. The status of Abkhazia and Ossetia, whose independence Russia has supported in 2008, remains a source of international disagreement.

The west

Russia is a part of the west not only geographically (as a part of Europe) but also culturally. It is interested in maintaining stable and productive political, cultural, and economic relations with all western states. However, numerous problems have existed in the past, and there continue to be problems in Moscow's relations with most European countries and North America.

There are still no better than lukewarm relations between Russia and the former European socialist countries, including the Baltic republics. A defining moment in determining Russia's attitude to these countries was their decision to join NATO. Although Russia has made continuous attempts to improve economic and political ties, the older shadow of the Soviet Union and unfortunate memories of the past continue to dominate its relationship with these countries. Very often Russia labels the policies of these countries as "unfriendly." In a similar fashion, Russia's policies (such as trade wars or gestures in support of the Russian-speaking population in the Baltic countries) are criticized as irresponsible.

Russia's relations with Western Europe are ambivalent. It pursues a robust policy of cooperation with any European country that is willing, in turn, to cooperate with it. It is a strategic foreign-policy goal of Russia to be a respectable partner and an effective G-8 member. Yet one of Russia's key interests is to diminish the influence of the United States on European affairs, or plant disagreements between Washington and Western Europe.

Of all West European countries, the United Kingdom is probably the most inconvenient partner from Russia's point of view. Several events have contributed to the worsening of mutual relations between these two countries. In 2003 Russia requested the extradition (legal expulsion) from Great Britain of several Russian citizens who were under criminal investigation in Russia. One was Boris Berezovsky, a billionaire and close ally of former President Boris Yeltsin. Berezovsky had sought and received political asylum in the United Kingdom, and the extradition request was refused, which caused significant displeasure in Moscow. In 2007 it was London's turn to ask for an extradition. This time, the case was related to the poisoning with a radioactive substance of a former Russian security officer, Alexander Litvinenko, who died in London under suspicious circumstances (you can read more about this case on the book's website). The British government wanted to extradite from Russia a main suspect in this case. The Kremlin refused, citing a law prohibiting the extradition of Russian citizens to foreign countries. These and other disagreements have unfortunately disrupted contacts in business, diplomatic, and cultural areas.

Russians speak their mind ...

... On the Litvinenko case. Percentage of Russians believing that the Litvinenko murder was committed by Russian secret agents: 10. Percentage believing that the murder was an anti-Russian provocation: 36.

Source: WCIOM (2009h).

Table 12.1   *The general attitudes of Russians to the United States*

Attitude/ year	1990	1995	2000	2005	2009
Very good/good	73	65	67	60	46
Very bad/ bad	7	13	22	32	40
Don't know	20	22	12	8	14

Source: Levada (2009q).

On paper, Russia has tried to build up its relations with the United States, taking into account mutually advantageous bilateral trade, economic, scientific and technological, and other forms of cooperation. Russia acknowledges the key US influence on global strategic stability. Moscow wants to have a continued dialogue with the United States on foreign policy, security, and strategic stability issues. Unfortunately, since 2003 the relations between these two countries have deteriorated. Opinion polls reflect these political difficulties (Table 12.1). There are several reasons for Russia's failure to get on with the United States.

Moscow disapproved of the US war in Iraq, did not support the expansion of NATO, opposed the US proposal to install an early warning radar system in Central Europe (which Russia claimed would reduce Russia's capability for nuclear response should it be attacked), criticized Washington's support of Ukraine, and was furious about US support for Georgia during the 2008 conflict. Russian foreign policy officials insist that the United States treats Russia as a second-tier country, important only because of its possession of nuclear weapons. The Russian government has continued to promote a negative image of the United States and its western allies (Simes, 2007: 47). The United States, in turn, criticizes Russia for its attempts to restore the imperial might of the Soviet Union, its support of several countries unfriendly to the United States (such as Venezuela and Iran), and numerous moves which suggest unfriendly intentions toward the United States and its partners.

Since President Obama came to power in the White House, both sides have attempted to "reset" their relations and resolve their differences. According to Moscow, Russia's long-term policy priority should be to put its relationship with the United States on a foundation of pragmatism and respect for the balance of interests (Concept, 2008). One of the main concerns for Russia is its relations with America regarding nuclear security. This is discussed in Chapter 13.

Russians speak their mind …

… **On Obama.** Percentage of Russians who supported Obama as a candidate for the US presidency: 35. Percentage supporting McCain: 14. Other people did not have a preference or did not know much about the US elections.

Source: Levada (2008g).

In relation to NATO, Russia claims that it is trying to be less ideological and more practical (Concept, 2008). Russia sees several possible areas of cooperation related to responses to common threats, such as terrorism, the proliferation of weapons of mass destruction, regional crises, drug trafficking, and natural and human-induced disasters. The NATO–Russia Council, created in 2002, is an international institution to coordinate the interaction between NATO and Russia. The council contains more than 25 subdivisions including formal permanent committees, less formal working groups, and informal expert gatherings. These bodies are working on diplomatic issues, assessments of global and regional threats, and antiterrorist and anti-drug trafficking training. However, several problems began to rise during the past few years.

Russia continues to oppose NATO's plans to expand eastward. Moscow has softened its language about the expansion, arguing primarily that the people of Ukraine and Georgia must decide this issue themselves without foreign pressure (Medvedev, 2009). The NATO countries, on the other hand, opposed the decision of the Kremlin in 2007 to reintroduce Russian Air Force long-range air patrols over the Atlantic Ocean for the first time since the Cold War. NATO was also alarmed by Russia's decision in 2007 to suspend its participation in the Treaty on Conventional Armed Forces in Europe. This 1992 treaty established limits on conventional forces in Europe to provide guarantees that no country would take advantage of others by a sudden military move. Russia argued that the new realities of post-Cold War Europe have changed, and not in its own favor. A bigger NATO puts Russia in a vulnerable position.

Russians speak their mind …

… **On NATO.** Percentage of Russians in 1997 believing that Russia had reasons to be afraid of the NATO countries: 60. Percentage of Russians in 2009 believing that Russia has reasons to be afraid of the NATO countries: 62. Percentage of Russians thinking that NATO membership would serve Russia's interests: 3.

Source: Levada (2009m).

Eurasia and China

Russia's Eurasian policies are not limited to the former Central Asian republics of the Soviet Union. The country's fundamental goal in this region is to create a favorable geopolitical environment to provide stability, security, and economic growth. A stable central Asia is vital for Russia's security. Therefore, security concerns frequently overshadow other interests and policies. Russia pays serious attention to any radical violent groups in the region, and assists local governments in counter-terrorism activities. The second major goal is economic. Russia needs to sell its natural resources to the energy-demanding economic regions of Asia, and receive manufactured products from Asian countries such as China.

Russia's concern about China's growing economic might is coupled with both countries' desire to expand their mutual ties. From the economic standpoint their cooperation is mutually beneficial. China needs Russia's natural resources, including gas and oil; Russia needs Chinese manufactured products. Both countries are interested in maintaining stability in Asia, and both oppose ethnic separatism, including Islamic fundamentalism. A common unifying goal for Moscow and Beijing is to create a global center of power to counterweight both the United States and Western Europe. However, this is a very delicate issue: Russia does not want to see a very powerful China at its borders. Russian nationalist groups insist that the ultimate goal of China is to capture Russian resources, and not necessarily through the use of force. There are several peaceful ways, such as deepening Russia's dependency on Chinese products, or the migration of Chinese peasants and workers into the vast areas of Russian Siberia and Far East.

Meanwhile, in 2001 Russia and China signed a new cooperation treaty. The previous treaty, signed in 1950, had expired in 1980, when relations between the two countries were tense. In 2005 the State Duma ratified an agreement between China and Russia on state borders. In the political sphere, Moscow supported Beijing's anti-separatist policies in Tibet, and received support for its own actions in Chechnya. Russia also supports the "one China" policy, and believes that Taiwan (now a self-proclaimed independent state) is an inseparable part of China. Both countries also need each other in their dealings with North Korea.

In 1996 Russia and China, together with Kazakhstan, Kyrgyzstan, and Tajikistan, formed a group that became in 2001 the **Shanghai Cooperation Organization**. Uzbekistan joined the group later that year. The initial purpose of the group was to eliminate border disputes, reduce the presence of the countries' military forces near state borders, and coordinate efforts related to the countries' mutual security. One mutual concern is the fight against ethnic separatism and terrorism. Mutual activities of the group also include joint military antiterrorism training and cooperation in antidrug policies. The countries have also begun to coordinate their efforts in economic, investment, and trade areas. China is pushing for more economic cooperation. Russia, however, gives top priority to the field of international security.

Russia also maintains a positive attitude about creating a strategic alliance between India, China, and Russia. However, all three countries realize that such an alliance might cause an alarming reaction from the rest of the world. Most countries would see this development as an attempt to destabilize the global situation, which could eventually lead a significant arms race in Eurasia. Therefore, China and India tend to be cautious about joining new alliances. See the book's website for updates related to Russia's foreign policy in the Middle East, Africa, Latin America, and Moscow's relations with Iran and other countries.

Critical thinking about foreign policy

How can we understand Russia's foreign policy and the changes that have taken place in Moscow's relations with other countries since the late 1990s? Any country's foreign policy is based on its security concerns and on specific economic and political interests and aspirations. Foreign policy is also based on a country's *ideology*, a predominant set of beliefs about its position in the world, friends and foes, role in international affairs, and the direction of global developments.

Does Russia have enemies?

A popular position in Moscow is that Russia is surviving in a primarily hostile environment dominated by foes led by the United States and its most loyal western allies. Russia's mission in this international context is to resist foreign threats and form alliances to counterweight the power of these opponents. This point of view was at the core of the Soviet Union's foreign policy strategy. A similar view is still maintained by the current Communist Party of Russia, which continues to see most domestic and international developments from the prism of class struggle, and poor nations' fight for economic and political independence against western imperialism.

The idea that Russia is surrounded by sworn enemies also finds support among many noncommunist groups of nationalistic persuasion. They see most global developments from either geopolitical or cultural perspectives. Accepting in general the idea about the "clash of civilizations," they maintain that Russia as a Slavic and Christian Orthodox nation is under siege.

Big corporations, the Catholic Church, Islam, and Asian cultures, are all trying to diminish Russian influence globally. Some representatives of this diverse group insist that Russia should conduct isolationist policies. Others, like the Liberal Democratic Party, prefer to pursue pragmatic alliances with China and India against Western Europe and America. These views do not find open support in the Kremlin. Both Medvedev and Putin promote Russia's global leadership position and an active role in international affairs.

Russia has interests

It appears that the Kremlin is leaning toward another strategy in foreign policy. This is based on the belief that Russia must actively pursue its strategic interests. Very often, these interests are different from the interests of other states, so the goal of Russia's foreign policy is to win as many strategic battles as possible by peaceful means, including diplomacy or economic incentives.

In fact, experts have showed that Russia does have different strategic interests from the United States (and other western countries) (Simes, 2009). For example, Russia needs to sell its energy resources such as oil and gas in large quantities and for a high price. The West consumes natural resources from Russia but is interested in buying them at a lower price. Therefore, Russia would support any international developments that eventually lead to higher energy prices. The west, naturally, would oppose such developments. Next, Russia emphasizes its role as an energy producer. It does not hesitate to put pressure on its neighbors such as Ukraine by cutting off gas supplies. The west generally rejects such policies. Russia also has a vital interest is in keeping foreign powers away from Central Asia to thwart their attempts to gain access to natural resources there. Moreover, most western governments support the idea of preserving the NATO alliance. Russia does not believe that this organization is necessary. Moscow believes that the west wants to continue to oppose Russia politically and militarily. The list of differences can be easily continued.

How can Russia use these differences to advance its strategic interests? Several possibilities exist. For instance, by opposing the NATO expansion, Russia could compel the west to bargain with Moscow, which could eventually gain significant economic and political benefits out of that bargain (Clover and Blitz, 2009). Alternatively, by offering economic incentives to China, Russia could secure Beijing's support at the United Nations. It might also supply Iran with antimissile land systems, which would make it a very important player in the complex relations between the west and Iran.

Do other views exist of Russian foreign policy, different from the "carrots and sticks" approach? How popular are nonconfrontational approaches?

Russia as part of the west

Supporters of this point of view maintain that both ideological and "national interest" doctrines are ineffective and dangerous. In the end, these strategies would devastate Russia financially, isolate it politically, create new enemies, and reverse the democratic gains of the past decade.

The critics of the hawkish approach to foreign policy have a point. As far as their argument goes, since Putin came to power, despite significant gains in the number of diplomatic contacts, signed treaties and protocols, Russia's position in the world has become less secure. In the westward direction, Russia probably has only one reliable partner, Belarus. Relations with the Baltic states were at a historic low in the early 21st century. It has not succeeded in improving its relations with the former socialist countries of Central Europe including Poland, the Czech Republic, and Hungary, and has worsened its relations with the United Kingdom and the United States. Russia's actions in Georgia produced overwhelming international condemnation, which Russia refused to understand, making things even worse. Moscow continues to accommodate North Korea, whose dangerous behavior has irritated Japan, South Korea, and many other countries. It continues to support an unpopular nuclear program in Iran, again distancing itself from many countries. In Latin America, Russia supports left-wing governments, sacrificing its vital relations with Washington by embracing Hugo Chavez in Venezuela and the antiquated communist regime in Cuba.

Overall, Russia's position has worsened, and the only way to reverse the negative trend is to accept a radically different approach to foreign policy. A change in Russian polices would remove many trade barriers between Russia and the United States, improve Moscow's relations with Europe, and contribute to substantial changes in global affairs. Accommodation is better than confrontation. This point of view, however, although it was popular in the early 1990s, does not now find significant support in the government or the media. The changes proposed by the Obama administration in 2009 were considered by some commentators in Russia as concessions Washington made as a result of Moscow's tough line in foreign policy. Therefore, quite a few American experts suggest that Washington needs to facilitate Russia's integration into global markets, but reject Russia's attempts to pursue anti-American policies (Cohen and Ericson, 2009). Many predict that relations between Russia and the west could be tense for years to come.

Choosing a tough line

At the beginning of the 21st century, Russian foreign policy strategists generally rejected the accommodationist approach and focussed on the strategic national interest. Quite often, ideological elements are also used to justify Russian activity in global affairs. Several factors, both domestic and international, have shaped this policy.

The first group of factors is related to the foreign policy of other states. Russia chose to overlook many positive development in Russia–west relations during the 1990s (Rivera and Rivera, 2009) and began to focus on problems instead. For example, the continuing NATO expansion has been an issue of major concern to Moscow. The civil war in Bosnia in the early 1990s and the conflict in Kosovo were seen differently in Moscow from how they were perceived in Paris, London, and Washington. The Russians believed that the conflict in the former Yugoslavia was for the most part a coordinated western aggression against Serbia. When the US-led coalition forces invaded Iraq in 2003, Russian–American relations reached their lowest point since the Cold War. The western support of Georgia in 2008 convinced many Russians that Moscow's foreign policy actions are simply not welcome in the west.

The second group of factors is related to Russia's domestic situation. Russia has learned that it can act independently and decisively against threats such as separatism in Chechnya. In the wake of terrorist attacks on Russian soil, including suicide bombings in Moscow, airplane crashes, and the killing of hundreds of children and adults in Beslan (see Chapter 13 for details), most Russians showed their support for the federal authorities in their pledge of world-wide unilateral actions against terrorism. Nevertheless, many Russian officials are convinced that their country is not allowed to confront terrorism, in Chechnya in particular, in the way Moscow wants to fight it. Many people saw this as another proof that the west applies one set of rules to its own policies and another set to Russia's.

The third factor was cultural-psychological. Washington's crucial error back in the 1990s was its tendency to treat post-Soviet Russia as a defeated opponent. The United States and the west might have "won" the Cold War, but this did not mean defeat for Russia (Simes, 2007: 36). By the mid-2000s, Russian foreign policy had become nationalistic. In numerous statements coming from the Kremlin and other federal offices, Russia constantly reminded its western neighbors that it is a formidable power to reckon with (Legvold, 2007). For a decade, Russians have been repeating the arguments about the world's multi-polarity, with Russia as a power center. An increasing number of Russians have come to doubt that American economic models, the principles of free market capitalism, and civil liberties can take root in Russia.

Considering these factors, some commentators suggest that Moscow is simply not interested in having good relations with Washington or the west (Golz, 2009). Anti-western policies could actually benefit Russia. First, having an external enemy will help the government to mobilize people around the idea that their nation is in danger. Second, by annoying Washington or London, for example, Russia could gain bargaining chips and earn substantial concessions.

However, there is some reason for hope about several constructive trends in Russia's foreign policy.

Looking for common ground

Presidents Putin and Medvedev have tended to maintain a pragmatic foreign policy aimed at an effective, although somewhat limited, partnership with the west, and the United States in particular. Many analysts admit that although relations between the Kremlin and the White House have indeed often been unfriendly and tense, Russia has never been a direct adversary of the United States (Trenin, 2003; Simes, 2007).

The first issue that brought Russia and the west closer together was the possibility of joint action against international terrorism. A working coalition between Moscow and Washington, for example, created a convenient and reliable basis for broader cooperation (Goldgeier and McFaul, 2003). In addition, an umbrella of "collective action" would allow Moscow and Washington to pursue independently their national objectives: fighting specific violent radical groups.

Second, Russia shares a growing international concern over the proliferation of weapons of mass destruction. After 2000, Russia began to work on policies and specific programs to secure nuclear, chemical, and biological materials all over the world.

Third, Russia shares global concerns about regional security, and in particular the situation in Afghanistan, Iraq, Pakistan, and around Iran. Russia as a member of the Security Council, did not support the 2003 US-led war in Iraq, but it is not motivated to see an unstable regime in Baghdad. Russia also wants to see a peaceful and stable Afghanistan and genuinely concerned about the ongoing war in this country while supporting the US anti-Taliban policies there (Katz, 2009)

The fourth shared issue is related to oil. The "oil card" has increasingly played, and will continue to play, a very important role in Russian foreign policy, and this is likely to tie together Russian and western interests. In fact, Russia might become a main supplier of oil to the United States and Western Europe, and help drive energy prices down as a means to win a share of the western market.

Conclusion

As a sovereign and powerful country, Russia is developing an independent foreign policy and pursues its own strategic interests. These interests often differ from the interests of the United States, the United Kingdom, Germany, and their allies. In the geopolitical context, Russia feels insecure about NATO and its possible expansion in the future. Having its own oil and gas supplies, Russia uses them as bargaining chips in foreign policy. Russia is also becoming a viable competitor for global energy resources. Ideology sometimes becomes a serious factor determining Russia's international moves. For example, Russia is extremely sensitive about its treatment as a junior partner; it is determined to become an equal player in global affairs. Russia continues to commit significant errors in foreign policy, and in fact its relations with many countries have worsened over the past few years. However, Russian foreign policy is more pragmatic and predictable than it was ten years ago. Russia is interested in global stability. Moscow pursues nuclear nonproliferation, supports antiterrorist policies, and hopes to expand trade and other forms of economic cooperation.

Probably these few points of agreement and areas of cooperation are not the only goals that Russia hoped to achieve in its ambitious foreign policy. In many ways, the government in the Kremlin hoped for a break from the Soviet past. Unfortunately, it remains shackled to it.

Chapter 13

Defense and Security Policies

Key developments
The commander in chief
The Defense Ministry of the Russian Federation
Military policies
The Federal Security Service
The External Intelligence Service
Counter-terrorism policies
Critical thinking about defense and security policies
Conclusion

Money, bribery, extortion, amnesty for old crimes—these are their methods of recruitment.
Nikolai Patrushev, Former chair of the Federal Security Service (2007), on foreign attempts to undermine Russia's security

Both the traditional Russian religions and a nuclear shield are the components that strengthen Russia's statehood, and create conditions for providing both external and internal security of the country.
Vladimir Putin, press conference, February 1, 2007

Do western countries have reasons to be afraid of Russia? When asked this question in a national poll, 32 percent of Russians agreed. Does Russia have reasons to be afraid of the west? More people, 62 percent, agreed (Dubin, 2008c). Many Russian people genuinely believe that Russia is surrounded by enemies attempting to harm their country, steal its secrets, buy the country's domestic political opposition, lie about the Kremlin leaders, weaken the military, and reduce birth rates. After a brief period of "relaxation" in the 1990s, the Russian government began a new campaign of boosting national security and creating an impression that Russia was under constant threat.

Key developments

Defense and security are two major and interrelated areas of concerns of every state. Defense policies typically involve the use of a country's armed forces, while security policies commonly include a broader set of actions including military and nonmilitary responses. Several developments have influenced the current state of Russia's defense and security policies.

Soviet policies

Defense and security were key policies of the former Soviet Union, heavily influenced by the imperatives of the communist ideology. During more than 70 years, the Soviet Union's official defense doctrine included the central idea that the country was surrounded by powerful enemies. The Soviet ideology maintained a belief in the inevitability of a conflict between communism and western imperialism. The Military-Industrial Commission, a powerful division of the central apparatus of the Communist Party of the Soviet Union, gained substantial power in the country, especially the 1970s. The officials of this Commission were allied with the Soviet military establishment, and supervised thousands of plans, factories, and scientific labs working on defense projects. By arguing that the Soviet armed forces were inferior to the US forces, they effectively manipulated the fears of powerful Communist Party leaders. As a result, the military-industrial lobbyists in the USSR could obtain significant resources from the government. Constant justification of the existence of foreign threats was part of the Soviet defense policies.

Security policies in the Soviet Union were directed and coordinated by a central agency, which has been known since 1954 as the *Committee of State Security*. This organization is better known as the KGB, according to its Russian abbreviation. The Constitution of the Soviet Union contained no mention of this agency, yet the KGB acquired significant political power, becoming virtually a special secret establishment under the direct control of the secretary general of the Communist Party. The main functions of the KGB included defending the country from foreign and domestic enemies, and protecting the country's borders (Petrov and Kokurin, 2003). However, the KGB is particularly known in history for its domestic activities against political opposition, independent thought, and free speech. Every large professional organization in the Soviet Union, such as a university, factory, or hospital, had a "supervisor" employed by the KGB whose responsibilities included gathering information about potential threats to the regime. Among these threats were serious actions such as spying or disclosing military secrets, as well as minor offences including critical comments about party leaders, reading religious literature, possession of foreign magazines, or foreign currency. Vladimir Putin, the future president and prime minister, served in a similar position at Leningrad State University.

Changes during perestroika and after

The last Soviet leader, Mikhail Gorbachev, came to believe that the security of his country could be achieved only within a broader context of international cooperation and disarmament. The policies of glasnost also diminished the importance of the KGB and domestic spying. Boris Yeltsin and the new Russian leaders after 1991 faced an extremely tough challenge. They inherited an incredibly large military infrastructure and the world's largest nuclear arsenal. On the other hand, Russia did not have enough resources and capabilities to maintain the military at full operational capability. Furthermore, when there was no pressing external enemy and there were mounting domestic problems, defense and security did not seem to be the most important policy issues.

The first attempts at military reform began in the early 1990s. Most believed that the country needed smaller, less expensive, but more efficient defense forces as it entered the 21st century. Opinions differed, however, about how small the military should be. Supporters of significant reductions argued that Russia had entered a new stage of international developments, and the Soviet-era military was no longer affordable or reasonable. Their opponents considered these arguments irresponsible and undermining Russia's national security.

The most significant changes in Russia's defense and security policies took place under President Putin. The concept that Russia is threatened by foreign enemies has been brought back, and became a central theme justifying the strengthening of Russia's defense and security. These policies largely continue under President Medvedev. Several key international events, such as the conflict in the former Yugoslavia, the NATO expansion eastwards, and the wars in Afghanistan and Iraq, have contributed to Russia's policies. Government officials saw these events as potential threats to Russia and its interests. The increasingly large resources available to the government during the economic boom of the early 2000s and as a result of high oil prices gave the Kremlin an opportunity to invest in defense and security. However, the economic crisis of 2008–09 forced the government to make adjustments and corrections.

Major challenges

According to the Military Doctrine of the Russian Federation approved by the president (Concept, 2000), Russia faces several potential and actual military threats. First, there are territorial claims from other countries. Second, some countries pose threats by opposing Russia's foreign policy and preventing Russia from playing its chosen role in global affairs. Next, any armed conflicts, or presence of foreign troops, especially close to

Russia's border, can be serious threats as well. Another threat is a continuous expansion of foreign military blocs (this is a direct reference to the NATO expansion in Europe).

Russia considers international terrorism as a substantial threat to the country's security. Any attempt to arm and train individuals with the purpose of sending them to Russia or to any allied country is also considered a security challenge. Any country's intent to disrupt Russia's defense capability, including its nuclear defense, is another perceived threat. Russia also includes in this class any form of discrimination against Russian citizens living abroad, particularly in other republics of the former Soviet Union.

To understand the security and defense policies, we first examine the government agencies responsible for these policies and their organization and functioning. Then we examine Russia's defense and security policies. As usual, in the critical thinking section we look at different views reflecting some past and present developments.

The commander in chief

Historically in Russia, the head of the state was also its commander in chief. During peacetime, he would exercise general management of the armed forces. During war, he was in charge of the country's defense. Stalin, for example, coordinated military actions during the 1941–45 war against Germany. Federal law contains provisions explaining the role and responsibilities of Russia's president as the country's top commander.

First, the president is responsible for the country's **military doctrine**, or a principal description of foreign threats against Russia and the general direction of Russia's defense policies. Twenty-five years ago, the Soviet Union's military doctrine was based on the strategic assumption of imminent threats coming from the United States, its allies, and some other countries (such as China). Today the military doctrine is different because the old Cold War problems have diminished. Russia's main concern is the integrity of its territory. For many years Russia ruled out the use of its military overseas, but a newly formulated defense doctrine of 2009 outlines four conditions under which the president can use Russia's armed forces abroad: for the protection of Russians living abroad, and against acts of piracy, actions against Russia's foreign bases, or actions against friendly states (Orlov, 2009). The Duma adopted this new doctrine in September 2009.

Second, the president is also responsible for outlining general military policies based on the country's military doctrine. President Medvedev, for instance, approves strategic plans for development and modernization of the armed forces, approves plans for civil defense in the event of war, and outlines general principles of interaction between the military and the economy. Russian men are obliged to serve in the military, and therefore the president is responsible for the national draft. Third, the president also signs international agreements related to military cooperation with other countries, and coordinates both military and foreign policies.

The president has the exclusive right to declare martial law in emergency situations, including severe natural disasters, massive public unrest, war, or other extraordinary conditions. Russian law prescribes that the president must inform the United Nations and the European Council should Russia temporarily suspend any international agreements because of the establishment of martial law. This presidential power is limited, however: the Federation Council has the right to reject such decisions (see Chapter 4).

Russians speak their mind ...

... **On the armed forces.** Percentage of Russians believing in 2009 that their armed forces can protect the country in the event of a real military threat from other states: 73. Percentage of Russians stating the same in 2000: 60.

Source: Levada (2009n).

The Defense Ministry of the Russian Federation

The legal foundation for the Ministry of Defense's performance is provided in a Presidential Decree of August 16, 2004. The decree names three major tasks of the ministry: institutional, military, and social.

The institutional tasks involve drafting and exercising military policies, coordinating the activities of various federal institutions in terms of defense policy, and coordinating the work of the subjects of the Federation related to defense of the country. The ministry also cooperates with its counterparts in other countries. The military tasks are related to maintaining appropriate military capabilities according to the country's military doctrine. In short, the ministry must guarantee that the country has enough technical and human resources for self-defense. The social tasks are complex. For instance, the ministry is responsible for exercising draft policies. In theory, every young man must serve in the military at 18 years of age (see later in the chapter). The Ministry must coordinate its efforts with federal, regional, and local authorities in order to achieve this. The social tasks also include social protection (benefits, pensions, and health plans) for members of the armed forces and their families. Finally, the ministry is

Table 13.1   *Basic policies of the Ministry of Defense of the Russian Federation*

Policy field	Description of policies
Institutional	Drafting and exercising military policies, coordinating the activities of various federal institutions in terms of defense policy, and coordinating the work of the Subjects of the Federation
Military	Maintaining appropriate military capabilities according to the country's military doctrine
Draft	Exercising draft policies: planning, drafting, and releasing individuals from the mandatory military service
Social	Social protection of the members of the armed forces during service and retirement from it
Civil defense	Civil defense policies or preparations related to protection of the civil population and economic infrastructure during war or in some cases of natural disaster
International	Developing international contacts and cooperation with other countries in the fields of defense policies

Source: Presidential Decree of August 16, 2004.

responsible for civil defense policies. It is in charge of protection of the civil population and economic infrastructure during war, and in some cases of natural disaster. See Table 13.1.

Structure of the Defense Ministry

The Defense Ministry in major countries such as Russia, China, and the United States is typically large and extremely complex. According to the Constitution, the president is in charge of the ministry. The president appoints the minister of defense based on a recommendation from the prime minister. The defense minister prepares strategic plans, controls the daily operations of the ministry, and reports to the president, and in some cases to the prime minister. See Figure 13.1.

The minister of defense and their deputies together coordinate the activities of Russia's armed forces. The state secretary coordinates policies related to personnel, their selection and training, as well as interaction with other federal ministries and services. The executive body of the Ministry of Defense is the General Staff of the Armed Forces of the Russian Federation. It is commanded by the chief of general staff, who is also appointed directly by the president. The Ministry of Defense, like other ministries in Russia, has adopted principles of collective management. There is, for instance, a

Figure 13.1   *Structure of the Defense Ministry*

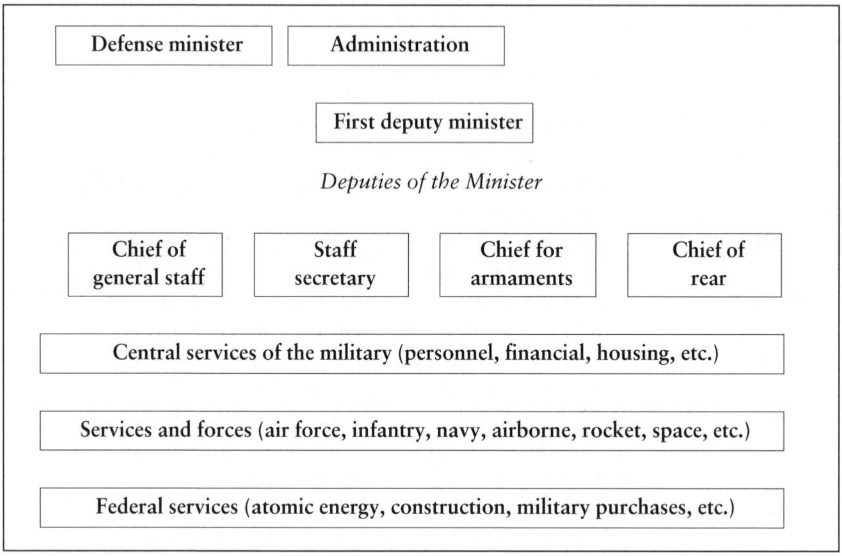

Defense minister	Administration

First deputy minister

Deputies of the Minister

Chief of general staff	Staff secretary	Chief for armaments	Chief of rear

Central services of the military (personnel, financial, housing, etc.)

Services and forces (air force, infantry, navy, airborne, rocket, space, etc.)

Federal services (atomic energy, construction, military purchases, etc.)

Ministry Council, which consists of the minister, the deputies, and several defense officials.

Russians speak their mind ...

... **On the armed forces.** Percentage of Russians believing that their country's armed forces are in good condition: 17. That the armed forces are in bad shape: 25. Percentage of Russians considering the state of affairs in the military as "normal": 48. Percentage of Russians who believe that their country must increase its military budget: 71. Percentage of those who want the budget reduced: 3.

Source: WCIOM (2009h).

The military draft

For many years Russia has had a **military draft**, or a legal and mandatory requirement for men to perform military service. This policy is common in many countries including Iran, Israel, and South Korea. In the past, the special role that the Soviet Union played in the world's affairs, the dangerous context of the Cold War, and the sheer size of the Soviet military gave the draft an especial importance: almost 4 percent of the entire adult male population was in the military at any given moment. We will discuss the consequences of the military draft in the critical thinking part of the chapter. Meanwhile, consider several important elements of this policy.

The Soviet Union had draft policies for more than 65 years. A 1993 law of the Russian Federation and several legislative acts provided the legal ground for similar policies in Russia. The law says that citizens of the Russian Federation must defend their fatherland. To implement this policy, the Ministry of Defense maintains specialized military commissariats, or draft offices, in cities and towns across Russia. Each office is headed by a military officer. After 2008, most employees of these commissariats became state employees (before 2008 most of them should have been military officers). Each draft office has a list of the male population residing in the district under the office's jurisdiction. Every male in Russia must register at a local commissariat when he is 17 years old. Citizens are eligible for the draft when they are between 18 and 27 years of age. The draft is administered twice a year: first between April and June, and second between October and December, based on special orders of the president.

The most recent limit of service has been established at one year (Presidential Decree, March 8, 2007). Since 2008, as a result of a decision of the government of Russia (March 6, 2008, N 275), 68 Russian universities and colleges have included "military departments," or educational and training facilities for future officers of the armed forces. All students eligible for military service who are enrolled in these colleges and universities must undergo training in these departments. So they do not have to serve full-time in the military, but participate in infrequent, short-term training exercises instead. Also under the new law, 37 institutions of higher education are forming military educational centers (the Russian version of ROTC in US schools). Those who attend these centers receive a special grant (four times the average student grant provided by the government), and must serve in the military for three years as an officer. By the end of the first decade of the century, according to the Ministry of Defense, more than 20 percent of lower-ranked officers in the military (and 30 percent of infantry officers) were college graduates serving a limited term (Russian Ministry of Defense: http://www.mil.ru).

The law allows individuals to apply for a deferral (a postponement of service) or a permanent release from military service. Among the criteria for granting this are being a college student, poor health, difficult family circumstances (being a single father, a father of two or more, or taking care of a disabled family member), or a prior conviction for a serious crime (such as murder or rape). In addition, teachers and doctors working in rural areas receive deferrals. (Doctors and teachers are in short supply in Russia's rural areas, and the law in this case is designed to ensure their services are not lost.) Religious beliefs or moral opposition to war do not qualify as legitimate factors for release from service. Overall, about 50 percent of males receive official deferrals or waivers. These numbers are considered high. It is believed that many young men use any excuse to simply avoid the military draft. In 2009, estimates suggest, in Moscow alone there were about 60,000 draft dodgers from that and previous years (Golz, 2009a).

Military policies

Chapter 12 discussed Russia's foreign policy. Russia tends to define its strategic defense interests within the limits of its geographic location on the Eurasian continent. It also responds to apparent threats and makes adjustments to its defense strategies. Similar factors affect Russia's military policies. Among them are Russia's response to important geopolitical developments, domestic capabilities for military mobilization, the country's possession of nuclear weapons, and its increasing aspirations in international relations.

Geopolitics and mass military mobilization

From the geopolitical standpoint, Russia's defense policies are based on constant attempts at containment of emerging threats from different directions. West of Russia, defense strategists perceive a growing threat from NATO and the possibility that several new countries, including Ukraine, Georgia, and Moldova, might join that military and political organization, which continues to be dominated by the United States.

South of Russia, one of the major concerns is the possibility of a violent attempt to spark ethnic conflicts in the Caucasus region. Russia is interested in keeping stability in this region, and opposes any military build-up near its border. In particular, Russia is interested in a peaceful solution to the conflict between Armenia and Azerbaijan. At the same time for many years Russia has not perceived Iran's nuclear programs as threatening from a military standpoint. Strong economic ties with Iran and the desire to have a reliable partner override other strategic concerns.

In the southeastern and eastern directions, one of the major concerns is the prevention of foreign countries' attempts to establish a military presence in the former republics of the Soviet Union. Russia intends to maintain its potentially superior military capabilities in this region, which has tremendous strategic importance for the Kremlin.

How would Russia fight a war? In theory, Russia's military doctrine assumes that the country could fight a war only over a limited period and within a limited territory. Under these conditions, Russia would use its standing army, air force, and navy. The strategic anticipation is that very soon Russia will develop fully professional, well-equipped, and efficient armed forces capable of carrying out various military tasks. At present, however, Moscow still relies on the Soviet-era concept of mass mobilization of men to cope with any circumstances that exceed the full-time forces' capabilities. The draft policies ensure that many (in theory, most) men serve in the military for at least a short time, so the assumption is that during wartime the country would have a sufficient number of trained and experienced men to call on, both rank and file and officers, in addition to the full-time professionals. The military establishment continues to consider it necessary to maintain this large reserve of men capable of bearing arms.

Nuclear defense

Although the numbers might change due to ongoing negotiations and new agreements, it is worth providing some facts to indicate the strength of Russia's nuclear arsenal. Back in 2008 Russia had more than 700 carriers of nuclear weapons (that is, rockets) capable of delivering more than 3000 nuclear warheads. Each of these warheads was capable of destroying any large city in any country in the world. Russia and the United States both agreed in 2002 to reduce their number of warheads to roughly 2000 by 2012. Both Washington and Moscow pursue a strategy of aiming to maintain parity between their nuclear capabilities, while working toward disarmament.

Nevertheless, Russia opposes complete nuclear disarmament. Two arguments are used to justify this position. The first is that if the major nuclear powers disarmed, smaller countries might develop nuclear weapons secretly and thus gain a significant advantage over other countries. The second reason is that in a world without nuclear weapons, the United States would remain the most powerful country because of the sheer size and quality of its conventional weapons. This could put Russia in a vulnerable position. However, Russia supports nuclear nonproliferation for several reasons. One is that the acquisition of nuclear weapons by new states would increase international tension. Another is the threat of international terrorist groups getting access to weapons of mass destruction and using them against Russia to achieve their political goals. Russia cooperates with other nuclear powers including the United States to ensure that nuclear arsenals are kept secure.

Russia's top concern remains nuclear security, a major issue related to national and international security. Back in the 1970s, both the United States and the Soviet Union accumulated nuclear arsenals capable of destroying not just the other country, but the entire planet (Wohlstetter, 1979). Both countries were motivated to keep nuclear weapons for two reasons: first, to deter aggression against themselves (the argument is that those who might be aggressors in other circumstances would hesitate to attack a nuclear state, because its retaliation using its nuclear weapons would be so terrible); and second, should an attack take place regardless of this, to punish the aggressor by the use of nuclear weapons.

Initially, back in the 1960s, military strategists in both Moscow and Washington wanted to achieve nuclear superiority over their opponent. There were at least three potential ways of achieving this. The first possibility was to mobilize scientific and technological resources and build as many warheads as possible so that the opponent would fall behind, and one country would eventually reach nuclear superiority over the other. The second possibility was to create a nuclear defense system that could destroy the enemy's airplanes and missiles in midair, and the third involved improving the quality and destruction capability of missiles. For example, typically one missile carries one nuclear warhead, but if technological advances enabled a missile to carry two, five, or even ten warheads, this might make it possible to penetrate the enemy's antimissile defense systems.

Soon enough the countries realized that all these three strategies were ineffective and even dangerous. First, the nuclear race to achieve quantitative superiority was getting too costly. The second strategy, to create missile defense systems, though superficially attractive, presented a significant problem. If one country developed an effective missile defense shield that would make its opponent less secure, and tend to destabilize the international situation. For example, if it was the United States that installed an effective antimissile defense system, and Washington then decided to strike first, Russia would not be able to retaliate effectively. This potential problem became closely associated with the third one: if countries began to develop very sophisticated systems for the delivery of nuclear weapons, this too would tend to make the whole international situation unstable (Leffler, 2007). Gradually, both countries realized that the only way to solve the nuclear problem was arms control and subsequent arms reduction. Russia and the United States between them possess 95 percent of the world's nuclear arsenal, so they were the parties who needed to achieve this (Legvold, 2009: 78).

Since the 1970s, most diplomatic efforts have been aimed at the reduction and limitation of nuclear weapons and antimissile systems. An agreement against antimissile systems was signed between the two countries in 1972 (the Anti-Ballistic Missile Treaty, or ABM Treaty). The Strategic Arms Reduction Treaty of 1991 (START) between Washington and Moscow effectively cut both countries' nuclear arsenals by up to 80 percent. In 1993 Presidents George W. Bush and Boris Yeltsin signed a new agreement prohibiting the use of multiple warheads on nuclear missiles

(START II). However, despite the obvious benefits of nuclear weapons limitations, the further process did not go smoothly. Although the US Senate ratified this agreement, the Russian side continued to drag its feet until 2000. The Russian Duma and the Federation Council postponed ratification for both political and strategic reasons. From the political standpoint, many Russian politicians believed that the agreement could be taken to signal Russia's approval of US foreign policy actions in Europe, especially in Yugoslavia and on the NATO expansion issues. The Russian military also believed that the obligations imposed by the treaty would be too costly for Russia. If Russia was unable to build missiles with multiple warheads, it would still need to develop less sophisticated but very expensive systems, for which it did not have enough money.

In 2002 Washington decided to withdraw from the ABM Treaty, and Russia in response withdrew from START II. Although moving away from the ABM Treaty gave the United States the possibility of developing a missile defense system, and so building up the country's security (as some experts believed), in Russia this move was considered dangerous. Russia was not prepared to accept a situation where the United States felt capable of delivering a deadly blow against it without fearing effective retaliation. Because it would have been too expensive for Russia to develop a similar defensive system, Moscow believed it had no choice but to attempt to build a more sophisticated offensive missile system capable of penetrating America's defenses.

Despite disagreements about the US missile shield plans, Russia and the United States continue to work to reduce nuclear threats. See the book website for updates.

Ongoing military reform

Russia is attempting to reform its military according to the changing conditions of the 21st century. It needs relatively manageable and efficient armed forces. It was announced back in 2005 that within a few years, there would be about 80 new detachments made up of 144,000 all-volunteer service men and women (Ivanov, 2005). However, several factors slowed the reform. The first factor was ideological. Some Russian military officials maintained the belief that Russia cannot afford any cuts in its armed forces because this could negatively affect national security. The second factor is political. There are powerful lobbying groups in Russia that believe the ongoing military reform would reduce federal budget appropriations for the military. This might eventually affect many sectors of the Russian economy and undermine the country's strategic interests. Finally, the third factor is economic. The financial crisis of the 2008–09 significantly limited many programs because it led to a lack of federal funding.

Arms sales

The Federal Service for Military-Technical Cooperation in the Defense Ministry coordinates the sales of weapons to foreign countries. It gives licenses to private and state companies to purchase and sell weapons and military-related materials. According to official statistics, Russia exported arms worth more than US$6.725 billion in 2008, and orders for future years were for more than four times this sum (Isaykin, 2009). China was the biggest buyer of weapons from Russia: almost half of all the orders usually come from Beijing. India and China combined make up almost 80 percent of all Russian sales. Since 2001, China alone has paid US $16.1 billion for its military purchases from Russia. About 56 percent of all foreign sales are aircraft, and 17 percent are air defense systems. Infantry weapons make up 15 percent of sales, naval purchases account for 9 percent, and about 3 percent fall in the miscellaneous category. Recently Russia began to expand its weapons sales, and it now sells to Latin American countries including Venezuela, Mexico, Peru, Colombia, and Brazil. In Asia, Vietnam, Indonesia, and Malaysia remain steady buyers as well. Russia also sells weapons to the Middle East and Algeria. Most industries producing arms and equipment, including military aircraft, are under state control. The Russian government itself is of course a major customer. In 2009, for example, in one of the biggest deals in history, it bought 64 jets from Russia's major aircraft company, Sukhoi (Interfax, August 19, 2009).

Any country's defense policies are conducted in coordination with its security policies, and Russia is no exception. As was explained in Chapter 4, the president's Security Council develops the strategy for Russian national security (Strategy, 2009). The current strategy is set until 2020.

Russians speak their mind ...

... On military education. Percentage of Russians believing that military education should be restored in high schools: 81. Percentage suggesting that this subject should be introduced but remain elective: 29.

Source: WCIOM (2008d).

The Federal Security Service

The Federal Security Service (FSS) of the Russian Federation is the centralized system of federal services performing security-related tasks. It was created in 1995 under President Boris Yeltsin. According to federal law, the president is directly in charge of the FSS (Federal Law, April 3, 1995). Over the years, this institution has undergone several reorganizations designed to improve its efficiency. As an example, in 2003 President Putin moved Russian border patrol operations, previously managed by the Department of Defense, under the control of federal security services.

The Federal Security Service performs several functions. The first one is counter-intelligence. In very general terms, these are anti-spying activities. The FSS has to investigate, prevent, or interrupt by legal means any activity by the intelligence services of other countries, as well as individuals who are considered a threat to the security of the Russian Federation. Counter-terrorism is the second function. The service carries out investigative and preventive work against terrorist threats within the Russian territory as well as overseas. Russia has a policy of preventive or retaliatory measures against terrorists regardless of their location (Golz, 2007). Intelligence gathering is another function of the FSS. Next, the service also fights against organized crime, including corruption, and illegal sales of arms and narcotics. It deals with groups conspiring to change Russia's constitutional order. The list of illegal activities that FSS investigates and fights against can be extended or changed by the legal authorities.

The FSS is also responsible for border protection. In particular, its role is to prevent people and goods from entering Russia illegally. This role also involves protection of the country's economic interests within the zone of Russia's continental shelf, and certain forms of protection of fish resources. The FSS also organizes informational security related to the transmission of sensitive or secret information within Russia and overseas.

The structure of the FSS

The central office is located in Moscow. It directs and coordinates the work of regional offices, offices in the armed forces, and the border patrol units. In addition, there are specialized departments including research facilities, training and educational centers, medical and other investigative institutions necessary for the FSS's functioning. For example, the Economic Security Service within the FSS organizes measures against spying in the fields of science, technology, and economics. The Department of Military Counterintelligence is responsible for antispying activities within the armed forces. The Department of Self Security works on preventive measures against spying and other illegal activities within the FSS itself.

Security policies: current activities

Any national security organization should work in secrecy. However, in a democratic country, government institutions must provide information about nonclassified aspects of their work. Various interviews, press conferences, and analytical papers have provided information about the work of the FSS (Patrushev, 2007). At least three tasks appear central to FSS activities. The first and central task is to prevent all attempts, open or clandestine, to violate Russia's territorial integrity. The second task is to prevent attempts to stir up political instability in Russia. The third task is to prevent any actions that would undermine Russia's pursuit of its national interests at home and globally.

President Medvedev is particularly concerned with the problem of corruption in the country. In his televised interviews he frequently discusses the harmful nature of corruption in Russia (Medvedev, 2009). He considers corruption a dangerous threat to Russia's security, and this is why he has put anticorruption policy high on the list of tasks for the FSS. A new director of the FSS appointed in 2008 warned about other new and emerging threats, including nationalist groups that actively recruit the young and are becoming increasingly active across Russia, even in traditionally calm regions such as the northwest. Hate crimes against minorities are another major issue of concern to the government (Bortnikov, 2009).

To fulfill these tasks and address these and other emerging concerns, the FSS conducts a wide range of activities. One of its major activities is

Photo 6   *President Medvedev started a national anti-corruption campaign. Anti-bribery billboards appeared in big Russian cities. The sign reads: "Have you encountered corruption? Call 576-77-65"*

Table 13.2 *Examples of criminal activities prosecuted by the Federal Security Service of the Russian Federation*

Type of activity	Date	Place	Description
Prevention of economic crime	April 4, 2009	Khabarovsk region	A large group of illegal loggers, not licensed to cut trees or sell timber, was arrested, and 300 cubic meters of timber (oak, lime, and ash) was confiscated. Estimated damage: 20 million rubles (approximately US$600,000).
Defusion of an explosive device	April 1, 2009	Derbent, Dagestan republic	A home-made pipe bomb filled with about 20 lbs of explosives was defused in this city on the Caspian Sea.
Prevention of violent criminal activities	March 24, 2009	Bashkorstan (a republic south of the Ural) Mountains	A criminal group that specialized in illegal arms sales, improvised explosive devises, and is accused of conspiracy to commit murder was arrested.
Prosecution of serious crime (embezzlement)	March 24, 2009	Novosibirsk	A local court sentenced a man to more than five years in jail for an attempt to sell an undercover FSS agent a counterfeit treasury bond worth 10 million rubles (approximately US$300,000).
Prosecution of crime related to security (a fake terrorist threat)	March 16, 2009	Kemerovo region	The local court of appeals upheld the sentence of a lower court (a 50,000 ruble fine) given to a woman for placing a prank call in 2007 about two bombs placed in a local postal office.
Prevention of crime (illegal gambling)	February 20, 2009	Cities of Hasavurt and Kizlyar, Dagestan Republic	A coordinated FSS and Department of the Interior operation resulted in confiscation of more than 100 gambling machines. Gambling is illegal according to federal and local legislation.
Prosecution of crime related to security (internet security)	February 16, 2009	Sarov, a small town in the Nizhny Novgorod region	A resident was sentenced to 2 years and 6 months in jail for obtaining passwords of 61 individuals and using their bank accounts for his personal purposes. The loss was estimated at 6 million rubles (US$200,000).

Source: FSS.

counter-terrorism. Russia has regular contacts with more than 75 countries in the fields of counter-terrorism. It is engaged in preventive measures against foreign services and individuals gathering information about Russia's armed forces, the ongoing military reform, and Russia's nuclear arsenal. The FSS is also concerned about economic espionage, and particularly about those trying to gather facts about Russia's natural resources, their extraction and delivery. From 2003 to 2007, for example, the FSS claimed that it had exposed 270 foreign agents and 70 foreign professional spies. Among these individuals were 35 Russian citizens. Six Russian citizens attempted to pass state secrets to foreign services (Patrushev, 2007). Those Russians suspected of spying can expect to be charged with treason (under Article 275 of the Criminal Code).

Another activity of the FSS is the prevention of foreign organizations' attempts to collect information about Russia's political atmosphere, especially before and during federal elections. To this end the FSS takes measures to control the activities of foreign nongovernment organizations (NGOs) on Russian territory. It is particularly concerned to frustrate foreign services' attempts to recruit Russian citizens to spy on their behalf. In addition, the FSS provides protection for foreign missions in Russia and Russian missions overseas.

To learn more about the activities that the FSS prosecutes see Table 13.2.

Russians speak their mind ...

... **On terrorism.** Percentage of Russians supporting the "extermination" of terrorists: 56. Percentage supporting negotiations with terrorists to find mutually acceptable solutions: 24.

Source: Levada (2009o).

Percentage of Russians believing that the government could protect them from new terrorist attacks: 66. Percentage believing the government would fail to protect them: 21.

Source: WCIOM (2008e).

The FSS justifies its role

Nikolai Patrushev, former director of the FSS under President Putin and the secretary of the Security Council after 2008, justified the necessity to expand the activities of the FSS by referring to the growing foreign threats (Patrushev, 2007). This point of view is widely shared today in the government and security services of the Russian Federation. From Russia's official point of view, foreign countries:

- increase their intelligence operations against Russia and increase their intelligence-related budgets every year
- want to learn increasingly more about Russia's political situation, its economic development, and natural resources; they also gather information about scientific research in Russia
- pay special attention to studies of the military, its reorganization, and Russia's nuclear arsenal
- pay increased attention to former Soviet republics, the situation in the Caucasus region, Siberia, and the Far East
- attempt to study the Russian political atmosphere, especially before and during federal elections.

The FSS maintains that western nations try to undermine Russia's economic and social development. Western leaders remain "Cold Warriors," which is in effect anti-Russian. They do not want to see Russia as a fully accepted member of the world's community. The major blame is commonly laid on NATO countries, including the United States and the United Kingdom, for their attempts to interfere in Russia's domestic affairs. Georgia, the Baltic countries, and Poland are regularly accused of being servants of Washington and London. Other countries such as Pakistan attempt to study the situation in regions with a large proportion of Muslim population, and gain influence among Russia's Muslim elites. One of Russia's major security concerns is to prevent any radical political changes in the former Soviet republics in Central Asia that could affect negatively Russia's positions in this region. Russia watches carefully the development of any political movements that could oppose the ruling regime in Central Asian states (McGlinchey, 2009).

A special area of concern is NGOs working in Russia. They are frequently accused of gathering sensitive information about Russia (about the opposition, social problems, or public opinion). NGOs' activities are viewed as a hidden way to penetrate deep within Russia's society and thus influence its policies. Some NGOs are accused of financing terrorist groups in the Caucasus region. Russian officials and large segments of the Russian population believe that foreign services are behind most of the democratic political movements in Georgia, Ukraine, Moldova, and other countries.

These and other developments, according to the Russian government, give it no choice but to expand and improve the country's security operations, both inside the country and elsewhere. The function of gathering intelligence, however, is given to another federal service called the External Intelligence Service.

Russians speak their mind ...

... **On the FSS.** Percentage of Russians admitting that they know very little or nothing about the activities of the Federal Security Service: 50.

Source: Levada (2009e).

The External Intelligence Service

A 1996 federal law designated the External Intelligence Service (EIS) as a federal agency (Federal Law, January 10, 1996). The President appoints the EIS director. This service is part of a complex federal security system, one of several agencies that often play similar functions. At least two major functions of the EIS have been established. The first one is analytical. It involves gathering and analyzing information about the opportunities, actions, or intentions of foreign states, organizations, or individuals related to the vital interests of Russia. The second task is operational. It is about assisting with and conducting practical measures to enhance the security of the Russian Federation. The necessity for intelligence is determined by the president and the Federal Assembly within their jurisdiction.

The 1996 law allows the EIS to use various methods to obtain intelligence information, including help from volunteers or undercover agents. Intelligence may be conducted by open methods as well as surreptitiously. The agency must not harm the environment while conducting its operations, and should take care over the human beings involved. Intelligence information is received by the president, the Federal Assembly, or by other federal institutions and organizations designated by the president.

State secrets

Russia designates certain information as secret based on the law (Federal Law, July 21, 1993). This information is related to the military, foreign policy, economic intelligence, counterintelligence, or investigative activities. The EIS, the FSS, and other agencies are also involved in protection of Russia's state secrets. The prosecutor general of Russia and other prosecutors supervise the execution of the law related to state secrets. There is an intra-institutional commission that coordinates federal policies in this area. According to the law, revelation of a state secret may threaten Russia's security. Table 13.3 provides an overview of information that is considered secret if it affects Russia's security.

Table 13.3 *Information considered and not considered secret in Russia*

Information considered secret	Information not considered secret
Any military information About scientific or technical discoveries and technologies	About environmental problems About Russia's health care, sanitary conditions, demography, education, culture, agriculture, and criminal statistics
About reserves, extraction, transportation, and use of platinum and natural diamonds. There are also other natural resources about which the Government of the Russian Federation can classify information.	About the gold reserves of the Russian Federation
About Russia's operations with foreign states (except general assessments of debts)	About natural disasters, catastrophic events, accidents and other events threatening life and health of citizens (this information was largely classified in the Soviet Union)
About border security operations or activities to protect the economic zone, and continental shelf of the country	About financial and other types of compensation to government institutions and their employees
About federal budget appropriations for defense, security, and law enforcement	About violation of human rights and liberties. Information about the health of top Russian leaders.

Counter-terrorism policies

Since the 1990s, one of the prime concerns of Russia's defense and security officials has been counter-terrorism. How does Russia coordinate its counter-terrorist policies? Based on a presidential decree (February 15, 2006), it has created an Anti-Terrorist Committee to coordinate polices on the federal level. The president appoints its chair, who works with several federal agencies and other institutions. See Figure 13.2.

Russia claims that in the area of counter-terrorism it shares similar interests with the United States and many other countries. There are short-term and long-term priorities and goals. The most important short-term priority is to prevent immediate acts of terrorism on Russian territory. Several terrorist acts have taken place in Russia over the past few years, and they have caused a significant loss of human life. Both public opinion

Figure 13.2   *Structure of Russia's National Anti-Terrorism Committee*

National Anti-Terrorism Committee
Coordinates the activities of:

Federal Security Service	Ministry of Extraordinary Situations	Defense Ministry

Interior Ministry	External Intelligence Service

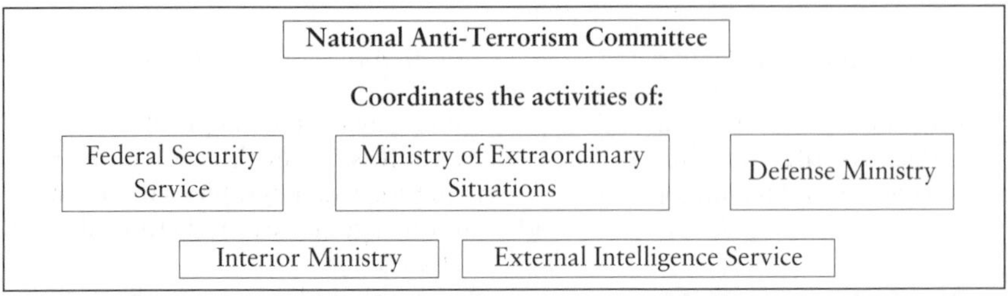

and political elites demand strong measures to prevent future attacks and punish their perpetrators. This task is also connected with immediate actions to prevent the escalation of tensions in certain Russian regions, and in particular, in the southern regions of Russia. Several agencies conduct policies to secure nuclear installations and radioactive materials. It is Russia's prime concern that these materials should not get into the hands of foreign governments or extremist groups.

The long-term priorities emerge out of the necessity to prevent the growth of Islamic fundamentalism as a potentially potent source of terrorism in the region, and in particular in the former republics of the Soviet Union. Pursuing this goal, Russia tends to supports authoritarian regimes for its southern neighbors, which provide protection against violent extremism and religious fundamentalism. Russia is also interested in ensuring stability in other countries in the region, such as Afghanistan and Iraq.

Case in point: Russia's speznaz

The Anti-Terrorist Committee does not have special structures or troops to enforce its decisions. Counter-terrorist actions can be undertaken by any federal unit designated for that purpose. There is a special term in Russia, *speznaz* (loose translation: a unit serving a special purpose), to refer to any type of special forces trained and permitted to use force in extraordinary situations such as hostage-taking. These can be any specially trained elite units under the direction of the FSS, internal troops of the Russian Ministry of Internal Affairs, or units controlled by the military intelligence service.

Critical thinking about defense and security policies

An accurate assessment of any country's capabilities involves the process of evaluation of this country's defense policies. These, in turn, often reflect the country's perceptions of its own and international security. How do

Russia's security and defense policies reflect the changes taking place in the world today?

Defense priorities

In any country, evaluating security risks and seeking adequate responses involves complicated analyses of multiple factors. If defense and security officials find out that the country is facing an external threat, they have several options to pursue. Four categories of these are:

- unilateral options: rapid strengthening of the military or actual military responses
- multilateral options: attempting to seek alliances with other states to resist the existing threat
- accommodationist options: negotiating and possibly granting concessions designed to reduce the existing threat
- isolationist options: withdraw from the conflict hoping to avoid the threat.

In the early 1990s, Russia on many occasions chose primarily isolationist and accommodationist polices. One of the reasons for choosing these policies was the weak state of Russia's economy and the poor condition of its military. Furthermore, the official policy was that Russia no longer had foreign enemies. From the late 1990s, Russia has been switching toward more active unilateral and multilateral options. For instance, it is actively involved in international military cooperation. The first priority in this area is friendly relations with the former republics of the Soviet Union south of Russia's border, and other neighboring states including China and India. The second priority is cooperation between Russia and western states. After 2001, Russia began to share and exchange military intelligence information related to emerging threats with the United States and other countries (Goldgeier and McFaul, 2003).

To justify its foreign and security policies, Russia needs to gather evidence about domestic and foreign threats. It appears that increasingly often, Russia has pursued a policy of emphasizing the existence of foreign threats. Here are some examples:

- President Putin used the terrorist acts against Russia in the early 2000s as examples of foreign penetration, reflecting the desire of certain forces outside of Russia to weaken the country.
- The NATO expansion to the east over the past 15 years was another source of frustration; in Russia's security doctrine, the expansion was an indication of significant and growing foreign threats.

- The attempts of several neighboring countries, including Ukraine and Georgia, both former Soviet republics, to distance themselves from Russia was interpreted in Moscow as a threat to Russia's strategic interests in the region.
- Most setbacks in Russia's foreign policy are interpreted as having been caused by the deliberate policies of foreign countries that work against Russia and its interests.
- The authorities in their interviews, speeches, and press conferences continue the strategy of trying to persuade people that foreign threats against Russia are on the rise.

These arguments resemble, to some degree, the point of view of the Military-Industrial Commission in the Soviet Union, discussed at the beginning of the chapter. Along with the practical and economic reasons used to emphasize foreign threats, there are other factors affecting Russia's defense and security policies.

Russian militarism?

Militarism is the set of attitudes and policies that revolve around the persistent aspiration to use military force in response to most foreign threats. Militarism is typically accompanied by the glorification of war, conquest, domination, weapons, and armed forces. Pacifism, on the other hand, as a combination of attitudes and policies, posits that international disputes should be settled by arbitration and other nonviolent means. Pacifism prioritizes nonviolence in international affairs, and glorifies restraint, mutual concessions, respect, and peace (Zinn, 2002). Both militarism and pacifism reflect the never-ending arguments between so-called "hawks" (supporters of military action) and "doves" (supporters of nonviolent policies) in the foreign policy of most countries. Russia is no exception.

The militarist tradition has always been part of Russia's defense policies. During the more than 70 years of existence of the Soviet Union, the country was managed as if it was a giant military camp. From the beginning of their lives people were told that their duty was to defend the country against imminent foreign aggression. In Russians' daily lives, in folklore, in songs, novels, and poetry learned in elementary, middle, and high school, the soldier, the defender, and the martyr were always glorified. From official documents reflecting core policies to everyday psychology and folklore, one of the most essential cultural aspects of the former Soviet Union was militarism (Shlykov, 2002).

In today's Russia, according to some critics the fundamental idea that the country must restore its might and glory is inseparable from so-called **civil militarism**, the strategic policy of adopting military goals, priorities, and values in domestic policies, and glorifying the military role in domestic defense (Golz, 2007). Although Russian officials declare that there is no longer a global rivalry between Russia and the United States, policies are still often based on the possibility of a confrontation. Most military and political experts in Russia suggest that there is nothing wrong with this doctrine because, as a common saying goes, it is better for Russia to be safe than sorry. However, foreign observers feel that Russia is sending the wrong message to the world: the Kremlin might not want to appear as a warmonger, but almost everything it does supports this image. Critics also maintain that such military and security policies could lead to unrestrained nationalism, and are a tremendous waste of useful resources. Skeptics suggest, though, that the threat of civil militarism in Russia is exaggerated. A fine illustration of the futility of militarism is the difficulties that Russia is experiencing with military reform.

The military reform

One of key problems for Russia is its military draft policies, one of the lasting legacies of the Soviet Union. The draft gives the state the necessary power and ability to control people and resources. To change the draft policy is to change the structure of the Russian military. It appears that if the reform is successful, Russia will have at least two sub-structures within its armed forces. One will be formed out of trained professionals serving in the military on a fixed-term basis, with individual legal contracts. The other structure will be based on hundreds of thousands of draftees who serve a one-year term and are then sent back home. Critics immediately point out that the differences between these two structures are profound. The people in the first group are trained, older, and motivated to serve. The second group are a inexperienced, generally unmotivated, and uneducated crowd of 18-year-olds.

Yet the diminished capability of the military would be acceptable if Russia changed its military strategy. Since the end of the Cold War Russia has no longer been capable of pursuing global military tasks. Estimates suggest that the Russian military is two to three times smaller than the military of the Soviet Union (Golz, 2007). However, the government is slow to admit such changes, or the fact that at least for some time, the Defense Ministry will have to deal with the country's worsening demographic situation. Every year, the number of 18-year-olds available to serve will decline. There were approximately 843,000 eligible for service in 2009. About half of them obtain deferrals and waivers, so only 400,000 can be drafted every year, which is barely half the number the military claims to need. In other words, the draft will remain a significant problem for the government unless this policy changes.

Another area of reform is drastic increases in compensation and benefits for military officers, which is supposed to achieve two goals: to retain existing officers and to recruit new ones to compensate for the continuous reduction in the number of military personnel. Prime Minster Putin promised to transform the pay structure of the military so that officers would see a significant wage increase. For instance, he promised that junior officers would earn approximately 50,000 rubles a month (roughly US$18,000 a year). Pay will be based on merit. Senior officers will be paid three or four times that amount. The government guarantees every officer an apartment by around 2010. At the same time, the government was planning to discharge almost 250,000 officers, expand the role of nonmilitary professionals, and reform the system of military education (RNS, 2009). With significant budget shortfalls in recent years, these tasks seem difficult to achieve.

The opposition argues that the state must end the draft. As a consequence, the size of the military would decrease and its efficiency improve. The second step would be a gradual expansion of civilian control over the military. In particular, the Duma should exercise greater control over the military budget. The Russian military establishment opposes these ideas.

Russians speak their mind ...

... On the military draft. Percentage of Russians supporting the mandatory military draft (for the male population only): 47. Percentage supporting contract-based forces: 43. By comparison, when Putin came to power in 2000, only 30 percent supported the military draft, and 63 percent wanted to make the military a contractual force.

Source: Levada (2009p).

Judging security policies

Two distinct points of view exist about Russia's security policies. The differences are primarily ideological, and are based on the critics' perception of Russia's global priorities and preferences in domestic policies.

It appears that today, the official security policy is based on the assumption that the country is surrounded by a growing number of enemies, and therefore must defend itself by all means available. The supporters of this approach try to find evidence, and justify their policies as a cautious response to the seemingly aggressive actions of foreign states, especially the United States. A strategic policy of restoring Russia as a great power on the world stage that is feared and respected is an important part of the Kremlin's plans (Kuchins, 2007). Russia's most immediate plan is to attempt to create a new security structure in Europe that would increase Moscow's influence on a number of post-Soviet states (Sestanovich, 2008: 27). This strategy was discussed in Chapter 12.

The critics of these policies immediately say that this hawkish approach to national security is another excuse for Russia's authoritarian strategy, based on a simple but faulty logic: to resist foreign threats and guarantee the success of social reforms, the country has no other alternative but a strong authoritarian system of government that will ensure public order, discipline, and national security (Golz, 2007). Unfortunately, the critics of the official course are in the minority. Over the past few years, government officials, political commentators, and policy analysts in Russia have generally accepted the "hostile environment" context for Russia's security policies (Umland, 2009).

Conclusion

Every country has the right to enhance its security and improve its defense policies. After all, this is a major responsibility of the government. The key question is always about the scope and depth of such policies. Historically, a large group of Russian elites supported by nationalist voices have believed that the government was not doing enough to protect the country. They demand a more hawkish approach to defense and security. Their critics maintain a completely different position, offering two major arguments. First, Russia cannot afford another massive military and security build-up. Second, this type of build-up is absolutely unnecessary because Russia does not have foreign enemies. The main reason, the critics argue, that the government accepts the nationalists' view of defense and security is that it allows the Kremlin to maintain its authoritative grip on society and its resources. The Kremlin disagrees with these assessments. In fact, the "hawkish" approach to Russian security and defense has gained strength in the past decade. Unfortunately, in politics it is always easy to stir up rows based on old grievances, emotions, and fears. It is far harder to calm them down.

Chapter 14

Summary and Conclusion

A brief review
The economy and economic policies
Social policies and dependency
Foreign policy and security
Government

> *An ineffective economy, semi-Soviet social sphere, weak democracy, negative demographic trends and an unstable Caucasus. These are very big problems even for a state like Russia.*
>
> Dmitry Medvedev, president of Russia, 2009

> *Russia is a great country. I admire it.*
>
> Nicolas Sarkozy, president of France, 2007

A brief review

From a historical viewpoint, the period from the early 1990s to the early 2010s was incredibly short. Yet these years were filled with remarkable and dramatic events that have few parallels in Russian or even world history. These were years of change and confusion, great hopes, and growing worries about the future (Kotkin, 2008).

An aftershock that followed the break-up of the Soviet empire was marked by an economic downturn and hyperinflation, trailed by the constitutional crisis of 1993. President Yeltsin used military force to disband the parliament inherited from the Soviet era, yet the populist and left-wing opposition won the legislative elections of 1993 and 1995. The devastating war in Chechnya became a painful thorn in the nation's side. The dramatic presidential campaign of 1996 kept Yeltsin in the Kremlin for three and a half years of his second term. A devastating financial crisis in 1998 had a profound and sobering effect on the country.

Yeltsin lost his effectiveness as a leader, and had enough courage to transfer power to his hand-picked successor, Vladimir Putin. The polls showed that the country was happy with the choice of president in 2000. A former KGB officer, Putin was young, busy, resilient, and relentless.

Table 14.1   *Russia yesterday and today: issues, problems, policies, consequences, and side-effects*

Issues, problems, and policies	Then: The USSR	Now: Russia	Actual consequences and side effects
Private property	Outlawed	Legal	Wealth polarization Illiberal economic management
Economy	Industries. Agriculture. Plan-oriented. State-controlled.	Industries. Agriculture. Free market. Private and state controlled.	Heavy emphasis on export of energy sources
Economic policies			A hybrid system of illiberal government control of the free market.
Party system	One party	Multi-party system	Dominance of a pro-government party
Civil liberties	Suppressed	Recognized	Selective censorship. Self-censorship.
Foreign policy	Ideology-driven	Pragmatic	Relatively confrontational and preoccupied with self-image
Judiciary and legislature	Not free	Relatively free and independent	Dominated by the executive branch
Freedom to emigrate	Absent	Granted	Visa system is in place for travel in most foreign countries
Birth rates	Low	Lower	Threat of depopulation

During his early presidency, Russia lived through deadly terrorist attacks and accidents, but it already showed some good signs of economic improvement. High oil prices and a mixture of public-sector and free market policies were helpful in boosting Russia's economic growth. Russia became more confident, and predictable even in the ways in which it was developing tensions with its close and distant neighbors. By the mid-2000s, one national party—United Russia—had become dominant in the country's multi-party political system. As in the case of Vladimir Putin, Russia witnessed another smooth transition of presidential power to Dmitry Medvedev in 2008.

What is Russia today, and what has the country achieved in the 21st century? See Table 14.1.

The economy and economic policies

On the surface, some economic figures related to Russia are encouraging. The average rate of economic growth was around 7 percent for several years. The global financial crisis of 2008–09 has slowed the growth, but all the signs suggest the global economy should recover and Russia's own recovery will be sustainable. Russia has almost paid off its foreign debt. Capital gains and personal income taxes are lower than in most economically developed countries. Since 2003, the minimum wage has risen more than 400 percent. The size of the average salary has doubled. The number of people below the poverty line has decreased by 50 percent. The government now backs loans and mortgages for those in need, and insures personal bank savings up to US$13,000. Russia has canceled its "death tax," so people can inherit money and property without paying a substantial financial penalty.

Yet Russia continues to rely too much on its energy resources at the expense of manufacturing. It is a free market economy, but it depends on raw material exports and state control over most important economic resources (Åslund, 2007). The economy depends heavily on oil and gas exports. If energy prices are low, federal revenues will be low too. Instead of investing in low-profit but important areas of manufacturing, the Kremlin takes control over the most profitable industries: the oil, gas, other natural resources, and car manufacturing sectors (Nemtsov, 2008). Continuous inflation has almost canceled out the recent wage and pension increases. Russia is still far behind most European countries in the average size of people's wages and pensions. Overall, Russia has embraced illiberal economic policies, a mixture of authoritarian methods of government coupled with the acceptance, when it is convenient, of free market principles.

Social policies and dependency

Despite the significant economic transitions that have taken place in Russia over the past 20 years, the authorities are still very much responsible for practically every element of people's lives—from establishing new laws and paying state salaries to distributing apartments; from hot water rationing, changing bus routes, and building health care clinics, to changing the Constitution in a record-breaking short time. Most people remain ultimately dependent on the authorities. This reliance on somebody else's power can develop a sense of dependency. The culture of dependency generates support for the leaders already in power, because most people start to believe, especially in times of crisis, that only powerful authorities can help them, the poor and the hopeless, to overcome difficulties and protect them from new challenges.

Foreign policy and security

With the ending of the Cold War, the world has seemingly buried the mutual fears and threats that had been haunting both Moscow and its opponents for more than 40 years. Russia as an international actor rewrote its old script. In the 1990s Moscow dropped ideology as a factor of foreign policy and declared a transition to a new, pragmatic approach. This process of transition was anxious, complicated, and somewhat disappointing in the end. Russia, is seeking a new place in the global world and pursuing an increasingly assertive foreign policy (Cohen, 2009). However, the old shadow of a foreign threat is back in the area of public debate and policymaking. Moscow pursues a policy of strengthening its influence on the countries that are former republics of the Soviet Union. It increases the pressure on the states that resist its influence. Russia supports authoritarian regimes that remain friendly to the Kremlin. It also uses its oil and gas as instruments of political pressure on some foreign countries.

While most democratic countries tend to criticize Russia, the Kremlin attributes the worsening of relations to a number of western policies. The message is simple: if western powers too had chosen a different foreign policy in the past, then the relations between the countries would have been different. Among its grievances are:

- America and Europe should not have supported Bosnian Muslims in the conflict in the former Yugoslavia in 1992–96. Washington and NATO should not have dropped bombs on Serbia, which fought for its own territorial integrity in 1999.

- The west should not have granted independence to Kosovo, thus punishing Serbia and annexing a part of its territory.
- NATO should have halted any further eastward expansion in 1996 and later.
- America should not have attacked Iraq unilaterally in 2003. Other western countries, including the United Kingdom, should not have supported Washington in this war.
- The United States and the European Union should not have supported the anti-Russian side during the elections in Ukraine in 2004–05.
- The world should not have supported Georgia in its military conflict with Russia in 2008.

There were some domestic ideological and political causes for the increased tensions between Russia and most western countries (Kuchins, 2007). First, Russian military and security leaders had a hard time coping with the country's status as an ex-superpower, and never planned to give up their gargantuan military goals. Second, the anti-western sentiment across Russia is not only a response to international developments, but also a reflection of Russia's growing nationalism and authoritarianism. Third, the Kremlin has a legitimate interest in maintaining the popular belief that Russia is surrounded by enemies. Russia's power may grow and carry the country's ambitions with it (Sestanovich, 2008: 28).

History shows that maintaining a permanent image of a foreign enemy helps the authorities to preserve national unity and rally people around the government.

Government

History also shows that political transition in any country is a painful process. Over just two decades Russia had to be reassembled in every sense: recreating a legitimate government, economic and military power, a multi-ethnic state, and democracy. These challenges were daunting. Privation and lawlessness at the early stages, several economic crises, terrorist attacks, and scores of other obstacles and problems slowed down the development of a new civil society. In general, the political restructuring in Russia was a transition to a democracy. Yet the type of democracy built in Russia today is unique and full of contradictions.

According to the Constitution, Russia has three independent branches of government. However, the executive power is disproportionately strong, and getting even stronger as additional amendments and presidential decrees are passed every year. Russia has an increasingly personal form of political rule (Umland, 2008a).

Russia has a functional multi-party system, but it also has a dominant, government-backed, ruling party, United Russia. Other parties have very little chance of power, or even to become a serious opposition.

From the inception of the Soviet Union to the end of the first decade of the century, Russia had already had nine scheduled national elections (four presidential and five parliamentary). Nevertheless, the rules for the Duma elections constantly change to increase the chances of Kremlin supporters. Since 1996, Russia has not had truly competitive presidential elections: the Kremlin candidate has always been expected to win.

From a legal point of view, Russia enjoys a full spectrum of political liberties. From a practical standpoint, however, the government has developed an effective system of regulating free speech by selectively pressurizing journalists. Self-censorship is becoming a necessary habit for reporters.

In politics, some commentators on Russian politics anticipate increased democratic competition and the surfacing of a stronger civil society. Other observers, however, see Russia sliding toward an authoritarian regime managed by security service professionals (Kuchins, 2007; Shleifer and Treisman, 2004).

Studies show that Putin and later Medvedev won electoral votes based on people's positive perception of the economy, the restoration of order, and the reinstatement of Russia's standing in the world (Colton and Hale, 2009). However, polls show that around two-thirds of Russians do not trust the establishment institutions, including the courts, political parties, and labor unions. At the same time, the approval ratings for the president and prime minister are very high, around 70 percent. People might disapprove of their policies, but they support the system and the government. Such a tendency to remain loyally unhappy is another paradox of the Russian political psychology (Gudkov, 2008a; Dubin, 2008b).

Meanwhile Russia as a country, an energy supplier, a nuclear power, and a trade partner, will remain a major player in global affairs in the 21st century. The main question is which direction of development it will choose. If Russian political leaders are to make Russia democratic and free, the time is now. The years before 2015 could become the most important in Russia's history.

References

Abalkin, L. (1995) *Ekonomicheskaya reforma: Zigzagi sydby i uroki na budushchee* (Economic reform: Zigzags of fate and lessons for the future). Moscow: Institute of Economics, RAS.

Adomeit, H. (1998) *Imperial Overstretch: Germany in Soviet Policy from Stalin to Gorbachev.* Baden-Baden: Nomos.

Albertazzi, D. and McDonnell, D. (2008) *Twenty-First Century Populism: The Spectre of Western European Democracy.* New York and London: Palgrave Macmillan.

Alekseeva, M. I., Bolotova, L. D., Vartanova, E. L., Voronova, O. A., and Zasurskij, I. I. (2008) *Sredstva Massovoj Informacii v Rossii* (Russia's Mass Media). Moscow: Aspect Press.

Arendt, H. (1951) *The Origins of Totalitarianism.* London: Secker & Warburg.

Åslund, A. (2007) *Russia's Capitalist Revolution: Why Market Reform Succeeded and Democracy Failed.* Washington, D.C.: Peterson Institute.

Åslund, A. and Kuchins, A. (2009) *The Russia Balance Sheet.* Washington, D.C.: Peterson Institute for International Economics.

Avtorkhanov, A. (1990) *Lenin v sudbakh Rossii: Razmyshleniia istorika.* Prometheus-Verlag.

Bahry, D. and Silver, B. D. (1990) "Soviet citizen participation on the eve of democratization." *American Political Science Review,* 84(3), pp. 821–47.

Barner-Barry, Carol (1999) "Nation building and the Russian Federation," pp. 95–108 in B. Glad and E. Shiraev (eds), *The Russian Transformation: Political, Sociological, and Psychological Aspects.* New York: St Martin's Press.

Bastrykin, A. I. (2008) "Interview with the First Deputy of the Prosecutor General of the Russian Federation." March 25. http://www.sledcomproc.ru/smi/543/ (accessed November 11, 2009).

Bastrykin, A. I. and Naumov, A. V. (2007) (eds) *Ugolovnoe Pravo Rossii. Prakticheskij Kurs* (Russian Criminal Law. Practical Course), 3rd edn. Moscow: Wolters Kluwer.

Bauman, Z. (1994). "A revolution in the theory of revolutions." *International Political Science Review,* 15(1), pp. 15–24.

Benderskaya, E. G. (2008) "Zaochnoe RAzbiratelstvo Ugolovnyh Del v Stranah SNG" (Processing of Criminal Cases in Absentia in CIS Countries). *Vestnik Moskovskogo Universiteta,* 5, 99–112.

Boldin, V. (1994) *Ten Years that Shook the World.* New York: Basic Books.

Bolhsakov, (2004) "Epokha Voennogo Kapitalizma" (An epoch of military capitalism). *Dengi Magazine,* 32(487), August 16. http://www.kommersant.ru (accessed November 11, 2009).

Bortnikov, A (2009) "President met with Director of FSS." Moscow, December 25, ITAR-TASS.

Boxer, V. and Hale, H. (2000) "Putin's anti-campaign campaign: presidential election tactics in today's Russia." *AAASS NewsNet, Newsletter of the American Association for the Advancement of Slavic Studies,* 40(3), May.

Brazhnikov, I. (2008) "Den Ochicheniya Gosudarstva" (The day of the state's purification). http://ei1918.ru/drevnjaja_rus/48.html (accessed November 11, 2009).

Brinton, C.(1938) *The Anatomy of Revolution.* New York: W.W. Norton.

Brown, A. (2009) *The Rise and Fall of Communism.* New York: HarperCollins.

Brownlee, J. (2007) *Authoritarianism in an Age of Democratization.* New York: Cambridge University Press.

Brumberg, A. (1991) "Russia after perestroika." *New York Times Book Review,* June 27.

Bruter, V. (1999) "Istoriya Sovremennykh Rossiyskih Vyborov, 1993" (A History of Modern Russian Elections, 1993). International Institute of Humanitarian-Political Studies. http://www.igpi.ru/info/people/bruter/1085749185.html (accessed November 11, 2009).

Brzezinski, Z. (1966). "The Soviet political system: transformation or degeneration? *Problems of Communism,* 15(1), pp. 1–15.

Bunich, I. (1992) *Zoloto Partii* (The Party's Gold). St Petersburg: Shans.

Carnaghan, E. (2008). *Out of Order. Russian Political Values in an Imperfect World.* University Park, Pa.: Penn State University Press.

Carr, E. H. (1958) *Socialism in One Country,* Vol. 1. London: Macmillan.

Chernyaev, A. (1993) *Shest lets Gorbachevym* (Six Years With Gorbachev). Moscow: Progress-Kultura.

Chernyaev, A. (2000) *My Six Years With Gorbachev.* University Park, Pa.: Penn State University Press.

Chetverikov, A. (2009) "O Zemelnom Kodekse" (On the Land Code). http://www.spravedlivo.ru/news/position/951.php (accessed November 11, 2009).

Chistyakov, O. (ed). (1994) "Manifesto, 17 October 1905," p. 41 in *Rossijskoe Zakonodatelstvo 10–20 Vekov* (Russian Law from the 10th to 20th Centuries). Moscow: Yuridicheskaya Literatura.

Churov, V. (2009) (ed.) *Izbiratelnoe Zakonodatelstvo i Vybory v Sovremennom Mire* (Electoral Law and Elections in a Modern World). Moscow: Central Electoral Commission.

Churov, V. (2009a) "Vybory—Osnova Demokratii" (Elections are a Foundation of Democracy). An interview. *VIP* (7–8). http://www.cikrf.ru/newsite/news/actual/2009/07/24/int_churov_vip.jsp (accessed November 11, 2009).

Clover, C. and Blitz, J. (2009) "Icy winds threaten US–Russia thaw." *Financial Times,* May 8. http://www.ft.com/cms/s/0/f3edbc88-3c17-11de-acbc-00144feabdc0.html (accessed November 11, 2009).

Cohen, A. (2009) "Russia and Eurasia: a realistic policy agenda for the Obama administration," paper by the Heritage Foundation, March 27. http://www.heritage.org/Research/RussiaandEurasia/sr0049.cfm (accessed November 11, 2009).

Cohen, A. and Ericson, E. (2009) "Russia's economic crisis and U.S.–Russia relations: troubled times ahead," paper by the Heritage Foundation, November 2.

http://www.heritage.org/Research/RussiaandEurasia/bg2333.cfm (accessed November 11, 2009).

Cohen, S. F. (2001) *Failed Crusade: America and the Tragedy of Post-Communist Russia*. New York: W.W. Norton.

Collins, N. (2007) *Through Dark Days and White Nights: Four Decades Observing a Changing Russia*. Washington, D.C.: Scarith.

Colton, T. and Hale, H. (2009) "The Putin vote: presidential electorates in a hybrid regime," *Slavic Review*, fall, pp. 473–503.

Communist Party of the Russian Federation (CPRF) (2009) *The Program of the Communist Party of the Russian Federation*. http://kprf.ru/party/program/ (accessed November 11, 2009).

Conquest, R. (1986) *Harvest of Sorrow: Soviet Collectivization and the Terror–Famine*. New York: Oxford University Press.

Davies, R. W. (1997) *Soviet History in the Yeltsin Era*. London: Macmillan.

Dobrynin, A. (1995) *In Confidence: Moscow's Ambassador to America's Six Cold War Presidents (1962–1986)*. New York: Random House.

Dobrynin, A. (1997) *Sugubo Doveritelno* (Very Confidentially). Moscow: Avtor.

Dobson, R. (1996) *Russians Choose a President. Results of Focus Group Discussions*. June. Washington, D.C.: USIA.

Doder, D. and Branson, L. (1990) *Gorbachev: Heretic in the Kremlin*. New York: Viking.

Dubin, B. (2008) An interview. *Novaia gazeta*, 23, April 3, pp. 8, 9.

Dubin, B. (2008a) An interview. *Novaia gazeta*, 40, June 5, pp. 12, 13.

Dubin, B. (2008b) An interview. *Novaia gazeta*, 46, June 30, pp. 6, 7.

Dubin, B. (2008c) An interview. *Novaia gazeta*, 63, August 28, pp. 16, 17.

Erlichman, V. V. (2004) *Poteri Narodonaseleniya v 20 Veke* (Population Loss in the 20 Century). Moscow: Russkaya Panorama.

ESP (1994) *Ekonomicheskie I Sotsialnye Peremeny: Monitoring Obshchestvennogo Mneniya* no. 6, 63.

Ferguson, G. (1996) "Parties and politics in Russia." *The Public Perspective*, 2, p. 44.

Feshbach, M (2008) "Behind the bluster, Russia is collapsing," *Washington Post*, October 5, p. B03.

Filatov, S. (2008) "Interview," October 6, Radio Station Ekho Moskvy. http://www.echo.msk.ru/programs/svoi-glaza/544670-echo (accessed November 11, 2009).

Fillipov, A. (2009) *Noveyshaya Istoriya Rossii, 1945–2006* (A Modern History of Russia, 1945–2006). Moscow: Prosveshenie.

Fish, S. (2005) *Democracy Derailed in Russia: The Failure of Open Politics*. New York: Cambridge University Press.

Fitzpatrick, S. (1986) "New perspectives on Stalinism." *Russian Review*, 45(4), pp. 357–73.

Fossato, F., Lloyd, J., and Verkhovsky, A. (2008) *The Web that Failed*. Oxford: Reuters Institute for the Study of Journalism.

Freedom House (nd) *The Freedom in the World*. www.freedomhouse.org (accessed November 11, 2009).

Freedom House (2009) *Russia. An annual report compiled by Robert W. Orttung.* http://www.freedomhouse.hu/images/nit2009/russia.pdf (accessed November 11, 2009).

Gaddy, C. and Ickes, B. (2009) *Russia's Addiction: The Political Economy of Resource Dependence.* Washington, D.C.: Brookings Institution.

Gaidar, Y (2002) *The Economics of the Russian Transition.* Boston, Mass.: MIT Press.

Gaidar, Y. (2007) *Collapse of an Empire: Lessons of Modern Russia.* Washington, D.C.: Brookings Institution.

Gatman-Golutvina, O. V. (2000) *Byurokratija ili Oligarkija?* Moscow.

Gelman, V. (2006) *Vozvrawenie Leviafana? Politika recentralizacii v sovremennoj Rossii.* Moscow: Polis, pp. 91–2.

Gibson, J. L. (1996). "A mile wide but an inch deep: the structure of democratic commitments in the former USSR," *American Journal of Political Science,* 2 (May), pp. 396–420.

Glad, B. and Shiraev, E. (1999) (eds) *The Soviet Transformation.* New York: St Martin's Press.

Goldgeier, J. (1999) *Not Whether but When: The U.S. Decision to Enlarge NATO.* Washington, D.C.: Brookings Institution.

Goldgeier, J. and McFaul, M. (2003) *Power and Purpose: U.S. Policy Toward Russia After the Cold War.* Washington, D.C.: Brookings Institution.

Golz, A. (2007) "Rossiyskaya Imperiya i Rossiyski Militarism" (Russian Empire and Russian Militarism), in I. M. Kliamkin (ed.), *Posle imperii.* Moscow: Fond Liberal'naia missiia.

Golz, A. (2009) "Ono im Nado?" (Do they need it?), *Ezhednevnyj Zhurnal,* http://ej.ru/?a=note&id=8846 (accessed November 11, 2009).

Golz, A. (2009a) "Prizyv v Nikuda" (A draft to nowhere), *Ezhednevnyj Zhurnal,* http://ej.ru/?a=note&id=8933 (accessed November 11, 2009).

Gorbachev, M. (1985) "Interview with *Time Magazine,*" *Pravda,* September,1–2, p. 1.

Gorbachev, M. (1995a) *The Search for New Beginning: Developing a New Civilization.* San Francisco: Harper.

Gorbachev, M. (1996) *Memoirs,* 1st edn. New York: Doubleday.

Gorbachev, M. and Mlynar, Z. (1994) *Conversations with Gorbachev on Perestroika, the Prague Spring, and the Crossroads of Socialism.* New York: Columbia University Press.

Gozman, L. and Etkind, A. (1992) *The Psychology of Post-Totalitarianism in Russia.* London: Centre for Research into Communist Economies.

Graham, T. (2008) *U.S.–Russia Relations: Facing Reality Pragmatically.* Washington, D.C.: Center for Strategic and International Studies.

Graham, T. (2008a) "Sneak peek: the friend of my enemy," *National Interest Online,* April 1. http://www.nationalinterest.org/Article.aspx?id=17266 (accessed November 11, 2009).

Granovskij, S. A. (2004) *Obshaja i Priklandnaya Politiologiya* (General and Applied Political Science). Moscow: Izdatelstvo Flinta.

Greenberg, R. (2008) "Director of the Institute of Economics, Russian Academy of Sciences: An interview." *Ekho Moskvy Radio,* August 3. http://www.

echo.msk.ru/programs/albac/531344-echo.phtml (accessed November 11, 2009)

Grossman, V. (1970) *Vse techet* (Everything flows). Frankfurt: Posev.

Grunt, V., Kertman, G., Pavlova, T., Patrushev, S., and Khlopin, A. (1996) "Rossiyskaya Povsednevnost I Politicheskaya Kultura: Problemy Obnovleniya" (Russian everyday's life and political culture: problems of renovation), *Polis,* 4, pp. 56–72.

Grushin, B. (1994) "Does fascist dictatorship threaten Russia?" *Mir Mnenii i Mnenia o Mire,* October, pp. 8–12.

Gudkov, L. (2008) "An interview." *Novaia gazeta,* 23, April 3, pp. 8, 9.

Gudkov, L. (2008a) "An interview." *Novaia gazeta,* 40, June 5, pp. 12, 13.

Gudkov, L. (2008b) "An interview." *Novaia gazeta,* 63, August 28, pp. 16, 17.

Gudkov, L., Klyamkin, I., Satarov, G., and Shevtsova, L. (2009) "False choices for Russia," *Washington Post,* June 9.

Gumilev, L. (2004) *Poiski vymyshlennogo tsarstva.* Moscow: AST.

Gusev, V. (2003) "An interview: Rossiyskaya Federacija Segodnja" (The Russian Federation today). http://www.russia-today.ru/2003/no_06/6_SF_5.htm (accessed November 11, 2009).

Hale, H. (2005) *Why Not Parties in Russia? Democracy, Federalism, and the State.* New York: Cambridge University Press.

Hale, H. (2005a) "Why not parties? Supply and demand on Russia's electoral market." *Comparative Politics,* 37(2), January, pp. 147–66.

Hammerschlag, M. (2007) "Putin's children," *New York Times,* July 5. http://www.nytimes.com/2007/07/05/opinion/05iht-edhammer.1.6509812.html?_r=2 (accessed November 11, 2009).

Haslam, S. A. and Reicher, S. D. (2007) "Beyond the banality of evil: the dynamics of an interactionist social psychology of tyranny," *Personality and Social Psychology Bulletin,* 33(5), pp. 615–22.

Hewett, E. A. (1988) *Reforming the Soviet Economy.* Washington, D.C.: Brookings Institution.

Hosking, G. A. (1992) *The First Socialist Society: A History of the Soviet Union from Within,* 2nd edn. Boston, Mass.: Harvard University Press.

Hughes, J. (1996) "Moscow's bilateral treaties add to confusion," *Transition,* September 19, pp. 39–43.

Hughes, L. (2004) *Peter the Great: A Biography.* New Haven, Conn.: Yale University Press.

Imse, A. (1990) "Soviets' one and only is Gorbachev," *The State,* March 15.

Interfax (2009) "Ministry of Defense signs a record contract with Sukhoi," http://www.newsru.com/russia/18aug2009/sdelkamaks.html (accessed November 11, 2009).

Isaev, B. A. (2008) *Teoriya Partij I PArtijjnykh System.* Moscow: Aspect Press.

Isaev, B. and Baranov, N. (2009) *Politicheskie otnoshenija I politicheskij process v sovermennoj Rossii.* St Petersburg: Piter.

Isaykin, A. (2009) "Russia sold arms in 2008 worth $6.7 billion," www.newsru.com, April 10 (accessed November 11, 2009).

Ivanov, I. (2001) "Russian foreign minister's interview," *Argumenty I Facty,* June 27.

Ivanov, S. (2005) "Nam Nyzhna Millionnaya Armiya" (We need a million-men army), *Izvestiha,* February 22.

Ivanov, V. (2009) *Edinaja Rossiya* (United Russia). Moscow: Evropa.

Just Russia (2007) "Political platform," adopted February 26. http://www. spravedlivo.ru/information/section_11/section_12/ (accessed November 11, 2009).

Kara-Murza, S. (1996) "An editorial," *Sovetskaya Rossia*, May 5, p. 1.

Karaganov, S. (2007) "Novaya Epokha: Chto Delat?" (A new epoch: What to do?), September 12. http://www.globalaffairs.ru/redcol/0/8282.html (accessed November 11, 2009).

Karatsuba, I. V., Kurukin, I. V., and Sokolov, N. P. (2006) *Vybiraya Svoyu Istoriyu. Razvilki na Puti Rossii* (Choosing its own history: forks in Russia's road). Moscow: Colibri.

Katz, M. (2009). "Afghanistan: Russia genuinely concerned that America is losing it," *Eurasianet*, September 24. http://www.eurasianet.org/departments/ insightb/articles/eav092409a.shtml (accessed November 11, 2009).

Katz, M. (1991) *The USSR and Marxist Revolutions in the Third World*. New York: Cambridge University Press.

Kenez, P. (2006) *A History of the Soviet Union from the Beginning to the End*. New York: Cambridge University Press.

Khasbulatov, R. I. (2004) *Velikaya Rossiyskaya Tragediya* (The Great Russian Tragedy). Moscow: Al-Kods.

Khasbulatov, R. (2008) "Interview October 6," Radio Station Ekho Moskvy. http://www.echo.msk.ru/programs/svoi-glaza/544670-echo (accessed November 11, 2009).

King, C. (2008) "The five-day war: managing Moscow after the Georgia crisis," *Foreign Affairs*, November/December, 2(11).

Kliamkin, I. M. (ed.) (2007) *Posle imperii*. Moscow: Fond Liberal'naia missiia.

Komissarov, V. S. (2005) (ed.) R*ossijskoe Ugolovnoe Pravo* (Russian Criminal Law). St Petersburg: Piter.

Korotich, V. (2000) *Ot Pervogo Litsa* (From the First Person). Kharkov, Ukraine: Folio.

Kort, M. (2006) *The Soviet Colossus: History and Aftermath*. New York: M.E. Sharpe.

Korzhakov, A. (1997) *Boris Yeltsin ot Rassveta do Zakata* (Boris Yeltsin from Dawn to Dusk). Moscow: Intebook.

Kotkin, S. (2008) *Armageddon Averted: The Soviet Collapse, 1970–2000*. New York: Oxford University Press.

Kotz, D. (1997) *Revolution from Above: The Demise of the Soviet System. New York*: Routledge.

Kozlova, N. (2009) "Dolgi po nasledstvy" (Inherited debts), *Rossiyskaya Gazeta*. #4884, Federal Issue, April 9. http://www.rg.ru/2009/04/08/precedent.html (accessed November 11, 2009).

Kozyrev, A. (1991) "An interview with Russia's foreign minister," *Izvestia*, October 2, p. 3.

Krivosheev, (2001) "Rossiya I SSSR v Voynah 20 Veka" (Russia and the USSR in 20th-century wars), http://www.soldat.ru/doc/casualties/book/ (accessed November 11, 2009).

Krotkov, A. (2003) "Mosques from Tver to Moscow." *Ogonek*, June, 22/4801.

Krylova, N. E. (2000) *Ugolovnoe Pravo (*Criminal Law*)*. Moscow: Vuzlib.

Kryshtanovskaya, O. (2005) *Anatomija Rossijskoj elity* (The Anatomy of Russia's Elite). Moscow: Zakharov.

Kuchins, A. (2007) "Alternative futures for Russia to 2017," Report of the Russia and Eurasia Program Center for Strategic and International Studies. http://www.csis.org/files/media/csis/pubs/071210-russia_2017-web.pdf (accessed November 11, 2009).

Kukushkin, Y. (ed.) (1996) "Highest Manifesto, 29 April 1881," in *Russian State: Power and Society, Selection of Documents*. Moscow: Moscow State University.

Kulikov, V. (2008) "Insurance without a name." *Rossiyskaya Gazeta,* Federal Issue, # 4638, April 15. http://www.supcourt.ru/news_detale.php?id=5281 (accessed November 11, 2009).

Kurganov, O. (1996) "Zhdite" (Wait), *Izvestiia*, August 24.

Lankina, T. (2004) *Governing the Locals: Local Self-Government and Ethnic Mobilization in Russia*. Lanham, Md.: Rowman & Littlefield.

Lavrov, A. (2009) "Court prohibits manufacturing of candy that look like Rafaello," *Komsomolskaya Pravda*, April 15. http://www.kp.ru/daily/24278/473648/print/ (accessed November 11, 2009).

Lavrov, S. (2008) "Speech of the Russian Foreign Minister at the Institute of International Relations," Moscow, September 1. http://newsru.com/russia/01sep2008/lavrov.html (accessed November 11, 2009).

Lebed, A. (1996) Press Conference. Moscow, May 13.

Lebedev, V. (2008) "Chair of the Supreme Court of the Russian Federation: an interview," *Rossiyskaya Gazeta*, 4803, Federal Issue, December 2. http://www.supcourt.ru/news (accessed November 11, 2009).

Ledeneva, A. (2006) *How Russia Really Works: The Informal Practices that Shaped Post-Soviet Politics and Business*. Ithaca, N.Y.: Cornell University Press.

Leffler, M. (2007) *For the Soul of Mankind: The United States, the Soviet Union, and the Cold War*. New York: Hill & Wang.

Legvold, R. (ed.) (2007) *Russian Foreign Policy in the 21st Century and the Shadow of the Past*. New York: Columbia University Press.

Legvold, R. (2009) "The Russia file: how to move toward a strategic partnership," *Foreign Affairs*, July/August, pp. 78–93.

Lenin, V. (1916/1969). *Imperialism, the Highest Stage of Capitalism*. Moscow: International Publishing.

Lenin, V. (1917/2006) *The State and Revolution*. Moscow: Kissinger Publishing.

Lenta (2007) "Medvedev offered Putin the premiership post," December 11. www.renta.ru (accessed November 11, 2009).

Lenta (2007a) "Kasparov announced the end of his presidential run," December 12. www.renta.ru(accessed November 11, 2009).

Levada (2007) Poll of 21–27 September. http://www.levada.ru

Levada Center (2007a) "Survey on Russia's electoral attitudes," http://www.levada.ru/press/2007091305.html

Levada (2008) Poll of May 5. http://www.levada.ru

Levada (2008a) Poll of August 18. http://www.levada.ru

Levada (2008b) Poll of December 24. http://www.levada.ru

Levada (2008c) Poll of September 8. http://www.levada.ru

Levada (2008d) Poll of November 20. http://www.levada.ru

Levada (2008e) Poll of September 9. http://www.levada.ru

Levada (2008f) "Survey on Russian higher education." http://www.rambler.ru/
    news/science/statistics/565896127.html

Levada (2008g) Poll of October 20. http://www.levada.ru

Levada (2009) Poll of March 25. http://www.levada.ru

Levada (2009a) Poll of February 9. http://www.levada.ru

Levada (2009b) Poll of May 6. http://www.levada.ru

Levada (2009c) Poll of February 27. http://www.levada.ru

Levada (2009d) Poll of June 26. http://www.levada.ru

Levada (2009e) Poll of February 18. http://www.levada.ru

Levada (2009f) Poll of January 27. http://www.levada.ru

Levada (2009g) Poll of July 22. http://www.levada.ru

Levada (2009h) Poll of March 20–23. http://www.levada.ru

Levada (2009j) Poll of April 27–29. http://www.levada.ru

Levada (2009k) Poll of February 11. http://www.levada.ru

Levada (2009l) Poll of February 25. http://www.levada.ru

Levada (2009m) Poll of April 1. http://www.levada.ru

Levada (2009n) Poll of March 5. http://www.levada.ru

Levada (2009o) Poll of January 27. http://www.levada.ru

Levada (2009p) Poll of March 30. http://www.levada.ru

Levada (2009q) Poll of August 11. http://www.levada.ru

Levchenko, A. (2007) "Vybory Protiv Vseh" (Elections against everybody).
    http://gazeta.ru/politics/elections2007/info/s2366166.shtml (accessed November
    11, 2009).

Levesque, J. (1997) *The Enigma of 1989: The USSR and the Liberation of Eastern
    Europe.* Berkeley, Calif.: University of California Press.

Levinson, A. (2008) "An interview," *Novaia gazeta*, 23, April 3, pp. 8, 9.

Levinson, A. (2008a) "An interview," *Novaia gazeta*, 40, June 5, pp. 12, 13.

Levy, D. (1997) *Tools of Critical Thinking.* Boston, Mass.: Allyn & Bacon.

Liberal Democratic Party of Russia (LDPR) (2009) Party Program.
    http://www.ldpr.ru/partiya/prog/ (accessed November 11, 2009).

Ligachev, Y. (1996) *Inside Gorbachev's Kremlin.* Boulder, Colo.: Westview Press.

Lipman, M. (2008) "Putin's puppet press," *Washington Post,* May 20, p. A13.

Lukov, V. (2009) "Russian institutions of higher education through students'
    eyes," *Zhanie, Poinmanie, Umenie,* 3, http://www.zpu-journal.ru/e-zpu/
    2009/3/lukov/ (accessed November 11, 2009).

Lyskov, D. (2009) "Panica po Stalinu" (A panic about Stalin), *Pravda*, June 25.
    http://www.pravda.ru/politics/parties/cprf/315334-1/ (accessed November 11,
    2009).

Malcolm, N. (1995). "Russian foreign policy decision-making," pp. 23–51 in P.
    Sherman (ed.), *Russian Foreign Policy Since 1990.* Boulder, Colo.: Westview Press.

Manikhin, O. (2003) "Vozniknovenie Jabloka" (Jabloko Creation).
    http://www.yabloko.ru/Elections/2003/History_Yabloko (accessed November
    11, 2009).

Margelov, M. (2006) "Nam Est S Chem Vernytsya V Afriku" (We have something to return to Africa), *Rossijskaya Gazeta*, no. 4185, October 2.

Materialy Politburo (1990) *Moscow: A Special Publication*, March 12. Moscow: Materialy Politburo.

Matlock, J. (2005) *Reagan and Gorbachev: How the Cold War Ended*. New York: Random House.

Mau, V. and Starodubrovskaya, I. (2001) *The Challenge of Revolution: Contemporary Russia in Historical Perspective*. New York: Oxford University Press.

McFaul, M. (1997) *Russia's 1996 Presidential Election: The End of Polarized Politics*. Stanford, Calif.: Hoover Press.

McFaul, M. and Stoner-Weiss, K. (2008) "The myth of the authoritarian model: how Putin's crackdown holds Russia back," *Foreign Affairs*, January/February, pp. 68–84.

McGlinchey, E. (2009). "Central Asian Protest Movements," in A. Wooden and C. Stefes (eds), *Tempting Two Fates in Central Asia and the Caucasus? The Political Legacies and Emerging Policy Challenges of Transition*. New York: Routledge.

Medvedev, D. (2009) "An interview with NTV," July 26. www.Interfax.ru http://www.newsru.com/russia/26jul2009/tv.html (accessed November 11, 2009).

Medvedev, D. (2009a) "An interview with Novaya Gazeta," April 15. http://en.novayagazeta.ru/data/2009/039/00.html (accessed November 11, 2009).

Medvedev, V. (1994). *V Komande Gorbacheva* (In Gorbachev's Team). Moscow: Bylina.

Mikulski, K.. I. (ed.) (1995) *Elita Rossii o Nastoyashem I Budushem Strany* (The Russian Elite on the Country's Present and Future). Moscow: Vekhi.

Ministry of the Interior of the Russian Federation (2009) "Structure of the Ministry of the Interior," http://www.mvd.ru/struct/3297/3353/ (accessed November 11, 2009).

Mironov, S. (2009) "Interview with Interfax," July 26. http://www.newsru.com/russia/26jul2009/nasel.html (accessed November 11, 2009).

Mironov, S. (2009a) "Speech during the 4th Congress of the Just Russia Party," Moscow, June 25. http://www.mironov.ru/firstface/speeches/333.html (accessed November 11, 2009).

Mitofsky, W. J. (1996) "Exit polling on the Russian elections," *Public Perspective*, August–September, pp. 41–4.

Morozov, A. (2004) *Diplomatia Putina* (Putin's Diplomacy). St Petersburg: Izmailovsky Publishing.

National Projects (2009) "Presidents' council on the implementation of priority national projects and demographic policy," http://www.rost.ru/main/what/01/01.shtml (accessed November 11, 2009).

Nemtsov, B. (2002) "Interview with Voice of America," June 14, Washington, D.C. http://www.voanews.com/russian/archive/2002-06/a-2002-06-14-1-1.cfm?moddate=2002-06-14 (accessed November 11, 2009).

Nemtsov, B. (2008) "An interview with Ekho Moskvy Radio," August 3, http://www.echo.msk.ru/programs/albac/531344-echo.phtml (accessed November 11, 2009).

Neumann, I. (1996) *Russia and the Idea of Europe: A Study in Identity and International Relations*. New York: Routledge.

New Politics [Novaya Politika] (2009) "There are new problems in the pension system. Review of the press," April 20. http://www.novopol.ru/text66277.html

Newsru.com (2007) "Students of the Department of Journalism of MSU will be 'persuasively convinced' that the ideology of the party of power is the most correct," www.newsru.com, August 27. (accessed November 11, 2009).

Nikiforov, I. (1995) *The World Factbook of Criminal Justice Systems under Grant No. 90-BJ-CX-0002 from the Bureau of Justice Statistics to the State University of New York at Albany.*

Nikitinsky, L. (1994) "An interview," *Izvestia*, July 16.

Nikonov, V. (2003) *Konstitutsionnyj Dizajn*. Moscow: Sovrem'ennaja Rossijskaja Politika.

Novaya Politika (New Politics) (2009) "V Pensionnoi Sisteme Voznikayut Novye Problemy" (There are new problems appearing in the pension system: a review of the press). News review, April 20, http://www.novopol.ru/text66277.html (accessed November 11, 2009).

Odelburg, S. S. (1949/1991) *Tsarstvovanie Imperatora Nikolaya II* (The Reign of the Emperor Nicolas II). St Petersburg: Petropol.

Odom, W. E. (1990) "The Soviet Military in Transition," *Problems of Communism*, May–June.

Openkin, L. (1996) "Reka v Poiskah Beregov" (A river in search of its banks), *Polis*, 1, pp. 171–4.

Orlov, A. S., Georgiev, V. A., Georgieva, N.G., and Sivokhina, T. A. (2008) *Istoriya Rossii* (A History of Russia). Moscow: Prospect.

Orlov, P. (2009) "The General Staff reports about a new military doctrine," *Rossiyskaya Gazeta* , no. 4971, August 11.

Osborn, D. (2009) "Dmitry Medvedev surprises Russia with attack on 'humiliating' economy," *Telegraph*, September 11. http://www.telegraph.co.uk/news (accessed November 11, 2009).

Palazhchenko, P. (1997) *My Years With Gorbachev and Shevardnadze: The Memoir of a Soviet Interpreter*. University Park, Pa.: Pennsylvania State University Press

Panyushkin, V. (2006*) Mikhail Khodorkovksy. Uznik Tishiny* (Mikhail Khodorkovksy: A Prisoner of Silence) Moscow: Secret Firmy.

Patrushev, N. (2007) "An interview," *Argymenty i Facty*, 41 (1406), October 10. http://www.fsb.ru/fsb/comment/rukov/ (accessed November 11, 2009).

Pearson, D. E. (1987) *KAL 007: The Cover-up*. New York: Summit Books.

Petrov, N. and Kokurin, A. (2003) *Lubyanka: 1917–1991*. Moscow: Democracy International Foundation.

Pifer, S. (2009) "An agenda for U.S.–Russian relations in 2009. Testimony before the House committee on foreign affairs," http://www.brookings.edu/testimony/2009/0225_russia_pifer.aspx (accessed November 11, 2009).

Pipes, R. (1984) *Survival is not Enough*. New York: Simon & Schuster.

Pipes, R. (2007) "An interview," *Chayka*, 4(87), February 15. http://www.chayka.org/article.php?id=1451 (accessed November 11, 2009).

Platonov, S. F. (1937/2009) *Ocherki po istoruii Smutnogo Vremeni* (Essays on the History of the Time of Troubles). Moscow: AST.

Politkovskaya, A. (2008) *Putin's Russia: Life in a Failing Democracy*. New York: Holt.

Public Opinion Foundation (2001) March 22, http://bd.fom.ru/report/cat/ smi/dd011011 (accessed November 11, 2009).

Putin, V. (2000) "An interview with *Le Figaro*," *Le Figaro*, October 26.

Putin, V. (2009) "Comments during the meeting with the WHO director," June 26. www.newsru.com (accessed November 11, 2009).

Putin, V. (2009a) "Speech in Davos, Switzerland," January 29. http://www.vesti.ru/doc.html?id=246949 (accessed November 11, 2009).

Radzihovsky, L. (2009) "An interview," *Ekho Moskvy*, July 21, http://www.echo. msk.ru/programs/opponent/606888-echo/ (accessed November 11, 2009).

Raikov, G. (2008) "An interview," *RIA Novosti*, February 19.

Remington, T. (2001) *The Russian Parliament: Institutional Evolution in a Transitional Regime, 1989–1999*. New Haven, Conn.: Yale University Press.

Rb.ru (2009) "Russian business," http://www.rb.ru/topstory/economics/2009/ 06/05/100507.html (accessed November 11, 2009).

Rivera, D. W. and Rivera, S. W. (2009) "Yeltsin, Putin, and Clinton: presidential leadership and Russian democratization in comparative perspective," *Perspectives on Politics*, 7, 3, September, pp. 591–610.

RNS (Russian news services) (2009) http://bratishka.ru/index.php?id=618 (accessed November 11, 2009).

Rostow, W. (1967) *The Dynamics of Soviet Society*. New York: W. W. Norton.

Rodionov, A. (2007) *Nalogovye Shemy, za Kotorye Posadili Hodorkovskogo* (Tax Scams for Which Khodorkovsky was Busted). Moscow: Vershina.

Rozov, V. S. (1997) "A transcript of a comment: 'Piat Let Posle Belovezhia.'" (Five years after the Belovezh Agreement). Moscow, April 85, pp. 57–9.

Ruble, B. (1990) *Leningrad: Shaping a Soviet City*. Berkeley, Calif.: University of California Press.

Sabvennikova, I. V. (2002) *Rossiyskaya Emigraciya (1917–1939)* (Russian Emigration, 1917–1939). Tver: Federal Archive Service.

Sakwa, R. (1993) *Russian Politics and Society*. London: Routledge.

Sakwa, R. (1999) *The Rise and Fall of the Soviet Union: 1917–1991*. New York: Routledge.

Sanford, G. (2009) *Katyn and the Soviet Massacre of 1940: Truth, Justice, and Memory*. New York: Routledge.

Sestanovich, S. (2008) "What has Moscow done? Rebuilding U.S.–Russian relations," *Foreign Affairs*, November/December, pp. 12–28.

Shakhnazarov, G. (1997) "Transcript of a presentation: 'Piat Let Posle Belovezhia,'" (Five years after the Belovezh Agreement). Moscow: April-85, pp. 10–20.

Shakkum, M. (2006) "Koncepcii Promyshlennoi Politiki u Pravitelstva Net" (The government does have a theory of industrial politics), *RF Today*. http://www.russia-today.ru/2006/no_01/01_topic_1.htm (accessed November 11, 2009).

Sheehy, G. (1990) *The Man Who Changed the World*. New York: HarperCollins.

Shevtsova, L. (2005) *Putin's Russia*. Washington, D.C.: Carnegie Endowment for International Peace.

Shiraev, E. (1999a) "Attitudinal changes during the transition," in E. Shiraev and B. Glad (eds), *The Russian Transformation*. New York: St Martin's Press, pp. 155–66.

Shiraev, E. (1999b) "The new nomenclature and increasing income inequality," in E. Shiraev and B. Glad (eds), *The Russian Transformation*. New York: St Martin's Press, pp. 109–18.

Shiraev, E. (2008) "Sizing up Obama in Russia: the first encounter," *Harvard International Review*, December 19. http://hir.harvard.edu/index.php?page=article&id=1811 (accessed November 11, 2009).

Shiraev, E. and Bastrykin, A. (1988) *Moda, Kumiry, I Sobstevennoe Ya* (Fashion, Idols, and the Self). Leningrad: Lenizdat.

Shiraev, E. and Terrio, D. (2003) "Russian decision-making regarding Bosnia: indifferent public and feuding elites," in R. Sobel and E. Shiraev (eds), *International Public Opinion and the Bosnia Crisis*. Lexington, Md.: Rowman & Littlefield.

Shiraev, E. and Zubok, V. (2000) *Anti-Americanism in Russia: From Stalin to Putin*. New York: Palgrave.

Shlapentokh, V. (1988) "The changeable Soviet image of America," pp. 157–71 in T. Thornton (ed.), *Anti-Americanism: The Annals of the American Academy of Political and Social Science*, Vol. 497. Newbury Park, Calif.: Sage.

Shlapentokh, V. (2009) *Putin is Smarter than the Soviet Leaders*. November. http://shlapentokh.wordpress.com/ (accessed November 11, 2009).

Shlapentokh, V. and Shiraev, E. (eds) (2002) *Fears in Post-Communist Societies: A Comparative Perspective*. New York: Palgrave.

Shlapentokh, V., Shiraev, E., and Carroll, E. (2008) *The Soviet Union: Internal and External Perspectives on Soviet Society*. New York: Palgrave.

Shlapentokh, V. and Woods, J. (2007) *Contemporary Russia as a Feudal Society: A New Perspective on the Post-Soviet Era*. New York: Palgrave.

Shlapentokh, V., Woods, J., and Shiraev, E. (2005) *America: Sovereign Defender or Cowboy Nation?* London: Ashgate.

Shleifer, A. and Treisman, D. (2004) "A normal country," *Foreign Affairs*, March/April.

Shlykov, V. (2002) *Chto Pogubilo Sovetskij Soyuz: Generalnyi Shtab i Ekonomika* (What Brought Down the Soviet Union: the General Staff and the Economy). Moscow: MFIT.

Sigelman, L. and Shiraev, E. (2002) "The rational attacker in Russia? Negative campaigning in Russian presidential elections," *Journal of Politics*, 64, pp. 45–62.

Simanov, S. (2009) "Andropov: Seven Tajn Genseka s Lubjanki" (Seven secrets of the General Secretary from Luybyanka), http://libereya.ru/biblus/Andropov/Andropov.htm#t1 (accessed November 11, 2009).

Simes, D. (2009) "Coping with areas of US–Russian disagreement and conflicts of national interest," paper for Designing U.S. Policy Toward Russia, Library of Congress Conference, March 27.

Simes, D. (2007) "Losing Russia: the costs of renewed confrontation," *Foreign Affairs*, November/December, pp. 36–52.

Skrynnikov, R. (2006) *Russkaya istoriya IX–XVII vekov* (Russia's History from the 9th–17th Centuries). St Petersburg: SPSGU.

Skrynnikov, R. (2006a) *Ivan III*. Moscow: Tranzitkniga AST.

Smith, H. (1990) *The New Russians*. New York: Avon Books.

Sobchak, A. (1992). *For a New Russia*. New York: Free Press.

Sokolov, N. (2008) "Vek Surka Ili Kratkaya Istoriya Kolovrashenia Rossijskih Uchebnikov Istorii" (A groundhog century, or a brief history of the tribulations of Russian history textbooks), http://www.polit.ru/analytics/2008/10/15/history.html (accessed November 11, 2009).

Solonevich, I. L. (2005) *Narodnaya Monarkhiya* (People's Monarchy). Moscow: Rimis.

Solzhenitsyn, A. (1976) *Lenin in Zurich*. New York: Penguin.

Sorokin, V. (2004) "An interview," arba.ru, January. http://www.arba.ru/art/849/7 (accessed November 11, 2009).

State, The (1989) "Gorbachev reveals Soviet defense budget," *The State,* May 31.

Stavrakis, P. J. (1996) "Russia after the elections: democracy or parliamentary Byzantium?" *Problems of Post-Communism,* 43(2), pp. 13–20.

Stephen, P. B. (1991) "Perestroika and property: the law of ownership in the post-Socialist Soviet Union." *American Journal of Comparative Law,* 39, Winter, pp. 35–65.

Stoner-Weiss, K. (2006) *Resisting the State: Reform and Retrenchment in Post-Soviet Russia*. New York: Cambridge University Press.

Stoner-Weiss, K. (2006a) "When the wave hits a shoal: the internal and external dimensions of Russia's turn away from democracy," CDDRL Working Papers, May. http://cddrl.stanford.edu (accessed November 11, 2009).

Strayer, R. (1998) *Why Did the Soviet Union Collapse? Understanding Historical Change*. New York: M.E.Sharpe.

Surkov, V. (2006) "Vladislav Surkov Razvel Demokratiju" (Vladislav Surkov compartmentalized democracy), *Kommersant,* June 29, 116 (3447) http://www.kommersant.ru/doc.aspx?DocsID=686274 (accessed November 11, 2009).

Taubman, P. (1987) "Gorbachev, citing party's failures, demands changes," *New York Times,* January 28.

Tetlock, P. Lebow, R., and Perker, G. (eds) (2006) *Unmaking the West. "What if?" Scenarios That Rewrite History*. Ann Arbor, Mich.: University of Michigan Press.

Transparency International (2009) *Corruption Perception Index*.

Treisman, D. (1996) "Moscow's struggle to control regions through taxation," *Transition,* 19, September, pp. 45–9.

Treisman, D. (1996a) *How Yeltsin Won*. Unpublished manuscript, University of California, Los Angeles.

Treisman, D. (1996b) "Why Yeltsin won," *Foreign Affairs,* September/October, pp. 64–77.

Treisman, D. (1999–2000) "Russia 2000: after Yeltsin comes ... Yeltsin," *Foreign Policy,* Winter, www.foreignpolicy.com (accessed November 11, 2009).

Treisman, D. (2008) "What keeps the Kremlin up all night," *Moscow Times,* February 18, no. 3844, p. 10.

Trenin, D. (2003) "Russian–American relations: two years after September 11th, a briefing." *Moscow's Carnegie Center,* 5(8), August.

Trenin, D. (2006) *Vrag Naroda* (An Enemy of the State). Moscow: Algoritm.

Trofimova, E. (2003) "Zhirinovsky: Russia should occupy Iraq," March 11, www.ytro.ru.

Trofimova, E. V. (2008) "Zaochnoe sudebnoe razburatel'stvo po ugolovnym delam. Ponjatie I perspektivy primenenija" (Court criminal proceedings in absentia. Meaning and possibilities of use), *Vestnik VGU. Seriya Pravo*, 2, pp. 313–22.

Trunin, I. (2009) "Interview with the director of the Department of Tax and Tariff Policies of the Finance Ministry," April 21. http://top.rbc.ru/economics/21/04/2009/295773.shtml (accessed November 11, 2009).

Tucker, R. C. (1961) "Toward a comparative politics of movement regimes," *American Political Science Review*, 55(2), pp. 281–93.

Tucker, R. C. (1990) *Stalin in Power: The Revolution from Above, 1928–1941*. New York: W. W. Norton.

Umland, A. (2009) "Will it be the second Crimean War?" *Zerkalo nedeli/Dzerkalotyzhnia*, 15(743), pp. 25–29, April.

Umland, A. (2008) "The pseudo-issue of Ukraine's NATO membership." April 3, http://www.opednews.com/articles/opedne_andreas__080403_the_pseudo_issue_of_.htm (accessed November 11, 2009).

Umland, A. (2008a). "Russia's constitutional ailments," *International Relations and Security Network: Security Watch [ETH Zurich]*, December 3.

United Russia (2007) Electoral Program adopted by the 8th Congress, October 1, Moscow. http://edinros.er.ru/er/rubr.shtml?110099 (accessed November 11, 2009).

Uzelac, A. (2001) "Terror may be tie that binds," *Moscow Times*, September 13.

Valenty, L. and Shiraev, E. (2001) "The 1996 Russian presidential candidates: a content analysis of motivational configuration and conceptual/integrative complexity," in O. Feldman and L. Valenty (eds), *Profiling Political Leaders: Cross-Cultural Studies of Personality and Behavior*. Santa Barbara, Calif.: Greenwood.

Voroshilov, D. (2009) *Mass Media are not Free Yet*. Freedom House. http://www.rian.ru/society/20090501/169782000.html May 1. (accessed November 11, 2009).

Vox Populi (1995) "Polls conducted by Boris Grushin's Vox Populi service," reported in *Izvestia*, October 13, p. 6.

Walt, S. (2005) "Taming American power." *Foreign Affairs*, September/October, pp. 105–120.

WCIOM (All-Russian Center for Study of Public Opinion) (2007) Poll of June 6. http://wciom.ru

WCIOM (2009) Survey of Attitudes about corruption cf *Vremya Novostey*, 2009-04-28 12:38, www.newsru.com (accessed November 11, 2009).

WCIOM (2008) Poll of November 17. http://wciom.ru

WCIOM (2008a) Poll of January 21. http://wciom.ru

WCIOM (2008b) Poll of December 2. http://wciom.ru

WCIOM (2008c) Poll of December 16. http://wciom.ru

WCIOM (2008d) Poll of September 10. http://wciom.ru

WCIOM (2008e) Poll of September 4. http://wciom.ru

WCIOM (2009) Poll of February 18. http://wciom.ru

WCIOM (2009a) Poll of May 20. http://wciom.ru

WCIOM (2009b) Poll of May 6. http://wciom.ru

WCIOM (2009c) Poll of April 15. http://wciom.ru

WCIOM (2009d) Poll of July 19. http://wciom.ru

WCIOM 2009g) Poll of April 23. http://wciom.ru

WCIOM (2009h) Poll of February 20. http://wciom.ru

WCIOM-RBK (2008) Poll of March 3. http://wciom.ru/novosti/v-centre-vnimanija/publikacija/single/9755.html

Welu, C. and Muchnik, E. (2009) "Corruption: Russia's economic stumbling block," *Business Week*, August 27. http://www.businessweek.com (accessed November 11, 2009).

White, S., Rose, R., and McAllister, I. (1996) *How Russia Votes*. Chatham, N.J.: Chatham House.

White, S. (2007) "Russia's client party system," pp. 21–52 in P. Webb and S. White (eds), *Party Politics in New Democracies*. Oxford: Oxford University Press.

White, S. (2008) *Politics and the Ruling Group in Putin's Russia*. New York: Palgrave.

Wohlstetter, A. (1979) *Swords from Plowshares: The Military Potential of Civilian Nuclear Energy*. Chicago: University of Chicago Press.

World Resource Institute (WRI) (2009) *Global Forest Watch: Carbon Assessment for Russia*. http://www.globalforestwatch.org/english/russia/ (accessed November 11, 2009).

World Bank (1997). GNP Estimates for various countries. www.worldbank.org (accessed November 11, 2009).

Wyman, M. (1997) *Public Opinion in Postcommunist Russia*. London: Macmillan.

Yakobson, L. (2009) "A Vice-Rector of the Moscow Higher School of Economics interview," Polit.ru. http://www.polit.ru/analytics/2005/10/03/med1.html (accessed November 11, 2009).

Yanin, V. L. and Aleshkovsky, M. H. (1971) "Proishozhdenie Novgoroda" (The Origin of Novgorod). *USSR History*, 2, 32–61. http://www.russiancity.ru/books/b39.htm (accessed November 11, 2009).

Yeltsin, B. (1994) *Zapiski Presidenta*. Moscow: Ogonjok.

Zaslavsakya, T. I. (2004) *Sovremennoe Rossijskoe Obwestvo: Social'nyj Mekhanism Formirovanija*. Moscow.

Zatulin, K. (2009) "Delo Sdelano ... Zabudte? Desyat Let Spustya Vojny NATO s Yugoslavijej" (Done Deal and ... Forget? Ten years after the NATO war against Yugoslavia), *Politicheskii Klass*, 3(51), March 30. http://www.zatulin.ru/index.php?&section=digest&id=403 (accessed November 11, 2009).

Zinn, H. (2002) *The Power of Nonviolence: Writings by Advocates of Peace*. Boston, Mass.: Beacon Press.

Zorkaya, N. (2004) "Dumskie Vybory 1993-2003" (Duma elections in 1993–2003), *Vestnik Obshestvennogo Mnenya*, 4 (72), pp. 19–30.

Zubok, V. (2007) *A Failed Empire: The Soviet Union in the Cold War from Stalin to Gorbachev*. Durham, N.C.: University of North Carolina Press.

Zubok, V. (2009). *Zhivago's Children: The Last Russian Intelligentsia.* *Cambridge*, Mass.: Harvard University Press.

Zyuganov, G. (1996) "Interview. Russia TV channel," Moscow, May 17.

Zyuganov, G. (2009) Speech at a meeting with young deputies of all levels representing four Parliament factions in the State Duma. Interfax, June 17.

Legislation and official documents

Concept (2000) The Military Doctrine of the Russian Federation. Approved by Vladimir. V. Putin, President of the Russian Federation, on April 21, 2000.

Concept (2000a) The Foreign Policy Concept of the Russian Federation. Approved by Vladimir V. Putin, President of the Russian Federation, on June 28, 2000. http://www.fas.org/nuke/guide/russia/doctrine/econcept.htm

Concept (2008) The Foreign Policy Concept of the Russian Federation. Approved by Dmitry A. Medvedev, President of the Russian Federation, on July 12, 2008.

Constitution of the USSR (1936) http://www.hist.msu.ru/ER/Etext/cnst1936.htm

Constitutional Court of the Russian Federation (2009) Ruling of February 27, 2009, http://www.ksrf.ru

Constitutional Court of the Russian Federation (2009) Ruling of April 20, 2009, http://www.ksrf.ru

Federal Law (1992) *The Prosecution Service of the Russian Federation.* N 2202-1, January 17.

Duma (2007) Rulings on October 9 2007; N 5134-4GD.

Federal Law (1993) *On State Secrets.* N 5485-1, July 21.

Federal Law (1994) *The Presidium of the Supreme Court.* N 50-FZ, October 28.

Federal Law (1995) *Continental Shelf of the Russian Federation.* N 187-FZ, November 30.

Federal Law, April 3, 1995 N 40-FZ *On Federal Security Service of the Russian Federation.*

Federal Law (1995) *Arbitration Courts of the Russian Federation.* N 1-FKZ, April 28.

Federal Law (1996) *On External Intelligence.* N 5-FZ, January 10.

Federal Law (1996) *On Undergraduate and Graduate Professional Education.* N 125-FZ, August 22.

Federal Law (1998) *On Inner Sea Waters, Territorial Sea, and the Adjacent Zone of the Russian Federation.* N 155-FZ, July 31.

Federal Law (1998) *On Exclusive Economic Zone of the Russian Federation.* N 191-FZ, December 17.

Federal Law (1991) *On Medical Insurance of the Russian Federation's Citizens.* N 1499-1, June 28.

Federal Law (1993) *Foundations of the Legislation of the Russian Federation on Health Care of Citizens.* N 5487-1, July 22.

Federal Law (2003) *On Elections of the President of the Russian Federation.* N 19-FZ, January 10.

Federal Law (2004) *On Jurors of Federal Courts of General Jurisdiction on the Russian Federation.* N 113-FZ, August 20.

Federal Law (2004) *On changes in the Federal Law "On Political Parties."* N 168-FZ O, December 20.

Federal Law (2007) *Additional Measures of Federal Support of Families with Children.* N 256 FZ, January 1.

Land Codex (2001) *The Land Codex of the Russian Federation.* N 136-FZ, October 25.

Ministry of the Interior of the Russian Federation (2009) Structure of the Ministry of the Interior. http://www.mvd.ru/struct/3297/3353/

Organizational Procedures of the Duma (1998) Adopted on January 22, 1998. N 2134-II GD

Presidential Decree (1991) #239. November 25. Source: *Vedomosti Syezda Narodnyh Deputatov RSFSR I Verhovnogo Soveta RSFSR*, 1991, N 48, p 1677.

http://lawrussia.ru/texts/legal_689/doc689a672x233.htm

Presidential Decree (1993) "On a gradual constitutional reform in the Russian Federation, No. 1400, October 21.

Presidential Decree (2004) "Questions of the Ministry of Justice of the Russian Federation," N 1313, October 13,

Presidential Decree (2004a) "Regulations about Ministry of Defense of the Russian Federation," N1082, August 16

Presidential Decree (2006) "About means of counteraction against terrorism," N116, February 16.

Presidential Decree (2007) "On changes in the Regulations about Military Service," No. 303, March 8.

Presidential Decree (2007a) "About changes in the bylaws of the Foreign Ministry," N 865, January 26.

Strategy for National Security of the Russian Federation until 2020 (2009) May 12, http://www.scrf.gov.ru/documents/99.html

Websites

Federal Security Service of the Russian Federation (FSS): http://www.fsb.ru

Federal Service of State Statistics(Gosstat): http://www.gks.ru

Legal Acts of the Russian Federation: http://www.interlaw.ru

Ministry of the Interior of the Russian Federation http://www.mvd.ru

Russian Center for Public Opinion: http://wciom.ru/

Russian Federal Statistical Service (Rosstat): www.gks.ru

Smi.ru (2009) http://www.smi.ru/sources/16/

Index

Communist Party of the Soviet Union
  Article 6 of the Soviet Constitution, 69,
    70
  atheism, 49
  Bolsheviks, 39, 40
  Central Committee, 47, 69, 100, 196
  democratic centralism, 47
  dictatorship of the proletariat, 49
  diversity quotas, 111
  founding, 37
  membership, 166
  mobilization, 49
  outlawed, 113
  Party Regulations, 47, 69
  Politburo, 47, 64, 74, 77, 256
  reforms during perestroika, 69, 70, 80
Community Chamber, 110
Constituent Assembly, 39, 40, 131
Constitution
  of 1918, 41
  of 1924, 45
  of 1936, 91, 175, 279
Constitution of the Russian Federation,
    xviii, 91, 92, 94, 95, 103, 105, 107,
    112, 113, 117, 118, 122, 124, 125,
    127, 130, 131, 136, 138, 139, 149,
    151, 173, 178, 190, 201, 208, 209,
    260, 283, 308
constitutional amendments, 122, 123
Constitutional Commission, 92
Constitutional Court of the Russian
    Federation
  establishment in 1991, 138
  impeachment, 94
  judges, 127, 129, 149
  legislative initiative, 136
  rulings, 140, 150
constitutional crisis of 1993, 92, 118, 138,
    139, 304
corruption, 13, 14, 63, 104, 112, 135, 147,
    166, 168, 169, 177, 201, 230, 242,
    292
Corruption Perception Index, 13
counter-terrorism, 149, 163, 165, 258, 271
coup of August 1991, 79, 85, 166
crime, 75, 86, 143, 147, 293
Crimean War, 33
Criminal Code, 143, 144, 145
critical-liberal view of history, 57
critical thinking
  convenient assumptions, 20
  emotional judgments, 20
  multiple causes of events, 22
Cuba, 76, 274

cultural inconsistencies, 6
cynicism, 56
Czars of Russia
  Alexander I, 33, 34, 109
  Alexander II, 34, 35
  Alexander III, 35
  Alexis I, 29
  Catherine II (empress), 33
  Elizabeth (empress), 33
  Ivan III, 27, 28
  Ivan IV the Terrible, 28, 60
  Mikhail, 29
  Nicolas I, 33
  Nicolas II, 35, 38, 39, 175
  Pavel I, 33
  Peter the Great, 30, 31, 60, 137
Chavez, Hugo, 274
Czech Republic, 257, 274
Czechoslovakia, 76
Czechoslovakian revolt of 1968, 53

death penalty, 150
Decembrist Revolt, 34
Democratic union, 157
defense policy
  Air Force, 270
  armed forces, 281
  Armenia, 286
  arms sales, 290
  authoritarian strategy, 303
  Azerbaijan, 286
  Caucasus, 286
  changes under Putin, 280
  China, 281
  defense priorities, 299
  deferral from service, 285
  draft dodgers, 286
  former republics of the Soviet Union, 286
  geopolitics, 286
  Georgia, 286
  global military tasks, 301
  hawkish approach, 303
  Iran, 286
  "military departments" in colleges, 285
  Military Doctrine of the Russian
    Federation, 280, 281, 282, 286
  military draft, 165, 282, 284, 285, 286,
    302
  military officers, 302
  military reform, 280, 289, 301
  Moldova, 286
  NATO, 286
  nuclear defense, 287
  nuclear disarmament, 287

Shakhrai, Sergei, 93
Shanghai Cooperation Organization, 271
Shevarnadze, Eduard, 156
shock therapy, 216
shortages, 62, 86, 240
Sibneft, 234
Singapore, 217
Slovakia, 92, 257
Slovenia, 257
Sobchak, Mikhail, 65
social policy, 237, 307
    dilemmas, 245
    education, 242, 243, 248, 249
    health care, 140, 239, 240, 247
    housing, 241, 242
    policy options, 245, 246
    paradox, 237
    pensions, 163, 240, 241, 253
    welfare system, 238
socialist economic system, 46, 64, 72
socialist entrepreneurship, 66
Socialist Revolutionaries Party, 37
Solzhenitsyn, Alexander, 67
Sorokin, Vladimir, 202
South Korea, 208, 217, 274, 284
sovereign democracy, 17, 57, 114, 187,
    189, 205
Sovetskaya Rossiya (newspaper), 77, 196
Soviet-German Pact of 1939, 51
Soviet Union, 15, 18
    beliefs in socialism, 62, 65
    bureaucracy, 47, 63, 66, 84
    caste system, 63
    coup of 1991, 79
    crime, 8, 75, 86
    criminal code, 144
    defense doctrine, 279
    democratic opposition, 77, 78, 168
    disappearance, 72, 81
    economy, 63, 71, 72, 75, 82, 83, 86
    enemy-searching, 279
    foreign policy, 50, 51, 53, 55, 73, 74, 76,
        78, 87
    foundation, 43, 45
    growth rate, 62
    ideology, 20, 53
    imperial overstretch, 83
    intellectual opposition, 56, 78
    life expectancy, 239
    military, 51, 74, 77, 80, 82
    nationalist movements, 72, 77
    Parliament of 1989, 70
    political mobilization, 49
    power struggle, 78, 84

shortages, 63, 75
social apathy, 63
social problems, 63
space launches, 21
state subsidies, 63
television, 68
transformation, 83, 86
trial system, 137
Union Treaty, 79
welfare state, 238
Sovietologists, 59
Soviets, 39
Spanish Civil War, 50
sports, 124, 195
stagnation period, 55, 62
Stalin, Josef, 8, 10, 48, 49, 50, 52, 54, 55,
    61, 67, 68, 75, 208
Stalingrad battle, 51
Starovoitova, Galina, 78
START II, 289
State Council, 109
state of emergency, 125, 129
state secrets, 207, 296, 297
Stolypin, Pyotr, 36
St Petersburg, 30, 31, 34, 38, 40, 51, 65,
    70, 78, 80, 97, 104, 112, 139, 250
St Petersburg State University, 97, 243, 279
Strategic Arms Reduction Treaty (START),
    288
Strategic Defense Initiative, 82
strategic national interests, 262, 273, 274,
    275, 277
Subjects of the Russian Federation, 103,
    104, 105, 120
superpower, 76, 308
Supreme Court of Arbitration of the
    Russian Federation, 129, 136, 142
Supreme Court of the Russian Federation,
    129, 136, 141, 142
Synod, 30

taxes, xviii, 112, 168, 218, 220, 222, 225,
    306
teachers, 249
terror, 42, 50, 54
terrorism, 109, 143, 151, 183, 258, 267,
    275, 287, 291, 294, 297, 299, 306
Teutonic knights, 27
Thailand, 218
thaw (political), 54
Time of Troubles, 29
traditional power, 17
transparency, 104, 119, 150, 151, 175, 249
Transparency International, 13